The Toastmaster's Treasure Chest

Herbert V. Prochnow
and Herbert V.
Prochnow, Jr.

HARPER & ROW, PUBLISHERS

1817

NEW YORK, HAGERSTOWN,
SAN FRANCISCO, LONDON

FIRST EDITION

Library of Congress Cataloging in Publication Data

Prochnow, Herbert Victor, DATE
  The toastmaster's treasure chest.
  1. Public speaking—Handbooks, manuals, etc.
2. Wit and humor. 3. Quotations, English.
4. Anecdotes. 5. Proverbs. I. Prochnow,
Herbert Victor, 1931- II. Title.
PN4193.I5P737   080'.24'85   78-2161
ISBN 0-06-013447-X

79 80 81 82 83 10 9 8 7 6 5 4 3 2 1

Contents

Preface

The response to *The Public Speaker's Treasure Chest* over many years has been extremely gratifying, with 500,000 or more users of the book. The authors believe that a companion book for toastmasters might be equally helpful to the large numbers of persons who serve as toastmasters or have occasion to lead discussions, conferences, or seminars. Their needs are somewhat different from those of the principal speaker and call for short items which can be used to lighten and enliven brief introductory remarks.

Consider the thousands of meetings held every month by Rotary, Kiwanis, Lions, Toastmasters and Optimists Clubs, Chambers of Commerce, parent-teacher associations, church groups, and professional, business, and trade organizations. At each one of these meetings someone must be fully prepared to preside and to assure those present that they will benefit by their attendance. The number of hours spent each year in meetings of all kinds is unbelievably large. The responsibility for conducting the meetings effectively and interestingly is correspondingly great. It is imperative that the toastmaster have well-prepared, stimulating "impromptu" remarks!

This book has been written for three groups of persons—first, those who must preside at luncheons, dinners, discussions, convention sessions, or meetings of various types; second, those who must make brief speeches; and, third, those who enjoy reading humorous stories, epigrams, amusing definitions, illustrations from biography, inspiring quotations, and anecdotes. In this book there are over 5,000 items on hundreds of subjects to help the toastmaster or speaker to discharge his responsibilities effectively. These items come from a great many past and present authors, philosophers, statesmen, businessmen, teachers, lawyers, and scientists. Men and women with brilliant minds and from numerous walks of life have made challenging, humorous, and inspiring observations.

It is inexcusable for a toastmaster to be dull. His remarks normally are brief as he introduces a speaker or a subject for discussion. Anything the person in charge of a meeting can do to make his own comments sparkle, arouse the interest of an audience, and win its attention, will help greatly to make a meeting successful. That means thorough preparation by the toastmaster if his performance is to be competent.

The book contains over 700 humorous stories, more than 1,300 epigrams, almost 725 examples of the wit and wisdom of world political leaders and famous persons, 200 inspirational quotations and illustrations, 240 toasts and sentiments for special occasions, more than 300 amusing and unusual definitions, over 200 unusual facts, stories, and quotations from biography, 350 proverbs of many nations, 160 stimulating thoughts of distinguished Americans, and hundreds of other items to help the toastmaster.

We believe this book presents an unusual amount of material which has not previously been so organized for toastmasters. The book is meant to be a practical, helpful reference book not only for toastmasters, but also for lawyers, teachers, salespeople, businessmen, ministers, union officials, and those in political positions who are called on frequently or occasionally for brief remarks. General readers will find humor, wisdom, and inspiration in the more than 5,000 items the book contains.

H.V.P.
H.V.P., Jr.

Humorous Stories, Anecdotes, and Verse

1   *Good Reason*

First mechanic: "Which do you prefer, leather or fabric for the upholstery in cars?"

Second mechanic: "I like fabrics. Leather is too hard to wipe your hands on."

2   *It Was Fresher Then*

A young army recruit was sent, by others in his company, to the commanding officer to complain that the bread served to them at mealtime wasn't too good.

"If George Washington had had that bread at Valley Forge, he would have eaten it with relish!" snapped the C.O.

"Yes, sir," replied the recruit, "but we don't have any relish!"

3   *A Whole Day*

The visitor to London was quite disgusted. "Rain, rain, rain, fog, fog, fog," he shouted to his guide. "When do you have summers in England?"

"I say," replied the guide. "That is a difficult question. Last year I believe it came on a Wednesday."

4   *Can't Change Them*

In her school essay on "Parents," a little girl wrote: "We get our parents at so late an age that it is impossible to change their habits."

1

5   *Not Difficult*

Major General Wilton B. Persons was President Eisenhower's favorite story-teller among White House staffers. Mr. Persons was the author of Ike's favorite story—the one about the duck hunters who had been waiting hours for some ducks to show up. Finally a lone duck flew by and everybody missed except one hunter who had been belting away at a bottle of whiskey.

His pals asked him how on earth he had hit the thing.

"That's easy," he replied, "you ought to be able to hit something when a flock that big goes by."—*Andrew Tully, Scripps-Howard Newspapers*

6   *He Told Him*

An elderly man entered a railroad car where there were three empty seats. He approached the person next to the first empty seat and said, "Before I sit down, do you have any grandchildren?"

"Yes, I have two," was the reply.

The man went on and repeated the scene at the second empty seat and received the same reply. Finally the man in the third empty seat answered, "No, I am sorry, I have no grandchildren."

With a smile the man took the seat and said, "Good, I will tell you all about mine."

7   *Couldn't Take a Chance*

Teacher: "Give me a sentence using the word 'tariff.'"
Boy: "My pants are so tight they'll tariff I bend over."

8   *Specialized*

A man who had just been promoted to vice-president boasted so much about it to his wife that she finally retorted: "Vice-presidents are a dime a dozen. Why, in the supermarket they even have a vice-president in charge of prunes."

Furious, the husband phoned the supermarket in the expectation of refuting his wife. He asked to speak to the vice-president in charge of prunes.

"Which kind?" was the reply. "Fresh or dried?"

9   *Our Debt*

Rockabye, baby, why do you fret?
Are you aware of the national debt?
Father has gone round the corner to vote
Millions in bonds for his snookums to tote.
Are you suspicious? Sleep while you can;
You can squirm later, dear, when you're a man.
Highways of Happiness

10   *We Understand*

Two teen-agers on a tour of a modern art gallery found themselves alone in a room of modern sculpture. Staring at the twisted pipes, broken glass, and tangled shapes, one of them said, "Let's get out of here before they accuse us of wrecking this place."

11   *Probably Not*

A group of small boys at Sunday School listened intently as the teacher told them the parable of the Prodigal Son.

After emphasizing the disagreeable attitude of the older brother, the teacher described the household's rejoicing at the return of the Prodigal Son.

"In the midst of the celebration, however," said the teacher, "there was one who failed to share in the festive spirit! Now, does anyone know who it was?"

Waving his hand frantically, one small boy said, "The fatted calf!"

12   *Inquisitive*

The class had been reading the story of Moses. Afterward one boy asked, "Did Moses have the same after-dinner illness my pop's got?"

Puzzled, the teacher asked him what he meant.

"Well," he said, "it says here the Lord gave Moses two tablets."

13   *Correct Name*

"Do you know the name of the little boy who sits behind you, Rosalie?" mother asked the first-grader.

"His name is Jimmy," Rosalie answered.

"Jimmy who?" asked mother.

"His whole name is Jimmy Sitdown," said Rosalie. "That's what the teacher calls him."

14   *Faith*

This is a country of faith. On the installment plan you can buy what you can't afford. On the stock market you can sell what you don't own.

15   *Serious*

At the end of the day, the bank officer was closing the door behind him when he noticed a customer outside with packages in his arms and a perplexed look on his face, staring at the night depository. The officer approached him and asked if he could help.

The man replied excitedly, "My wife will divorce me!"

"What happened?"

"I dropped the wrong package down the chute."

"What was in it?"

"Pork chops."

16   *Reference Only*

A new patron of the Cincinnati Public Library was astounded at the supply of freely lent material. He stood in the record department gazing around and gripping his card.

"You mean," he said, "with this card I can take out any record I want?"

Assured of this, he went on, "And I can take out any color film you have?"

Another assurance didn't stop the dazzled patron, who persisted, "With this card can I take out any librarian?"

Here the woman at the record desk sweetly informed him, "The librarians, sir, are for reference only."—*Cincinnati Enquirer*

17   *Choice*

If you've ever wanted a definition of ultimatum, consider the farmer, pail in hand, who looked at his cow and said, "Well, Bossy, what'll it be? Milk or hamburger?"

18   *Conscience*

I stole a kiss the other night,
My conscience hurts, alack!
I think I'll go again tonight,
And put the darned thing back.

19   *Fair Exchange*

The wise teacher mailed this note home to parents the first day of school: "If you promise not to believe everything your child says happens at school, I'll promise not to believe everything he says happens at home."

20   *First Things First*

At Moscow University the distinguished professor was excitedly explaining to his students how interplanetary junketing was in the cards for the not-too-distant future. "We will be able to travel to Mars, Pluto and Venus regularly," he declared. "Are there any questions?"

A student at the back of the room raised his hand. "When," he asked, "can we travel to Vienna?"

21   *Opportunity*

Two men were walking by a fish market in New York. They noticed there were two tubs or barrels of lobsters. One said, "Lobsters, $3.00 a pound," and the other said, "Lobsters, $6.00 a pound." As they watched, one of the lobsters in the $3.00 barrel very, very laboriously made it to the top, up, up, up, teetered over the top for a second and fell into the $6.00 barrel. One man turned to the other and said, "You know, that could only happen in America."

22   Only One Who Could Answer

His name was Johnny, and one day he came home from school looking so miserable that his mother was worried. "What is wrong?" she finally asked. Out of his trousers pocket, Johnny fished a note from the teacher which said: "Johnny has been a very naughty boy. Please have a serious talk with him."

"What did you do?" asked Mother.

"Nothing," sobbed Johnny. "Except that the teacher asked a question and I was the only one who could answer it."

"H'm," murmured Mother. "What was the question?"

"Who put the dead mouse in my drawer?" answered Johnny.

23   People

A six-year-old girl submitted the following composition on "People" to her teacher: "People are composed of girls and boys, also men and women. Boys are no good at all until they grow up and get married. Boys are an awful bother. They want everything they see except soap. My ma is a woman and my pa is a man. A woman is a grown up girl with children. My pa is such a nice man that I think he must have been a girl when he was a little boy."

24   What Lincoln Did

Father: "Get up, son. When Lincoln was your age, do you know what he was doing?"

Son: "No, Dad, I don't. But I do know what he was doing when he was your age."

25   That's Telling Him

A car screeched to a halt at an intersection, barely missing a white-haired old lady. Instead of giving the driver a tongue lashing, she smiled sweetly, and pointed to a pair of baby shoes dangling from the rear-view mirror.

"Young man," she asked, "why don't you put your shoes back on?"

26   Good Answer

Interviewing an applicant for a chauffeur's job, a man said: "Now, I want a very careful chauffeur, one who doesn't take the slightest risk."

The applicant responded: "I'm your man, sir. Can I have my salary in advance?"

27   Tact

Leaving a plush dinner club one night, a miserly gentleman stalked right past the doorman without tipping him.

Nevertheless, the doorman helped the man into the car with a flourish and said pleasantly, "By the way, in case you happen to lose your wallet on the way home, sir, just remember that you didn't pull it out here."

28   No Bird Watcher

A wife pointed to her husband stretched out in the hammock and explained to her friend: "Fred's hobby is letting birds watch him."

29   Annoys the Squirrels

"It's no use planting tulip bulbs one foot deep."
"I know, but it sure annoys the squirrels."

30   Next Question

There is the story of a famous scholar who found himself sharing a seat in a bus with a farmer, and proposed an exchange of riddles to help pass the time.

"When I miss a riddle," suggested the scholar, "I'll pay you a dollar, but since obviously I've had more opportunity than you to acquire knowledge, when you miss a riddle you need pay me only fifty cents."

The farmer nodded agreement. "I have my first riddle ready for you right now," he said. "What is it that weighs six hundred pounds on the ground and only fifteen pounds when it flies?"

"I don't know," confessed the scholar, "so here's my dollar."

"I don't know either," admitted the farmer, and handed back fifty cents.

31   Good Question

The librarian went over to the small, noisy boy. "Please be quiet!" she admonished. "The people near you can't read!"

"They can't?" the lad said inquisitively. "Then what are they doing here?"

32   Why?

If it's true the world's getting smaller, why do they keep raising the price of postage?

33   Age of Wisdom

The father having trouble with his young son said to his wife, "Perhaps we'd do him a favor if we let him start shifting for himself . . . while he still knows everything!"

34   Man Is an Animal

Yes, man is an animal. During his lifetime he may be many different animals. First, he is a little lamb, then a kid, or maybe a little pig. As he grows older he may become a good-for-nothing pup, or even a skunk, or a rat.

He meets a girl who can make a monkey of him. For a while he is a stag; then, getting married, he becomes a goat or a stubborn mule. He sometimes becomes a little cuckoo, and in his old age he may become a wise old dog, or a sly old fox.

Yes, man may become many different animals during his lifetime, but, unlike other animals, he can be skinned more than once.

35 *Inflation*

Our opinion of the dollar? Confidentially, it shrinks.

36 *Good Reason*

A mother asked her son who had just returned from a youth group's car-washing project, "What was the least amount anyone paid you?"

He replied, "One man gave us just fifty cents."

His mother said, "That's not very much."

"I know," he explained, "but maybe it's because we hosed his car before the windows were rolled up."

37 *Loans*

Sign in a finance company window: "Loans—for those who have everything but haven't paid for all of it yet."

38 *Typical*

A wife was telling her neighbor about her fishing trip with her husband.

"I did everything wrong on the trip. I talked too loud, I made too much noise. I used the wrong bait, I reeled in too soon, and I caught more fish than he did."

39 *Striking Need*

A teacher emphasizing the need of good handwriting said: "If you do not learn to write well, no one will be able to read your picket signs."

40 *Taking No Chance*

Six-year-old Peter lost no time telling his playmates all about his recent tonsillectomy.

"And do you know what?" he concluded. "All the nurses had blindfolds over their mouths!"

41 *Fond of Him*

"I suppose the baby is fond of you," said the visitor to the new father.

"Fond of me? Why, he sleeps all day when I'm not at home and stays up all night to enjoy my company," answered the proud father.

42   *Out of Circulation*

The couple was shopping for wedding rings. "I don't want too wide or too tight a band; it might cut off the circulation," he said.

"It's going to do that anyway," she said, smiling meaningfully.

43   *Dear Alice*

An executive had hired a new secretary. Upon being called out of town suddenly, he told her to write Allis-Chalmers in Milwaukee and inform them that he wouldn't be able to keep his appointment. When he returned to his office four days later, he found this carbon copy:

"Alice Chalmers, Milwaukee, Wis. Dear Alice: I'm off for Texas and can't keep our date."

Horrified, he immediately phoned Allis-Chalmers. "I hope you haven't received a certain letter."

"Received it?" was the reply. "It's been on the bulletin board for three days."

44   *Just the Top*

Two sailors, at sea for the first time, were looking out over the mighty ocean. Said one, "That's the most water I ever saw."

The other replied, "You ain't seen nothin' yet. That's just the top of it."

45   *There Are Lots of Them*

Every baseball team could use a man who plays every position superbly, never strikes out, and never makes an error. The trouble is there's no way to make him lay down his hot dog and come down out of the grandstand.

46   *Some Other Reason*

The Postal Service's credo, updated: "Neither snow nor rain, nor gloom of night stays these couriers from the swift completion of their appointed rounds —so there must be some other reason."

47   *A Long Time*

Greta Garbo was invited to a Hollywood dinner which was attended also by Dr. Albert Einstein. Having some vague idea as to Dr. Einstein's status, Greta turned to him during the dinner and remarked, "Doctor, I understand that you have a great theory. Won't you please explain it all to me?"

"My dear lady," said Einstein, "I'm afraid there will not be time enough during the dinner to explain the Theory of Relativity, but perhaps I can tell you about the law of Gravitation, which is really a prerequisite."

So Dr. Einstein went on to tell her all about the phenomenon of Gravity and its consequences. Upon the conclusion of his discourse, Greta seemed very impressed and said to him, "Well, for goodness' sake, Doctor, how long has this been going on?"

48   Not Fair

Two fishermen sitting on a bridge, their lines in the water, made a bet as to which would catch the first fish. One of them got a bite on his line and got so excited that he fell off the bridge.

"Oh, well," said the other, "if you're going to dive for them, the bet's off!"

49   That's Bad

For three nights Father had struggled dutifully to help his little daughter with her arithmetic homework. They were not making much progress.

"Daddy, it's going to be even worse next week," she warned. "Then we start learning the dismal system."

50   Football

Seeing his first American football game, the Englishman watched one of the teams go into a huddle.

"What do you think of it?" asked his American friend.

"It's not a bad sport," he observed, "but they have too many committee meetings."

51   Typical

A young woman boarded a crowded bus with a pair of skis slung over her shoulder. An old Southern gentleman gallantly offered her his seat.

"Thank you, sir," she said, "but I prefer standing. I've been sitting all day."

52   Right

First duck: "Check that twin-engine jet that just went by; don't you wish you could fly that fast?"

Second duck: "Buddy, if I had two tails and they were both on fire—you wouldn't even see me!"

53   Our Dog

The little boy was making a manful effort to lead a large, shaggy dog. "Where are you taking him?" he was asked.

"I don't know yet," the lad replied, "but when he makes up his mind where he wants to go, I'm going to take him there."

54   *Good Question*

Dismayed by the size of the Newfoundland dog given to him for his birthday, the small boy wanted to know, "Is he for me, or am I for him?"

55   *Keep It Confidential*

"Don't you and your wife ever have a difference of opinion?"
"Sure we do—but I don't tell her about it."

56   *Stranger*

A young mother put her two children to bed, then changed into an oversized sweat shirt and an old pair of blue jeans and proceeded to wash her hair. All during the shampoo she could hear the youngsters growing wilder and noisier.

She finished as quickly as she could, wrapped a large towel around her head, stormed into the children's room, and put them back to bed with a stern warning to stay there.

As she left she heard her two-year-old say to his brother in a trembling voice, "Who was that?"

57   *College Bred*

"What does 'college bred' mean, Dad?" asked the young man.
"College bred," replied his father, "is a four-year loaf made from the flavor of youth and his old man's dough."

58   *Inflation*

"With the high price of food, my shopping habits have changed," commented the housewife. "Now I fill the shopping cart with money and put the food in my purse."

59   *What's Wrong?*

Judge: "And why did you park your car there?"
Motorist: "Well, the sign said, 'Fine for parking'!"

60   *Not That Bad*

"It looks like a bad storm is coming up," said the hostess. "You'd better stay for dinner."
"Oh, thanks," said the guest absently, "but I don't think it will be that bad."

61   *Frequent Trouble*

Three men at the office were discussing what most people want to get out of a new car.

"Dependability," said one fellow. "Styling," declared another. "Economy," stated the third.

Just then a fourth man, who had recently bought a new car, entered the room. They put the question to him. "What is the thing you'd like most to get out of your new car?"

"My teen-age son!" he replied.

62 Why Buy?

Woman at insurance counter at airport: "I used to buy flight insurance, but it doesn't seem to make any difference."

63 Won't Take Long

"I hope you don't think me too young for marriage with your daughter," said the young man anxiously.

"That's all right, my boy," was the cheerful reply. "You'll age fast enough!"

64 Phonetics

It is easy to make mistakes in print. A newspaper referred to a couple of very learned gentlemen as two "bibulous old flies." The reporter had phoned in the story and that was the typesetter's interpretation of "bibliophiles."

Upon receiving the protest from the offended, the editor undertook to right the wrong by printing their criticism, but in his comment he added that he thought they were too "fastidious."

He dictated his story and did not check the copy. The proofreader again distinguished himself with this mix-up: "two fast idiots."—*Sunshine Magazine*

65 Salesmanship

The sales manager was approached by some little Girl Scouts peddling cookies. "Why do you want to see me?" he asked.

"Because you are so handsome," smiled one little girl.

He bought twelve boxes and went back to his desk murmuring, "There is no brighter sales tool than truth."

66 A Great Ride

Little boy to Mother: "Did Dad take me for a ride! We passed two idiots, three morons, four fools, and I don't know how many knotheads!"

67 No Pressure

Life-insurance agent to prospect: "Don't let me frighten you into a decision. Sleep on it tonight and if you wake up in the morning let me know what you think."

68   *Easy*

"Pardon me, officer," the pedestrian said in a busy intersection, "can you tell me how to get to the City Hospital?"

"Yes," said the officer, "just stand right there a little longer."

69   *The Price Tag*

A new mother came home from the hospital with her baby son still wearing his hospital identification tag. The mother's three-year-old met his new brother, then asked, "Mama, when you gonna take off his price tag?"

70   *Too Formal*

Our relaxed style of life at home sometimes makes it difficult for our teen-agers to appreciate more formal situations. A fifteen-year-old, following a dinner at the home of a neighbor, said, "I hate dinners with two forks."

71   *Be Sure*

"If you raise your children 'by the book,' " our pastor told the Young Married Club at church, "better make up your mind which one—comic, bank, or Good Book."—*Burton Hillis*

72   *Accurate*

He had found fault with his secretary for altering a sentence in a letter he had dictated.

"I don't want you to think," roared the great man. "I want you to take down my words accurately and then type them, neither adding nor leaving out anything I may say."

Later in the afternoon the typist brought back the following letter:

"Dear Smyth: Spell it with a y, though that's pure swank on his part. In answer to your letter of—look up the date. We can quote you—tell me, Walter, what's the most we can charge this old buzzard? Very well. We can quote you $50 a ton for the goods. If he accepts we shall have to make sure of our money beforehand, for I don't trust him. Awaiting the pleasure of your valued order, Yours faithfully."

73   *Of Course*

A Bostonian was showing an Englishman the sights and finally took him out to the Bunker Hill Monument.

"This is where Warren fell, you know," he explained.

The Englishman looked up at the tall shaft. "Nasty drop! Killed him, of course?"

74   *Ideal Place*

Sue: "This is an ideal spot for a picnic."
Anne: "It must be. Fifty thousand insects can't be wrong."

75   *Be a Good Boy*

"Now, Johnny, be a good boy and say 'Ah-h-h' so the doctor can get his finger out of your mouth."

76   *It Changed Him*

"I'm glad to find you as you are," said the old friend. "Your wealth hasn't changed you."

"Well," replied the candid millionaire, "it has changed me in one thing. I'm now 'eccentric' where I used to be impolite, and 'delightfully witty' where I used to be rude."

77   *Specialists*

Surgeon leaving operating room: "That was close!"
Second surgeon: "What do you mean?"
First surgeon: "An inch either way and I would have been out of my specialty."

78   *A Problem*

The new minister's family was presented with a pie baked by one of the congregation who was a rather poor cook. The pie was inedible, so the minister's wife reluctantly threw it into the garbage.

The preacher was faced with the problem of thanking the lady, while at the same time being truthful. After much thought, he sent the following note:

"Dear Mrs. Jones: Thank you for being so kind and thoughtful. I can assure you that pie like yours never lasts long at our house!"

79   *Last Raise*

An office worker, slicing a gaily decorated cake at his desk, said to his boss: "Hope you don't mind, sir. Just a little celebration on the tenth anniversary of my last raise."

80   *Patience*

It's extremely important that parents with small children save something for a rainy day: their patience.

81   *Expensive*

When you eat at some fancy restaurants these days you need an after-dinner mint—like the one in Denver.

82   *Her Prayer*

Louise, a little girl who had begun life in a happy-go-lucky household, went to spend a few days with a very strict aunt.

One evening, after a trying day when she had been scolded for her small faults even more than usual, she said her evening prayer. As the aunt passed the bedroom door, she heard: ". . . and please, please, make all the bad people good, and the good people a little easier to live with."

83   *Probably Will*

"Mother," asked Bobby, "is it true that an apple a day keeps the doctor away?"

"So I understand, Bobby, but why do you ask?"

"Well, I've kept away six doctors this morning, but I'm afraid one will have to come this afternoon."

84   *Prospect*

One secretary to another at the Internal Revenue office: "Here's another good one, Mabel. Bachelor, no dependents, thirty-five thousand dollars a year."

85   *Not Too Difficult*

"With a single stroke of the brush," said the schoolteacher taking his class through the National Gallery, "Joshua Reynolds could change a smiling face into a frowning one."

"So can my mother," said one of the small boys.

86   *Slight Difference*

A Dutchman was explaining the red, white, and blue Netherlands flag to an American. "Our flag is symbolic of our taxes," he said. "We get red when we talk about them, white when we get our tax bills, and blue after we pay."

The American nodded. "I know what you mean. It's the same in the U.S.A., only we see stars, too."

87   *Come Again?*

When we change to the metric system, we'll have to relearn such common expressions as these:

A miss is as good as 1.609 kilometers.

A decigram of salt.

Beat him within 2.54 centimeters of his life.
28.350 grams of prevention is worth 453.59237 grams of cure.
Peter Piper picked 8.81 liters of pickled peppers.

88 Couldn't Help

Internal Revenue agent to taxpayer: "We sympathize with your problems, but they won't fit into our computer."

89 Tried to Be Helpful

On a crowded bus: "Madam, would you like me to get you a strap to hang on to?"
"No, thank you, I have one."
"Then would you mind letting go of my necktie?"

90 Puzzled

A mother, with her little son, was calling on a neighbor. The boy suddenly said, "Mrs. Jones, may I see your new bedroom rug?"
"Why, Tommy, how nice of you to be interested! Of course, you may go in and look."
The little boy went into the bedroom, then soon reappeared. "Gee, Mommy," he said, puzzled, "it didn't make *me* sick!"

91 Missed Coffee Breaks

Then there was the fellow who wanted to know if he could have a day off with pay. When asked why, he said, "I want to catch up on the time I missed for coffee breaks when I was on vacation."

92 A Diplomat

A diplomat is a gentleman who can tell a lie in such a manner to another gentleman (who is also a diplomat) that the second gentleman is compelled to let on that he really believes the first gentleman, although he knows that the first gentleman is a liar, who knows that the second gentleman does not believe him, yet both let on that each believes the other, while both know that both are liars.

93 Our Side

A little old lady was sightseeing in Washington, D.C., and wasn't sure which side of C Street the State Department was on. She stopped a passing Marine and queried: "Which side is the State Department on?"
He replied, "Ours, I think!"

94   *General William C. Westmoreland Speaks*

Mr. Chairman and Distinguished Guests at the head table, and Members of The Chicago Executives' Club, when I left home en route here, my wife asked me where I was going.

I said, "To Chicago, to address The Executives' Club."

She replied, "That's an accolade we must note on our tombstone."

I said, "That's a good idea, but let's not rush it."

You'll miss my wife today because every time I am on a podium she throws me a kiss. Everybody thinks it's a mark of affection, but it's K-I-S-S: "Keep It Short, Stupid."

95   *One Horse to Another*

I don't remember your mane, but your pace is familiar.

96   *He Had an Idea*

The little boy studied the Ten Commandments until he thought he had them letter-perfect. But when it came to putting them down on paper during a Sunday School test, he fumbled over the fifth and wrote: "Humor thy father and mother."

97   *Bookkeeping*

In an effort to display her business proficiency in running the home, the little woman submitted to hubby a detailed account of expenses for the month. Asked to explain an entry marked "ESP—$26.98," she replied, "ESP means, 'Error Some Place.'"

98   *She is Learning Fast*

Mary, a first-grader, was listening as her older brother and friends exchanged hints on how to read quickly. Finally, Mary decided to give some advice of her own, announcing, "I've found you can read a lot faster if you don't stop to color the pictures."

99   *Tough Winter*

During last winter's violent snowstorms, one Red Cross rescue team was carried by helicopter to within a mile of a mountain cabin all but covered by deep snowdrifts.

The rescuers struggled on foot through the deep drifts and finally arrived at the cabin, where they shoveled away enough snow to clear the door. They knocked, and when their summons was answered by a mountaineer, one rescuer stepped up and said, "We're from the Red Cross."

"Well," said the mountaineer, scratching his head. "It's been a right tough winter and I don't see how we can give anything this year."

100 What's Gobbledygook?

The following, allegedly from the British Admiralty, is a classic example: "It is necessary for technical reasons that these warheads should be stored upside down, that is, with the top at the bottom and the bottom at the top. In order that there may be no doubt as to which is the bottom and which the top, for storage purposes, it will be seen that the bottom of each warhead has been labeled with the word 'Top.' "—*Cadillac Commentator*

101 Yesterday's Carpool Rules

In view of today's trend to carpooling due to high energy costs, keep in mind the following carpool rules, culled from a 100-year-old list from Wells, Fargo and Company: "Abstinence from liquor is requested, but if you must drink, share the bottle. Forgo smoking, as smoke and odor are repugnant, especially to ladies. Chewing tobacco is permitted. Gentlemen must refrain from strong language. Don't snore loudly, or friction with fellow travelers may result. Firearms may be kept, but don't fire them for pleasure—the sound frightens the horses. Gents guilty of unchivalrous behavior toward lady passengers will be put off the stage. It's a long walk back."—*Cadillac Commentator*

102 Modern Youth

Mother (horrified): "Kissing a man you just met! You never saw *me* doing that!"
Daughter: "No, but I'll bet Grandma did."

103 Inflation

In some Latin American countries a price rise of over 40 percent is called inflation, 20 to 40 percent is called stability, and a price rise of 20 percent or less, deflation.—*Gottfried Haberler*

104 Both Mistaken

An author once praised another writer heartily to a third person.
"It is strange," replied the other, "that you speak so well of him, for he says you are a quack."
"Oh," replied the author, "it is very likely that both of us may be mistaken."

105 That's Better

Mother: "You were a very tidy boy not to throw your orange peel on the floor of the bus. Where did you put it?"
Johnny: "In the pocket of the man next to me."

106   *Acting Up*

Woman showing well-dented car to garageman: "The fender's been acting up again."

107   *Not Easy*

"Above all," the doctor said, "you must eat more fruit, and particularly the skin of the fruit. The skin contains all the vitamins. What is your favorite fruit?" The patient looked gloomy. "Coconuts," he said.

108   *Diplomat*

When a diplomat says "yes," he means "perhaps"; when he says "perhaps," he means "no"; when he says "no," he is no diplomat.

109   *We Live It Up*

The dinner started with cream of tomato soup. The main course was rib roast with mashed potatoes and broccoli. Soft rolls with two pats of butter to a plate were served. Dessert was apple pie with ice cream. There was coffee with cream and sugar.

The speaker of the evening cleared his throat and began, "We are a bankrupt nation."

110   *Modern Life*

Two old friends got together after many years and soon fell to discussing their husbands' faults.

"We've been married fifteen years," one woman said, "and every night after dinner my husband complains about the food."

"How terrible," exclaimed the other. "Doesn't it bother you?"

"Why should it bother me," her friend replied, "if he can't stand his own cooking?"

111   *Smart Lad*

Boy: "I made a hundred in school today, Mom."
Mom: "Good! What did you make it in?"
Boy: "Well, I made forty in reading, thirty in spelling, and thirty in arithmetic."

112   *She Is Through*

Mama Bear to Papa Bear: "This is positively my last year as den mother!"

113   *Fair Question*

Judge: "You say you have known the defendant all your life. Tell the jury whether you think he would be guilty of stealing this money."
Witness: "How much was it?"

114   *Modern Mathematics*

How old are you? When a census taker asked a certain woman this, she said, "Well, now, let me figure it out. I was eighteen when I married and my husband was thirty. He is now sixty, or twice as old as he was then, so I am now thirty-six."

115   *Hard to Define*

All of the adult members of the family had gone off in a flurry of best clothes and excitement to attend a wedding. Four-year-old Billy asked his seven-year-old sister Sue, "What's a wedding?"

"You're too young to understand," answered the sophisticated young lady, "but it's something between dancing school and a funeral."

116   *Indian Advice*

Sign on a car driven by an Indian in New Mexico: "Love America or give it back."

117   *Advice*

Before offering your seat to a girl—make certain that she is.

118   *Perfect Pair*

Overheard at a party: "They're a perfect pair. He's a pill and she's a headache."

119   *Smart Dog*

Several hunters were sitting around one night bragging about the dogs they owned. Noting that an elderly native was listening intently, they laid it on thick.

"Take my setter," said one man. "When I send him to the store for eggs, he refuses to accept them unless they're fresh. What a nose that dog has!"

"That's nothing," boasted another. "My springer goes out for my cigars and refuses to accept any but my favorite brand. Not only that, he won't smoke any until he gets home and I offer him one."

"Say, old-timer," said another man, turning to the native, "did you ever hear of any dogs as smart as ours?"

"Just one—my brother's dog," was the reply. "I think he's maybe a bit smarter."

"How?" he was asked.
"Well," replied the native, "he runs the store where your dogs trade."

120   *In Trouble*

The guest at the dinner party, arriving late, found a seat reserved for him near the head of the table, where a goose was being carved.
"Oh," he exclaimed, "so I'm to sit by the goose."
Then, observing the lady on his left, he made haste to amend an awkward phrase. "I mean," he said, "the roasted one, of course."

121   *Correct*

Applicants for jobs on a state dam project had to take a written examination. The first question was: "What does hydrodynamics mean?"
One applicant hesitated a minute, then wrote: "It means I don't get the job."

122   *No Response*

"How was the applause after your speech?" asked the wife when her husband, an aspiring politician, returned home after an evening meeting.
"Terrible, terrible!" he moaned. "It sounded like a caterpillar in sneakers romping across a field of clover."

123   *Difficult Question*

An elderly lady zoomed past a state trooper. He gave chase, and when he had brought her to a stop he asked for her driver's license.
The elderly woman looked at him sharply. "Young man," she said, "how can I be expected to show you my driver's license when you people keep taking it away from me?"

124   *Golf*

He was as usual churning up the golf course, leaving a trail of raw earth in his wake.
"I'd move heaven and earth to be able to break a hundred," he moaned to his caddy.
"You've moved all the earth there is," the caddy answered, "so heaven is about all you have left."

125   *Elegant*

A wealthy Easterner moved to Wyoming, where he bought a large ranch. He gave an enormous housewarming at which only the finest foods and refreshments were served. It was an elegant affair. Afterward, a cowhand was telling some friends about it. "We ate fer more'n two hours," he said, "an' the only thing I recognized was an olive!"

126   *The Job He Wanted*

A young fellow in the naval reserve was telling his friends that if he was ever called for active duty he would like to be assigned as commander of an LMD. "What is an LMD?" asked a friend.

The young fellow quickly replied: "Why, it's a Long Mahogany Desk!"

127   *Advertising*

A sign on a butcher shop in London proclaims proudly: "We make sausage for the Queen."

Across the street, on a rival shop, is another sign: "God save the Queen!"

128   *Tact*

When a woman parishioner called at her clergyman's home, the minister's little son blurted out, "My, how ugly you are!"

Horrified, his mother exclaimed, "Johnny, whatever do you mean by saying such a thing?"

"I only meant it for a joke, Mother," Johnny stammered.

"Well," his mother purred unwittingly, "how much better the joke would have been if you had said to Mrs. Smith, 'How pretty you are!' "

129   *He Wanted to Help*

"Those poor children next door have no mummy nor daddy, and no Aunt Jane," said a mother to her little boy. "Wouldn't you like to give them something?"

"Yes," replied the little boy. "Let's give them Aunt Jane."

130   *Why a Man Needs a Wife*

Every man needs a wife because things sometimes go wrong that you can't blame on the government.

131   *Where They Came In*

Two elderly ladies arrived at a baseball game just as the batter hit a home run. Twenty minutes later the same batter came up to bat and hit another home run. One of the old ladies turned to the other: "Let's go. This is where we came in."

132   *Frank*

When William Howard Taft was teaching in the Yale Law School, he was annoyed one day because the students began to fidget and whisper before his lecture ended. "Just a minute, gentlemen," he said, "I have still a few more pearls to cast."

133   *Tactful*

To a man who asked if he was making a bore of himself by talking too much, Franklin P. Adams replied: "Well, sir, I would put it this way—you never seem to have an unexpressed thought."

134   *Hard to Believe*

Wife to husband as the tailor measured his waist: "It's quite amazing when you realize that a Douglas fir with that much girth would be ninety feet tall!"

135   *Two Egotists*

What happens when two egotists meet? It's an I for an I.

136   *Powerful Vitamins*

A man walked into a restaurant, handed the waiter two vitamin pills, and asked him to dissolve them in a bowl of clam chowder.

After a long interval he asked why he hadn't been served yet. "You'll get your soup, sir," said the waiter, "as soon as we can get the clams to lie down."

137   *Stowaway*

The elderly couple were on their first trip abroad. They were going over on one of the big luxury liners. The wife, who took a lively interest in fellow passengers, remarked to her husband, "Did you notice the huge appetite of the man opposite us at dinner?"

"Yes," replied her husband dryly. "He must be what they call a stowaway."

138   *Good System*

"Did I hear you correctly?" asked the new secretary. "Make twenty-six copies of every letter?"

"That's right," answered the boss, "please do."

"May I ask why?"

"We file one under each letter of the alphabet, then we are sure of finding them," replied the harried man.

139   *Smart Lad*

In class, there was a discussion of the origins of the word "manuscript." The teacher noted that it came from the Latin words *manu* and *scriptus:* written by hand. "But actually," he laughed, "what other kind of writing could there have been in those days?"

"Footnotes?" suggested a pupil.

140 *Too Late Then*

Wife to husband, who is helping their small son with his homework: "Help him now while you can. Next year he goes into the fourth grade."

141 *Takes Time*

Barber: "What kind of a haircut do you want, little boy?"
Boy: "The kind like my father's with the hole in the middle."

142 *Valuable Information*

A hen never lays an egg—she drops it. She may sit on the nest before she "lays," but the actual "laying" of the egg is done standing up.

143 *Balancing the Budget*

Harried wife, figuring at a desk, to husband and children: "Well, I worked out a budget, but one of us will have to go."

144 *How Much a Meter?*

The clerk at the supermarket handed a woman customer the long tape itemizing her purchases. After glancing at it, she said, "That's about right. I usually pay twenty-five dollars a foot for my groceries."

145 *How to Avoid Agony*

The youngster advised his little brother that he could be spared much agony and toil by refusing to spell his first word.

"The minute you spell 'cat' you're trapped," he said. "After that, the words get harder and harder."

146 *Trouble Ahead*

Concerned about her husband in the Navy, a young wife sent a note to her pastor. It reached the pulpit. It read, "John Anderson having gone to sea, his wife desires the prayers of the congregation for his safety." Looking it over hastily, the minister read aloud, "John Anderson, having gone to see his wife, desires the prayers of the congregation for his safety."

147 *First—Some Film*

The boy rushed into the drugstore and yelled, "My Dad was painting and the ladder fell down. He's hanging on the side of the house by his fingertips."

"Want me to call for help?" asked the clerk.

"Not yet. First I want you to help me put a new roll of film in my camera."

148   *What Marriage Teaches*

Marriage teaches you loyalty, forbearance, self-restraint, meekness—and a great many other qualities you wouldn't need if you had stayed single.

149   *Now She Knows*

Mother heard her five-year-old son screaming and found that the baby daughter was pulling his hair.

"Never mind," she tried to comfort him, "your baby sister doesn't understand that it hurts you."

She had not been out of the room for a minute when more shrieks sent her back. This time the baby was crying.

"What's the matter?" she asked the boy.

"Nothing much," he replied calmly. "Only now she knows."

150   *Thankful*

Little Toby was telling his mother about the day in school. "Mother," he said, "today our teacher asked me whether I had any brothers or sisters, and I told her I was the only child."

"And what did she say?" asked his mother.

"She said, 'Thank goodness!' "

151   *Couldn't Fool Him*

A traffic cop who had stopped a young lady driver said: "Your driver's license says you should be wearing glasses. Where are they?"

"I have contacts," the young lady answered.

"I don't care who you know," snapped back the cop. "I'm giving you a ticket anyway."

152   *Perhaps Not*

Customer: "Waiter, I can't find any oysters in this oyster stew."

Waiter: "Well, you wouldn't expect to find any angels in an angel-food cake, would you?"

153   *It Was Different*

When Tim went to visit his grandparents, they took him to a posh restaurant as a special treat—and were surprised when the nine-year-old ordered a hamburger. "In a place like this," his grandfather smiled, "don't you want to try something different? Something you've never had?"

"That's what I'm doing," announced the lad. "I've sure never had a three-dollar hamburger before!"

154   *Good and Bad News*

A distinguished scientist was participating in a panel discussion on the results of the nation's future water supply. "Gentlemen," he said, "I have some good news and some bad news for you. Our study shows that by the year 2000 everyone will be drinking recycled sewage from his water tap."

"Great Scott!" came a shout from the audience. "Quick, tell us the good news."

"That *was* the good news," answered the scientist. "The bad news is that there won't be enough to go around."

155   *Confused*

I overheard a scrap of conversation between a couple of businessmen in New York the other day. "Confused?" one of them was saying. "Of course I'm confused. I have a son at Vassar and a daughter at Yale."—*Preston R. Tisch*

156   *Couldn't Help It*

Driver to officer arresting him for speeding: "But, officer, I couldn't slow down while you were going so fast right behind me!"

157   *Take It Easy*

"Stick to your washing, ironing, scrubbing, and cooking," a husband exhorted his wife. "No wife of mine is going to work."

158   *Hard Times*

A: "What time is it by your watch?"
B: "Quarter to."
A: "Quarter to what?"
B: "I can't tell. Times got so bad I had to lay off one of the hands."

159   *Education*

Mama Mouse was introducing her offspring to the ways of the world when they were confronted by a cat. Mama immediately began barking like a dog. The cat took off.

Turning back to her young, Mama announced, "That shows the importance of learning a second language!"

160   *Follow Me*

"Now in case anything should go wrong with this experiment," said the professor of chemistry, "we and the laboratory will be blown sky high. Now come a little closer, boys, that you may follow me."

161   *Not Easy*

A prospective employer asked a job applicant, "Do you live within your income?"

"Just can't do it," the man replied. "It's all I can do to live within my credit."

162   *Curious*

"What is your name, sir?" the bank clerk asked politely.

"Don't you see my signature?" snapped the indignant customer.

"Yes, sir, that's what aroused my curiosity."

163   *Farm Outlook*

"Now that you've won the sweepstakes," the news reporter asked the lucky farmer, "what are you going to do with all that money?"

"Well, I reckon," drawled the farmer, "I'll just keep on a-farmin' till it's all gone."

164   *He Heard Him*

"As an economy measure," said a political-rally committeeman, "we're going to dispense with a dinner. We've decided we'd rather hear the Senator speak than eat."

"That suits me," said another member. "I've heard him eat."

165   *Poor Art Work*

An American tourist in a Madrid restaurant wanted to order steak and mushrooms. He spoke no Spanish, the waiter knew no English.

The diner drew a picture of a mushroom and a cow. The waiter brought him an umbrella and a ticket to the bullfight.

166   *Not on His TV*

The geography teacher asked Bobby a question about the English Channel.

"I don't know about that one," he answered. "There's no such channel on our television set."

167   *He Flunked*

The pupils had all been photographed and the teacher was trying to persuade them each to buy a copy of the group picture.

"Just think how nice it will be to look at it when you are all grown-up and say, 'There's Rose; she's married,' or 'That's Billy, he's a sailor.' "

A small voice at the back of the room piped up, "And there's teacher; she's dead."

168   *Naturally*

What happens when ducks fly upside down?
They quack up.

169   *A Satisfactory Substitute*

A neighbor boy knocked at the door.
"Can Timmy come out and play with me?" he asked.
"I'm sorry, but Timmy is taking his nap," she replied.
"Then can Timmy's new bike come out and play?" he inquired hopefully.

170   *No Use*

"When that boy threw stones at you," the mother scolded her son, "why didn't
you come and tell me instead of throwing stones back at him?"
"What good would that do?" asked the boy. "You couldn't hit the side of a
barn."

171   *Is That Clear*

Waiter: "We got some good zoop today. Want some?"
Customer: "Zoop? What is that?"
Waiter: "You know what hash is? Well, zoop is looser."

172   *Truth in Advertising*

"This clock I bought from you loses fifteen minutes every hour," complained
the irate customer.
"Didn't you see the 'twenty-five percent off' sign when you bought it?" asked
the store owner.

173   *That's Different*

The rookie pitcher had more determination than skill. He was in deep trouble
when the manager came to the mound and said, "Son, I think you've had
enough."
"But I struck out this guy the last time he was up," the pitcher protested.
"I know," the manager said, "but this is the same inning!"

174   *Typical*

A politician who had changed his views radically was congratulated by a
colleague, who said, "I'm glad you've seen the light!"
Came the terse reply, "I didn't see the light—I felt the heat!"

175   *Correct*

John: "Do you know what vehicle doesn't burn gas but is the most expensive to operate?"
Mary: "No. What vehicle is that?"
John: "A supermarket cart."

176   *Is That Clear?*

Farmer Jones was going down the road, and noticed his neighbor raising his barn. When asked why he was doing that, the neighbor said that his mule's ears were so long they were getting sores from rubbing on the door.
"Why don't you just dig out a little under the door? It would be much easier and just as good."
"I said it was the ears that were too long," the man answered, "nothing wrong with his legs!"

177   *Simple*

The children next door told their mother she wasn't to lift a finger on Mother's Day. They were going to do all the cooking. So, they got out three pots, two frying pans, a double boiler, three mixing bowls, a chopping board, six measuring spoons, eight serving dishes—and Mom was delighted. She said it was the best Jell-O she ever tasted.

178   *Wrong Fork*

A man and his wife, hiking in the woods, suddenly realized they had lost their way.
"I wish Emily Post were here," said the husband. "I think we took the wrong fork."

179   *Keeping Up*

A friend has decided against moving from his present house into a new one in the better part of town. The reason, he says, is that most people try to keep up with the Joneses, and where he lives now, he's Jones.

180   *Sounds Reasonable*

As an assignment for schoolwork, the young girl was questioning a quarry worker about the different specimens of rock and stone, what they were used for, and how they could be sold for profit.
As she looked around, the girl discovered the big hole from which the rock was taken, and she asked: "And then, what do you do with this great big hole?"
"Oh, we make a profit on that too," replied the worker. "We cut it up and sell it for basements."

181   *The R's of Life*

The three R's of life:
    At 25. . . . . Romance
    At 45. . . . . Rent
    At 65. . . Rheumatism

182   *Sweetest Phrases*

Language specialists claim that the five sweetest phrases in English are: "I love you." "Dinner is served." "All is forgiven." "Sleep until noon." "Keep the change." There are those who choose to add: "You've lost weight."

183   *Reducing*

Doctor handing bottle of pills to a paunchy patient: "You don't eat them. Just spill them on the floor three times a day and pick them up one at a time."

184   *Smart Machine*

A man returning from Europe landed at Kennedy Airport and stepped on a weighing machine which reports weights by voice instead of by card. Dropping in a dime, he heard the voice say: "You are 5 feet 10 inches tall, weigh 185 pounds, and you are taking a plane to Chicago." He tried it again and got the same answer. To test it out thoroughly, he stepped aside, put on a different-colored coat and tie, pulled his hat down over his ears, stooped over, climbed on the machine, and received this startling answer: "You are 5 feet 10 inches tall, weigh 185 pounds. Your plane left for Chicago while you were changing your coat."

185   *Slow Pay*

A country doctor parked his old jalopy on the street to run an errand. When he returned, a group of small boys were crowded around the vehicle, laughing at it.

The doctor climbed in, saying mildly, "The car's paid for, boys." Then, looking around from one lad to another, he added, "You're not, and you're not, and you're not."

186   *How About Answers?*

What did one math book say to the other math book? "I've got problems."

187   *Salesmanship*

When a sheik returned home from his first vacation in the United States, a friend asked what had impressed him the most.

"American salesmen," he replied, strapping on his skis.

188   *Wanted to Help*

Professor: "If there are any dumbbells in the room, please stand up."
A long pause, then a lone freshman stood up.
Professor: "What! Do you consider yourself a dumbbell?"
Freshman: "Well, not exactly that, sir, but I hate to see you standing all alone."

189   *Tooth Tax*

Internal Revenue agent to taxpayer: "We try to be lenient, sir, but we just can't allow this as a medical deduction: '$50 to the tooth fairy'?"

190   *Just the Old Geese*

Game warden: "Say, you're hunting with last year's license!"
Hunter: "Yeah. But I'm only shooting at the ones I missed last season."

191   *Modern Spider*

Little Miss Muffet sat on a tuffet eating her curds and whey.
Along came a spider, who sat down beside her and said, "Curds have cholesterol, whey is fattening, and sitting on that tuffet will give you back trouble before you're forty."

192   *The Good Old Days*

A little boy ran to his father and excitedly said: "Wow! You oughta see the great lawn mower our neighbors have. It doesn't need gas or anything. You just push it!"

193   *Difficult Case*

A frightened householder reported to the police that he'd been struck down in the dark outside his back door by an unknown assailant. A young policeman was sent to investigate and soon returned to headquarters with a lump on his forehead and a glum look on his face.
"I solved the case," he muttered.
"Amazingly fast work," his superior complimented him. "How did you accomplish it?"
The young cop explained, "I stepped on the rake, too."

194   *Easy Question*

One Sunday morning a group of children in a Sunday School class were asked this seeming run-of-the-mill question: "Why did the Pilgrims invite the Indians to the very first Thanksgiving dinner?"

"Because," said one straightforward thinker, "there wasn't anybody else to invite."

195 *Substitute*

Roses are red, violets are blue;
Orchids are $10.95—will dandelions do?

196 *In School*

"John have you whispered today without permission?"
"Only wunst."
"Robert, should John have said wunst?"
"No'm; he should have said twict."

197 *Move to the Rear*

The bus had become so crowded that there didn't seem to be room for any more passengers. Surveying the situation, the driver sang out cheerfully, "Kindly push each other to the rear, please!"

198 *Wonderful Thing to Do Also*

A university English instructor recently introduced to his class what he termed "one of the finest, most elegant lines of poetry in the English language."
" 'Walk with light,' " he quoted, and then repeated softly, " 'Walk with light.' Now, isn't that a wonderful thing to say to someone?"
The class agreed and wished to know the author.
"I suppose it's anonymous," said the instructor. "It's written on a sign at the intersection of Main and Ninth Streets."

199 *That Would Be Bad*

A Phoenix teacher was explaining to her third-graders the importance of penmanship. "If you can't write your name, when you grow up you'll have to pay cash for everything."

200 *Busy*

An Oxford don describing another don: "What time he can spare from the adornment of his person, he devotes to the neglect of his duties."

201 *Mixed Up*

"My family is politically mixed up," the woman told the canvasser. "I'm a Republican; the old man's a Democrat; the kid's wet; the cow's dry; and the cat's on the fence."

202   *Modern Art*

A modern sculptor is a man who can take a rough block of stone or wood, work on it for months, and make it look like a rough block of stone or wood.

203   *Wrong Way*

An elderly motorist who couldn't see too well was going the wrong way down a one-way street. A policeman stopped him.

"Do you know where you're going?" he asked sternly.

"No," the motorist admitted, "but I surely must be late. Everybody else is coming back!"

204   *Safe*

Wife: "You look tired, dear. Did you have a bad day at the office?"

Husband: "I'll say. I took an aptitude test, and, believe me, it's a good thing I own the company!"

205   *Mystery*

Police inspector to driver whom he had stopped: "Your driving license seems to be valid, madam. Now suppose you tell me how in the world you got it!"

206   *Smart Girl*

Bridegroom: "And now, dear, that we are married, let's have an understanding about our affairs. Do you wish to be president or vice-president?"

Bride: "Neither. You be both. I'll just be the treasurer."

207   *Inflation*

A man went to the meat market the other day and ordered a dollar's worth of steak. The meat man replied, "Brother, you said a mouthful!"

208   *Quick Recovery*

Doctor, to very sick patient: "I'll have you up and complaining about my fee before you know it."

209   *Cool It*

Mother cat reprimanded her kitten for playing away from home so long. "Something dreadful will happen to you," she meowed.

"Cool it, Ma," purred Kitty, "and let me do my own thing with at least one of my lives."

210   *He Punished Him*

Alice: "Isn't Coby a naughty dog, Mommy? He ate my dolly's slipper."
Mother: "Yes, dear. He must be punished."
Alice: "I did punish him. I went out to his kennel and drank his milk."

211   *Simple Question*

Two secretaries sat discussing their bosses during coffee break.
"He's in a bad mood again," moaned one. "All I asked him was whether he wanted the carbon copies double-spaced, too."

212   *Home Cooking*

Grandma's day was not a lark,
She slaved in kitchen, dawn to dark,
But today's wife, she cooks with ease,
All she does is just "unfreeze."

213   *High-powered*

Customer: "Are you sure these field glasses are high-powered?"
Ambitious Salesman: "Lady, when you use these glasses, anything less than ten miles away looks as if it were behind you!"

214   *Fully Insured*

Insured for every accident and policies all paid for,
He drove as madly as he wished—else what's insurance made for?
And then one day he hit a truck—awhile his spirit hovered.
And now one reads above his head the words: "Completely covered."

215   *Worried*

"Just where are you going?" asked the wife of her husband, who was heading for a bank where he intended to try to renew a mortgage loan.
"Oh," replied the harried husband, "I have a rendezvous with debt."

216   *Smart*

Old Lady: "Isn't it wonderful how these filling-station people know where to set up pumps and get gas?"

217   *Collective Noun*

Teacher: "Give me an example of a collective noun."
Pupil: "Garbage can."

218   *Not Easy*

The teacher had asked her pupils who the nine greatest Americans were. All pupils had turned in their papers except Johnny.

"Can't you finish your list, Johnny?" asked the teacher.

"I'm still undecided," replied Johnny, "about the first baseman."

219   *Good Question*

Mother: "Be sure to wash your arms before you put on a clean shirt."

John: "Shall I wash them for long or short sleeves?"

220   *Not Difficult*

When my nephew was five years old, he surprised me one day by saying, "I guess I'll go outdoors and play ball with God."

"How do you play ball with God?" I asked.

"Oh, it's not hard at all," he explained. "I just throw the ball up and God throws it back down to me."

221   *Left the Rabbits*

Little Ricky was delighted when he received two baby rabbits for an Easter present. He enjoyed them even more as they grew up, but they became a nuisance to his parents.

Mom and Dad considered various ways of getting rid of the rabbits. Dad finally decided a brisk, blunt approach would be best. One day he said to his wife, "Dear, how about having one of those rabbits for dinner tonight?"

Ricky's face lit up. Before Mom could answer, he cried, "Say, that would be swell, Daddy. Do you think he can hold his spoon?"

They still have the rabbits.

222   *Feel Older*

Nothing makes you feel older than the discovery that today's children are studying in history class what you studied in current events.

223   *Good Sight*

Lawyer: "You say you were about thirty-five feet away from the scene of the accident? Just how far can you see clearly?"

Witness: "Well, when I wake up in the morning I see the sun, and they tell me it's about ninety-three million miles away."

224   *Could Be Different*

Employer (to applicant for position who had handed in testimonials from two ministers): "We don't work on Sundays. Haven't you a reference from someone who sees you on weekdays?"

225 *Wonderful*

"Senator, your speech was superfluous, simply superfluous," gushed the woman admirer.

"I'm glad you liked it," responded the Senator, tongue in cheek. "I hope to have it published posthumously."

"Wonderful! Just wonderful!" she replied. "I do hope it will be soon."

226 *Dumbbells*

Professor (after a trying first-hour class): "Some time ago my doctor told me to exercise early every morning with dumbbells. Will the class please join me tomorrow before breakfast?"

227 *It Depends*

A tourist stopped where a farmer was erecting a building. "What are you building?" he asked.

"Wal," answered the farmer, "if 'n I can rent it, it's a rustic cottage, an' if 'n I can't, it's a cowshed."

228 *Moldier*

The man was lecturing his daughter on snobbishness. "Remember," he pointed out, "we're all made from the same mold."

"Of course that's true, Pop," the daughter replied, "but some are moldier than others."

229 *We Saw It*

Real-estate man to young couple: "Yes, I do have something for ten thousand dollars. Would you like to ride out with me and see if it is standing?"

230 *Employees*

A Munich, Germany, hotel has posted a sign in each room: "Please be courteous to our employees. They are harder to get than guests."

231 *Read the Fine Print*

Behold the warranty: The bold print giveth, and the fine print taketh away.

232 *Really Tough*

Three little boys were talking about how tough they were.

"I'm so tough I wear out a pair of shoes every week," said the first little boy.

"Why, that's nothing," said the second boy. "I wear out a pair of blue jeans every day."

"You guys aren't so tough," piped up the third. "I wear out my grandma and grandpa in an hour."

233   *We Heard Them*

Wife (watching a youthful singing group on TV): "They say those boys alone have sold thousands of TV sets."
Husband: "I believe it. After seeing them, I feel like selling ours, too."

234   *When You Go Camping*

A camping tip: The best way to make a fire with two sticks is to be sure one of them is a match.

235   *Valuable Knowledge*

Americans swallow some seventeen billion aspirin tablets every year—an average of seventy-seven per person, according to research done at Duke University Medical Center.

236   *Correct*

A small boy was asked to write an essay in as few words as possible on two of life's greatest problems.
He wrote: "Twins."

237   *Every Family Needs One*

The father of the household called the telephone company and ordered a fifty-foot extension cord put on the phone. He explained, "I want my daughter to stay outside more now that the weather is nice."

238   *Comparatively Speaking*

> In every way in which we live,
> Our values are comparative.
> Observe the snail who, with a sigh,
> Says: "See those turtles whizzing by."

239   *She Probably Knew*

A farmer and his wife, married happily for almost half a century, were sitting in the front-porch swing in the cool of the evening. The sun was going down in a blaze of color, the birds were trilling their evening song, the soft breeze wafted the scent of honeysuckle across the porch. The moment was a moving one. The farmer felt strangely moved to speech, and blurted out, "Martha, sometimes I love you so much I can hardly keep from telling you."

240   *Smart Boys*

Two boys were talking together when one asked the other, "Did you hear about the four new states?"

"No!" the second boy said. "What are they called?"

"New York, New Jersey, New Hampshire, and New Mexico."

241   *Unreasonable*

Employee: "I'd like to have next Wednesday off, sir."

Boss: "Why?"

Employee: "It's our silver anniversary and my wife and I want to go out and celebrate."

Boss: "Are we going to have to put up with this every twenty-five years?"

242   *Different*

As the Sunday School teacher was describing how Lot's wife looked back and turned into a pillar of salt, little Norman interrupted.

"My mother looked back once while she was driving," he announced triumphantly, "and she turned into a telephone pole!"

243   *Takes Her Work Home*

Two hard-working secretaries were riding home from work on the bus and one said, "Isn't it fierce the way we have to work these days?"

"Fierce isn't the word. Why, I typed so many letters yesterday that last night I finished my prayers with 'yours truly.' "

244   *Not So Easy*

The four-year-old was absolutely fascinated with his grandfather's false teeth. After staring transfixed while they were removed for brushing and replaced, he asked to have the process repeated. The obliging grandfather did it several times for the youngster, then asked, "Now what?"

The child's eyes shifted momentarily and he said, "Take off your nose."

245   *Using Her Head*

We heard of an enterprising housewife who found a way to meet the crisis during a garbagemen's strike in her city. She put the family garbage in a box, wrapped the box very carefully with gift wrapping, put a nice ribbon around it, and then drove to a public parking lot and left it conspicuously on the front seat of her car, with the window open. When she returned to her car after a reasonable time, the box was gone every time.

246   *Fair Exchange*

Want ad: "Reliable and hardworking clerk who is paid on Friday and broke on Tuesday would like to exchange small loans with another who gets paid on Wednesday and is broke on Saturday."

247   *What He Heard*

One hot summer Sunday, a faithful member of the congregation invited the visiting minister and his family to come to dinner. Wanting to impress the guests, the mother asked her five-year-old son to say grace before the meal.

"But I don't know what to say," the boy exclaimed.

"Oh, just say what you heard me say, dear," the mother prompted.

Obediently, the boy bowed his head and murmured: "O Lord, why did I invite those people here on a hot day like this?"

248   *Fast Thinking*

A golfer stepped up to the first tee and took a mighty swing. The drive was a hole in one.

His opponent stepped to the tee, waggled his driver, and said, "Okay, Fred, now I'll take *my* practice swing—then we'll start."

249   *Not Certain*

A reporter asked the centenarian the inevitable, "To what do you attribute your long life?"

"Not sure yet," the old-timer replied, eyes a-twinkle. "I'm still negotiating with a mattress company and two breakfast-food firms."

250   *Thoughtful*

Said the kind old lady to the Internal Revenue clerk, "I do hope you'll give my money to some nice country."

251   *Typical Texas*

A little boy from Texas asked Santa Claus, "What can I do for you?"

252   *Still Young*

A young reporter asked the chic, vibrant, elderly woman if she'd mind telling her age.

"Not at all," she replied with a twinkle. "I'm plenty-nine."

253 *No Charge*

"There'll be no charge, lady," said the irate taxi driver to his fare. "You did the driving."

254 *Hard to Believe*

Two women on a tour of Mount Vernon, George Washington's beautiful home on the Potomac, were enthusiastically admiring the various rooms. "And did you notice, Grace," commented one, "everything's furnished in Early American?"

255 *It Will Sell*

There's a new tranquilizer out. It doesn't relax you, but it does make you enjoy being tense.

256 *Nothing New*

Excerpt from a letter by a fourteen-year-old girl reporting to a friend on the gifts she received after graduating from junior high: "And Grandma gave me a diary. It is a nice diary, but it is awfully late to start a diary now. Everything has happened."

257 *By Comparison*

One woman archeologist to another: "What I like about this work is that it makes me feel so young."

258 *Helpful*

Woman customer (after the tired assistant had pulled down blanket after blanket until there was only one left on the shelf): "I don't really want to buy a blanket today. I was only looking for a friend."

Clerk: "If you think she's in the other one, madam, I'll gladly take it down for you."

259 *Threatening Letters*

An angry little man bounced into the postmaster's office. "For some time now," he shouted, "I've been bothered by threatening letters, and I want something done about it."

"I'm sure we can help," soothed the postmaster. "That's a federal offense. Have you any idea who is sending you these letters?"

"Sure!" snapped the little man. "It's those pesky income-tax people!"

260   *Worried*

A businessman visited his banker and asked: "Are you worried about whether I can meet my note next month?"

"Yes, I am," confessed the banker.

"Good," said the client. "That's what I pay you eight percent for."

261   *Needs Glasses*

First burglar: "I need eyeglasses."

Second burglar: "What makes you think so?"

First burglar: "Well, I was twirling the knobs of a safe and a dance orchestra began to play."

262   *He Was Alone Then*

It was the minute of rest between the ninth and tenth rounds and the battered fighter sat on his stool, his seconds working furiously over his bleeding face.

"I think he's got you whipped," said his manager in disgust.

"Yeah," agreed the pugilist, gazing dizzily through nearly closed eyes. "I should have got him in the first round when he was by himself."

263   *Sounds Right*

A woman motorist was being examined for a driver's license.

Examiner: "And what is the white line in the middle of the road for?"

Woman: "Bicycles."

264   *A Real Problem*

"This is the fourth morning you've been late, Susan," said the mistress to her maid.

"Yes, ma'am," replied Susan, "I overslept myself."

"Where is the clock I gave you?"

"In my room, ma'am."

"Don't you wind it up?"

"Oh, yes! I wind it up, ma'am."

"And do you set the alarm?"

"Every night."

"But don't you hear the alarm in the morning, Susan?"

"No, ma'am. That's the trouble. You see, the thing goes off while I'm asleep."

265   *Easy Mistake*

The junior sales manager complained of aches and pains to his wife. Neither could account for his trouble. Arriving home one night from work, he informed her, "I finally discovered why I've been feeling so miserable. We got some ultramodern office furniture two weeks ago, and I just learned today that I've been sitting in the wastebasket."

266 Blast Off

After a long, dreary Saturday during which our two sons had been particularly rambunctious, my wife had reached the end of her patience. "Get ready for bed!" she commanded.

The boys headed for their room, and I overheard Tom—eight years old—say, "We'd better get a move on. She's on the countdown and ready to blast off."

267 He Knew

Teacher: "How did you get that swelling on your nose, Joseph?"
Joseph: "Yesterday I bent down to smell a brose."
Teacher: "'Joseph, there is no 'b' in 'rose.' "
Joseph: "There was in this one."

268 They're Scarce

Sign in a department-store window: "Wonderful bargain in shirts for men with sixteen and seventeen necks."

269 Perfect

"Professor," said the old grad at the class reunion, "now that I've made a lot of money, I want to do something for the dear old school. Let's see now, in what studies did I excel?"

"As I remember, sir, in my class you slept most of the time."

"Fine! Good suggestion! I'll build a dormitory!"

270 In the Springtime

Spring has sprung, The grass has riz;
I wonder where the birdies is!

271 Good Job

Weary of the constant disorder in her sons' room, a mother laid down the law: For every item she had to pick up off the floor, they would have to pay her a nickel.

At the end of a week, the boys owed her sixty-five cents. She received the money promptly—along with a fifty-cent tip and a note that read, "Thanks, Mom, keep up the good work!"

272   Trying

A mother, distressed about her daughter's report card, called the school. "Isn't she trying?" she asked the child's teacher. The teacher sighed wearily. "Yes, very."

273   Foolish Questions

A man, full of excitement, phoned the fire department: "Fire! Fire!" "Where is it?" "My house!" "I mean the location of the fire." "My kitchen!" "Yes, but how can we get to your place?" "You've got a fire engine, haven't you?"

274   He Helped

At a large park a conservationist guide wound up his lecture by shouting, "What did you ever do to preserve our forests?" One startled tourist blurted, "I—I shot a woodpecker as a boy."

275   Of Course

Foreman: "Sir, the employees are complaining that the lunches in the café are smaller these days." Manager: "Nonsense. They only look smaller since the café was enlarged."

276   Experience

Professor: "What happens when the human body is immersed in water?" Student: "The telephone rings."

277   Let Him Squeak

A local housewife aroused her husband at about two A.M. and said: "Get up, John. There's a mouse in this room. I can hear him squeaking." A sleepy reply came from John: "Well, what do you expect me to do—oil him?"

278   Tough Decision

Then there's the fellow who'd like to buy one of those electric toothbrushes, but doesn't know if his teeth are AC or DC.—F. G. Kernan

279   Expensive Advice

The doctor finally reached his table at a dinner, after breaking away from a woman who sought advice on a health problem.

"Do you think I should send her a bill?" the doctor asked a lawyer who sat next to him.

"Why not?" the lawyer replied. "You rendered professional services by giving advice."

"Thanks," the physician said. "I think I'll do that."

When the doctor went to his office the next day to send the bill to the woman, he found a letter from the lawyer. It read:

"For legal services, $50."

280   Helpers

Two women were talking about their husbands.

"Henry is perfectly helpless without me," said one.

"John is that way, too," said the other. "I don't know what would become of him if I went away for a week."

"Isn't that a fact!" sighed the first. "Sometimes I think my husband is a child, the way I have to look after him. Why, whenever he is sewing on buttons, mending his clothes, or even darning his socks, I always have to thread the needle for him."

281   Shrewd Salesmanship

"Grandma, were you once a little girl like me?" asked a youngster.

"Why, yes, dear," answered Grandma, smiling. "Why do you ask?"

"Then," continued the little girl, "I suppose you know how it feels to get an ice-cream cone when you don't expect it."

282   Golf

I shot a golf ball into the air.
It fell to earth, I knew not where.
I only knew, with woe immense,
That I had lost a good many cents!

283   Good Advice

The portly sales manager was getting ready to leave his doctor's office after a routine examination. "Here," said the doctor, "follow this diet, and I want to see three fourths of you back here for a check-up in three months."

284   Experience

Mark Twain once said this about experience: "We should be careful to get out of an experience only the wisdom that is in it—and stop there, lest we be like the cat that sits down on a hot stove-lid. She will never again sit on a hot stove-lid —and that is well, but neither will she ever sit down on a cold one."

285   *Gallant and Buoyant*

A plump old lady struggled up onto a bus without her husband making any attempt to help her. "Eh, Henry," she said, as she sank into a seat, "you ain't as gallant as you was when I was a gal."

"No, luv," he replied. "And you ain't as buoyant as you was when I were a boy."—*Tid-Bits, London*

286   *Shouldn't Kick*

The firing squad was escorting a Russian comrade to his place of execution. It was a dismal march in a pouring rain.

"What a terrible morning to die," muttered the prisoner.

"What are you kicking about?" asked the guard. "We gotta march back and live."

287   *They Help You*

A little boy was leading his sister up a mountain path. "Why," she complained, "it's not a path at all. It's all rocky and bumpy."

"Sure," he said, "the bumps are what you climb on."

288   *Hard to Explain*

Man puts up screens against insects, air-conditions his home, and then goes outside for a picnic.

289   *Bright Side*

Wife at breakfast table to grumpy husband: "Look on the bright side. In sixteen hours you'll be back in bed."

290   *Originality*

One of the big service clubs limits its members to one from each business or profession. It already had a member filling the classification "Religion—Protestant" when a Methodist bishop moved to town. His friends were eager to get him into the local club. They wound up by reclassifying their present member under the heading "Religion—Retail" and took in the bishop under "Religion—Wholesale."—*Chaplain*

291   *Informal*

Mark Twain calls on some new neighbors: "My name is Clemens; we ought to have called on you before, and I beg your pardon for intruding now in this informal way, but your house is on fire."—*Mark Twain*

292   *News*

Thieves broke into the Kremlin and stole the results of the next election.

293   *Wearing Out Early*

A four-year-old boy was severely sunburned and his skin began to peel. One day, as he washed his face, his mother heard him mutter: "Only four and wearing out already."

294   *Only Talked Sense*

Among the guests at a reception was a distinguished man of letters. He was grave and somewhat taciturn. One of the ladies present suggested to the hostess that he seemed to be out of place at such a party.

"Yes," replied the hostess, "he can't talk anything but sense."

295   *The Test*

New executive slogan: "If you haven't developed ulcers, you're not carrying your share of the load."

296   *Not Expensive*

A five-year-old boy was asked by a new neighbor how many there were in his family.

"Seven," was the reply.

"My, that many children must cost a lot," the neighbor exclaimed.

"Oh, no," said the child. "We don't buy them, we raise them."

297   *Hard Work*

A bum approached a man and asked for a dime. The man told him he didn't have a dime but he'd be glad to buy his breakfast.

"Man," the bum said, "I've had three breakfasts now, trying to get a dime."

298   *Not His Fault*

A small boy presented a worn, dirty book at the desk of the public library. The librarian glanced at the title, then at the size of the boy, and remarked, "This book is awfully technical, isn't it?"

Although a little embarrassed, the boy stood firm, looked her squarely in the eye, and answered, "It was that way when I got it."

299   *Just Practicing*

The paratroopers were aloft for their first jump. Everything went off in perfect order, until the last man came forward to jump. "Hold it!" shouted his commanding officer. "You're not wearing your parachute!"

"Oh, that's all right, sir," retorted the recruit. "We're just practicing, aren't we?"

300   Modern Youth

After teaching my second-graders "America the Beautiful," I listened while they sang it for me. And one voice rang out above the rest: "Oh, beautiful for space-ship skies . . ."—*Merilyn Kilby*

301   Spaceman

"Take me to Brigitte Bardot. I'll see your leader later."

302   Is That Nice?

Two rival authoresses met the other day. One had just had a new book published.
First: "Darling, I think it's a masterpiece. Who wrote it for you?"
Second: "I'm so glad you like it. Who read it to you?"

303   More Reliable

We were discussing various kinds of clocks in my kindergarten class. "Now you have an alarm clock at home, don't you?" I asked one of the pupils.
"Oh, no," he replied. "We don't need one. We have a grandmother."

304   It Won't Be Easy

Shoe Department manager to customer: "Yes, we have a selection of loafers. I'll see if I can get one to wait on you."

305   Not Tiring

The couple had just returned from a trip to the coast, and their neighbors asked about it.
"We drove five thousand miles in two weeks," the husband said.
The neighbors were impressed. "Some driving! Did it tire you?"
"Well, actually," the husband attempted to explain, "my wife did the driving."
"And you enjoyed the scenery?" asked the incredulous neighbor.
"Yes—that, and held the wheel."

306   No Wonder

"Has the laundry made a mistake?" asked Mr. Brown. "This shirt is so tight I can hardly breathe."
"Yes, it's your shirt all right," replied his wife, "but you've got your head through a buttonhole."

307 *Safe*

Business partner: "We forgot to lock the safe."
Other partner: "What difference does it make? We're both here."

308 *New Record Player*

A modern youngster came home from school and announced excitedly, "They've got a magic record player at our school."
"Magic record player?" asked his puzzled mother.
"Yes, you don't have to plug it into electricity—you don't even need electricity to make it play. All you have to do is wind up a crank."

309 *His Observation*

From a student's examination paper: "A circle is a round straight line with a hole in the middle."

310 *Standing By*

After a traffic accident, one woman rushed out of the gathering crowd to lean over the victim. She was pushed aside by a man who directed, "Step back, please. I've had a course in first aid."
The woman stood and watched the man's ministrations for a few minutes, then tapped him on the shoulder. "When you get to the part about calling a doctor," she said, "I'm already here."

311 *Break It Gently*

Weatherman to radio announcer: "Better break it to them gently. Just say 'Partly cloudy with scattered showers followed by a hurricane.' "

312 *Couldn't Believe It*

Inviting a friend to his wedding anniversary, the man explained, "We're on the seventh floor, apartment 7D. Just touch the button with your elbow."
"Why should I use my elbow?"
"For goodness' sake, man, you're not coming empty-handed, are you?"

313 *Just a Little Dent*

Wife to husband: "I scratched the front fender a little, dear. If you want to look at it, it's in the trunk."

314   *Slowly*

A couple vacationing in Rome were being shown through the Colosseum. "Now this is the room," said the guide, "where the slaves dressed to fight the lions."

"But how does somebody dress to fight lions?" asked the wife.

"Very slowly," replied the guide.

315   *Small Meeting*

A small boy lowered his head at the dinner table one night and told his parents there was to be a small PTA meeting next day. "Well, if it's just a small one, do you think we ought to go?" asked his mother.

"I'm afraid so," said the youngster. "It's just you, me, and the principal."

316   *Smart Student*

Teacher: "Name some of Thomas Edison's contributions to science."

Student: "If it weren't for Edison, we'd all be watching television by candlelight."

317   *They'll See Through It*

Bob: "My boss wants a pane of glass nine by eleven inches."

Clerk: "Haven't any that size. Will a pane eleven inches by nine inches do?"

Bob: "Well, I'll try it. Maybe if I slip it in sideways, nobody will notice."

318   *How He Felt*

Young Jim spent his first week away from home at a summer camp. He was not much of a letter writer, but one day his mother got a card from him: "Dear Mom: There are 50 boys here this week, but I sure wish there were only 49. Jim."

319   *No Doubt*

Father was sitting in the armchair one evening when his little son came in and showed him a new penknife which he said he had found in the street.

"Are you sure it.was lost?" inquired the father.

"Of course it was lost! I saw the man looking for it!" replied the youngster.

320   *No Guest*

Hotel patron: "May I have some stationery, please?"

Clerk: "Are you a guest of the hotel, sir?"

Patron: "I should say not! I'm paying fifty dollars a day!"

321   *Changing World*

With moccasins, loafers, casuals, and buckles, a person can earn a Ph.D. and never have to learn how to tie a shoelace.

322   *Health Hint*

Electric-toothbrush owners are advised to brush twice a day and see their electrician once a year.

323   *Only First Grade*

Little Barbara was walking home from school, holding hands with a boy about her own age. "This is my boyfriend," she told a friendly policeman.

"A pretty little girl like you has only one boyfriend?" he asked in mock surprise. "Well," Barbara said, wrinkling her small brow, "I'm only in the first grade."

324   *Already Knew*

"Why are you eating that banana with the skin on?"

"Why should I peel it? I know what's inside."

325   *Strange*

Two houseflies were conversing and the first said, "Sylvester, aren't people funny?" "Yes, George," said Sylvester, "but what made you think about it just now?" "Well," replied George, "I was just thinking how much money they spent building a beautiful ceiling like this—and then they walk on the floor."

326   *Good Reason*

A lady phoned her television serviceman, and complained that something was wrong with her set. The serviceman asked her whether there were any visible symptoms.

"Well, the newscaster is on right now," replied the lady, "and he has a very long face."

"Ma'am," replied the serviceman, "if you had to report what's happening in the world these days, you'd have a long face, too!"

327   *Pennsylvania Dutch*

Throw Papa down from the haymow, his hat.
Go out and tie the dog loose.
I belled the door, but it didn't make.
Don't eat yourself full, there's cake back yet.
Mary, eat your mouth empty before you say.

328   *Bald*

The advantage of being bald is that when you are expecting company, all you have to do is to straighten your tie.

329   *Saving*

Trying to sell a housewife a home freezer, a salesman pointed out, "You can save enough on your food bills to pay for the freezer."

"Yes, I know," the woman agreed, "but you see we're paying for our car on the carfare we save. Then, we're paying for our washing machine on the laundry bills we save, and we're paying for the house on the rent we're saving. We just can't afford to save any more right now."

330   *He Warned Them*

A farmer who was troubled by trespassers during the nutting season consulted with a botanical friend. The botanist furnished him with the technical name of the hazel, and the farmer placed the following notice at conspicuous points about his premises:

"Trespassers, take warning! All persons entering these woods do so at their own risk, for although common snakes are not often found, the Corylus Avelana abounds everywhere and never gives warning of its presence."

The place was unmolested that year, and the farmer gathered his crop in peace.

331   *Wrong*

"Who can tell us something about Ruth?" asked the Sunday School teacher.

"I can, ma'am," said Johnny. "They called him The Bambino."

332   *She was Listening*

A small girl was entertaining the visitors while her mother was in the kitchen. One woman guest cast an appraising look at the little girl and then whispered to her friend, "Not very p-r-e-t-t-y."

"No," answered the child, "but awfully s-m-a-r-t."

333   *Success*

"My garden was such a success this year," boasted a gentleman farmer, "that my neighbor's chickens took first prize at the poultry show."

334   *Frank*

A group of second-graders were struggling to compose a thank-you letter to send to the manager of a farm they had visited. One suggested version was, "We want to thank you for wasting your time on us and showing us the farm and the animals."—*Harry B. Gorton*

335   *He Really Pays*

He who dances must pay the fiddler—also the waiter, the florist, the hatcheck girl, the doorman, and the parking attendant.

336   *Couldn't Win*

Mrs. Biggs: "Don't you dare tell me, Doctor, that I am overweight."

Doctor: "Then, according to my height and weight chart, you are four inches too short."

337   *Baseball*

The Little Leaguer put all his sixty pounds into a swing and connected—barely. The ball scraped the bottom of the bat, jiggled straight back to the pitcher, who fumbled it. There was time to nail the batter at first, but the pitcher's throw soared over the first baseman's head. The slugger flew on toward second base. Somebody retrieved the ball. The next throw sailed into left field.

The hitter swaggered into third, puffing through a man-sized grin, then continued to cross the final plate.

"Oh, boy!" he said. "That's the first home run I ever hit in my whole life!"

338   *The Difference*

The four-year-old daughter of a busy father had acquired a fixation for the story "The Three Little Pigs," and demanded that he read it to her night after night. The man, pleased with himself, tape-recorded the story. When the child next asked for it, he simply switched on the playback.

This worked for a couple of nights, but then one evening the little girl pushed the storybook at her father.

"Now, honey," he said, "you know how to turn on the recorder by yourself."

"Yes," she said, "but I can't sit on its lap."

339   *Not Easy*

As they window-shopped at the furniture store, the new bride said to her husband, "I just cannot see how they make all that nice furniture out of those crinkly little old walnuts."

340   *New Song*

Mother: "What did you do at the party?"

Little Laura: "We sang the refrigerator song."

Mother: "How does that go?"
Little Laura: "Freeze a jolly good fellow . . ."

341 Not Time to Ride

Two men carrying briefcases stopped in front of a traffic snarl. One glanced at his watch and looked at the traffic.

"Hmmmm," he said to his companion, "do we have time to take a cab or shall we walk?"

342 Knotholes

"Daddy, what are those holes in the board for?"

"Those are knotholes."

"Well, if they are not holes, what are they?"

343 It Isn't Easy

Said the sweet young thing, tripping up to the bank cashier's window: "Tell me how to make out a check so that the money will come out of my husband's half of our joint bank account."

344 Same Old Tie

"Well, Coach," said the team captain, "we're going to present you with a victory for your birthday."

"Good!" replied the coach happily. "I was expecting the same old tie!"

345 Didn't Know

Two hitchhikers had to find a place to spend the night. They asked a farmer for a handout and a place to sleep.

"Cut a batch of kindling," said the farmer, "and I'll give you a good meal and let you sleep in the barn tonight."

Neither hitchhiker had ever handled an ax, but they were too hungry to say no. Five minutes later the farmer came back to see how they were doing. One of the men was leaning on his ax staring at the other, who bounced around the yard in an amazing series of ballet leaps, flip-flops, and somersaults.

"Say," exclaimed the farmer in admiration, "I didn't know your partner was an acrobat."

"I didn't either," replied the hitchhiker, "until I accidentally hit him on the shins with this ax."

346 Early Shaver

A tourist was traveling through the mountains and stopped for gas. In back of the station was a mountaineer boy shaving himself with a bowie knife.

"My," said the tourist, "that looks dangerous. Did you ever cut yourself?"

"Well," said the mountain boy, "I have been shaving nigh on to two years now and I haven't cut myself either time."

347   Her Weight

When a woman refuses to tell her weight, you can be sure she weighs one hundred and plenty.

348   Three Months

While traveling through Maine they stopped at a country store. The husband attended to the buying while the wife pored over a road map. Suddenly she realized an elderly man was looking at their New York license plate.

"The first one of those I've seen through here this spring," he explained. "Great state, New York!"

"Yours is a great state, too," she responded.

"Yes, Maine's a great state. Only bad thing about it is the weather. There's three months in the year you can't depend on the sleighin' bein' any good—June, July, and August."

349   Both Broke

First clerk: "I don't know what Bill does with his money. He's broke again."

Second clerk: "Was he trying to borrow from you?"

First clerk: "No! I wanted to borrow from him."

350   Is the Line Busy?

A man bought a parrot and in trying to make him talk he kept repeating, "Hello, hello."

Finally, the parrot opened one sleepy eye and said, "What's the matter? Line busy?"

351   Hard Decision

The deep-sea diver had scarcely reached the bottom when a message came from the surface which left him in a dilemma.

"Come up quick," he was told, "the ship is sinking!"

352   Cautious

Uncle Ben, a very cautious and frugal old man, put on his best clothes one day and went down to have a look at the city.

As he was standing on a street corner, a ragged stranger approached, asking, "Will you give me a quarter for a sandwich?"

Uncle Ben gave him a good looking over, then said, "Lemme see the sandwich first."

353 *Knocking*

Used-car dealer, driving up a hill: "This is the opportunity of your lifetime."
Customer: "Yes, I can hear it knocking."

354 *The Horse*

"I had some trouble with my horse while cantering about the park this morning," confessed the intrepid horseman. "He wanted to go one way, and I wanted to go the other way."
"How did you settle it?"
"Oh," replied the rider airily, "the horse tossed me for it."

355 *Is that Clear?*

The job applicant tried his best to fill out the employment form. On the line asking, "Length of residence at present address," he thought and thought, and finally wrote: "About forty feet not counting the garage."

356 *Be Careful*

Captain: "So you desire to become my son-in-law?"
Private: "Well, no, I don't, but I can't see how I'm going to get out of it if I marry your daughter, sir."

357 *The First Buzzards*

An old man was sitting on the porch of a little village store when a big, shiny car drove up with two strangers in it.
"Hey, Grandpa," one of them called out, "how long has this burg been dead?"
The old man looked at them carefully over the rim of his spectacles before he replied: "Not long, you're the first buzzards I have seen."

358 *Good Reason*

Waiting in line at the parachute-jumping club, a new member nervously inquired of an old veteran, "What made you decide to become a jumper?"
The older man replied: "A plane with three dead engines."

359 *Enough*

Gas-station attendant to teen-age motorist with dented fender: "I don't know if I should sell you any gasoline or not. It looks to me like you've had enough."

360 *Great Except*

Wife to her accordion-player husband: "I thought your part was great, except when you pinched yourself."

361   *Heaping*

Home Economics teacher: "When the sauce begins to boil, put in a tablespoon of water."

Sweet young thing: "Level or heaping?"

362   *The Same—Except*

A collector of antiques passed through a small town in Illinois one day and stopped to watch an old man splitting some logs. "That's a very old ax you have there," he volunteered.

"Yes," replied the old man, "and it once belonged to Abe Lincoln."

"You don't say!" exclaimed the collector. "But it doesn't look quite that old."

"Well," said the old man, "it ain't exactly. It's had four new handles and two new heads since Lincoln had it."

363   *Better Rug*

The wealthy playboy had been showing his guests the trophies he had brought back from a hunting expedition in India. Indicating a tiger-skin rug, he said, "When I shot this tiger it was a case of him or me!"

One of the rather uncultured guests stared at the tiger skin, and then at the host. "Well, old boy," he declared, "he sure makes a better rug!"

364   *Too Smart for Dad*

"Young man," said the angry father from the head of stairs, "didn't I hear the clock strike four when you brought my daughter in?"

"You did," admitted the boy friend. "It was going to strike eleven, but I grabbed it and held the gong so it wouldn't disturb you."

The father muttered, "Wonder why I didn't think of that one in *my* courting days!"

365   *That's the Problem*

Husband to wife: "I'll say this for television—the more unsuitable the program, the quieter it keeps the children!"

366   *He Owns One*

A West Texan pulled up in front of Houston's Shamrock Hotel in a cruiser-length car. He fished a ten-dollar bill out of his pocket and handed it to the doorman. "Take good care of the car," he said patronizingly.

"I sure will," answered the doorman. "I own one myself."

367   *Nippy*

"In your advertisement you said that there was a nip in the air after sundown," complained the tourist.

"Well," replied the resort owner, "take a look at those mosquitoes."

368   *He Behaves*

"Do you behave in church?" an interested relative asked Junior when he came to visit.

"I guess I do," said Junior. "I heard a lady behind me say she never saw a child behave so."

369   *What a Beach*

An American tourist was in his bathing suit in the middle of the desert. An Arab rode by and blinked in amazement.

"I'm going swimming," the tourist explained.

"But the ocean's eight hundred miles from here," said the Arab.

"Eight hundred miles!" exclaimed the tourist. "Boy! What a beach!"

370   *He Was Ready*

Boss: "You can't just ask for a raise, you must work yourself up."

Employee: "I have, sir. I'm trembling all over."

371   *Not Too Smart*

A motorist was driving in the country when suddenly his car stopped. He got out and was checking the spark plugs when an old horse trotted up the road.

The horse said, "Better check the gas line," and trotted on.

The motorist was so frightened that he ran to the nearest farmhouse and told the farmer what had happened.

"Was it an old horse with a flopping ear?" inquired the farmer.

"Yes! Yes!" cried the frightened man.

"Well, don't pay any attention to him," replied the farmer. "He doesn't know much about cars."

372   *Really Short*

Policeman: "Can you describe your missing cashier?"

Banker: "He is about five feet five inches tall and seven thousand dollars short."

373   *Really Serious*

"How long have you been driving without a tail light, buddy?" demanded the policeman.

The driver jumped out, ran to the rear of his car, and gave a low moan. His distress was so great that the cop was moved to ease up on him a bit.

"Aw, come now," he said, "you don't have to take it so hard. It isn't that serious."

"It isn't?" cried the motorist. "What happened to my trailer?"

374   No Luck

Two commuters were waiting for the morning special to take them into the city.

"Did I get a surprise this morning," said one. "I put on a suit I hadn't worn since last fall, and in one of the pockets I found a roll of bills I had forgotten!"

"Boy," said the other, "how lucky can you get?"

"Oh, I don't know," said the first. "Not a one of them was receipted!"

375   Not His Plan

Sam: "They tell me your brother is going to be married."

Jake: "I don't think that's so. He's in school and studying for a bachelor's degree."

376   Insulting

Stout blonde: "On the bus today three men jumped up and offered me their seats."

Slender brunette: "And did you take them?"

377   A Good Driver

A young girl was going on her first date, and the naturally nervous father inquired: "Are you sure this fellow is a good driver?"

"Oh, yes," his daughter replied. "He has to be. One more speeding ticket and he loses his license."

378   Old Phrases Used Today

Here are some common phrases used every day. See if you have any idea where they came from:

"Thanks for nothing."

"No limits but the sky."

"To give the devil his due."

"A peck of troubles."

"Let the worse come to the worst."

"A finger in every pie."

"Every dog has his day."

"A wild-goose chase."

Give up? Every one of them appeared in one book, *Don Quixote,* written more than 350 years ago by Miguel de Cervantes.

379   *Language Barrier*

There is a law in Ethiopia that all school instruction above the sixth grade must be done in English instead of the native Amharic. For youngsters not well grounded in English, this stress results in some bloopers. Some of the definitions:
Bride: Past tense for broad.
Coffin: A place to have coffee.
Ankle: My father's brother.
Use "vice" in a sentence: "I hear the Vice of America on the radio."
Name the planet that has rings around it: "Saturday."

380   *Of Course*

Teacher: "Why do wild geese fly south in the autumn?"
Pupil: "Walking would take too long."

381   *Times Change*

> The world is so full of a number of things,
> Most of them so chaotic,
> That those of us who are happy as kings
> Must either be boobs or psychotic.

382   *Hard Job*

"I'm sorry to be late, Mom," said ten-year-old Jimmy as he rushed home from school. "We were making a science display, and I had to stay to finish the universe."

383   *He Is Not Clean*

Mother: "I'm ashamed of you, Betty! Why are you whipping the kitty?"
Betty: " 'Cause he's dirty. He spits on his feet and wipes them on his face."

384   *A Crooked Oyster*

A lady oyster had just returned from her first date with a lobster, and was telling her oyster friends about it.
"He was wonderful," she confided. "First he looked deep into my eyes, then he put his arms around me, then he . . ."
A look of horror crossed her face. "They're gone!" she shrieked. "My pearls!"

385 *Watt For?*

Did you hear about the man who thought he would like to make gardening his hobby?

He planted some 25-watt bulbs, hoping by fall to get some 75- and 100-watt sizes. During the summer there was a lot of lightning and all he got was flash bulbs.

386 *Oversight*

He took her hand in marriage, but made the basic blunder
Of letting her withhold from him a thumb to keep him under.

387 *It Did*

Bill Muffet said his car couldn't skid:
This monument shows that it could—and did.

388 *On Her Right Hand*

Hostess (to small boy at party): "Will you sit on my right hand, Johnny?"
Johnny: "If you wish, Mrs. Manning, but won't you need to use it?"

389 *Salesman*

The cub realtor asked his manager if he could refund the money to an irate customer who discovered that the lot he bought was underwater.

"What kind of a salesman are you, anyway?" demanded the manager. "Go out there and sell him a motorboat."

390 *Frank*

An American couple decided to take a little orphan girl from a refugee camp with the hope of adopting her later. When she arrived at their home, they showed her a neat little room, a closet full of new, clean clothes, and told her how much they wanted a little girl like her.

They promptly introduced the child to daily bathing. Although unaccustomed to it, the child took the vigorous soaping and scrubbing without complaint. After a week of it, she decided maybe she had had enough.

That night, immersed in a tub of hot water with her face and body smothered in suds, she looked up at her new mother and said, "You folks don't want a little girl. What you want is a duck."

391 *No Artist*

A kindergarten teacher putting her charges through a psychological test set them to work carving soap. "Panda, dog, man, table, tree, gun, car," she wrote

as the tots told her what they were making. Then she came to a lad whose work appeared to defy description. "What's this?" she asked.
"Soap flakes," said he.

392 Optimist

"How many fish have you caught?" asked someone, seeing an old villager fishing on the banks of a stream.
"Well, sir," replied the old fisherman thoughtfully, "if I catch this one I'm after, and two more, I'll have three."

393 They Only Read Slowly

Little Johnnie rushed home from school one afternoon and breathlessly announced to his mother that his class was going to be split into two divisions.
"I'm going to be in the top one," he explained, "and the other one's for backward readers.
"But," he added confidentially, "we don't know who's going to be in the other one because there's not a pupil in the room who can read backwards."

394 Helpful

Man: "I want to buy a pillowcase."
Salesgirl: "What size?"
Man: "I'm not sure, but if it'll help, I wear a size seven hat."

395 Safe

Little sister: "Bobby, quick, I've dropped my cookie under the table. Don't let Rover eat it!"
Bobby: "Don't worry. I have my foot on it."

396 Pushed

A man had rescued a person from drowning, and on reaching the shore someone said, "It was splendid of you to jump from such a magnificent height and save this man's life."
"What I want to know," snarled the hero, "is who pushed me?"

397 He Got the Job

The company's personnel director was examining several applicants for a job. The first was ushered into his office and seated beside his desk.
Director: "What's your experience, young man?"
Applicant: "Sir, I've been a gag writer for TV shows."

Director: "Let's see you invent a gag."

The applicant opened the office door, leaned out into the hall, and said: "Okay, you guys, you can go home. The job's taken."

398   *Good Part*

"Dad, guess what! I've got my first part in a play," enthused the budding young actor. "I play the part of a man who's been married for twenty-five years."

"That's a good start, son," replied his dad. "Just keep at it and one of these days you'll get a speaking part."

399   *On the Rims*

The little girl was telling her teacher about her baby teeth coming out. One tooth was loose and she already had lost three.

She said: "Pretty soon I'll be running on the rims."

400   *He Will*

Onlooker: "What a glorious scene! I wish I could take these colors home with me."

Artist: "You will. You're sitting on my paintbrushes!"

401   *Not So Bad*

An old gentleman was riding in an airplane for the first time. At Phoenix, Arizona, the plane made a beautiful landing, and immediately a little red wagon rushed up to refuel it. The next stop was Fort Worth, Texas, and again a little red wagon rushed up. The same thing happened in Nashville, Tennessee.

A fellow passenger commented to the old gentleman, "These planes certainly make wonderful time."

"Yes," replied the old man, "and that little red wagon ain't doin' so bad, either."

402   *The Blessing*

A young minister, sitting down to dinner, was asked by his wife to say grace. He opened the casserole dish she had prepared from a new recipe and countless leftovers.

"Well, I dunno," he said dubiously, "seems to me I've probably blessed this before."

403   *Compassion*

Some boys made a snowman on a side street and put a shovel in his hands. A couple of days later a government foreman came along and gave him a check.

404   *The Rooster*

I love to watch a rooster crow.
He's like so many men I know.
Who brag and bluster, rant and shout,
And beat their manly chests without
A single thing to brag about.

405   *All That Is Left*

Two fools had cars they thought perfection.
They met one day at an intersection,
Tooted their horns and made a connection.
A police car came and made an inspection;
An ambulance came and made a collection.
All that is left is a recollection,
And two less voters in the next election.

406   *Language*

The farmer had driven his team of mules to town, and was late returning home.
"What took you so long?" his wife asked.
"On the way back," he explained, "I picked up the minister, and from then on, them mules didn't understand a thing I said!"

407   *Biblical*

An exasperated salesman parked his car in a no-parking zone, and left this note for the policeman, who he felt sure would spot it: "I've circled this block twenty times. I have an appointment and must keep it or I will lose my job. Forgive us our trespasses!"
Upon returning, he found this note: "I've circled this block for twenty years. If I don't give you a ticket, I'll lose my job. Lead us not into temptation!"

408   *It Is a Problem*

Uncle Joe says this getting up and going to work every morning breaks into his whole day.

409   *Gallant Effort*

At a dinner party a shy young man had been trying to think of something nice to say to his hostess. At last he saw his chance when she turned to him and remarked, "What a small appetite you have tonight, Mr. Jones."
"To sit next to you," he replied gallantly, "would cause any man to lose his appetite."

410   *He Knew*

While mother and daughter were in the kitchen washing dishes, father and seven-year-old Johnny were in the living room. Suddenly they heard a crash of falling dishes. They listened.

"It was Mom," said Johnny.

"How do you know?" asked his father.

"Because," answered Johnny, "she isn't saying anything."

411   *Don't Ask Me*

Voice: "Is this the weather bureau? How about a shower tonight?"

Forecaster: "Don't ask me. If you need one, take it."

412   *Half Serious*

Said the reluctant young man: "My girl and I are only half serious about getting married: I am and she isn't."

413   *Advice*

"My advice," said the mechanic, "is that you keep the oil and change the car."

414   *Not His Troubles*

The school bus pulled up in front of the gate. Six-year-old Bobby appeared as his mother hustled him out the door. Then the morning ritual began. Bobby dropped his books, laboriously picked them up, patted the dog, and struggled with the gate. His mother implored, begged, and threatened Bobby on his way. At last Bobby clambered onto the bus.

"Are you having troubles this morning?" the bus driver asked.

"No," Bobby replied, "but I think my mother is."

415   *Of Course*

"When it comes to eating, you've got to hand it to Venus de Milo."

"Why?"

"How else could she eat?"

416   *The Reason*

The warden began to feel sorry for one of the prisoners. One visitors' day, while most of the prisoners received kinfolk, this fellow sat alone.

One visiting day, the warden called him into the office. "Ben," he said kindly, "I notice you never have any callers. Don't you have any friends or family?"

"Oh, sure," replied Ben happily, "but they're all in here."

417   *Good Rating*

Freshman coed to new roommate: "I wrote to fifteen colleges, but this one had the best rating—2,500 boys, 132 girls."

418   *Logical*

The Smithsons went away for their summer vacation and gave Jane, the maid, a month's wages, then sent her on her way rejoicing.

On their return four weeks later, Jane demanded higher wages or no work.

Mrs. Smithson was horrified. "Gracious," she exclaimed, "you've just had a vacation for a whole month with full pay! You should consider yourself very fortunate."

"That's just it," replied Jane. "You paid me that money for doing nothing, so it isn't fair to expect me to do all this work now for the same wages."

419   *You Should Know*

The young woman was breezing along in the left-hand lane when suddenly, and without warning, she made a sharp right turn and almost slammed into another car.

"Lady, why didn't you signal?" yelled the other driver.

"Don't be ridiculous," came the indignant reply. "I always turn at this corner."

420   *Tact*

The minister's wife was visiting a member of the congregation, and mentioned, with particular pride, that her daughter had won first prize in a musical recital.

"I know just how you must feel," said her hostess understandingly. "I remember how pleased we were when our pig got the blue ribbon at the fair last year."

421   *Yesterday*

A sad-faced man came into a florist shop early one morning. The clerk was ready to take his order for a funeral piece, but he guessed wrong. The customer wanted a basket of flowers sent to his wife for their anniversary.

"And what day will that be?" the clerk asked.

Glumly the poor man replied, "Yesterday."

422   *The Reason*

Little Johnnie had to stand in the corner at school for putting mud in a little girl's mouth.

His mother was horrified when she heard about it. "Why in the world did you put mud in Margaret's mouth?"

"Well," said Johnnie, shrugging his shoulders, "it was open."

423   The English Language

Among the English language's many puzzling words is "economy," which means the large size in soap flakes and the small size in autos.

424   All the Details

One woman to another: "I won't go into all the details; in fact, I've already told you more about it than I heard myself."

425   On the Safe Side

People don't always believe everything they hear, but often repeat it just to be on the safe side.

426   It's Purty

"What a purty bird that is!"

"Yeah, it's a gull."

"I don't care if it's a gull or a boy; it's purty."

427   Still Sleepy

The alarm clock rings and to life's lofty duel,
I rise like a rocket—just out of fuel.

428   He Knew

"Now, children," said the teacher, "I want you to write me an essay without a theme—just put down what is in you."

Then minutes later Jimmy handed in the following:

"In me there is a heart, a lung, and an appendix. And then there is a stomach with two pieces of bread and butter, an apple, and five caramels."

429   The Catch

"And if I take the job I'm to get a raise every year?"

"Yes, provided, of course, that your work is satisfactory."

"Ah! I thought there was a catch somewhere."

430   Art Objects

A cynical-minded man was standing in front of an exhibit of modernism, labeled "Art Objects."

"Well," he announced to the attendant, "I can't say I blame Art for objecting."

431 *No One Thinking*

The plaintiff was wholly unused to court proceedings. He was disturbed to see that the defendant corporation had two men from its legal staff on the case. During the recess, he turned to his own lawyer and said, "I ought to have a second lawyer on my side."

"What's the matter?" demanded his astonished counsel. "I think I am presenting your case very effectively. I don't see how we can lose."

The plaintiff explained, "I notice the corporation has two lawyers. When one of them is up speakin' for their side, the other is sittin' there thinkin'. When you're up speakin' for our side, there ain't nobody thinkin'."

432 *Literary Advice*

The budding author sent a poem to an editor and wrote: "Please let me know at once if you can use it, for I have other irons in the fire."

The editor wrote back: "Remove irons and insert poem."

433 *A Tale with a Moral*

Mary had a little cold, but wouldn't stay at home,
And everywhere that Mary went, the cold was sure to roam.
It wandered into Molly's eyes and filled them full of tears;
It jumped from there to Bobby's nose, and thence to Jimmie's ears.
It painted Anna's throat bright red, and swelled poor Jennie's head;
Dora had a fever, and a cough put Jack to bed.
The moral of this little tale is very quickly said—
Mary could have saved great pain with just one day in bed!

434 *Too Frank*

Visiting a parishioner's home for Sunday dinner, the minister placed some green beans on his plate.

Intently watching, the small daughter of the family suddenly exclaimed, "Look, Daddy, he took some beans! You said he didn't know beans!"

435 *Fussy*

Bricklayer: "I'd like to work here, but I can't find a place to park my car."
Foreman: "I guess you won't do. We want to employ only bricklayers with chauffeurs."

436 *Bank Titles*

The city banker was visiting the countryside.

The banker, nodding toward a figure in the farmyard: "I suppose that's the hired man."

Farmer, with tongue in cheek: "Well, that's the first vice-president in charge of cows."

437 *To the Dentist*

Overheard in a bus: "The tooth aches so badly that it's driving me to extraction!"

438 *Always Time*

> "I haven't time!" These idle words
> Are not exactly true,
> Because I always find the time
> For things I want to do.

439 *Poor Fit*

Said the sergeant to the recruit: "How does the new uniform fit?"

"The pants are all right, but I'd be afraid to run in this jacket for fear my feet would get tripped up in the pockets."

440 *All He Did*

A customer in a crowded restaurant slumped to the floor from his seat at one of the tables. Another customer rushed to his side from a nearby table and urged him to lie still till a doctor could examine him. By this time two waiters were also trying to help, and a crowd had gathered.

"What's all this commotion about?" asked the man on the floor. "All I did was drop my fork, and fell off my chair when I tried to pick it up."

441 *A Particular Noise*

Two riveters were busy on a job. One man said: "Joe, I wish you'd stop your noise. You are making me nervous."

"What noise?" queried the other, still riveting.

"That constant humming to yourself," was the reply. "You're a full octave too high."

442 *Makes a Difference*

Bill: "Shall I cut this pie into six or eight pieces?"

Jim: "Better cut it in six—I don't think I can eat all eight pieces."

443 *Helpful*

"Sir, can you help a man in trouble?"

"Sure. What kind of trouble do you want to get in?"

444 *Pseems Psilly*

The examination question was a real puzzler. It asked why "psychic" was spelled with a "p."

The young man on the far corner didn't have the answer, but he felt he could not let the question go unheeded. Shaking his head, he wrote: "It pcertainly does pseem psilly."

445 *The West End*

The proofreader for a small-town daily newspaper was a woman of great precision and extreme propriety. One day a reporter succeeded in getting into print an item about "Willie Brown, the boy who was burned in the West End by a live wire."

On the following day the reporter found a frigid note on his desk, which asked, "Which is the West End of a boy?"

It took him only an instant to reply: "The end the son sets on, of course!"

446 *The Tin Can*

A pedestrian was waiting to cross the street when a huge Saint Bernard dog came by and knocked him into the street. As he was trying to get up, a small foreign car came by and ran over him. A passerby rushed up and asked him if he was hurt.

The man replied, "I didn't mind when that dog knocked me over, but that tin can tied to his tail nearly killed me."

447 *Bride's Lament*

The honeymoon is over, though loudly I begrudge it—
I've been taken off my pedestal and placed upon a budget!

448 *Really Inferior*

A woman went to a psychiatrist complaining of an inferiority complex. After an extended series of sessions, in which she poured out her whole life story to the analyst, he told her, "Madam, I hate to tell you this, but you don't have a complex at all. You really are inferior."

449   *Correct*

The peak of mental activity must be between the ages of four and seventeen. At four they know all the questions; at seventeen, all the answers.

450   *We Understand*

A Chinese telephone company was preparing to publish a directory. They finally abandoned the project when it was discovered there were thousands of Wings and Wongs, and this would result in too much winging the wong number.

451   *He Was Busy*

"And what did my little boy do all day?"

"I played postman, Mommy. I put a letter in every mailbox on the block. Real letters, too. I found them in your drawer, tied up in pink ribbon."

452   *On a Bun*

Professor, rapping on desk: "Order, please!"

Sleepy voice from the back row: "I'll take a hamburger with onions."

453   *Used*

Wife: "Honey, I'll be needing a new fur coat this winter."

Husband: "Why, you've worn that one only two seasons."

Wife: "Yes, but it was secondhand when I got it—the fox wore it for five years before that."

454   *A Purpose*

"Senator, many of your constituents can't understand from your speech last night just how you stand on the question."

"Fine! It took me eight hours to write it that way."

455   *She Did Not*

First Typist: "Why did you tell the boss what time I came in this morning?"

Second Typist: "I did not!"

First Typist: "Who did, then?"

Second Typist: "I don't know. When he asked me, I said I didn't notice because I was too busy getting ready to go to lunch."

456   *Say That Again*

A foreign student at the university assured his faculty advisor: "I'm glad to say I have no trouble with the English language—just the idiotisms."

457   *News to Him*

"I see by the paper," said a wife to her husband, "that the concert we attended last night was a huge success."

"Yes," he said, "I had no idea we enjoyed it half so much at the time."

458   *Missed Nothing*

Overheard at the ball game:
"What inning is it?"
"It's the top of the fourth."
"What's the score?"
"Nothing to nothing."
"Oh, goody, goody! We haven't missed anything!"

459   *Hard to Tell*

A mother summed up the problems of parenthood by explaining, "My oldest is in college, and my youngest is in nursery school, and some days you can hardly tell the difference."

460   *No Other Kind*

Boy: "Tell me, do you really like conceited men as well as you do the other kind?"
Girl: "What other kind?"

461   *The Answer*

The chicken farmer was losing a lot of his flock, and wrote to the Department of Agriculture: "Gentlemen: Something is wrong with my chickens. Every morning when I come out, I find two or three lying on the ground cold and stiff with their feet in the air. Can you tell me what is the matter?"

Eight weeks later he received this letter from Washington: "Dear Sir: Your chickens are dead."

462   *Smart Dad*

The junior Murray had become involved in a financial tangle. In a moment of weakness he had loaned a friend $500 in cash without a written note, or even a receipt, indicating the amount loaned. In the meantime the young man had found he needed his money. In desperation, he consulted his father.

After a moment of consideration, the father said, "Oh, that's easy, son. Write him and say you need the $1,000 you loaned him."

Young Murray said, "You mean $500."

"That I do not," said the father. "You say $1,000, and he will write back that he owes you only $500. Then you will have it in writing."

463 *Okay*

Park keeper (to man in pond): "Hey, you! Can't you see the notice 'No Swimming'?"
Man: "I'm not swimming, I'm drowning."
Park keeper: "Oh, that's all right, then."

464 *Obvious*

Husband: "Where has all the grocery money I gave you gone?"
Wife: "Stand sideways and look in the mirror."

465 *Smart Dog*

When John Jones took his hunting dog out in the fields to show him off to several strangers, to his amazement the dog pointed at one of them.
"He's smarter than you think," said the man. "My name happens to be Partridge."

466 *Hold It*

Customer: "You say this hair restorer is very good, do you?"
Druggist: "Yes, sir, I know a man who took the cork out of a bottle of this stuff with his teeth and he had a mustache that had to be trimmed the next day."

467 *That Was All He Had*

It was a testimonial dinner for the town's leading citizen. He told his story in a quiet voice. "Friends," he said, "when I came here forty-seven years ago, I came in no limousine. I walked into your town down a muddy dirt road. I had only one suit, one pair of shoes on my feet, and all my possessions were wrapped in a red handkerchief over my shoulder. Now, forty-seven years later, I am on the board of directors of your leading bank. I own apartment buildings and office buildings; I am on the board of your leading clubs; I own three concerns with branches in thirty-nine cities. Yes, friends, your town has been good to me, and I have walked a long way since I first walked down your muddy dirt road."
After the banquet, an awed youngster approached the great man and asked timidly: "Tell me, sir, what did you have in the red handkerchief over your shoulder when you walked into our town forty-seven years ago?"
"Let me think, son. If I recall rightly, I was carrying about $300,000 in cash and $750,000 in negotiable securities."

468 *It Often Happens*

At a vacation camp for children, a little girl fished for a while, then threw down her pole and cried, "I quit."
Asked for an explanation, she said, "I just can't seem to get waited on."

469   *News*

A reporter from a big-city newspaper stopped to visit with a friend who operated a little country weekly. He asked his friend, "How can you keep up your circulation in a town where everyone already knows what everyone else is doing?"

The editor grinned and said, "They know what everyone's doing, all right, but they read the paper to see who's been caught at it!"

470   *Is That Clear?*

A man called for information at the telephone office. "I want to speak to Mr. Dill," he said.

The operator asked, "Is it 'B' as in Bill?"

The man answered, "No—'D' as in Pickle."

471   *TV and Newspapers*

TV will never replace the newspaper—you can't swat flies with it!

472   *Honeymoon*

The honeymoon is over when he stops helping her with the dishes—and does them himself.

473   *Remember*

When you feel like criticizing the younger generation, just remember who raised them.

474   *Think About It*

> If I should spend in working,
> The intellect and care
> I use on crossword puzzles,
> I'd be a millionaire!

475   *Wrong Order*

"There's a man at the door with a package marked C.O.D."

"Tell him to keep it—I ordered salmon."

476   *Modern Methods*

A tourist spotted an Indian sending up smoke signals in the desert. He had a fire extinguisher strapped to his side.

"What's the idea of the fire extinguisher?" asked the tourist.

The rugged redskin replied, "If me mispellum word, me erasum."

477 Working Part-time

The story is told of a great musician who took his orchestra on tour, and during his travels received a note from a well-meaning person in one of his audiences. This is what the note said:

"I think it is only fair to inform you that the man in your orchestra who blows the instrument that pulls in and out, only played during the brief intervals when you were looking at him."

478 The Solution

One of the men on the job spoke up: "I dug this hole where I was told to, and began to put the dirt back like I was supposed to. But all the dirt won't go back in. What'll I do?"

For a long while the foreman pondered the problem, then he said, "I have it!" Rubbing his chin and still calculating, he remarked, "There is only one thing to do. You'll have to dig the hole deeper."

479 Excelsior!

The shades of night were falling fast.
The fool stepped on it and he sped fast.
A crash—he left without a sound.
They opened up his head and found—
Excelsior!

480 No Money

Student: "You look broken up. What's the matter?"
Roommate: "I wrote home for money for a study lamp."
Student: "Well?"
Roommate: "They sent a lamp!"

481 That Explains It

The shoemaker was explaining to a complaining customer the reason for the poor quality of the soles. "All the good leather," he said, "is going into steaks."

482 Good for a Time

"I like the sound of the job, but the last place I worked paid more."
"Did they give you rest periods?"
"Yes."
"Furnish life insurance?"
"Yes."
"Vacation with pay?"

"Yes, and a $100 holiday bonus."
"Hmmmm! Why did you leave?"
"The company went busted."

483   *Not Easy*

At a recent shipyard launching, the woman who was to christen the boat was quite nervous.

"Do you have any questions before we start?" inquired the master of ceremonies.

"Yes," she replied, "how hard do I have to hit the boat to knock it into the water?"

484   *First Question*

"I hear you have a boy in college. Is he going to become a doctor, an engineer, or a lawyer, perhaps?"

"That I do not know," was the slow, wistful answer. "Right now the big question is: Is he going to become a sophomore?"

485   *Full of Energy*

Prospect being given a demonstration ride in a used car: "Say, what makes it jerk when you put it in gear?"

Salesman: "Ah, that proves it to be a real car. It's anxious to get started."

486   *Costly Expert*

"That efficiency expert charged me so much to tell me how badly I was running my business that I couldn't afford to pay him even if I were doing so well that I didn't need him," grumbled the businessman.

487   *Wonderful Vocabulary*

Teacher: "Johnny, give me a sentence containing the words deduct, defeat, defense, and detail."

Johnny, after some thought: "Defeat of deduct gets over defense before detail."

488   *Remember*

Children may tear up a house, but they never break up a home.

489   *TV Dinners*

Have you heard about the woman who has served so many TV dinners that she thinks she is in show business?

490   *Small World*

After a 1,000-mile trip in two hours, it's a small world—until you drive in from the airport.

491   *Debt*

Never have so many people lived so well so far behind before.

492   *It Comes Early Now*

Office boy: "Isn't this a beautiful morning we're having?"
Boss: "We? All of a sudden you're a partner?"

493   *Not Sure*

Judge: "Have you ever been up before me?"
Accused: "I don't know. What time do you get up?"

494   *Too Early*

"I hear that both Smith and Jones proposed to Joan; I wonder which one is the lucky fellow."
"It's too early to say yet, but she accepted Smith."

495   *Listen Carefully*

"My dears," gushed the matron at the bridge party, "my resolution this year is never to repeat gossip, so for heaven's sake listen carefully the first time."

496   *Not Many*

"Everybody is talking about Mr. and Mrs. Smith, and how they're always fighting," said Mrs. Jones to Mr. Jones. "Some people are taking her part, and others are taking his part."
"I know," said Mr. Jones to Mrs. Jones. "And I suppose a few eccentrics are minding their own business."

497   *The Reason*

"But your story has such a hollow ring," said the lady to the panhandler.
"Yes, lady," he said, "that's on account of I'm speaking on an empty stomach."

498   *It Works*

Woman to bridge-club members: "I have the most marvelous recipe for goulash—all I have to do is mention it to my husband and he says, 'Let's eat out.' "

499   *A Good Many of Us*

The teacher, lecturing on perseverance, said: "He drove straight to his goal. He looked neither to the right nor to the left, but pressed forward, moved by a definite purpose. Neither friend nor foe could delay him, nor turn him from his course. All who crossed his path did so at their own peril. What would you call such a man?"

Student: "A truck driver!"

500   *It's Not My Fault*

Mother, reprimanding her small son: "You mustn't pull the cat's tail."
Son: "I'm only holding it, Mom. The cat's doing the pulling."

501   *Good Children*

Our children are as good as gold,
And always do as they are told;
Psychology we've used for years,
Then, too, we've spanked their little rears.

502   *Warning*

"Anyone found near my chicken house at night," reads a notice in a country newspaper, "will be found there the next morning."

503   *Washington*

A man went down to Washington,
His needs were simply stated;
He had a simple problem,
But they made it complicated.

504   *He Sure Did*

Eagle Scout: "Did you fish with flies while at camp?"
Tenderfoot: "We sure did! We fished, cooked, ate, slept, and hiked with flies."

505   *Helpful*

Man (in hotel): "Boy, run up to room 1204 and see if my briefcase is there. My train leaves in nine minutes."
Eight minutes passed.
Boy (panting): "Yes, it's still right there."

506   *Naturally*

Bill: "Did you see what happened to the plant in the math teacher's room?"
Fred: "No, what?"
Bill: "It grew square roots."

507   *Different View*

"So you think you should have a raise?" the boss bellowed. "I suppose you
have often thought what you would do if you had my income, haven't you?"

His faithful clerk smiled wryly. "No, sir," he replied, "but I have often
wondered what you would do if you had mine!"

508   *He Got the Idea*

A teacher was getting acquainted with her new class of first-graders. "What's
your name?" she asked one little boy.

"Jule."

"Not Jule," she said. "You shouldn't use nicknames; your name is Julius."
Turning to the next boy, she asked him his name.

"Billious," he answered.

509   *Guess*

Big-game hunter: "Once when I was sitting down resting in the jungle, a tiger
came so close to me that I could feel his moist breath on the back of my neck.
Do you know what I did?"

Bored listener: "Now don't tell me. Let me guess. You turned up your collar,
I betcha!"

510   *Believed Him*

Fisherman: "I tell you it was t-h-a-t long! I never saw such a fish!"
Friend: "I believe you."

511   *Plus All Your Guests*

> Little drops of water,
> Little grains of sand
> Make the summer cottage
> More than I can stand.

512   *Typical Grandparents*

Two grandmothers were bragging about their grandchildren and one, quite
impressed, asked, "How old are your grandsons?"

"Well," replied the other, "the doctor's two and the lawyer's four."

513 *Not in Tune*

Daisy: "When did your daddy stop singing in the choir?"

Mazie: "Since the Sunday he was absent, and everyone thought the organ had been tuned."

514 *Tarzan*

After playing outdoors, a little boy came in and asked his mother, "Who am I?"

"Tarzan?" she guessed.

"That lady down the street was right," exclaimed the lad. "She said I was so dirty even my own mother wouldn't know me!"

515 *Puzzle*

A bird sat on a bookshelf,
And shook his head in doubt;
He wondered where those bookworms were
He'd heard so much about.

516 *He Taught Him*

Five-year-old Billy ran into the house to tell his mother that four-year-old Johnny had fallen into the pool. She ran out and found Johnny submerged up to his neck. After rescuing him, she asked Billy how it had happened.

"I kept telling him that he was going to fall into the pool if he got too close to the edge."

"But what made him fall in?" demanded his mother.

"I pushed him," was the matter-of-fact reply.

"What?" cried the mother.

"Yes, I pushed him," Billy repeated. "I wanted to show him what would happen if he didn't mind."

517 *Wise Crack*

An Easterner was being driven by a rancher over a blistering and almost barren stretch of West Texas when a gaudy bird, new to him, scurried in front of them. The Easterner asked what it was.

"That is a bird of paradise," said the rancher.

The stranger rode on in silence for a time and then said, "Pretty long way from home, isn't he?"

518 *Growing Up*

The teen-ager was traveling home from a movie and remarked to her friend: "You know, I must be really growing up. I don't feel sick any more watching love scenes."

519 *Then He Created Girls*

The Sunday School teacher asked one little girl if she knew the story of Adam and Eve. "First God created Adam," she said, "and then He looked at him and said, 'I think I can do better.' So He created girls."

520 *Would Not Help Much*

Principal to small boy: "It's very generous of you, Tommy, but I don't think your resignation would help our crowded school situation."

521 *It's Okay*

Smart son: "Dad, I just siphoned a couple of gallons of gas out of your car for my old bus. It's okay, isn't it?"

Smarter father: "Sure, it's okay, son. I bought that gas with your allowance for next week. So run along and have a good time."

522 *Modern Art*

A proud father was showing a friend some of the modern painting his daughter had done. He pointed out one in particular which he called a gorgeous sunset. When the friend hesitated to express anticipated praise, the father thought he would add to his daughter's prestige by saying, "She studied abroad, you know."

"Ah, that explains everything," cried the friend in relief. "I knew I had never seen anything like that called a sunset in this country."

523 *Just Three*

A guest at a restaurant asked, "What flavors of ice cream have you today?"

The pretty waitress answered in a hoarse whisper, "Vanilla, chocolate, and strawberry."

Wishing to be sympathetic, the guest said, "You got laryngitis?"

"No," replied the waitress, with an effort, "just vanilla, chocolate, and strawberry."

524 *He Did*

"Didn't I tell you to notice when the soup boiled over?"

"I did. It was ten-thirty."

525 *Be Precise*

"I'll order a pork chop," said the diner, "and make it lean."

"Yes, sir," replied the waitress. "Which way?"

526 *He Knew*

Father (to daughter's boyfriend): "She will be right down. Care for a game of chess?"

527   *New Method*

As the county agent sat relaxing, he was suddenly startled by a fellow who came into the office lugging a sack of dirt and asking where he could get his samples of soil tested.

"How did you take your samples?" asked the agent.

The farmer replied, "Well, I'll tell you. I waited for a rainy day, drove the tractor all over the farm, an' then just cleaned off the tires!"

528   *How He Felt*

"Grand Coulee!" shouted the bishop when he hit his thumb with a hammer.

"Grand Coulee?" asked a friend softly, with a smile.

"Yes!" exclaimed the bishop. "It's one of the world's biggest!"

529   *Pretty Bad*

"I'm a magician."

"That's interesting. What's your best trick?"

"I saw a woman in half."

"Is it difficult?"

"It's child's play. In fact, I learned it while I was a child."

"Are there any more children at home yet?"

"I have several half-sisters."

530   *The Rule*

New patient to nurse: "I don't need to undress—I just want to see the doctor for him to look at my sore toe."

Nurse: Our rule is that everyone undresses."

Patient: "Dumb rule, making me undress to look at my toe."

Voice from the next room: "That's nothing, I came in to fix the telephone."

531   *Modern Movies*

Considering some of today's movies, one can understand why the idea of adding odor to the sound was dropped.

532   *Fooling People*

You can't fool all of the people all the time, but those highway interchange signs come pretty close to doing it.

533   *Just for a Moment*

Photographer: "Look pleasant, please. As soon as I snap this picture, you can resume your natural expression."

534 *Running the Country*

It's not easy to run a home. It's easier to go down to the filling station, sit on a bench, and run the country.

535 *Laborsaving*

There are so many labor-saving appliances on the market today that you have to work all your life to pay for them.

536 *Oversight?*

Thomas Jefferson composed the epitaph for his own grave. It read thus: "Here was buried Thomas Jefferson, Author of the Declaration of American Independence, of the Statute of Virginia for Religious Freedom, and Father of the University of Virginia."

He neglected to mention that he was once President of the United States!

537 *A Poor Driver*

He's such a poor driver the police gave him a season ticket.

538 *In the Past*

The person who lives in the past has one thing going for him—it's cheaper.

539 *Three Wishes*

Wives who cook and do the dishes
Should be granted these three wishes:
A grateful mate, a well-kissed cheek,
And a restaurant dinner every week.

540 *Modern Youth*

Teen-ager placing battery in a radio: "I'm doing a transistor transplant."

541 *He Is Useful*

For fixing things around the house, nothing beats a man who's handy with a checkbook.

542 *How You Can Tell*

The honeymoon is over when your wife starts complaining about the noise you make when you are getting breakfast.

543 *Clever Artist*

Janie: "Sit still. I'm drawing your picture."
Susie: "How's it coming?"
Janie: "Not so good. I guess I'll put a tail on it and make it a dog."

544 *The Others Were Dumb*

There was a lad who had the reputation of not being very bright. People had fun with him by placing a dime and a nickel on the open palm of his hand, and telling him to take his pick of the two. In each case the boy would take the nickel and the crowd would laugh.

A kind-hearted woman asked him one day if he didn't know the difference between a dime and a nickel—that a dime, though smaller, was worth more.

"Sure, I know it," he replied, "but they wouldn't try me out on it anymore if I took the dime."

545 *Next Question*

Teacher: "Can you give me a sentence with the word 'officiate' in it?"
Pupil: "A man got sick from a fish he ate."

546 *Broad Worries*

After working laboriously over his homework, the little boy turned to his father.

"Dad," he said wearily, "what's the use of this education stuff?"

"Why, son," said his father, "there's nothing like it! A good education enables you to worry about conditions everywhere in the world."

547 *Help*

Teen-age mother: "Oh, dear, I don't know what to do to make the baby stop crying."

Teen-age father: "You've got to do something. Where's the book of instructions that came with the baby?"

548 *It Pays to Advertise*

The codfish lays a million eggs, the helpful hen but one,
But the codfish doesn't cackle to tell you what she's done.
And so we scorn the codfish coy while the helpful hen we prize,
Which indicates to thoughtful minds—it pays to advertise!

549 *Come Now*

I'm practically dead from lack of sleep
And from counting erratic sheep;

And one sheep's left that should have gone,
But his tail got caught in the crack of dawn.

550   *Good Question*

Tommy, the football enthusiast, said to his little sister, "Well, we won the game, nuthin' to nuthin'!"
"Who made the first nuthin'?" she asked.

551   *Be Careful*

Station attendant: "Where is your radiator cap?"
Driver: "On the front end of the car, but don't call me 'Cap.' "

552   *Too Risky*

First inmate: "Betcha you can't climb up that beam of light shining in the window."
Second inmate: "Do you think I'm crazy? I'd get halfway up and you'd turn it off."

553   *His Fault*

Billy: "Mother, Bobby broke a window."
Mother: "How did he do it?"
Billy: "I threw a rock at him and he ducked."

554   *Is That Fair?*

"I expect my husband to be just what he is now twenty years from today."
"But that's unreasonable."
"Yes, that's what he is now."

555   *Half Time*

A mother was talking to her little boy. "Now, Billy, you shouldn't be selfish with your toys. I've told you to let your younger brother play with them half the time."
"That's what I've been doing," said Billy. "I take the sled going downhill, and he takes it going up."

556   *Tough Case*

The famous detective arrived on the scene. "Heavens," he said, "this is more serious than I thought—the window is broken on both sides."

557   *Good Reason*

Johnny came home from school and told his mother, "I wish you'd let me take my bath in the morning instead of at night."

"Why?" asked his mother.

"Because every day in health class the teacher asks us if we had a bath today. I haven't been able to say 'yes' once this year."

558   *What's the Use?*

The chap who says, "What's the use?"
Is never the engine, always the caboose.

559   *He Knew It*

The first-grader was talking about the recent fire in his school.

"I knew it was going to happen," he said, "because we've been practicing for it all year."

560   *An Old One*

A story appeared a hundred years or so ago about a Senator. There was a hanging in Wichita, Kansas, and 35,000 people gathered to witness it. The criminal was confronted with the Governor, who said, "The United States Senator has come from Washington to be here, and before you are hung, we yield to you five minutes so that you can say anything you want."

The criminal stood up and said, "No, just get on with the hanging."

The Senator got up and said, "Would you yield your five minutes to me?"

And he said, "Yes, but hang me first."

561   *Always There*

Two boys were talking. One said to the other, "Aren't ants funny little things? They work and never play."

"Oh, I don't know about that," replied the other boy. "Every time I go on a picnic they're always there."

562   *Smart Lad*

At a little party of young folks there were just enough cookies for each to have three. But little Bobby took four.

"You're supposed to get only three cookies, Bobby," said the hostess. "You ought to put the fourth one back."

"Can't," exclaimed Bobby, "I ate that one first."

563   *One on Him*

Auctioneer: "What am I offered for this beautiful bust of Robert Burns?"

Man in crowd: "That's not Burns, it's Shakespeare."

Auctioneer: "Well, folks, that's one on me. Shows how little I know about the Bible."

564 *Holding Her Own*

Willis: "I've taken three lessons in French from a correspondence school."
Gillis: "So. Could you carry on conversation with a Frenchman?"
Willis: "Oh, no, but I could talk to anybody else who had had three lessons."

565 *Times Change*

Father: "When I started on my business career, I worked twelve hours a day at my first job."
Son: "Yes, but, Dad, in these fast times anyone who takes twelve hours to do a day's work would get fired!"

566 *Seems Logical*

The teacher asked a class, discussing the North American Indian, if anyone could tell what the leaders of the tribes were called.
"Chiefs," said a little girl.
"Correct," said the teacher. "And what were the women called?"
A sharp little lad answered promptly, "Mischiefs."

567 *Advertising*

Travel agency sign: "Please Go Away!"

568 *Precise*

A tourist was visiting New Mexico. While gazing at the dinosaur bones, he met an old Indian who acted as an official guide.
"How old are these bones?" asked the tourist.
"Exactly one hundred million and three years old," was the Indian's reply.
"How can you be so definite?" asked the tourist.
"Oh," replied the Indian, "a geologist told me they were one hundred million years old, and that was exactly three years ago."

569 *Good Reason*

She: "Why does the man behind the hitter wear such a big bib, honey? He looks silly."
He: "That, my dear, is to keep the catcher's shirt from getting all mussed up in case a ball happens to knock his teeth out."

570 *Common Experience*

After boasting of his prowess as a marksman, the hunter took aim on a lone duck overhead. "Watch this," he commanded his listeners.

He fired, and the bird flew on.

"My friends," he said with awe, "you are now viewing a miracle. There flies a dead duck!"

571   Make-believe

Little Doris was lying on her back on the floor singing. A little later when her mother came into the room again, Doris was on her stomach now, still singing lustily.

"Playing a game, Doris?" asked mother.

"Yes," replied Doris seriously, "I'm a record, and I've just turned myself over."

572   Experience

Doctors will tell you that if you eat slowly you will eat less. It is particularly true if you're a member of a large family.

573   To Be Eligible

Social Security agent to applicant: "Feeling sixty-five isn't good enough—you have to *be* sixty-five."

574   Just Like Home

One day, instead of serving the usual hot meal, the school cafeteria handed out peanut-butter-and-jelly sandwiches.

After lunch, a satisfied first-grader marching out the door complimented the cafeteria manager: "Finally, you gave us a home-cooked meal."

575   Rummage Sale

"I've sold everything out of that room," said the helper at the rummage sale, proudly.

"Dear, dear," cried the minister's wife, "that was the cloakroom."

576   Not Serious

One girl to another: "Well, it's true we are having a little disagreement. I want to have a big church wedding and he wants to break off the engagement."

577   Even Prettier

Nice old lady: "You're pretty dirty, aren't you?"

Little girl: "Yes, and I'm even prettier clean."

578 *Why He Came*

As the man pulled the small boy out of a hole in the frozen river, he asked: "How did you come to fall in?"

"I didn't come to fall in," the boy gasped. "I came to skate."

579 *Smart*

Tim: "If you have ten potatoes and must divide them equally between seven persons, how would you do it?"

Sam: "I'd mash them."

580 *Right*

An airline pilot was explaining to a group of listeners how he had miraculously escaped from a serious crash. "We were flying along and suddenly just happened to get into an air pocket."

Said a sympathetic old-lady listener: "Oh, dear! And there was a hole in it!"

581 *Broke*

Departing vacationer to neighbor: "We'll be back in about $500."

582 *Get the Details*

The managing editor was very explicit in his instruction to the cub reporter. Among other things, he emphasized that names be obtained in writing all items. "In fact," he stressed, "names are essential."

Later the cub reporter handed in the following item:

"Last night lightning struck a barn northwest of town belonging to Ike Davis, and killed three cows. Their names were Rosie, Isabel, and Mabel."

583 *Economy Costs Money*

The couple shopping for a new automobile were startled by the price quoted for a compact car.

"But that's almost the cost of a big car!" they protested.

"Well," shrugged the salesman, "if you want economy, you gotta pay for it."

584 *Read the Fine Print*

"You say you were once stranded on a desert island entirely without food. How did you live?"

"Well, I had an insurance policy in my pocket and I found enough provisions in it to keep me alive till I was rescued."

585   *We've Seen It*

Sign in a cluttered, old-fashioned hardware store: "We've got it if we can find it."

586   *Thirty Days*

Sign on a country road: "Thirty days hath September, April, June and November. Also anyone driving over 55 MPH on this road."

587   *Self-service*

"I've finally learned the routine at a self-service filling station," the woman told her husband. "I let the gas run until it overflows the tank, smear the windshield with a dirty rag, forget to check the oil, pay the attendant exact change—then thank myself and drive off, leaving the gas cap on top of the pump."

588   *Doubtful*

Said one taxpayer to the other: "You shouldn't be grumbling about taxes. Just think how wonderful it is to live in a country like ours. You should pay your taxes with a smile."

Said the second taxpayer: "Well, I'd be glad to, but do you think the government would settle for that?"

589   *Too Late*

Talkative Mrs. Brown was reporting to her husband the events of her club meeting the previous night.

"The gossip was exciting," she said, "but it got so late I could hardly keep my mouth open."

590   *Too Tense*

America has become so tense and nervous it has been years since I've seen anyone asleep in church—and that is a sad situation.—*Norman Vincent Peale*

591   *They Are Also Slow Starters*

Old truck drivers never die—they just can't make the grade.

592   *How to Succeed*

A woman never knows how much she can do until she cries.
If at first she doesn't succeed, she has to cry, cry again.

593   *School Motto*

School motto: "Laugh and the class laughs with you, but you stay after school alone."

594   *Impossible*

There's a catch to it: A Sunday School teacher asked her young class how Noah spent his time on the ark.

As there was no response, she asked: "Do you suppose he did a lot of fishing?"

"What?" responded a six-year-old, "with only two worms?"

595   *Off Course*

Two inexperienced yachtsmen were storm-tossed on the Atlantic, headed for New York harbor. One turned from his chart table to the other and said: "I think you ought to take off your hat."

"Why?" asked his worried shipmate.

"Because," replied the amateur navigator, "according to my calculations, we're inside St. Patrick's Cathedral!"

596   *To Be on Time*

"Good news, dear," called the husband as he came into the house. "I picked up two tickets for the theatre on the way home from work."

"Oh, that's wonderful," said the wife, "I'll start dressing right away."

"That's a good idea," he said. "The tickets are for tomorrow night."

597   *Making Certain*

The obituary editor of a Boston newspaper was not one who would admit his mistakes easily. One day he got a phone call from an irate subscriber who said his name had been printed in the obituary column.

"Really?" was the calm reply. "Where are you calling from?"

598   *Smart Cat*

And there was the cat who ate cheese and waited by the mouse hole with baited breath.

599   *Excuse Me*

"Excuse me for coming up to the door to get your daughter," explained the young-man suitor to his lady love's mother, "but my horn isn't working."

600 *Felt Better*

A motorist lost control of his car and ran into a telephone pole. When he came to, he was on the ground clutching telephone wires.

"Thank goodness," he murmured, "it's a harp."

601 *Not Santa*

"For Christmas," a woman remarked to her friend, "I was visited by a jolly, bearded fellow with a big bag over his shoulder. My son came home from college with his laundry."

602 *A Baseball Dog*

"Speaking about baseball, I've got a baseball dog."

"What makes you call him a baseball dog?"

"Because he wears a muzzle, catches flies, chases fowls, and beats it home when he sees the catcher coming."

603 *He Knew*

Sunday School teacher: "What parable do you like?"

Jimmie: "The one about the multitude that loafs and fishes."

604 *Not Fair*

It takes years of painstaking effort and study before a woman considers herself a really good cook. But all a man needs is a sack of charcoal, a tall white hat, and an apron with funny sayings printed on it.

605 *Two Rules*

There is an old story of an Eastern merchant who was about to send his eldest son forth into the world. "My son," said the merchant, "there are two precepts I would have you keep ever in mind. The first of these is, 'Always keep your word once you have given it.' "

"Yes, Father," said the son. "And the second?"

"Never give it."

606 *A Hit*

Jane: "That speaker last night sure made a hit."

Jenny: "What did he talk about?"

Jane: "About five minutes."

607 *Satisfied*

Asking for a recommendation, a worker received this note: "Jack Jones worked for us a week. We're satisfied."

608　*Please Complain*

A little boy called to the new neighbor and said, "If you are annoyed by the piano playing next door, be sure to complain to my mother."

609　*A Good Reason*

Dad: "You usually talk on the phone for two hours, but this time it was only forty-five minutes. Why?"
Daughter: "Well, this time it was a wrong number."

610　*Detective*

"Are the criminals you encounter in your daily routine as clever as those presented on the TV screen?"
"Well, no," said the candid cop. "But neither are we as resourceful as the TV sleuths, so it just about evens up."

611　*Naturally*

Why did the doctor tiptoe past the medicine box? He didn't want to wake the sleeping pills.

612　*Not Quite*

Fond mother: "I hope my little darling has been as good as gold all day."
Baby-sitter: "No, ma'am, he went off the gold standard about ten o'clock."

613　*Smart Customer*

The butcher placed his last roast on the scale. "That'll be $3.95," he told the customer."
"That one's too small; don't you have anything larger?" the woman asked.
The canny butcher returned the roast to the refrigerator, paused a moment, then took it out again. "This one," he announced, "will be $4.80."
"Fine," the customer smiled. "I'll take them both."

614　*Next Question*

A schoolteacher was outwitted by a clever pupil. She was questioning the class in social studies. "Can anyone tell me what the equator is?"
"Yes, I can," answered one boy. "It's an imaginary line drawn around the earth equally distant from the poles."
That sounded to her like a memorized definition. "Do you really know what that means?" she demanded. "Could you, for example, tie a knot in the equator?"
"Yes," he stated promptly.
"Could you, indeed?" was her rejoinder. But the bright pupil was not dismayed.
"An imaginary knot, teacher," he countered.

615   *The Reason*

The man went to the doctor with a severe headache. The doctor examined him carefully.

"I don't know what is causing your headaches," the doctor said, "but I advise you to give up smoking and drinking, go to bed earlier at night, and get more rest."

"But," cried the patient, "I don't smoke or drink, and I'm always in bed by ten o'clock. I never fail to get at least nine hours' sleep in a night."

"In that case," the doctor said, "I know what is causing the headaches. Your halo is on too tight."

616   *The Hearse in Verse*

Than drinking and driving there's nothing worse.
It's putting the quart before the hearse.

617   *Never Tried*

Dear old lady: "Pardon me, sailor, but do those tattoo marks wash off?"
Old salt: "Couldn't say, ma'am."

618   *Most of Us*

Said the enthusiastic lecturer, describing his travels, "There are some spectacles we never forget."

An old lady approached him after the lecture and asked, "Please, sir, where can I get the kind of spectacles you mentioned? I'm always forgetting mine."

619   *Ask Dad*

Little Alice was allowed to sit in her mother's place at the dinner table one evening when her mother was absent. Her slightly older brother, resenting the arrangement, sneered, "So you're the mother tonight. All right, how much is two times seven?"

Without a moment's hesitation, Alice replied nonchalantly, "I'm busy. Ask your father."

620   *Honest*

Two horse traders engaged in a rather bitter discussion. Said one, "That horse you sold me is almost blind."

"Well," replied the other, "remember I told you he was a fine horse but that he didn't look good."

621   *Only Thirteen*

"Johnny, name the fifty states," instructed the teacher.

"I can't, teacher."

"Why, when I was your age I could name all the states," she scolded.

"Yeah, but then there were only thirteen," answered Johnny.

622   *Like Dad*

Little Johnny was in one of his very bad and disobedient moods. In answer to his mother's remonstrations that he behave himself, he said: "Give me a quarter, and I'll be good."

"Give you a quarter!" she scolded. "Why, Johnny, you shouldn't be good for a quarter, you should be good for nothing—like your father."

623   *Preparing Himself*

A business executive stopped his car each morning as he passed a state institution. In the yard one of the inmates was going through the motions of winding up and pitching an imaginary ball.

His friend asked, "Why do you stop each morning and watch that unfortunate fellow go through his act?"

"Well," he answered, "if things go the way they are, I'll be there someday catching for that guy and I want to get into his curves."

624   *Close Enough*

Last summer a girl told her sweetheart she couldn't think of marrying him until he had saved at least a thousand dollars.

Toward the end of the year, she asked him how much he had saved.

"Oh, about ten dollars."

"Well," she said, "that's close enough."

625   *Can't Trust Anyone*

Judge: "Tell me—did you commit this theft alone?"

Crook: "Yes, Your Honor, you can't trust anyone these days."

626   *It Leaked Out*

In looking around the church the visiting bishop was surprised to see that the congregation consisted of precisely two old ladies and two children under the age of ten. However, he went through the service and gave the address he had prepared.

Later the bishop said to the clergyman, "Did you tell the parishioners that I was going to be present here this morning?" The clergyman replied, "No, it must have leaked out somewhere."

627   *Good as New*

"For sale" sign on a used television set: "This TV is as good as new. It was owned by a little old lady who hated soap operas, Westerns, and re-runs."

628   *Only Saw One*

A city slicker, walking along a country road, thought he would have some fun with a farmer working in a field. He called to him: "Say, mister, did you see a truckload of monkeys go by here?"

"No, sir," replied the farmer. "Did you fall off?"

629   *Naturally*

Two workmen sat down to eat their lunches. One began to unwrap a package some eighteen inches long.

"What's that?" asked the other.

"My wife's away," said the first, "so I made myself a pie."

"A bit long, isn't it?" his friend asked.

"Long? Sure, it's long. It's rhubarb."

630   *Is That Clear*

Mr. Newlywed: "You mean there's only cheese for dinner?"

Mrs. Newlywed: "Yes, dear. When the chops caught fire and fell into the dessert, I had to use the soup to put out the fire."

631   *No More Weapons*

It used to be that Dad dealt out a stern code of discipline to Junior. Then the electric razor took away his razor strap, the furnace took away the woodshed, and tax worries took away his hair and the hairbrush. That's why youngsters are running wild today. Dad ran out of weapons.

632   *In a Nutshell*

"Now, if you have that in your head," said a professor, who had just explained a theory to his students, "it's all in a nutshell."

633   *What Politicians Forget*

A lot of politicians make the mistake of forgetting that they've been appointed, instead of annointed.

634   *Uncertain*

Many a wife has helped her husband to the top of the ladder and then left him there—while she made up her mind whether the picture would look better on some other wall.

635   *Being a Grandparent*

The quickest way to be convinced that spanking is unnecessary is to become a grandparent.

636   *Trying To Forget*

"By the way, Bill, have you forgotten that you owe me five dollars?"
"Not yet. I'm a slow forgetter. Gimme time and I will."

637   *Ready*

Two foremen were comparing notes. "Do all the boys in your shop drop their tools the moment the whistle blows?" asked one.
"No, not at all," replied the other foreman. "The orderly ones have their tools all put away before that time."

638   *Not Badly*

"Your hair needs cutting badly," remarked the barber.
"It does not," exclaimed the customer, sitting down in the chair. "It needs cutting nicely. You cut it badly last time."

639   *Progress*

"I hear that your son is getting on quite well."
"Oh, definitely! Only two years ago he was wearing my old suits. Now I wear his."

640   *So Would I*

Teacher: "How would you punctuate this sentence? 'I saw a five-dollar bill on the street.' "
Student: "I would make a dash after it."

641   *Fair Question*

When the first-grader asked his mother why Daddy brought home a briefcase full of papers every night, the mother replied, "Daddy has so much to do that he can't finish it all at the office. That's why he has to work at night."
"Well," said the child, "why don't they put him in a slower group?"

642   *The Secret*

You will always stay young if you live honestly, eat slowly, sleep sufficiently, work industriously, worship faithfully—and lie about your age.

643   *Conscience?*

Judge: "You have been found not guilty."
Prisoner: "Does that mean I can keep the money?"

644   *Lost Control*

"As I backed out of the garage I hit the door, ran over my son's bicycle, tore up the lawn, hit our neighbor's house, crushed a stop sign, and crashed into a tree."
"Then what happened?" the officer inquired.
"Then I lost control of the car," replied the driver.

645   *Prose and Poetry*

Little Tommy was asked the difference between prose and poetry. After a brief thought, he said, "There was a young man named Rees, who went wading up to his ankles."
After a pause, he went on. "That's prose," he said, "but if the water had been a few inches higher, it would have been poetry."

646   *Unbelievable*

"Does Bill know what caused his fainting spell?"
"He says his son asked for the keys to the garage and came out with the lawn mower."

647   *Cheap*

Sign on the windshield of an old, beat-up jalopy at a used-car lot: "Price $2,300. Rebate $2,100."

648   *Lucky*

"What are you smiling at?" asked Noah.
"I was just thinking," replied his wife, "how lucky it was we could go ahead and build this ark without waiting for an appropriation from Congress."

649   *Modest Man*

Father of teen-age daughter when answering telephone: "No, this isn't Dreamboat. This is the Supply Ship."

650   *Seems Fair*

After the race the owner was giving the jockey a piece of his mind. "A fine jockey you are!" he said. "I distinctly told you to come away with a rush at the corner. Why didn't you?"

"Well," retorted the jockey tartly, "it didn't seem quite sporting to leave the horse behind."

651 *Wrong Lesson*

The minister's theme was the beneficent wisdom of God who knows which of us grow best in the sunlight and which of us need the shade. He took an example from the flower garden.

"You know you plant roses in the sunlight," he said, "but if you want your fuchsias to grow they must be kept in the shade."

After church a woman came up to him, her face radiant. "I am so grateful for your wonderful sermon," she said. "It did me so much good."

A glow of pride warmed the minister's heart, but it vanished a moment later.

"Yes," continued the woman. "I never knew before just what was the matter with my fuchsias."

652 *Statues*

You can say some things in favor of statues of politicians. They do keep their mouths shut. They also don't create big budget deficits and raise your taxes.

653 *Confidence*

We sometimes find that confidence is that quiet, absolutely assured feeling you have just before you fall flat on your face.

654 *The Secret Ballot*

A peasant in a Communist country went to the polls on election day and was handed a sealed envelope to drop into the ballot box. He began to tear the envelope open, but an official shouted, "What do you think you are doing?"

The peasant said he wanted to see for whom he was voting.

"Are you crazy?" exclaimed the official. "This is a secret ballot."

655 *Get on the Ball*

An inept golfer once drove his tee shot onto an anthill. After many swings he demolished the anthill, but still had not hit the ball. At this point one of the two ants still alive turned to the other and said, "If we're going to survive, we'd better get on the ball!"

656 *Instructions*

Traveling lady: "Tell me which platform to go to for the train to Boston."
Conductor: "Just turn to the left and you'll be right."

Lady: "Young man, don't be so smart-alecky!"
Conductor: "Okay, lady, then just turn right and you'll be left."

657   *Speakers*

Speakers come and speakers go.
Some of 'em say, "I told you so";
Some of 'em start to "show their stuff";
Some of 'em try to "throw a bluff."
Some of 'em try to "be real funny";
Some of 'em come to "get the money."
But the one who makes us all feel happy
Is the "ten-minute bird" who makes it "snappy."

658   *Foreigner*

Inquired the Sunday School teacher of her class: "Who was the first man?"
"George Washington," promptly announced a restless boy.
"Oh, no," corrected the instructor, with an amused smile.
"Well, then, I suppose it was Adam," muttered the boy, "if you're counting them foreigners."

659   *Oversight*

It was the first day on the job for the pretty blonde steno just out of school. Her boss picked up the first of her finished letters, and with a sigh said, "You can't spell very well, can you? I see you spelled sugar 's-u-g-g-e-r.' "
"Oh, dear, so I have!" she exclaimed. "How do you suppose I came to leave out the 'h'?"

660   *Late*

The harsh, Scrooge-like boss berated his employee who was due at eight but did not get in until nine.
"Look at me," said the employee, holding up a bandaged arm. "I fell out of a second-story window."
The boss asked angrily, "Did that take an hour?"

661   *Don't Ask Him*

Texan to son: "Son, I just heard you asking that man if he was from Texas. Now, my boy, I want you always to remember that if a man comes from Texas, he'll tell you, and if he isn't from Texas, there's no need to embarrass him."

662　*Heap Big Winner*

A deserted farmhouse in a gullied field was pictured in a farm magazine some time ago, and a prize was offered for the best 100-word description. The award was given to an Indian who submitted the following:

"Picture show white man crazy. Cut down trees. Make big tepee. Plow hill. Water wash. Wind blow soil. Grass gone. Door gone. Window gone. Whole place gone. Buck gone. Papoose gone. Squaw too. No chuckaway. No pigs. No corn. No plow. No hay. No pony. Indian no plow land. Keep grass. Buffalo eat grass. Indian eat buffalo. Hide make tepee. Make moccasin. Indian make no terrace. No make dam. All time eat. No hunt job. No hitchhike. No ask relief. No shoot pig. Great Spirit make grass. Indian no waste anything. Indian no work. White man loco."

663　*Baseball*

Professor: "Joseph, describe hibernation to the class."

Joe: "To hibernate is to pass the winter in a state of torpor, as do certain animals. It is a sort of suspended animation during which life flickers low and the animal barely exists through the cold, dark part of the year."

Professor: "Correct. Give us an example."

Joe: "A baseball fan."

664　*A Sure Sign*

Early to bed and early to rise is a sure sign that you are fed up with television.

665　*Responsible*

Employer: "For this job we want a responsible man."

Applicant: "Then you want me. Everywhere I've worked, when something went wrong they said I was responsible."

666　*Good Advice*

A kind-hearted gentleman saw a little boy trying to reach a doorbell. He rang the bell for him, then said: "What now, my little man?"

"Run like crazy," said the boy. "That's what I'm going to do!"

667　*Honest*

Mother: "Did you eat those tarts I had in the pantry?"

Jack: "I didn't touch one."

Mother: "Well, there is only one left."

Jack: "That's the one I didn't touch."

668   *Shorthand*

"Anyone here know shorthand?" asked the sergeant of the recruits.
Two men stepped forward.
"Good," he said, "go help with the potato peeling. They're short-handed there!"

669   *Two Whistles*

Happiest man on earth: "How much is this sparkling diamond?"
Jeweler: "That one is $1,000."
The young man looked startled and then gave a whistle. He pointed to another one. "And this one?"
Jeweler: "That one is two whistles."

670   *Cancel His Order*

"Tell me what you eat and I'll tell you what you are," said a lunch-counter philosopher.
Whereupon a meek little man, sitting a few stools away, called to the waitress: "Cancel my order for shrimp salad, please."

671   *Keep Trying*

If nobody knows the trouble you've seen, you're not talking to the right people.

672   *Full of Hot Air?*

Do you know what one young uninflated balloon said to the other? "What are you gonna be when you blow up?"

673   *Inflation*

The old-timer says that in the good old days inflation was just something you did to the kids' balloons on the Fourth of July.

674   *The Iron Curtain*

The latest joke behind the Iron Curtain: "What is the difference between an optimist and a pessimist?" Answer: "An optimist is content to know Russian, but a pessimist is busy learning Chinese."

675   *Miracle Drug*

Every parent knows that a miracle drug is any medicine you can get the kids to take without screaming.

676   *The Cough and the Sneeze*

> I coughed a cough into the air,
> Germs fell to earth, I know not where.
> For who has eyes so keen and bright
> That they can see where microbes light?
> I sneezed a sneeze into the air,
> The virus flew most everywhere.
> For who has hand so quick to lug
> His hanky out and top his mug?
> Not long afterward on a bed
> I found a neighbor almost dead.
> For he that day was standing by,
> And now has flu, the same as I.

677   *How to Tell*

If you can't hear a pin drop, ten to one there's something wrong with your bowling.

678   *No Argument*

Teacher: "What's the shape of the earth, Johnny?"
Johnny: "It is round."
Teacher: "How do you know it's round?"
Johnny: "All right, it's square, then. I don't want to start an argument about it."

679   *No Hero*

A couple of young boys walked into the dentist's office. One faced him boldly and said, "Doc, I want a tooth took out and I don't want no gas 'cause I'm in a hurry."

"I must say you're a brave boy," said the doctor. "Which tooth is it?"

The little boy turned to his silent friend and said, "Show him your tooth, Albert."

680   *Unfortunately*

Usually the first screw to get loose in a person's head is the one that controls the tongue.

681   *Age*

By the time a man can afford to lose a golf ball, he can't knock it that far.

682 *Ain't It the Truth!*

We heard about a place where "ain't" is used properly—in the roadside grocery store in the hills:

Customer: "Ain't got no fr sh eggs, is you?"

Clerk: "I ain't said I ain't!"

Customer: "Ain't asked you ain't you ain't. I asked you ain't you is."

683 *Big Deal*

Dad took his six-year-old boy for a ride in the family's bright new station wagon.

"Well, David, how did you like it?" the father asked after the ride was over.

"It's swell, Dad!" the youngster replied. "Two great big seats and a big, back recreation room!"

684 *Golf Caddie*

About the only person who can smile when everything around him goes wrong.

685 *Husband Around the House*

If you want a thing well done, don't do it yourself—unless you know how.

686 *Quiz*

If you were to list the ten smartest people you know, who would be the other nine?

687 *Real Bad*

Richard Burlin of Chatham, Massachusetts, won the world's liar championship of the Burlington, Wisconsin, Liars' Club when he said, "Fishing around here was so bad sometimes this summer that even the biggest liars didn't catch any."

688 *Wrong Advice*

David, who was better in arithmetic than in spelling, was at the blackboard trying to spell a word. Meaning to be helpful, a classmate said, "Just add 'e.' " David looked irritably over his shoulder: "I am not adding. I am spelling."

689 *Good Question*

The little boy looked up and down the street, then sorrowfully approached a policeman standing on the corner.

"Sir," he asked, "did you see a lady going by without me?"

690   *The Difference*

Opportunity only knocks. Temptation kicks in the door.

691   *Among Those Present*

> The bridal veil was fragile net,
> The bridal gown was lace.
> The bride wore slippers on her feet,
> A smile upon her face.
>
> The bride wore gloves of softest silk,
> And garlands in her hair.
> The bride's bouquet was white.
> P.S. The groom was also there.

692   *Prosperity*

We have reached an age of such prosperity in this country that living within your means is considered almost unpatriotic.

693   *Better Idea*

Instead of having the students work their way through college, maybe it would be better to have the colleges work their way through the students.

694   *Under Oath*

"You seem to have plenty of intelligence for a man in your position," sneered the attorney to the man on the witness stand.

"Thank you," answered the witness. "If I weren't under oath I'd return the compliment."

695   *Breakable*

A woman was mailing the old family Bible to a brother in a distant city.
Postal clerk: "Does this package contain anything breakable?"
Lady: "Only the Ten Commandments."

696   *Handicap*

"Children," said the teacher, "be diligent and steadfast, and you will succeed. Take the case of George Washington. Do you remember my telling you of the great difficulty George Washington had to face?"

"Yes, ma'am," said a boy. "He couldn't tell a lie."

697   *Gaining on Him*

The proud owner of one of those new cars, half a block long and loaded with chrome, zoomed into the gas station and called out airily, "Fill 'er up, son!"

The filling-station attendant dutifully stuck the gas hose into the tank. After some time had passed, the attendant stuck his head in the window and complained, "Better shut off your engine, mister—you're gaining on me."

698   *Why Bother?*

> Thirty days has September.
> All the rest I can't remember.
> The calendar hangs there on the wall—
> Why bother me with this at all!

699   *Dream Come True*

"Gentlemen," stated the portly member of the study club, "I now firmly believe in dreams—in their reality and in the power of prophecy. Last night, while sound asleep, I dreamed that I was at a concert, and when I awoke, I was at a concert."

700   *Their Toys*

If you have wondered what the difference is between men and boys, one difference certainly is the price of their toys.

701   *Just an Hour*

Jane: "Have I kept you waiting long?"

Wayne: "No, but did you know that there are 3,692 polka dots on your wallpaper?"

702   *Failure*

When a new lighthouse was erected on a dangerous shore, a couple of Eskimos appointed themselves sidewalk superintendents. They were constantly on hand to watch operations.

Then one night a heavy fog blew. One Eskimo turned triumphantly to the other. "I told you white igloo-builder no good," he exulted. "Light shine, bell ding-dong, horn woo-woo, but fog come rolling in just the same."

703   *Civil Service Jargon*

Undue multiplicity of personnel assigned either concurrently or consecutively to a single function involves deterioration in the resultant product as compared with the product of the labor of an exact sufficiency of personnel.

In plain English: Too many cooks spoil the broth.

704   *Changing Times*

In 1878 a sign in a restaurant read: "Count your change before leaving." Now the sign reads: "Don't count on leaving with any change."

705   *Saving Time*

"Since I bought a new car, I don't have to walk to the bank to make my deposits."

"Now you drive over?"

"No. I just don't make any."

706   *Wonderful*

The young couple sat together on a park bench. After a long pause, she asked dreamily, "Do you think my eyes are like stars?"

"Yeah," he replied.

"And do you think my teeth are like pearls?" she continued.

"Yeah," he said.

"And do you think my hair is like spun gold in the moonlight?"

"Yeah," he repeated.

"Oh, Joe!" she exclaimed ecstatically. "You say the most wonderful things!"

707   *Not Much*

An artist who wanted a home among the Taconic Hills of Vermont was talking the matter over with a farmer who allowed he had a house for sale.

"I must have a scenic view," said the artist. "Does your house offer a good view?"

"Well," drawled the farmer, trying to be honest, "from the front porch yuh kin see Ed Snow's barn, but beyond that there ain't nothin' but a bunch of mountains."

708   *Frank*

Several women at a party were chatting with the little daughter of their hostess. "I suppose that you are a great help to your mother," commented one of them.

"Oh, yes, ma'am," replied the child, "and so is Ethel; but today it's my turn to count the spoons after you have gone."

709   *Thankful*

One optimistic minister had the habit in his opening prayer each Sunday of thanking God for the weather. On a particularly cold, icy, windy, slushy Sunday morning, the people who had ventured out wondered how the minister could possibly refer to the weather in his morning prayer with any sense of gratitude. To their surprise, he said in the beginning of his prayer, "Dear God, we thank Thee that Thou dost send us so few Sundays like today."

710   *Logical*

Teacher: "What inspired the old-time pioneers to set forth in their covered wagons?"
Pupil: "Well, maybe they didn't want to wait thirty years for a train."

711   *Frank*

Departing guest: "Well, good night—hope I haven't kept you up too late."
Host: "Not at all. We'd have been getting up about now anyway."

712   *Should Flunk Them*

Dinner Guest: "Will you pass the nuts, Professor?"
Professor: "I suppose so, although I really should flunk them."

713   *He Was Flat*

Jack: "When I sat down to play the piano, they all laughed."
Tim: "Why?"
Jack: "There wasn't any piano stool."

714   *How to Meditate*

When we were kids, our parents taught us how to meditate. They said, "Sit down and shut up."

715   *With Inflation*

There was a time when a fool and his money were soon parted. Now it happens to everybody.

716   *Please Call*

A newspaper carried this classified ad: "The man who picked up my wallet on Market Street was recognized. He is requested to return it."
A few days later this ad appeared: "The recognized man who picked up your wallet on Market Street requests the loser to call and get it."

717   *Progress*

Every year it takes less time to fly across the ocean and longer to drive to work.

718   *Help*

Because of the current enthusiasm for class visits to science museums, the attendants are gradually going crazy. Recently in Chicago a youngster, obviously lost, approached the lost-and-found desk. She inquired hopefully: "Has any teacher been turned in this afternoon?"

719   *Worrier*

If you're a born worrier, you were born at the right time.

720   *Sounds Reasonable*

Teacher: "Why are the days longer in summer and shorter in winter?"
Student: "During summer, heat expands, and in winter, cold contracts. Therefore, the days are long in summer and short in winter."

721   *How to Save Money*

When in supermarkets you should exercise shelf-control.

722   *Very Courteous*

"Well, dear," sighed the husband after viewing the crumpled fender, "did the officer scold you for hitting one of the city's trees?"
"No, he was just lovely, John," explained the new driver. "He said the city planted them just to keep drivers from getting up on the people's porches."

723   *You Must Dig*

We like this little ditty—it has a lot to say—
So go ahead and read it now, and remember it each day:
"Sitting still and wishing makes no person great.
The good Lord sends the fishing, but you must dig the bait!"

724   *Helpful*

The diner was annoyed because he had a knife and ، fork, but no spoon.
"This coffee is pretty hot to stir with my finger," he chided the waitress.
The waitress hurried to the kitchen, returning shortly with another cup of coffee.
"This one isn't so hot, sir," she beamed.

725   *Painters*

Not every husband with a green thumb is a good gardener—some are just careless painters.

Interesting and Useful Quotations

726   In the last analysis, it is our conception of death which decides our answers to all the questions that life puts to us.—*Dag Hammarskjold*

727   A straw vote only shows which way the hot air blows.—*O. Henry*

728   One machine can do the work of fifty ordinary men. No machine can do the work of one extraordinary man.—*Elbert Hubbard*

729   Little minds are interested in the extraordinary; great minds in the commonplace.—*Elbert Hubbard*

730   What was one day a sheep's hind leg and leaves of spinach was the next part of the hand that wrote, the brain that conceived the slow movement of the Jupiter Symphony.—*Aldous Huxley*

731   Armaments, universal debt, and planned obsolescence—those are the three pillars of Western prosperity.—*Aldous Huxley*

732   A nation is a society united by a delusion about its ancestry and by a common hatred of its neighbors.—*W. R. Inge, Dean of St. Paul's*

733   Summer afternoon—summer afternoon; to me those have always been the two most beautiful words in the English language.—*Henry James*

734   The war against hunger is truly mankind's war of liberation.—*John F. Kennedy*

735   The most exhausting thing in life, I have discovered, is being insincere. That is why so much social life is exhausting; one is wearing a mask.—*Anne Morrow Lindbergh*

736   If one sets aside time for a business appointment, a trip to the hairdresser, a social engagement, or a shopping expedition, that time is accepted as inviolable. But if one says: I cannot come because that is my hour to be alone, one is considered rude, egotistical or strange. What a commentary on our civilization, when being alone is considered suspect; when one has to apologize for it, make excuses, hide the fact that one practices it—like a secret vice!—*Anne Morrow Lindbergh*

737   Well, yes. You could say we have independent means.—*John D. Rockefeller III*

738   We have gone completely overboard on security. Everything has to be secured, jobs, wages, hours—although the ultimate in security is jail, the slave labor camp and the salt mine.—*Cola Parker*

739   Our people have always been endowed with a sense of mission in the world. They have believed that it was their duty to help men everywhere to get the opportunity to be and do what God designed.—*John Foster Dulles*

740   Any song that moves you to joy or tears has greatness. Everything in life should be enjoyed for what it is.—*Marguerite Piazza, Metropolitan Opera star.*

741   The parent who could see his boy as he really is would shake his head and say: "Willie is no good: I'll sell him."—*Stephen Leacock*

742   If you're there before it's over, you're on time.—*Mayor James J. Walker*

743   To give an accurate and exhaustive account of that period would need a far less brilliant pen than mine.—*Max Beerbohm*

744   It is impossible to enjoy idling thoroughly unless one has plenty of work to do.—*Jerome K. Jerome*

745   It is a sin to believe evil of others, but it is seldom a mistake.—*H. L. Mencken*

746   It is better to have loafed and lost than never to have loafed at all.—*James Thurber*

747   One of the principal troubles about inflation is that the public likes it. —*Lord Woolton*

748   The way to crush the bourgeoisie is to grind them between the millstones of taxation and inflation.—*Nikolai Lenin*

749   Our federal government is the biggest employer, the biggest tenant, the biggest debtor, the biggest banker, and the biggest spender in all the history of the world. Big government and big taxes, plus unrestrained regulatory control of business, spell big trouble for every American.—*James D. Finley*

750   Life is no brief candle to me. It is a sort of splendid torch which I have got hold of for the moment, and I want to make it burn as brightly as possible before handing it on to future generations.—*George Bernard Shaw*

751   The ultimate purpose of man is not merely to fly from Chicago to London in seven hours—eating a ten-course dinner en route. The great goal of free men is not simply to create a sleek and self-satisfied culture of comfort, leisure, and fun. . . . The final measure of greatness is whether you and I have increased the freedom of man, enhanced his dignity, and brought him nearer to the nobility of the divine image in which he was created.—*Herbert V. Prochnow*

752   Fifteen minutes a day devoted to one definite study will make one a master in a dozen years.—*Edward Howard Griggs*

753   Doing an injury puts you below your Enemy; Revenging one makes you but even with him; Forgiving it sets you above him.

754   Other things being equal, that is the best government which most liberally lets its subject or citizen alone. Through the whole range of authority, he governs best who governs least.—*Arthur Stevens Phelps*

755   Pythagoras used to say life resembles the Olympic Games; a few men strain their muscles to carry off a prize; others bring trinkets to sell to the crowd for a profit; and some there are who seek no further advantage than to look at the show and see how and why everything is done. They are spectators of other men's lives in order better to judge and manage their own.—*Michel de Montaigne*

756   Life is a progress from want to want, not from enjoyment to enjoyment.
—*Samuel Johnson*

757   The game of life is not so much in holding a good hand as playing a poor hand well.—*H. T. Leslie*

758   The goal of all life is death.—*Sigmund Freud*

759   The minority is always wrong—at the beginning.—*Herbert V. Prochnow*

760   No man is an island, entire of itself; every man is a piece of the continent, a part of the main.—*John Donne*

761   In nothing do men approach so nearly to the gods as doing good to men.—*Cicero*

762   The American reading his Sunday paper in a state of lazy collapse is perhaps the most perfect symbol of the triumph of quantity over quality. . . . Whole forests are being ground into pulp daily to minister to our triviality.—*Irving Babbitt*

763   Children will watch anything, and when a broadcaster uses crime and violence and other shoddy devices to monopolize a child's attention it's worse than taking candy from a baby. It is taking precious time from the process of growing up.—*Newton Minow*

764   We are drowning our youngsters in violence, cynicism and sadism piped into the living room and even the nursery. The grandchildren of the kids who used to weep because the Little Match Girl froze to death now feel cheated if she isn't slugged, raped and thrown into a Bessemer converter.—*Jenkin Lloyd Jones*

765   My life has been nothing but a failure.—*Claude Monet*

766   It is not the employer who pays wages—he only handles the money. It is the product that pays wages.—*Henry Ford*

767   The finest eloquence is that which gets things done.—*David Lloyd George*

768   There is nothing that fails like success.—*G. K. Chesterton*

769   In the world there are only two tragedies. One is not getting what one wants and the other is getting it.—*Oscar Wilde*

770   I always avoid prophesying beforehand, because it is much better policy to prophesy after the event has already taken place.—*Winston Churchill*

771   The trouble with our times is that the future is not what it used to be. —*Paul Valéry*

772   When I get back to familiar sights of the farmlands, the corn and the wheat, the vast horizons, the friendly people with whom I was raised, I feel more at home than I do any other place in this world that I have been roaming for long over forty years.—*Dwight D. Eisenhower*

773   May the Lord bless you real good.—*Billy Graham*

774   In cities, no one is quiet but many are lonely; in the country, people are quiet but few are lonely.—*Dr. Geoffrey Fisher, Archbishop of Canterbury*

775   It is well known that the older a man grows, the faster he could run as a boy.—*Red Smith*

776   I do not think Rome is burning at such a pace we should sacrifice our lunch.—*Andrei Vishinsky*

777   I realize that advice is worth what it costs—that is nothing.—*Douglas MacArthur*

778   When I had got my notes all written out, I thought that I'd polish it off in two summers, and it took me twenty-seven years.—*Arnold Toynbee, on completing the ten volumes known as A Study of History*

779   With sixty staring me in the face, I have developed inflammation of the sentence structure and a definite hardening of the paragraphs.—*James Thurber*

780   All I know is, it is better to tell the truth than to lie, better to be free than a slave, better to have knowledge than be ignorant.—*H. L. Mencken*

781   On the whole, I haven't found men unduly loath to say, "I love you." The real trick is to get them to say, "Will you marry me?"—*Ilka Chase*

782   We cannot get grace from gadgets. In the bakelite house of the future, the dishes may not break, but the heart can. Even a man with ten shower baths may find life flat, stale and unprofitable.—*J. B. Priestley*

783   Thanks a thousand.—*Nelson Rockefeller*

784   The common man is a man who believes in only what he sees and he sees only what he can put his hand on. . . . He is on speaking terms with progress and progress must be in spite of him, although for him.—*Frank Lloyd Wright*

785   Time is a dressmaker specializing in alterations.—*Faith Baldwin*

786   People have got to think. Thinking isn't to agree or disagree. That's voting.—*Robert Frost*

787   The sum of the whole matter is this, that our civilization cannot survive materially unless it be redeemed spiritually. It can be saved only by becoming permeated with the spirit of Christ and being made free and happy by the practices which spring out of that spirit.—*Woodrow Wilson*

788   Science, freedom, beauty, adventure: What more could you ask of life? Aviation combined all the elements I loved. . . . I began to feel that I lived on a higher plane than the skeptics of the ground; one that was richer because of its very association with the element of danger they dreaded, because it was freer

of the earth to which they were bound. In flying I tasted the wine of the gods of which they could know nothing. . . .—*Charles A. Lindbergh*

789   The soul of a civilization is its religion, and it dies with its faith.—*Will and Ariel Durant*

790   . . . I was at a party feeling very shy because there were a lot of celebrities around, and I was sitting in a corner alone and a very beautiful young man came up to me and offered me some salted peanuts and he said, "I wish they were emeralds" as he handed me the peanuts and that was the end of my heart. I never got it back.—*Helen Hayes*

791   The most important thing a father can do for his children is to love their mother.—*Theodore M. Hesburgh*

792   If you have an important point to make, don't try to be subtle or clever. Use a pile driver. Hit the point once. Then come back and hit it a second time —a tremendous whack.—*Winston Churchill, advice to the young Prince of Wales on speechmaking*

793   Never invest your money in anything that eats or needs repainting. —*Billy Rose*

794   A man never knows what a fool he is until he hears himself imitated by one.—*Sir Herbert Beerbohm Tree*

795   Advertising agency: eighty-five percent confusion and fifteen percent commission.—*Fred Allen*

796   One fifth of the people are against everything all the time.—*Robert F. Kennedy*

797   Prisoner to his cellmate: "I'm going to study and improve myself, and when you're still a common thief I'll be an embezzler."—*Comic postcard*

798
>   Out where the handclasp's a little stronger,
>   Out where the smile dwells a little longer,
>   That's where the West begins.
>   —*Arthur Chapman*

799   I'm living so far beyond my income that we may almost be said to be living apart.—*Saki*

800   If Botticelli were alive today he'd be working for *Vogue.*—*Peter Ustinov*

801   Every artist writes his own autobiography.—*Havelock Ellis*

802   An artist must know how to convince others of the truth of his lies.
—*Pablo Picasso*

803   Nobody dast blame this man. You don't understand: Willy was a
salesman, there is no rock bottom to the life. He don't put a bolt to a nut, he
don't tell you the law or give you medicine. He's a man way out there in the blue,
riding on a smile and a shoeshine. And when they start not smiling back—that's
an earthquake. And then you get yourself a couple of spots on your hat, and
you're finished. Nobody dast blame this man. A salesman is got to dream, boy.
It comes with the territory.—*Arthur Miller*

804   His studies were pursued but never effectually overtaken.—*H. G. Wells*

805   In the midst of life we are in debt.—*Ethel Watts Mumford*

806   I kissed my first woman and smoked my first cigarette on the same day;
I have never had time for tobacco since.—*Arturo Toscanini*

807   Don't talk about yourself, it will be done when you leave.—*Addison
Mizner*

808   If you can actually count your money, then you are not a really rich
man.—*Paul Getty*

809   There are few sorrows, however poignant, in which a good income is
of no avail.—*Logan Pearsall Smith*

810   You must not suppose, because I am a man of letters, that I never tried
to earn an honest living.—*George Bernard Shaw*

811   In these times you have to be an optimist to open your eyes when you
awake in the morning.—*Carl Sandburg*

812   You will find that the truth is often unpopular and the contest between
agreeable fancy and disagreeable fact is unequal. For, in the vernacular, we
Americans are suckers for good news.—*Adlai E. Stevenson*

813   With the supermarket as our temple and the singing commercial as our
litany, are we likely to fire the world with an irresistible vision of America's
exalted purposes and inspiring way of life?—*Adlai E. Stevenson*

814   I'm very healthy. And I have an eternal curiosity. Then, I think I'm
not dependent on any person. I love people, I love my family, my children.
. . . But inside myself is a place where I live all alone and that's where you renew
your springs that never dry up.—*Pearl Buck*

815   I write at high speed because boredom is bad for my health. It upsets my stomach more than anything else. I also avoid green vegetables. They're grossly overrated.—*Noel Coward*

816   I'd just as soon play tennis with the net down.—*Robert Frost, on writing "free verse"*

817   Now what is history? It is the centuries of systematic explorations of the riddle of death, with a view to overcoming death. That's why people discover mathematical infinity and electromagnetic waves, that's why they write symphonies. . . .—*Boris Pasternak*

818   The instability of the economy is equaled only by the instability of economists.—*John H. Williams, Harvard University professor*

819   There is no such thing as "soft sell" and "hard sell." There is only "smart sell" and "stupid sell."—*Charles Brower*

820   Our national flower is the concrete cloverleaf.—*Lewis Mumford*

821   The end of all political effort must be the well-being of the individual in a life of safety and freedom.—*Dag Hammarskjold*

822   It's no good shutting your eyes and saying "British is best" three times a day after meals and expecting it to be so. We've got to work for it by constantly criticizing and improving.—*Duke of Edinburgh*

823   Education is the ability to listen to almost anything without losing your temper or your self-confidence.—*Robert Frost*

824   The true business of liberal education is greatness.—*Nathan M. Pusey*

825   I assert that the cosmic religious experience is the strongest and the noblest driving force behind scientific research.—*Albert Einstein*

826   If you achieve success, you will get applause, and if you get applause, you will hear it. My advice to you concerning applause is this: Enjoy it but never quite believe it.—*Robert Montgomery*

827   Now see here! I cut my own hair. I got sick of barbers because they talk too much. And too much of their talk was about my hair coming out.—*Robert Frost*

828   It might be said now that I have the best of both worlds: a Harvard education and a Yale degree.—*John F. Kennedy*

829   Man wants a great deal here below, and Woman even more.—*James Thurber*

830 I'm sixty-five and I guess that puts me in with the geriatrics. But if there were fifteen months in every year, I'd only be forty-eight. That's the trouble with us. We number everything. Take women, for example. I think they deserve to have more than twelve years between the ages of twenty-eight and forty.—*James Thurber*

831 America is a large, friendly dog in a very small room. Every time it wags its tail, it knocks over a chair.—*Arnold Toynbee*

832 What passes for optimism is most often the effect of an intellectual error.—*Raymond Aron*

833 In the midst of winter, I finally learned that there was in me an invincible summer.—*Albert Camus*

834 We sit at breakfast, we sit on the train on the way to work, we sit at work, we sit at lunch, we sit all afternoon . . . a hodgepodge of sagging livers, sinking gall bladders, drooping stomachs, compressed intestines, and squashed pelvic organs.—*Dr. John Button, Jr.*

835 Striving to outdo one's companions on the golf course and tennis court or in the swimming pool constitutes several socially acceptable forms of suicide. —*Dr. George Griffith*

836 Archeology sounds like dull sport in five syllables. It isn't. It's the Peeping Tom of the sciences. It is the sandbox of men who care not where they are going; they merely want to know where everybody else has been.—*Jim Bishop*

837 I think and think for months and years. Ninety-nine times, the conclusion is false. The hundredth time I am right.—*Albert Einstein*

838 Not so long ago, when I was a student in college, just flying an airplane seemed a dream. But that dream turned into reality.—*Charles A. Lindbergh*

839 I'm leaving because the weather is too good. I hate London when it's not raining.—*Groucho Marx*

840 A politician is a man who understands government, and it takes a politician to run a government. A statesman is a politician who's been dead ten or fifteen years.—*Harry S. Truman*

841 Whenever a fellow tells me he's bipartisan, I know he's going to vote against me.—*Harry S. Truman*

842 Duty, honor, country: Those three hallowed words reverently dictate what you ought to be, what you can be, what you will be. They are your rallying point to build courage when courage seems to fail, to regain faith when there

seems to be little cause for faith, to create hope when hope becomes forlorn.—
Douglas MacArthur

843   When I've had a rough day, before I go to sleep I ask myself if there's anything more I can do right now. If there isn't, I sleep sound.—*L. L. Colbert*

844   Business more than any other occupation is a continual dealing with the future; it is a continual calculation, an instinctive exercise in foresight.—
Henry R. Luce

845   Perfection of planning is a symptom of decay. During a period of exciting discovery or progress, there is no time to plan the perfect headquarters. The time for that comes later, when all the important work has been done.—*C. Northcote Parkinson*

846   I look back on my life like a good day's work, it was done and I am satisfied with it. I was happy and contented, I knew nothing better and made the best out of what life offered.—*Anna Mary Moses (Grandma Moses)*

847   I've sometimes thought of marrying—and then I've thought again.—
Noel Coward

848   To be out of jail. To eat and sleep regular. To get what I write printed in a free country for free people. To have a little love in the home and esteem outside the home.—*Carl Sandburg*

849   God cannot alter the past, but historians can.—*Samuel Butler*

850   History is the great dust-heap . . . a pageant and not a philosophy.—
Augustine Birrell

851   History is indeed little more than the register of the crimes, follies, and misfortunes of mankind.—*Edward Gibbon*

852   What history teaches us is that men have never learned anything from it.—*Georg Wilhelm Hegel*

853   The men who make history have no time to write about it.—*Prince von Metternich*

854   I would rather men should ask why no statute has been erected in my honor, than why one has.—*Cato*

855   No person was ever honored for what he received. Honor has been the reward for what he gave.—*Calvin Coolidge*

856   There are well-dressed foolish ideas just as there are well-dressed fools.
—*Nicolas Chamfort*

857   Anyone who has begun to think places some portion of the world in jeopardy.—*John Dewey*

858   It is impossible to defeat an ignorant man in argument.—*William Gibbs McAdoo*

859   I have never met a man so ignorant that I couldn't learn something from him.—*Galileo Galilei*

860   Surely God would not have created such a being as man . . . to exist only for a day! No, no, man was made for immortality.—*Abraham Lincoln*

861   At bottom every man knows well enough that he is a unique being, only once on this earth; and by no extraordinary chance will such a marvelously picturesque piece of diversity in unity as he is, ever be put together a second time.—*Friedrich Nietzsche*

862   How could a state be governed, or protected in its foreign relations if every individual remained free to obey or not to obey the law according to his private opinion?—*Thomas Hobbes*

863   He who builds a better mousetrap these days runs into material shortages, patent-infringement suits, work stoppages, collusive bidding, discount discrimination—and taxes.—*H. E. Martz*

864   We Jews have a secret weapon in our struggle with the Arabs—we have no place to go.—*Golda Meir*

865   I expect to pass through life but once. If, therefore, there be any kindness I can show, or any good thing I can do to any fellow being, let me do it now, and not defer or neglect it, as I shall not pass this way again.—*William Penn*

866   If the soul has food for study and learning, nothing is more delightful than an old age of leisure. . . . Leisure consists in all those virtuous activities by which a man grows morally, intellectually, and spiritually. It is that which makes a life worth living.—*Cicero*

867   The only liberty an inferior man really cherishes is the liberty to quit work, stretch out in the sun, and scratch himself.—*H. L. Mencken*

868   Leisure tends to corrupt, and absolute leisure corrupts absolutely.—*Edgar A. Shoaff*

869   Life is easier to take than you'd think; all that is necessary is to accept the impossible, do without the indispensable and bear the intolerable.—*Kathleen Norris*

870   When a man has pity on all living creatures, then only is he noble.—*Buddha*

871   Life can only be understood backwards; but it must be lived forwards. —*Sören Kierkegaard*

872   . . . my sense of my own importance to myself is tremendous. I am all I have, to work with, to play with, to suffer and to enjoy. It is not the eyes of others that I am wary of, but my own.—*Noel Coward*

873   Life is like playing a violin in public and learning the instrument as one goes on.—*Samuel Butler*

874   It is a socialist idea that making profits is a vice; I consider the real vice is making losses.—*Winston Churchill*

875   A hundred years from now, I dare say, some dreamy collector will pay a cool thousand for an old milk bottle, and I wish I had the equivalent for what my hot-water bag will bring in 2034. Why we should be so beguiled by the antique is a riddle that perhaps only the interior decorator can solve.—*Cornelia Otis Skinner*

876   What our generation has forgotten is that the system of private property is the most important guaranty of freedom, not only for those who own property, but scarcely less for those who do not.—*Friedrich Hayek*

877   Property is the fruit of labor: property is desirable; it is a positive good. —*Abraham Lincoln*

878   The function of government must be to favor no small group at the expense of its duty to protect the rights of personal freedom and of private property of all its citizens.—*Franklin D. Roosevelt*

879   Generous people are rarely mentally ill people.—*Dr. Karl Menninger*

880   Next to being witty yourself, the best thing is being able to quote another's wit.—*Christian N. Bovee*

881   The wisdom of the wise and the experience of the ages are perpetuated by quotations.—*Benjamin Disraeli*

882   Our concern is not how to worship in the catacombs but how to remain human in the skyscrapers.—*Abraham Joshua Heschel*

883   Reality is always more conservative than ideology.—*Raymond Aron*

884   A reform is a correction of abuses; a revolution is a transfer of power. —*Edward Bulwer-Lytton*

885   Man is great only when he is kneeling.—*Pope Pius XII*

886   The price of greatness is responsibility.—*Winston Churchill*

887   Many speak the truth when they say that they despise riches, but they mean the riches possessed by other men.—*Charles Caleb Colton*

888   If money is your hope for independence, you will never have it. The only real security that a man can have in this world is a reserve of knowledge, experience and ability.—*Henry Ford*

889   You can be sincere and still be stupid.—*Charles F. Kettering*

890   A government that robs Peter to pay Paul can always depend upon the support of Paul.—*George Bernard Shaw*

891   Blessed are the young, for they shall inherit the national debt.—*Herbert Hoover*

892   If Patrick Henry thought that taxation without representation was bad, he should see how bad it is with representation.—*Farmer's Almanac*

893   The job of a teacher is to excite in the young a boundless sense of curiosity about life, so that the growing child shall come to apprehend it with an excitement tempered by awe and wonder.—*John Garrett*

894   Every actor in his heart believes everything bad that's printed about him.—*Orson Welles*

895   Few people think more than two or three times a year. I have made an international reputation for myself by thinking once or twice a week.—*George Bernard Shaw*

896   Once lead this people into war and they will forget there ever was such a thing as tolerance.—*Woodrow Wilson*

897   Tolerance is the virtue of the man without convictions.—*G. K. Chesterton*

898   Natives who beat drums to drive off evil spirits are objects of scorn to smart Americans who blow horns to break up traffic jams.—*Mary Ellen Kelly*

899   A man who dares to waste one hour of time has not discovered the value of life.—*Charles Darwin*

900   Yet several common fallacies about urban America continue to persist —despite the lessons of New York City. One is that bigness brings greatness and the second that the continued urbanization of our country—no matter how

misdirected—is a fatalistic reality that is beyond our control.—*Charles N. Kimball*

901   In the fight between you and the world, back the world.—*Franz Kafka*

902   There never has been any thirty-hour week for men who had anything to do.—*Charles F. Kettering*

903   The world is full of willing people; some willing to work, the rest willing to let them.—*Robert Frost*

904   The world will never have lasting peace so long as men reserve for war the finest human qualities.—*John Foster Dulles*

905   War is only a cowardly escape from the problems of peace.—*Thomas Mann*

906   There are no warlike peoples—just warlike leaders.—*Ralph Bunche*

907   The only question with wealth is what you do with it.—*John D. Rockefeller, Jr.*

908   The best way I know of to win an argument is to start by being in the right.—*Quentin Hogg, M.P.*

909   The best thing about the future is that it comes only one day at a time. —*Abraham Lincoln*

910   Prayer of the modern American: "Dear God, I pray for patience. And I want it right now!"—*Oren Arnold*

911   Two things fill the mind with ever new and increasing wonder and awe —the starry heavens above me, and the moral law within me.—*Immanuel Kant*

912   Goethe said there would be little left of him if he were to discard what he owed to others.—*Charlotte Cushman*

913   I often say of George Washington that he was one of the few in the whole history of the world who was not carried away by power.—*Robert Frost*

914   Power is what men seek, and any group that gets it will abuse it. It is the same old story.—*Lincoln Steffens*

915   The care of human life and happiness . . . is the first and only legitimate object of good government.—*Thomas Jefferson*

916   I sit here all day trying to persuade people to do the things they ought to have sense enough to do without my persuading them. That's all the powers of the President amount to.—*Harry S. Truman*

917   No public man can be just a little crooked.—*Herbert Hoover*

918   Every man has an equal chance to become greater than he is.

919   The best way to keep a boy out of the mud puddle is to shine his shoes. And that goes for grown-ups, too.

920   It is the biggest mistake in the world to think you are working for someone else.

921   If we should repeal all the regulatory laws on our statute books, and enforce only the Ten Commandments, in ten years we would become the most law-abiding nation on earth.—*James R. Page*

922   Changing one thing for the better is worth more than proving a thousand things are wrong.

923   What governs men is the fear of truth.—*Henri Frédéric Amiel*

924   The law is reason free from passion.—*Aristotle*

925   It ain't what a man don't know that makes him a fool, but what he does know that ain't so.—*Josh Billings*

926   I never did anything worth doing by accident; nor did any of my inventions come by accident; they came by work.—*Thomas Alva Edison*

927   All free governments are managed by the combined wisdom and folly of the people.—*James A. Garfield*

928   Today the guns are silent. A great tragedy has ended. A great victory has been won. The skies no longer rain death—the seas bear only commerce—men everywhere walk upright in the sunlight. The entire world is quietly at peace. The holy mission has been completed. And in reporting this to you, the people, I speak for the thousands of silent lips, forever stilled among the jungles and the beaches and in the deep waters of the Pacific which marked the way. I speak for the unnamed brave millions homeward bound to take up the challenge of that future which they did so much to salvage from the brink of disaster.—*Douglas MacArthur*

929   There is no security on this earth; there is only opportunity.—*Douglas MacArthur*

930   I am closing my fifty-two years of military service. When I joined the Army, even before the turn of the century, it was the fulfillment of all my boyish hopes and dreams. The world has turned over many times since I took the oath on the Plain at West Point, and the hopes and dreams have all since vanished,

but I still remember the refrain of one of the most popular barracks ballads of that day, which proclaimed most proudly that old soldiers never die; they just fade away. And like the old soldier of that ballad, I now close my military career and just fade away, an old soldier who tried to do his duty as God gave him the light to see that duty. Goodbye.—*Douglas MacArthur*

931　If the distinguished *Senator* will allow me, I will try to extricate him from his thoughts.—*Former Senator Eugene Millikin*

932　He is forever poised between a cliché and an indiscretion.—*Harold Macmillan*

933　. . . When I was young I used to go into the practice room and lock the door behind me. I'd put a beautiful novel in with my sheet music and a box of cherries on the right-hand side of the piano and a box of chocolates on the left and play runs with my left hand and eat cherries with my right and all the time be reading my book.—*Arthur Rubinstein*

934　This hooby doopy, oop-shoop, ootie ootie, boom boom de-addy boom, scoobledy goobledy dump—is trash.—*Denver Post, reporting a reader's comment on "rock 'n' roll" music*

935　A boy has two jobs. One is just being a boy. The other is growing up to be a man.—*Herbert Hoover*

936　. . . If a political party does not have its foundation in the determination to advance a cause that is right and that is moral, then it is not a political party, it is merely a conspiracy to seize power.—*Dwight D. Eisenhower*

937　True, there is government harassment, but there still is that relative freedom to fight. I can attack my government, try to organize to change it. That's more than I can do in Moscow, Peking, or Havana.—*Saul Alinsky*

938　If that's art, I'm a Hottentot!—*Harry S. Truman*

939　Less is more.—*Mies van der Rohe*

940　Some see private enterprise as a predatory target to be shot, others as a cow to be milked, but few are those who see it as a sturdy horse pulling the wagon.—*Winston Churchill*

941　There are an enormous number of managers who have retired on the job.—*Peter Drucker*

942　Enthusiasm for conversation can be fashioned into a nasty weapon for those who dislike business on general principles.—*William F. Buckley, Jr.*

943   A great deal of the so-called government encroachment in the area of business, labor, and the professions has been asked for by the people misusing their freedom.—*J. Irwin Miller*

944   Assassination is the extreme form of censorship.—*George Bernard Shaw*

945   To enjoy freedom we have to control ourselves.—*Virginia Woolf*

946   If we in business cannot put the brakes on this creeping socialism, the free enterprise system will become a thing of the past.—*Barton A. Cummings*

947   I could not say I believe. I know! I have had the experience of being gripped by something that is stronger than myself, something that people call God.—*Carl Jung*

948   I could prove God statistically.—*George Gallup*

949   The only thing necessary for the triumph of evil is for good men to do nothing.—*Edmund Burke*

950   The world's great men have not commonly been great scholars, nor the great scholars great men.—*Oliver Wendell Holmes, Jr.*

951   What a wonderful life I've had! I only wish I'd realized it sooner.—*Colette*

952   One of the indictments of civilizations is that happiness and intelligence are so rarely found in the same person.—*William Feather*

953   The heart has its reasons which reason does not understand.—*Blaise Pascal*

954   If you would not be forgotten as soon as you are dead, either write things worth reading or do things worth writing.—*Benjamin Franklin*

955   The family is the nucleus of civilization.—*Will and Ariel Durant*

956   I can pardon everyone's mistakes but my own.—*Cato*

957   He that cannot forgive others breaks the bridge over which he must pass himself; for every man has need to be forgiven.—*Thomas Fuller*

958   People will sometimes forgive you the good you have done them, but seldom the harm they have done you.—*W. Somerset Maugham*

959   Adversity is the trial of principle. Without it a man hardly knows whether he is honest or not.—*Henry Fielding*

960   All of us have sufficient fortitude to bear the misfortunes of others.—
La Rochefoucauld

961   The Constitution . . . speaks of liberty and prohibits the deprivation of
liberty without due process of law. In prohibiting that deprivation the Constitution does not recognize an absolute and uncontrollable liberty.—*Charles Evans
Hughes*

962   When people are free to do as they please, they usually imitate each
other.—*Eric Hoffer*

963   At the desk where I sit, I have learned one great truth. The answer for
all our national problems—the answer for all the problems of the world—comes
to a single word. That word is "education."—*Lyndon B. Johnson*

964   America is the best half-educated country in the world.—*Nicholas
Murray Butler*

965   It is a curious fact that of all the illusions that beset mankind none is
quite so curious as that tendency to suppose that we are mentally and morally
superior to those who differ from us in opinion.—*Elbert Hubbard*

966   Your levelers wish to level down as far as themselves, but they cannot
bear leveling up to themselves.—*Samuel Johnson*

967   Real equality is not to be decreed by law. It cannot be given and it
cannot be forced.—*Raymond Moley*

968   The man who makes no mistakes does not usually make anything.—
Bishop W. C. Magee

969   The justification of majority rule in politics is not to be found in its
ethical superiority.—*Walter Lippmann*

970   Life is a series of experiences, each one of which makes us bigger, even
though sometimes it is hard to realize this.—*Henry Ford*

971   Education is the transmission of civilization.—*Will·and Ariel Durant*

972   You can't say that civilization don't advance, for in every war they kill
you a new way.—*Will Rogers*

973   I have always considered that the substitution of the internal combus-
tion engine for the horse marked a very gloomy milestone in the progress of
mankind.—*Winston Churchill*

974   Of all the tasks of government the most basic is to protect its citizens
against violence.—*John Foster Dulles*

975   Freedom of inquiry, freedom of discussion, and freedom of teaching—without these a university cannot exist.—*Robert Maynard Hutchins*

976   The theory of the Communists may be summed up in the single sentence: Abolition of private property.—*The Communist Manifesto*

977   The inherent vice of capitalism is the unequal sharing of blessings; the inherent virtue of socialism is the equal sharing of miseries.—*Winston Churchill*

978   A man who is not a Liberal at sixteen has no heart; a man who is not a Conservative at sixty has no head.—*Benjamin Disraeli*

979   To escape criticism—do nothing, say nothing, be nothing.—*Elbert Hubbard*

980   Being a Christian is more than just an instantaneous conversion—it is a daily process whereby you grow to be more and more like Christ.—*Billy Graham*

981   All cities are mad, but the madness is gallant. All cities are beautiful, but the beauty is grim.—*Christopher Morley*

982   The individual who pollutes the air with his factory and the ghetto kid who breaks store windows both represent the same thing. They don't care about each other—or what they do to each other.—*Daniel P. Moynihan*

983   The government of cities is the one conspicuous failure of the United States.—*James Bryce*

984   The city is not obsolete; it's the center of our civilization.—*Edward Logue*

985   Civilization is a stream with banks. The stream is sometimes filled with blood from people killing, stealing, shouting and doing things historians usually record, while on the banks, unnoticed, people build homes, make love, raise children, sing songs, write poetry and even whittle statues. The story of civilization is the story of what happened on the banks. Historians are pessimists because they ignore the banks for the river.—*Will and Ariel Durant*

986   To be able to fill leisure intelligently is the last product of civilization.—*Arnold Toynbee*

987   The oppressed are allowed once every few years to decide which particular representatives of the oppressing class are to represent and repress them.—*Karl Marx*

988   You can do anything with children if you only play with them.—*Prince Otto von Bismarck*

989   Parents are the last people on earth who ought to have children.—*Samuel Butler*

990   In every real man a child is hidden that wants to play.—*Friedrich Nietzsche*

991   Children are our most valuable natural resource.—*Herbert Hoover*

992   A boy may be a brilliant mathematician . . . at the age of thirteen. But I never knew a child of that age who had much that was useful to say about the ends of human life.—*Robert Maynard Hutchins*

993   I have now disposed of all my property to my family. There is one thing more I wish I could give them, and that is the Christian religion.—*Patrick Henry*

994   It is all one to me if a man comes from Sing Sing or Harvard. We hire a man, not his history.—*Henry Ford*

995   People are always ready to admit a man's ability after he gets there.—*Bob Edwards*

996   None of us can help the things life has done to us. They're done before you realize it, and once they're done they make you do other things until at last everything comes between you and what you'd like to be, and you have lost your true self forever.—*Eugene O'Neill*

997   Few people at the beginning of the nineteenth century needed an adman to tell them what they wanted.—*John Kenneth Galbraith*

998   The agnostic's prayer: "O God, if there is a god, save my soul, if I have a soul."—*Ernest Renan*

999   Americans are like a rich father who wishes he knew how to give his sons the hardships that made him rich.—*Robert Frost*

1000   This is still a very wealthy country. The failure is of spirit and insight.—*Governor Jerry Brown*

1001   This land of ours cannot be a good place for any of us to live in unless it is a good place for all of us to live in.—*Richard M. Nixon*

1002   We need some great statements about what America is about and what we can do about it.—*Theodore M. Hesburgh*

1003   The stream of time sweeps away errors, and leaves the truth for the inheritance of humanity.—*Georg Brandes*

1004   The American mind, unlike the English, is not formed by books, but, as Carl Sandburg once said to me, . . . by newspapers and the Bible.—*Van Wyck Brooks*

1005   The prophet and the martyr do not see the hooting throng. Their eyes are fixed on the eternities.—*Benjamin N. Cardozo*

1006   Religion and art spring from the same root and are close kin. Economics and art are strangers.—*Willa Cather*

1007   The Christian ideal has not been tried and found wanting. It has been found difficult, and left untried.—*G. K. Chesterton*

1008   If our democracy is to flourish, it must have criticism; if our government is to function, it must have dissent.—*Henry Steele Commager*

1009   Diversity of opinion within the framework of loyalty to our free society is not only basic to a university but to the entire nation.—*James Bryant Conant*

1010   The way of the superior man is threefold, but I am not equal to it. Virtuous, he is free from anxieties; wise, he is free from perplexities; bold, he is free from fear.—*Confucius*

1011   Collecting more taxes than is absolutely necessary is legalized robbery. —*Calvin Coolidge*

1012   Freedom lies in being bold.—*Robert Frost*

1013   Art is a collaboration between God and the artist, and the less the artist does the better.—*André Gide*

1014   If Carlyle could define a university as a collection of books, Socrates might have defined it as a conversation about wisdom.—*Sir Edward Grey*

1015   We shall soon with the help of God be in sight of the day when poverty will be banished from this nation.—*Herbert Hoover*

1016   In my opinion, we are in danger of developing a cult of the Common Man, which means a cult of mediocrity.—*Herbert Hoover*

1017   While democracy must have its organization and controls, its vital breath is individual liberty.—*Charles Evans Hughes*

1018   Anybody who feels at ease in the world today is a fool.—*Robert Maynard Hutchins*

1019   The world hates change, yet it is the only thing that has brought progress.—*Charles F. Kettering*

1020   The ideas of economists and political philosophers, both when they are right and when they are wrong, are more powerful than is commonly understood. Indeed, the world is ruled by little else.—*John Maynard Keynes*

1021   Worry affects the circulation, the heart, the glands, the whole nervous system. I have never known a man who died from overwork, but many who died from doubt.—*Charles H. Mayo*

1022   Sam Gompers once put the matter succinctly. When asked what the labor movement wanted, he answered "More." If by a better standard of living we mean not only more money but more leisure and a richer cultural life, the answer remains "More."—*George Meany*

1023   Remember, my son, that any man who is a bear on the future of this country will go broke.—*J. Pierpont Morgan*

1024   There is only one success—to be able to spend your life in your own way.—*Christopher Morley*

1025   A man is quite dishonorable to sell himself
                For anything other than quite a lot of pelf.
                                          —*Ogden Nash*

1026   The desire to take medicine is perhaps the greatest feature which distinguishes man from the animals.—*William Osler*

1027   In every generation there has to be some fool who will speak the truth as he sees it.—*Boris Pasternak*

1028   When war is declared, Truth is the first casualty.—*Arthur Ponsonby*

1029   The mark of the immature man is that he wants to die nobly for a cause, while the mark of a mature man is that he wants to live humbly for one.—*Wilhelm Stekel*

1030   Communism is the death of the soul. It is the organization of total conformity—in short, of tyranny—and it is committed to making tyranny universal.—*Adlai E. Stevenson*

1031   A person who is fundamentally honest doesn't need a code of ethics. The Ten Commandments and the Sermon on the Mount are all the ethical code anybody needs.—*Harry S. Truman*

1032   In the cause of freedom we have to battle for the rights of people with whom we do not agree; and whom, in many cases, we may not like. . . . If we do not defend their rights we endanger our own.—*Harry S. Truman*

1033   I shall never permit myself to stoop so low as to hate any man.—*Booker T. Washington*

1034   A good catchword can obscure analysis for fifty years.—*Wendell L. Willkie*

1035   Today it is not big business that we have to fear. It is big government. —*Wendell L. Willkie*

1036   It is our task not to produce "safe" men, in whom our safety can never in any case lie, but to keep alive in young people the courage to dare to seek the truth, to be free, to establish in them a compelling desire to live greatly and magnanimously, and to give them the knowledge and awareness, the faith and the trained facility to get on with the job. Especially the faith . . .—*Nathan M. Pusey*

1037   I believe that every right implies a responsibility; every opportunity, an obligation; every possession, a duty.—*John D. Rockefeller, Jr.*

1038   I tell you folks, all politics is apple sauce.—*Will Rogers*

1039   I believe in free enterprise—and always have. I believe in the profit system—and always have.—*Franklin D. Roosevelt*

1040   One truth stands firm. All that happens in world history rests on something spiritual. If the spiritual is strong, it creates world history. If it is weak, world history suffers.—*Albert Schweitzer*

1041   Liberty means responsibility. That is why most men dread it.—*George Bernard Shaw*

1042   Nothing has so much contributed to egotism, pride, conceit, swellhead-edness and braggadocio as the assumption that an "inferiority complex" is always wrong. If the failure to assert oneself . . . is the mark of a psychic disease, then satanic pride is on the throne.—*Bishop Fulton J. Sheen*

1043   Wealth comes from industry and from the hard experience of human toil. To dissipate it in waste and extravagance is disloyalty to humanity. This is by no means a doctrine of parsimony.—*Calvin Coolidge*

1044   I have noticed that nothing I never said ever did me any harm.—*Calvin Coolidge*

1045   The world is now too dangerous for anything but the truth, too small for anything but brotherhood.—*Arthur Powell Davies*

1046   Civilization begins with order, grows with liberty, and dies with chaos. —*Will Durant*

1047   They [the founders] proclaimed to all the world the revolutionary doctrine of the divine rights of the common man. That doctrine has ever since been the heart of the American faith.—*Dwight D. Eisenhower*

1048   The sun, the moon and the stars would have disappeared long ago, had they happened to be within reach of predatory human hands.—*Havelock Ellis*

1049   Pain makes man think. Thought makes man wise. Wisdom makes life endurable.—*John Patrick*

1050   There is no inevitability in history except as men make it.—*Felix Frankfurter*

1051   We are all of us more or less the slaves of opinion.—*William Hazlitt*

1052   All social disturbances and upheavals have their roots in crises of individual self-esteem, and the great endeavor in which the masses most readily unite is basically a search for pride.—*Eric Hoffer*

1053   On the whole, with scandalous exceptions, Democracy has given the ordinary worker more dignity than he ever had.—*Sinclair Lewis*

1054   All progress has resulted from people who took unpopular positions. —*Adlai E. Stevenson*

1055   When a government takes over a people's economic life it becomes absolute, and when it has become absolute it destroys the arts, the minds, the liberties and the meaning of the people it governs.—*Maxwell Anderson*

1056   When the outlook is steeped in pessimism, I remind myself, "Two and two still make four, and you can't keep mankind down for long."—*Bernard M. Baruch*

1057   The marvel of all history is the patience with which men and women submit to burdens unnecessarily laid upon them by their governments.—*William E. Borah*

1058   We have grasped the mystery of the atom and rejected the Sermon on the Mount.—*Omar N. Bradley*

1059   Merely having an open mind is nothing. The object of opening the mind, as of opening the mouth, is to shut it again on something solid.—*G. K. Chesterton*

1060   One can only hope the courage, integrity, and valiant spirit that rode the adventurous *Mayflower* in the storm-swept Atlantic, built log cabins in the rocky hills of New England, and with unbelievable hardship blazed new trails across the wide plains in covered wagons to stake out a new nation, still are somehow secure and sheltered deep in the hearts of the American people.— *Herbert V. Prochnow*

1061   The call of economic comfort is loud. But are the objectives today of leisure instead of labor, of more rights instead of more responsibilities, of spending instead of saving—are these the earmarks of a vigorous, advancing civilization, or evidences of disintegrating character?—*Herbert V. Prochnow*

1062   There are two kinds of discontent in this world: the discontent that works and the discontent which wrings its hands. The first gets what it wants and the second loses what it has.—*Gordon Graham*

1063   It pays to be in partnership with God, because spiritual bankruptcy is far more serious than financial loss could ever be.—*R. G. LeTourneau, industrialist*

1064   When I was a student at the Sorbonne in Paris I used to go out and riot occasionally. I can't remember now what side it was on.—*John Foster Dulles*

1065   If a nation values anything more than freedom, it will lose its freedom. And the irony of it is that if it is comfort or money that it values more, it will lose that, too.—*W. Somerset Maugham*

1066   Civilization is always in danger when those who have never learned to obey are given the right to command.—*Bishop Fulton J. Sheen*

1067   Is there no wisdom in the idea that to maintain its economic strength and to prevent the steady erosion of the value of its currency, a nation must sometimes put off spending until tomorrow what it cannot afford today?—*Herbert V. Prochnow*

1068   We need to recognize that no nation grows stronger by striving constantly for more leisure and less work.—*Herbert V. Prochnow*

1069   We are getting old when we do more and more things for the last time and fewer and fewer things for the first time.

1070   Soap and education are not as sudden as a massacre, but they are more deadly in the long run.—*Mark Twain*

1071   All business sagacity reduces itself in the last analysis to a judicious use of sabotage.—*Thorstein Veblen*

1072   My only solution for the problem of habitual accidents . . . is for everybody to stay in bed all day. Even then, there is always the chance that you will fall out.—*Robert Benchley*

1073   I have been told by hospital authorities that more copies of my works are left behind by departing patients than those of any other author.—*Robert Benchley*

1074   I don't know why it is that we are in such a hurry to get up when we fall down. You might think we would lie there and rest awhile.—*Max Eastman*

1075   What we call progress is the exchange of one nuisance for another nuisance.—*Havelock Ellis*

1076   My own personal reaction is that most ballets would be quite delightful if it were not for the dancing.—*Evening Standard*

1077   If you are scared to go the brink, you are lost.—*John Foster Dulles*

1078   I detest life-insurance agents; they always argue that I shall someday die, which is not so.—*Stephen Leacock*

1079   Gratitude looks to the past and love to the present; fear, avarice, lust and ambition look ahead.—*C. S. Lewis*

1080   He was nimble in the calling of selling houses for more than people could afford to pay.—*Sinclair Lewis*

1081   All I've got against it [golf] is that it takes you so far from the club house.—*Eric Linklater*

1082   Please accept my resignation. I don't want to belong to any club that will accept me as a member.—*Groucho Marx*

1083   Wealth is not without its advantages, and the case to the contrary, although it has often been made, has never proved widely persuasive.—*John Kenneth Galbraith*

1084   No society seems ever to have succumbed to boredom. Man has developed an obvious capacity for surviving the pompous reiteration of the commonplace.—*John Kenneth Galbraith*

1085   There are as many fools at a university as elsewhere. . . . But their folly, I admit, has a certain stamp—the stamp of university training, if you like. It is trained folly.—*William Gerhardi*

1086   In our era the road to holiness necessarily passes through the world of action.—*Dag Hammarskjold*

1087   I could think of no one among my contemporaries who had achieved so considerable a position on so little talent.—*W. Somerset Maugham*

1088   Women would rather be right than reasonable.—*Ogden Nash*

1089   The only alternative to co-existence is co-destruction.—*Jawaharlal Nehru*

1090   The American public's taste is impeccable. They like me.—*Noel Coward*

1091   Ultimately, this is what you go before God for: You've had bad luck and good luck and all you really want in the end is mercy.—*Robert Frost*

1092   In the theater, I was brought up in the tradition of service. The audience pays its money and you are expected to give your best performance—both on and off the stage.—*Helen Hayes*

1093   I do not think that winning is the most important thing. I think winning is the only thing.—*Bill Veeck, president, Chicago White Sox*

1094   Most of the trouble in the world is caused by people wanting to be important.—*T. S. Eliot*

1095   The reason why worry kills more people than work is that more people worry than work.—*Robert Frost*

1096   We shall succeed only so far as we continue that most distasteful of all activity, the intolerable labor of thought.—*Learned Hand*

1097   Experience is not what happens to you; it is what you do with what happens to you.—*Aldous Huxley*

1098   I want to be the white man's brother, not his brother-in-law.—*Martin Luther King, Jr.*

1099   Growing old is no more than a bad habit which a busy man has no time to form.—*André Maurois*

1100   Butler was a characteristic British personality. He looked stolid. He said little, and what he said was obscure.—*Winston Churchill*

1101   Literature is the art of writing something that will be read twice; journalism what will be grasped at once.—*Cyril Connolly*

1102   Whom the gods wish to destroy they first call promising.—*Cyril Connolly*

1103   This person was a deluge of words and a drizzle of thought.—*Peter De Vries*

1104   I smiled with Christianity out of one side of my face while with the other I expressed outrage.—*Peter De Vries*

1105   There are two problems in my life. The political ones are insoluble and the economic ones are incomprehensible.—*Sir Alec Douglas-Home*

1106   We know what happens to people who stay in the middle of the road. They get run over.—*Aneurin Bevan*

1107   Journalism largely consists in saying "Lord Jones Dead" to people who never knew Lord Jones was alive.—*G. K. Chesterton*

1108   There is a great man who makes every man feel small. But the real great man is the man who makes every man feel great.—*G. K. Chesterton*

1109   The meanest man is immortal and the mightiest movement is temporal, not to say temporary.—*G. K. Chesterton*

1110   Men will forgive a man anything except bad prose.—*Winston Churchill*

1111   Youth is the trustee of posterity.—*Benjamin Disraeli*

1112   We know that he [Ramsay MacDonald] has, more than any other man, the gift of compressing the largest amount of words into the smallest amount of thought.—*Winston Churchill*

1113   We are citizens of the world; and the tragedy of our times is that we do not know this.—*Woodrow Wilson*

1114   We are none of us infallible—not even the youngest of us.—*W. H. Thompson*

1115   Nothing matters very much, and very few things matter at all.—*Stanley Baldwin*

1116   London is a splendid place to live in for those who can get out of it. —*Lord Balfour of Burleigh*

1117   Men have never been good, they are not good, they never will be good. —*Karl Barth*

1118   Pay no attention to what the critics say; no statue has ever been put up to a critic.—*Jean Sibelius*

1119   Democracy is the art of running the circus from the monkey cage.— *H. L. Mencken*

1120   Democracy is the worst system devised by the wit of man, except for all the others.—*Winston Churchill*

1121   Sixty years ago I knew everything; now I know nothing; education is a progressive discovery of our own ignorance.—*Will Durant*

1122   All who have meditated on the art of governing mankind have been convinced that the fate of empires depends on the education of youth.—*Aristotle*

1123   Why should society feel responsible only for the education of children, and not for the education of all adults of every age?—*Erich Fromm*

1124   Call it what you will, incentives are what get people to work harder. —*Nikita S. Khrushchev*

1125   Free government is government by public opinion. Upon the soundness and integrity of public opinion depends the destiny of our democracy.—*Robert M. La Follette, Sr.*

1126   Private property was the original source of freedom. It still is its main bulwark.—*Walter Lippmann*

1127   I know war as few other men now living know it, and nothing to me is more revolting. I have long advocated its complete abolition, as its very destructiveness on both friend and foe has rendered it useless as a method of settling international disputes.—*Douglas MacArthur*

1128   The natural role of twentieth-century man is anxiety.—*Norman Mailer*

1129   Risk! Risk anything! Care no more for the opinion of others, for those voices. Do the hardest thing on earth for you. Act for yourself. Face the truth. —*Katherine Mansfield*

1130   The general idea, of course, in any first-class laundry is to see that no shirt or collar comes back twice.—*Stephen Leacock*

1131   This is the sort of English up with which I will not put.—*Winston Churchill*

1132   It is useless for the sheep to pass resolutions in favor of vegetarianism while the wolf remains of a different opinion.—*W. R. Inge, Dean of St. Paul's*

1133   Nothing is more costly, nothing is more sterile, than vengeance.— *Winston Churchill*

1134   The rich never feel so good as when they are speaking of their possessions as responsibilities.—*Robert Lynd*

1135   It is easier to fight for one's principles than to live up to them.—*Alfred Adler*

1136   His face was filled with broken commandments.—*John Masefield*

1137   The rise in the total of those employed is governed by Parkinson's Law and would be much the same whether the volume of work were to increase, diminish or even disappear.—*C. Northcote Parkinson*

1138   The result is a phenomenon that has often been observed but never yet investigated. It might be termed the Law of Triviality. Briefly stated, it means that the time spent on any item of the agenda will be in inverse proportion to the sum involved.—*C. Northcote Parkinson*

1139   Being a hero is about the shortest-lived profession on earth.—*Will Rogers*

1140   In the early days of the Indian Territory, there were no such things as birth certificates. You being there was certificate enough.—*Will Rogers*

1141   For every person wishing to teach there are thirty not wanting to be taught.—*W. C. Sellar and R. J. Yeatman*

1142   It had only one fault. It was kind of lousy.—*James Thurber, when asked his opinion of a play*

1143   He was born stupid, and greatly increased his birthright.—*Samuel Butler*

1144   I am not young enough to know everything.—*J. M. Barrie*

1145   A room without books is as a body without a soul.—*Sir John Lubbock*

1146   In the last analysis, ability is commonly found to consist mainly in a high degree of solemnity.—*Ambrose Bierce*

1147   All civilization has from time to time become a thin crust over a volcano of revolution.—*Havelock Ellis*

1148   Know thyself. A Yale undergraduate left on his door a placard for the janitor on which was written, "Call me at seven o'clock; it is absolutely necessary that I get up at seven. Make no mistake. Keep knocking until I answer." Under this he had written: "Try again at ten."—*William Lyon Phelps*

1149   No grand idea was ever born in a conference, but a lot of foolish ideas have died there.—*F. Scott Fitzgerald*

1150   The Nonconformist Conscience makes cowards of us all.—*Max Beerbohm*

1151   Some fellows get credit for being conservative when they are only stupid.—*Kin Hubbard*

1152   You see things; and say "Why?" But I dream things that never were; and I say "Why not?"—*George Bernard Shaw*

1153   We die before we have learned to live.—*Stephen Winstein*

1154   God will forgive me the foolish remarks I have made about him just as I will forgive my opponents the foolish things they have written about me, even though they are spiritually as inferior to me as I to thee, O God!—*Heinrich Heine*

1155   And the wind shall say "Here were decent godless people; their only monument the asphalt road and a thousand lost golf balls."—*T. S. Eliot*

1156   If all economists were laid end to end, they would not reach a conclusion.—*George Bernard Shaw*

1157   It was said that Mr. Gladstone could persuade most people of most things, and himself of anything.—*W. R. Inge, Dean of St. Paul's*

1158   A man may be a fool and not know it—but not if he is married.—*H. L. Mencken*

1159   Conversation is this country has fallen upon evil days. . . . It is drowned out in singing commercials by the world's most productive economy that has so little to say for itself it has to hum it. It is hushed and shushed in dimly lighted parlors by television audiences who used to read, argue, and even play bridge, an old-fashioned card game requiring speech.—*Whitney Griswold*

1160   You done splendid.—*Casey Stengel*

1161   Freedom of the press is not an end in itself but a means to the end of a free society.—*Felix Frankfurter*

1162   You know, acting makes you feel like a burglar sometimes—taking all that money for all that fun.—*Pat O'Brien*

1163   A chair is a very difficult object. A skyscraper is almost easier. That is why Chippendale is famous.—*Mies van der Rohe*

1164   When I was forty, my doctor advised me that a man in his forties shouldn't play tennis. I heeded his advice carefully and could hardly wait until I reached fifty to start again.—*Hugo Black*

1165   I would not seek your nomination for the presidency because the burdens of that office stagger the imagination. Its potential for good or evil now, and in the years of our lives, smothers exultation and converts vanity to prayer.—*Adlai E. Stevenson*

1166   It's a terribly hard job to spend a billion dollars and get your money's worth.—*George Humphrey*

1167   There are a number of things wrong with Washington. One of them is that everyone has been too long away from home.—*Dwight D. Eisenhower*

1168   The first step to knowledge is to know that we are ignorant.—*Lord David Cecil*

1169   My fellow citizens of the world, ask not what your country can do for you—ask what you can do for the freedom of man.—*John F. Kennedy*

1170   Politicians are the same all over. They promise to build a bridge even where there is no river.—*Nikita S. Khrushchev*

1171   The idea that you can merchandise candidates for high office like breakfast cereal—that you can gather votes like box tops—is, I think, the ultimate indignity to the democratic process.—*Adlai E. Stevenson*

1172   I find that a great part of the information I have was acquired by looking up something and finding something else on the way.—*Franklin P. Adams*

1173   We do not know one millionth of one percent about anything.—*Thomas Alva Edison*

1174   The more corrupt the state, the more numerous the laws.—*Tacitus*

1175   Anyone who stops learning is old, whether at twenty or eighty. Anyone who keeps learning stays young. The greatest thing in life is to keep your mind young.—*Henry Ford*

1176   All that I know I learned after I was thirty.—*Georges Clemenceau*

1177   Few women and fewer men have enough character to be idle.—*E. V. Lucas*

1178   A perpetual holiday is a good working definition of hell.—*George Bernard Shaw*

1179   A gossip is one who talks to you about others; a bore is one who talks to you about himself; and a brilliant conversationalist is one who talks to you about yourself.—*Lisa Kirk*

1180   Politics is the diversion of trivial men who, when they succeed at it, become important in the eyes of more trivial men.—*George Jean Nathan*

1181   He who slings mud generally loses ground.—*Adlai E. Stevenson*

1182   When you become forty, you should take it a little slower, work a little harder, take a little more time to think, and you will be all right. . . . I guess the best assurance of a long life is to get yourself a set of long-living parents like I did.—*Harry S. Truman*

1183   It is only governments that are stupid, not the masses of people.—*Dwight D. Eisenhower*

1184   I got all the schooling any actress needs. That is, I learned to write well enough to sign contracts.—*Hermione Gingold*

1185   It will be continually a challenge to government to sense the aspirations of the working people of our country, that all may have the opportunity to fairly share in the results of the productive genius of our time, from which come the material blessings of the present and a greater promise for the future.—*Dwight D. Eisenhower*

1186   I expressed the hope that our next meeting together might be in Washington. Someone said, "God willing." It was Stalin.—*Harry S. Truman*

1187   When a man sits with a pretty girl for an hour, it seems like a minute. But let him sit on a hot stove for a minute—and it's longer than any hour. That's relativity.—*Albert Einstein*

1188   For an actress to be a success she must have the face of Venus, the brains of Minerva, the grace of Terpsichore, the memory of Macaulay, the figure of Juno, and the hide of a rhinoceros.—*Ethel Barrymore*

1189   Has anybody ever seen a dramatic critic in the daytime? Of course not. They come out after dark, up to no good.—*P. G. Wodehouse*

1190   How can it be that mathematics, being after all a product of human thought independent of experience, is so admirably adapted to the objects of reality?—*Albert Einstein*

1191   The will to conquer is the first condition of victory.—*Marshal Ferdinand Foch*

1192   Exercise is bunk. If you are healthy, you don't need it: if you are sick, you shouldn't take it.—*Henry Ford*

1193   . . . they all laid their heads together like as many lawyers when they are gettin' ready to prove that a man's heirs ain't got any right to his property. —*Mark Twain*

1194   In statesmanship get the formalities right, never mind about the moralities.—*Mark Twain*

1195   To laugh often and much; to win the respect of intelligent people and the affection of children; to earn the appreciation of honest critics and endure the betrayal of false friends; to appreciate beauty; to find the best in others; to leave the world a bit better whether by a healthy child, a garden patch, or a redeemed social condition; to know even one life has breathed easier because you lived. This is to have succeeded.—*Ralph Waldo Emerson*

1196   What America really needs is more shortages. Americans have always been able to handle austerity, and even adversity. Prosperity is what's been doing us in.—*James Reston*

1197   This makes me so sore it gets my dandruff up.—*Samuel Goldwyn*

1198   Poor teeth have become the badge of civilization.—*C. C. and S. M. Furnas*

1199   The little I know I owe to my ignorance.—*Sacha Guitry*

1200   Many a man who would not dream of putting too much pressure in his automobile tires lays a constant overstrain on his heart and arteries.—*Bruce Barton*

1201   If you wish to make a man your enemy, tell him simply, "You are wrong." This method works every time.—*Henry C. Link*

1202   We all have weaknesses. But I have figured that others have put up with mine so tolerably that I would be much less than fair not to make a reasonable discount for theirs.—*William Allen White*

1203   The tendency is to be broad-minded about other people's security.—*Aristide Briand*

1204   Travel is fatal to prejudice. . . .—*Mark Twain*

1205   Her unselfishness came in pretty small packages well wrapped.—*F. Scott Fitzgerald*

1206   War is not a moral picnic.—*Lancelot Hogben*

1207   Certainly, we cannot say that our individual freedom is guaranteed if every twenty years we have to stop production of consumer goods and waste all our energies and resources in the manufacture of the tools of war.—*Emery Reves*

1208   The Army must get rid of the theory that an officer breathes special air and is a gentleman while the enlisted man is not.—*Bill Mauldin*

1209   We told that boy when he marched away that he was fighting a war to end all wars. He fell, believing.—*Bruce Barton*

1210   From birth to age eighteen, a girl needs good parents. From eighteen to thirty-five, she needs good looks. From thirty-five to fifty-five, a woman needs personality. And from fifty-five on, the old lady needs cash.—*Kathleen Norris*

1211   Any girl can be glamorous. All you have to do is stand still and look stupid.—*Hedy Lamarr*

1212   All say, "How hard it is that we have to die"—a strange complaint to come from the mouths of people who have had to live.—*Mark Twain*

1213   A capacity for self-pity is one of the last things that any woman surrenders.—*Irvin S. Cobb*

1214   Drying a widow's tears is one of the most dangerous occupations known to man.—*Dorothy Dix*

1215   The art of writing is the art of applying the seat of the pants to the seat of the chair.—*Mary Heaton Vorse*

1216   Repair shops have been built for motors, but we scrap men.—*Heywood Broun*

1217   The function of language is twofold: to communicate emotion and to give information.—*Aldous Huxley*

1218   I could hear the cadence of his voice and that was all, nothing but the measured rise and fall of syllables. . . .—*J. P. Marquand*

1219   We are likely to believe the worst about another because the capacity for evil is so pronounced in ourselves.—*Louis Nizer*

1220   Is there anything more soothing than the quiet whir of a lawn mower on a summer afternoon?—*F. Scott Fitzgerald*

1221   Architects cover their mistakes with ivy. The bride covers hers with mayonnaise.—*Atchison Globe, Atchison, Kansas*

1222   Ours seems to be the only nation on earth that asks its teen-agers what to do about world affairs and tells its golden-agers to go out and play.—*Julian F. Grow*

1223   We owe to the Middle Ages the two worst inventions of humanity—romantic love and gunpowder.—*André Maurois*

1224   The rain is famous for falling on the just and unjust alike, but if I had the management of such affairs I would rain softly and sweetly on the just, but if I caught a sample of the unjust outdoors I would drown him.—*Mark Twain*

1225   Tell me, George [Gershwin], if you had to do it all over, would you fall in love with yourself again?—*Oscar Levant*

1226   Idealists maintain that all nations should share the atomic bomb. Pessimists maintain that they will.—*Punch*

The Wit and Wisdom of Famous Persons

1227   I am different from Washington; I have a higher, grander standard of principle. Washington could not lie. I can lie, but I won't.—*Mark Twain*

1228   A celebrity is a person who works hard all his life to become well known, and then wears dark glasses to avoid being recognized.—*Fred Allen*

1229   After a fellow gets famous it doesn't take long for someone to bob up that used to sit by him at school.—*Kin Hubbard*

1230   A lot of parents pack up their troubles and send them off to a summer camp.—*Raymond Duncan*

1231   A fanatic is a man that does what he thinks the Lord would do if he knew the facts of the case.—*Finley Peter Dunne*

1232   She's generous to a fault—if it's her own.—*Arthur "Bugs" Baer*

1233   I wish my ulcers and I could get together on a mutually satisfactory diet.—*Irvin S. Cobb*

1234   Another good reducing exercise consists in placing both hands against the table edge and pushing back.—*Robert Quillen*

1235   Let us be thankful for the fools. But for them the rest of us could not succeed.—*Mark Twain*

1236   It's far easier to forgive an enemy after you've got even with him.—
Olin Miller

1237   When you're down and out, something always turns up—and it's usually the noses of your friends.—*Orson Welles*

1238   There are many in this old world of ours who hold that things break even for all of us. I have observed for example that we all get the same amount of ice. The rich get it in the summertime and the poor get it in the winter.—*Bat Masterson*

1239   A friend that ain't in need is a friend indeed.—*Kin Hubbard*

1240   He's the kind of man who picks his friends—to pieces.—*Mae West*

1241   In the battle of existence, Talent is the punch; Tact is the clever footwork.—*Wilson Mizner*

1242   When choosing between two evils, I always like to try the one I've never tried before.—*Mae West*

1243   Now I know what a statesman is: he's a dead politician. We need more statesmen.—*Bob Edwards*

1244   A statesman is any politician it's considered safe to name a school after.
—*Bill Vaughan*

1245   Have you ever seen a candidate talking to a rich person on television?
—*Art Buchwald*

1246   Now and then an innocent man is sent t' th' legislature.—*Kin Hubbard*

1247   Congress is so strange. A man gets up to speak and says nothing. Nobody listens—and then everybody disagrees.—*Boris Marshalov*

1248   I once said cynically of a politician, "He'll double cross that bridge when he comes to it."—*Oscar Levant*

1249   The boys are in such a mood that if someone introduced the Ten Commandments, they'd cut them down to eight.—*Senator Norris Cotton*

1250   A miser is a guy who lives within his income. He's also called a magician.—*Alliston Herald*

1251   The mayor was a man you had to know to dislike.—*Jim Bishop*

1252   We can't all be heroes because someone has to sit on the curb and clap as they go by.—*Will Rogers*

1253   There's one way to find out if a man is honest—ask him. If he says, "Yes," you know he's a crook.—*Groucho Marx*

1254   The more humble a man is before God, the more he will be exalted; the more humble he is before man, the more he will get rode roughshod.—*Josh Billings*

1255   I hope you have not been leading a double life, pretending to be wicked, and being really good all the time. That would be hypocrisy.—*Oscar Wilde*

1256   When I sell liquor, it's called bootlegging; when my patrons serve it on silver trays on Lake Shore Drive, it's called hospitality.—*Al Capone*

1257   When asked by an anthropologist what the Indians called America before the white man came, an Indian said simply, "Ours."—*Vine Deloria, Jr.*

1258   Do not always assume that the other fellow has intelligence equal to yours. He may have more.—*Terry-Thomas*

1259   A jury is composed of twelve men of average ignorance.—*Herbert Spencer*

1260   He was so benevolent, so merciful a man that he would have held an umbrella over a duck in a shower of rain.—*Douglas Jerrold*

1261   A specialist is one who knows everything about something and nothing about anything else.—*Ambrose Bierce*

1262   Some are bent with toil, and some get crooked trying to avoid it.—*Herbert V. Prochnow*

1263   For more than forty years I have been speaking prose without knowing it.—*Molière*

1264   In Paris they simply stared when I spoke to them in French; I never did succeed in making those idiots understand their own language.—*Mark Twain*

1265   The American arrives in Paris with a few French phrases he has culled from a conversational guide or picked up from a friend who owns a beret.—*Fred Allen*

1266   I care not who makes the laws of a nation if I can get out an injunction.—*Finley Peter Dunne*

1267   These detective series on TV always end at precisely the right moment—after the criminal is arrested and before the court turns him loose.—*Robert Orben*

1268   A liberal is a man who leaves the room when the fight begins.—*Heywood Broun*

1269   A liberal is a man who is willing to spend somebody else's money.—*Carter Glass*

1270   I can remember way back when a liberal was one who was generous with his own money.—*Will Rogers*

1271   Love doesn't make the world go 'round. Love is what makes the ride worthwhile.—*Franklin P. Jones*

1272   He has every attribute of a dog except loyalty.—*Senator Thomas P. Gore*

1273   There are a terrible lot of lies going about the world, and the worst of it is that half of them are true.—*Winston Churchill*

1274   The biggest liar in the world is They Say.—*Douglas Malloch*

1275   A man who won't lie to a woman has very little consideration for her feelings.—*Olin Miller*

1276   I got the bill for my surgery. Now I know what those doctors were wearing masks for.—*James H. Boren*

1277   The world is made of people who never quite get into the first team and who just miss the prizes at the flower show.—*Jacob Bronowski*

1278   There must be at least five hundred million rats in the United States; of course, I am speaking only from memory.—*Edgar Wilson Nye*

1279   Memory is what tells a man that his wife's birthday was yesterday.—*Mario Rocco*

1280   Middle age is when you're sitting at home on Saturday night and the telephone rings and you hope it isn't for you.—*Ogden Nash*

1281   At least I have the modesty to admit that lack of modesty is one of my failings.—*Hector Berlioz*

1282   The English instinctively admire any man who has no talent and is modest about it.—*James Agee*

1283   We sold our house and are moving into one of those Pandemoniums. —*Marie Aragon*

1284   Money is always there but the pockets change; it is not in the same pockets after a change, and that is all there is to say about money.—*Gertrude Stein*

1285   He had so much money that he could afford to look poor.—*Edgar Wallace*

1286   I'd like to live like a poor man with lots of money.—*Pablo Picasso*

1287   A neighborhood is where, when you got out of it, you get beat up.—*Murray Kempton*

1288   If your parents didn't have any children, there's a good chance that you won't have any.—*Clarence Day*

1289   In a museum in Havana there are two skulls of Christopher Columbus, "one when he was a boy and one when he was a man."—*Mark Twain*

1290   What happens to the hole when the cheese is gone?—*Bertolt Brecht*

1291   The trouble with being punctual is that nobody's there to appreciate it.—*Franklin P. Jones*

1292   It is a very sad thing that nowadays there is so little useless information.—*Oscar Wilde*

1293   No matter how thin you slice it, it's still baloney.—*Alfred E. Smith*

1294   A real patriot is the fellow who gets a parking ticket and rejoices that the system works.—*Bill Vaughan*

1295   Ask not what you can do for your country, for they are liable to tell you.—*Mark Steinbeck*

1296   Patriotism is your conviction that this country is superior to all other countries because you were born in it.—*George Bernard Shaw*

1297   Taking something from one man and making it worse is plagiarism.—*George Moore*

1298   I've known what it is to be hungry, but I always went right to a restaurant.—*Ring Lardner*

1299   Modesty is the only sure bait when you angle for praise.—*G. K. Chesterton*

1300   I am free of all prejudices. I hate every one equally.—*W. C. Fields*

1301   A psychiatrist is a fellow who asks you a lot of expensive questions your wife asks for nothing.—*Joey Adams*

1302   You learn more about yourself while campaigning for just one week than in six months spent with a psychoanalyst.—*Adlai E. Stevenson*

1303   No author is a man of genius to his publisher.—*Heinrich Heine*

1304   When a thing has been said and well said, have no scruple; take it and copy it.—*Anatole France*

1305   I've been rich and I've been poor; rich is better.—*Sophie Tucker*

1306   It doesn't matter if you're rich or poor, as long as you've got money. —*Joe E. Lewis*

1307   There is nothing more demoralizing than a small but adequate income. —*Edmund Wilson*

1308   A study of economics usually reveals that the best time to buy anything is last year.—*Marty Allen*

1309   The only reason I ever played golf in the first place was so I could afford to hunt and fish.—*Sam Snead*

1310   Then there is the man who drowned crossing a stream with an average depth of six inches.—*W. I. E. Gates*

1311   Behind every successful man is a woman—with nothing to wear.— *L. Grant Glickman*

1312   It takes twenty years to make an overnight success.—*Eddie Cantor*

1313   Tact: Ability to tell a man he's open-minded when he has a hole in his head.—*F. G. Kernan*

1314   The income tax has made more liars out of the American people than golf has. Even when you make a tax form out on the level, you don't know when it's through if you are a crook or a martyr.—*Will Rogers*

1315   There is just one thing I can promise you about the outer-space program: Your tax dollar will go farther.—*Wernher von Braun*

1316   I'm proud to be paying taxes in the United States. The only thing is —I could be just as proud for half the money.—*Arthur Godfrey*

1317   If a farmer fills his barn with grain, he gets mice; if he leaves it empty, he gets actors.—*Bill Vaughan*

1318   He thinks things through very clearly before going off half-cocked.—*General Carl Spaatz*

1319   Sixty minutes of thinking of any kind is bound to lead to confusion and unhappiness.—*James Thurber*

1320   The Vice Presidency is sort of like the last cookie on the plate. Everybody insists he won't take it, but somebody always does.—*Bill Vaughan*

1321   If at first you don't succeed you're running about average.—*M. H. Alderson*

1322   There's no trick to being a humorist when you have the whole government working for you.—*Will Rogers*

1323   A pun is the lowest form of humor—when you don't think of it first.—*Oscar Levant*

1324   He is as good as his word—and his word is no good.—*Seumas Mac-Manus*

1325   A farm is a hunk of land on which, if you get up early enough mornings and work late enough nights, you'll make a fortune—if you strike oil on it.—*"Fibber" McGee*

1326   One of the advantages of being poor is that it necessitates the cultivation of the virtues.—*Jerome K. Jerome*

1327   Much may be made of a Scotchman, if he be caught young.—*Samuel Johnson*

1328   Youth had been a habit of hers for so long that she could not part with it.—*Rudyard Kipling*

1329   There are only two ways of getting on in the world: by one's own industry, or by the stupidity of others.—*Jean de La Bruyère*

1330   New Year's Day is every man's birthday.—*Charles Lamb*

1331   They gave each other a smile with a future in it.—*Ring Lardner*

1332   We confess little faults in order to suggest that we have no big ones.—*La Rochefoucauld*

1333   Lots of times you have to pretend to join a parade in which you're not really interested in order to get where you're going.—*Christopher Morley*

1334   Gentility is what is left over from rich ancestors after the money is gone.—*John Ciardi*

1335   When one has had to work so hard to get money, why should he impose on himself the further hardship of trying to save it?—*Don Herold*

1336   There is nothing so absurd or ridiculous that it has not at some time been said by some philosopher.—*Oliver Goldsmith*

1337   He has spent all his life in letting down buckets into empty wells; and he is frittering away his age in trying to draw them up again.—*Sydney Smith*

1338   It got to a point where I had to get a haircut or a violin.—*Franklin D. Roosevelt*

1339   The race is not always to the swift, nor the battle to the strong—but that's the way to bet.—*Damon Runyon*

1340   When you have to make a choice and don't make it, that is in itself a choice.—*William James*

1341   It is always the best policy to speak the truth, unless of course you are an exceptionally good liar.—*Jerome K. Jerome*

1342   That fellow seems to me to possess but one idea, and that a wrong one. —*Samuel Johnson*

1343   On the Continent people have good food, in England people have good table manners.—*George Mikes*

1344   War hath no fury like a noncombatant.—*Charles Edward Montague*

1345   She was a singer who had to take any note above A with her eyebrows. —*Montague Glass*

1346   Everything in the world may be endured except continual prosperity. —*Johann Wolfgang von Goethe*

1347   Every absurdity has a champion to defend it.—*Oliver Goldsmith*

1348   Wagner's music is better than it sounds.—*Mark Twain*

1349   He has returned from Italy a greater bore than ever; he bores on architecture, painting, statuary, and music.—*Sydney Smith*

1350   The terrible thing about the quest for truth is that you find it.—*Remy de Gourmont*

1351   A college education shows a man how little other people know.—*Thomas Chandler Haliburton*

1352   Education is what remains when we have forgotten all that we have been taught.—*Sir George Savile*

1353   Some people have had nothing else but experience.—*Don Herold*

1354   He was the product of an English public school and university . . . that is to say, he was no scholar but essentially a gentleman.—*Henry Seton Merriman*

1355   Blessed are they who have nothing to say, and who cannot be persuaded to say it.—*James Russell Lowell*

1356   If you make people think they're thinking, they'll love you; but if you really make them think, they'll hate you.—*Don Marquis*

1357   I hate to see men overdressed; a man ought to look like he's put together by accident, not added up on purpose.—*Christopher Morley*

1358   There is nothing so consoling as to find that one's neighbor's troubles are at least as great as one's own.—*George Moore*

1359   Logic is an instrument used for bolstering a prejudice.—*Elbert Hubbard*

1360   To be good is noble, but to teach others how to be good is nobler—and less trouble.—*Mark Twain*

1361   No one is exempt from talking nonsense; the misfortune is to do it solemnly.—*Michel de Montaigne*

1362   Be nice to people on your way up because you'll meet them on your way down.—*Wilson Mizner*

1363   Some folks get credit for having horse sense that hain't ever had enough money to make fools of themselves.—*Kin Hubbard*

1364   Everything bows to success, even grammar.—*Victor Hugo*

1365   To his dog, every man is Napoleon, hence the constant popularity of dogs.—*Aldous Huxley*

1366   If a little knowledge is dangerous, where is the man who has so much as to be out of danger?—*Thomas H. Huxley*

1367   In dealing with Englishmen you can be sure of one thing only, that the logical solution will not be adopted.—*W. R. Inge, Dean of St. Paul's*

1368   Men are conservative after dinner.—*Ralph Waldo Emerson*

1369   By working faithfully eight hours a day, you may eventually get to be a boss and work twelve hours a day.—*Robert Frost*

1370   They spell it Vinci and pronounce it Vinchy; foreigners always spell better than they pronounce.—*Mark Twain*

1371   The trouble with the world is that the stupid are cocksure and the intelligent full of doubt.—*Bertrand Russell*

1372   You've no idea what a poor opinion I have of myself, and how little I deserve it.—*W. S. Gilbert*

1373   Youth is a blunder, manhood a struggle, old age a regret.—*Benjamin Disraeli*

1374   I've never any pity for conceited people because I think they carry their comfort about with them.—*George Eliot*

1375   The louder he talked of his honor, the faster we counted our spoons. —*Ralph Waldo Emerson*

1376   We reproach people for talking about themselves; but it is the subject they treat best.—*Anatole France*

1377   To bear other people's afflictions, everyone has courage and enough to spare.—*Benjamin Franklin*

1378   A man will sometimes devote all his life to the development of one part of his body—the wishbone.—*Robert Frost*

1379   It isn't so much what's on the table that matters, as what's on the chairs.—*W. S. Gilbert*

1380   There's always something about your success that displeases even your best friends.—*Mark Twain*

1381   No man needs a vacation so much as the person who has just had one. —*Elbert Hubbard*

1382   The greatest luxury of riches is that they enable you to escape so much good advice.—*Sir Arthur Helps*

1383   A hair in the head is worth two in the brush.—*Oliver Herford*

1384   Order is the first requisite of liberty.—*Georg Wilhelm Hegel*

1385   A rolling stone gathers no moss, but it gains a certain polish.—*Oliver Herford*

1386   Be kind and considerate to others, depending somewhat upon who they are.—*Don Herold*

1387   I must decline your invitation owing to a subsequent engagement.—*Oscar Wilde*

1388   The learned fool writes his nonsense in better language than the unlearned, but still 'tis nonsense.—*Benjamin Franklin*

1389   People who have no faults are terrible; there is no way of taking advantage of them.—*Anatole France*

1390   What a good thing Adam had—when he said a good thing, he knew nobody had said it before.—*Mark Twain*

1391   In composing, as a general rule, run your pen through every other word you have written; you have no idea what vigor it will give your style.   —*Sydney Smith*

1392   When I see a bird that walks like a duck and swims like a duck and quacks like a duck, I call that bird a duck.—*Richard Cardinal Cushing*

1393   I can believe anything, provided it is incredible.—*Oscar Wilde*

1394   When I am dead, I hope it may be said:
         "His sins were scarlet but his books were read."
                              —*Hilaire Belloc*

1395   There is nothing that people get tired of so quickly as the things they like the most.—*W. Burton Baldry*

1396   He's the kind of bore who's here today and here tomorrow.—*Binnie Barnes*

1397   A bore is a fellow who opens his mouth and puts his feats in it.—*Henry Ford*

1398   It is only people of importance who can afford to be dull.—*Constance Jones*

1399   If you would know the value of money, go and try to borrow some.—*Benjamin Franklin*

1400   Lend only what you can afford to lose.—*George Herbert*

1401   In Boston they ask, How much does he know? In New York, How much is he worth? In Philadelphia, Who were his parents?—*Mark Twain*

1402   A fellow who knows his business is allus reticent.—*Kin Hubbard*

1403   Do not put off till tomorrow what can be enjoyed today.—*Josh Billings*

1404   At one time I thought he wanted to be an actor. He had certain qualifications, including no money and a total lack of responsibility.—*Hedda Hopper*

1405   Bernard Shaw is an excellent man; he has not an enemy in the world, and none of his friends like him.—*Oscar Wilde*

1406   She has the answer to everything and the solution to nothing.—*Oscar Wilde*

1407   I have found that the best way to give advice to your children is to find out what they want and then advise them to do it.—*Harry S. Truman*

1408   Middle age is when your age starts to show around your middle.—*Bob Hope*

1409   The swaggering underemphasis of New England.—*Heywood Broun*

1410   The United States is the greatest law factory the world has ever known.—*Charles Evans Hughes*

1411   Great literature is simply language charged with meaning to the utmost possible degree.—*Ezra Pound*

1412   A child enters your home and makes so much noise for twenty years you can hardly stand it—then departs, leaving the house so silent you think you will go mad.—*Dr. J. A. Holmes*

1413   Don't stay away from church because there are so many hypocrites. There's always room for one more.—*A. R. Adams*

1414   A church is God between four walls.—*Victor Hugo.*

1415   City life: millions of people being lonesome together.—*Henry David Thoreau*

1416   The world tolerates conceit from those who are successful, but not from anybody else.—*John Blake*

1417   Every man has a right to be conceited until he is successful.—*Benjamin Disraeli*

1418   All you need is to tell a man that he is no good ten times a day, and very soon he begins to believe it himself.—*Lin Yutang*

1419   The world has achieved brilliance without conscience. Ours is a world of nuclear giants and ethical infants.—*Omar N. Bradley*

1420   Talk to a man about himself and he will listen for hours.—*Benjamin Disraeli*

1421   Gardens are not made by singing "Oh, how beautiful" and sitting in the shade.—*Rudyard Kipling*

1422   The best way to get on in the world is to make people believe it's to their advantage to help you.—*Jean de La Bruyère*

1423   He gave her a look that you could have poured on a waffle.—*Ring Lardner*

1424   If you would be a leader of men, you must lead your own generation, not the next.—*Woodrow Wilson*

1425   I can resist everything except temptation.—*Oscar Wilde*

1426   If your riches are yours, why don't you take them with you to the other world?—*Benjamin Franklin*

1427   A hero is no braver than an ordinary man, but he is brave five minutes longer.—*Ralph Waldo Emerson*

1428   I like Wagner's music better than anybody's; it is so loud, one can talk the whole time without other people hearing what one says.—*Oscar Wilde*

1429   He looked at me as if I was a side dish he hadn't ordered.—*Ring Lardner*

1430   He has occasional flashes of silence that make his conversation perfectly delightful.—*Sydney Smith*

1431   Before I got married I had six theories about bringing up children; now I have six children, and no theories.—*John Wilmot, Earl of Rochester*

1432   A little learning is not a dangerous thing to one who does not mistake it for a great deal.—*William Allen White*

1433   He knew the precise psychological moment when to say nothing.—*Oscar Wilde*

1434   Children have more need of models than of critics.—*Joseph Joubert*

1435   There is no wealth but life.—*John Ruskin*

1436   It is in the ability to deceive oneself that the greatest talent is shown. —*Anatole France*

1437   If men are so wicked with religion, what would they be without it?— *Benjamin Franklin*

1438   Fame is proof that the people are gullible.—*Ralph Waldo Emerson*

1439   No man has a good enough memory to make a successful liar.— *Abraham Lincoln*

1440   A sophistical rhetorician, inebriated with the exuberance of his own verbosity.—*Benjamin Disraeli*

1441   If fifty million people say a foolish thing, it is still a foolish thing.— *Anatole France*

1442   A jury consists of twelve persons chosen to decide who has the better lawyer.—*Robert Frost*

1443   He must have had a magnificent build before his stomach went in for a career of its own.—*Margaret Halsey*

1444   The rooster makes more racket than the hen that lays the egg.—*Joel Chandler Harris*

1445   Actors are the only honest hypocrites.—*William Hazlitt*

1446   It usually takes me more than three weeks to prepare a good impromptu speech.—*Mark Twain*

1447   God often visits us, but most of the time we are not at home.—*Joseph Roux*

1448   In America there are two classes of travel—first class, and with children.—*Robert Benchley*

1449   I do not mind lying, but I hate inaccuracy.—*Samuel Butler*

1450   I wish he would explain his explanation.—*Lord Byron*

1451   Experience is the best of schoolmasters, only the school fees are heavy. —*Thomas Carlyle*

1452   In France we leave unmolested those who set fire to the house, and persecute those who sound the alarm.—*Nicholas Chamfort*

1453   Be virtuous and you will be eccentric.—*Mark Twain*

1454   By persistently remaining single, a man converts himself into a permanent public temptation.—*Oscar Wilde*

1455   Work is the greatest thing in the world, so we should always save some of it for tomorrow.—*Don Herold*

1456   Give us the luxuries of life and we will dispense with necessaries.—*Oliver Wendell Holmes*

1457   Boys will be boys, and so will a lot of middle-aged men.—*Kin Hubbard*

1458   Your ignorance cramps my conversation.—*Anthony Hope*

1459   If you keep your mouth shut, you will never put your foot in it.—*Austin O'Malley*

1460   Edith was a little country bounded on the north, south, east, and west by Edith.—*Martha Ostenso*

1461   He admits that there are two sides to every question—his own and the wrong side.—*Channing Pollock*

1462   If there were no bad people, there would be no good lawyers.—*Charles Dickens*

1463   The road to success is filled with women pushing their husbands along.—*Lord Dewar*

1464   All heiresses are beautiful.—*John Dryden*

1465   It is perfectly monstrous the way people go about nowadays saying things against one, behind one's back, that are absolutely and entirely true.—*Oscar Wilde*

1466   I have never let my schooling interfere with my education.—*Mark Twain*

1467   My father taught me to work; he did not teach me to love it.—*Abraham Lincoln*

1468   The reason the way of the transgressor is hard is because it's so crowded.—*Kin Hubbard*

1469   The biggest fish he ever caught were those that got away.—*Eugene Field*

1470   The end of the human race will be that it will eventually die of civilization.—*Ralph Waldo Emerson*

1471   If a man could have half his wishes, he would double his troubles.—*Benjamin Franklin*

1472   I hate mankind, for I think myself one of the best of them, and I know how bad I am.—*Samuel Johnson*

1473   The right honorable gentleman is indebted to his memory for his jests, and to his imagination for his facts.—*Richard Brinsley Sheridan*

1474   If you pick up a starving dog and make him prosperous, he will not bite you; that is the principal difference between a dog and a man.—*Mark Twain*

1475   Part of the secret of success in life is to eat what you like and let the food fight it out inside.—*Mark Twain*

1476   My idea of an agreeable person is a person who agrees with me.—*Benjamin Disraeli*

1477   His conversation does not show the minute hand, but he strikes the hour very correctly.—*Benjamin Franklin*

1478   If I wished to punish a province, I would have it governed by philosophers.—*Frederick the Great*

1479   Methods of locomotion have improved greatly in recent years, but places to go remain about the same.—*Don Herold*

1480   Nothing succeeds like—failure.—*Oliver Herford*

1481   If you tell the truth, you don't have to remember anything.—*Mark Twain*

1482   Pretty much all the honest truth-telling there is in the world is done by children.—*Oliver Wendell Holmes*

1483   The path of civilization is paved with tin cans.—*Elbert Hubbard*

1484   Train your child in the way you now know you should have gone yourself.—*Charles Haddon Spurgeon*

1485   By all means marry; if you get a good wife, you'll become happy; if you get a bad one, you'll become a philosopher.—*Socrates*

1486   I never read a book before reviewing it; it prejudices one so.—*Sydney Smith*

1487 All reformers, however strict their conscience, live in houses just as big as they can pay for.—*Logan Pearsall Smith*

1488 One should always play fairly when one has the winning cards.—*Oscar Wilde*

1489 A self-made man? Yes—and worships his creator.—*William Cowper*

1490 When I was a boy I was told that anybody could become President; I'm beginning to believe it.—*Clarence Darrow*

1491 Home is the place where, when you have to go there, they have to take you in.—*Robert Frost*

1492 Idealism increases in direct proportion to one's distance from the problem.—*John Galsworthy*

1493 The disappointment of manhood succeeds to the delusion of youth.—*Benjamin Disraeli*

1494 Isn't it strange that I who have written only unpopular books should be such a popular fellow?—*Albert Einstein*

1495 Man is ready to die for an idea, provided that idea is not quite clear to him.—*Paul Eldridge*

1496 Blessed is the man who, having nothing to say, abstains from giving wordy evidence of the fact.—*George Eliot*

1497 To be a leader of men one must turn one's back on men.—*Havelock Ellis*

1498 Have a place for everything and keep the thing somewhere else; this is not advice, it is merely custom.—*Mark Twain*

1499 The old believe everything, the middle-aged suspect everything, the young know everything.—*Oscar Wilde*

1500 Everyone lives by selling something.—*Robert Louis Stevenson*

1501 'Tis known by the name of perseverance in a good cause, and obstinacy in a bad one.—*Laurence Sterne*

1502 The shepherd always tries to persuade the sheep that their interests and his own are the same.—*Stendhal*

1503 Everything happens to everybody sooner or later if there is time enough.—*George Bernard Shaw*

1504   He draweth out the thread of his verbosity
                      Finer than the staple of his argument.
                            —William Shakespeare

1505   If you aim at imperfection, there is some chance of your getting it; whereas if you aim at perfection, there is none.—*Samuel Butler*

1506   As soon as you cannot keep anything from a woman, you love her.—*Paul Géraldy*

1507   It's better to give than to lend, and it costs about the same.—*Philip Gibbs*

1508   He wasn't exactly hostile to facts, but he was apathetic about them.—*Wolcott Gibbs*

1509   One of the pleasures of reading old letters is the knowledge that they need no answer.—*Lord Byron*

1510   Make yourself an honest man and then you may be sure there is one rascal less in the world.—*Thomas Carlyle*

1511   Arguments are extremely vulgar, for everybody in good society holds exactly the same opinions.—*Oscar Wilde*

1512   It is an interesting question how far men would retain their relative rank if they were divested of their clothes.—*Henry David Thoreau*

1513   While he was not dumber than an ox, he was not any smarter.—*James Thurber*

1514   Always do right; this will gratify some people and astonish the rest.—*Mark Twain*

1515   The multitude of books is making us ignorant.—*Voltaire*

1516   I have already given two cousins to the war, and I stand ready to sacrifice my wife's brother.—*Artemus Ward*

1517   It was one of those parties where you cough twice before you speak and then decide not to say it after all.—*P. G. Wodehouse*

1518   Many of us spend half our time wishing for things we could have if we didn't spend half our time wishing.—*Alexander Woollcott*

1519   The printing press is either the greatest blessing or the greatest curse of modern times, one sometimes forgets which.—*J. M. Barrie*

1520   I am saddest when I sing; so are those who hear me; they are sadder even than I am.—*Artemus Ward*

1521   After a good dinner, one can forgive anybody, even one's own relatives. —*Oscar Wilde*

1522   I have received no more than one or two letters in my life that were worth the postage.—*Henry David Thoreau*

1523   Well, if I called the wrong number, why did you answer the phone?— *James Thurber*

1524   All you need in this life is ignorance and confidence, and then success is sure.—*Mark Twain*

1525   I know I am among civilized men because they are fighting so savagely. —*Voltaire*

1526   She used to diet on any kind of food she could lay her hands on.— *Arthur "Bugs" Baer*

1527   When in Turkey, do as the turkeys do.—*Honoré de Balzac*

1528   If *Hamlet* had been written in these days, it would probably have been called *The Strange Affair at Elsinore.*—*J. M. Barrie*

1529   Originality is nothing but judicious imitation.—*Voltaire*

1530   There are nowadays professors of philosophy, but not philosophers.— *Henry David Thoreau*

1531   Be good and you will be lonesome.—*Mark Twain*

1532   Let us all be happy and live within our means, even if we have to borrow the money to do it with.—*Artemus Ward*

1533   Arguments are to be avoided; they are always vulgar and often convincing.—*Oscar Wilde*

1534   There's nothing wrong with Oscar Levant—nothing that a miracle couldn't cure.—*Alexander Woollcott*

1535   Men will wrangle for religion; write for it; fight for it; die for it; anything but live for it.—*Charles Caleb Colton*

1536   The less one has to do, the less time one finds to do it in.—*Lord Chesterfield*

1537   Bachelors' wives and old maids' children are always perfect.—*Nicolas Chamfort*

1538   The urge to gamble is so universal and its practice so pleasurable that I assume it must be evil.—*Heywood Broun*

1539   I do most of my work sitting down; that's where I shine.—*Robert Benchley*

1540   When a man comes to me for advice, I find out the kind of advice he wants, and I give it to him.—*Josh Billings*

1541   There is a tide in the affairs of young men, which, if not skillfully dodged, effectually drowns them.—*Arthur M. Binstead*

1542   I have seen three emperors in their nakedness, and the sight was not inspiring.—*Prince Otto von Bismarck*

1543   It is not worth while to go round the world to count the cats in Zanzibar.—*Henry David Thoreau*

1544   Animals talk to each other; I never knew but one man who could understand them—I knew he could because he told me so himself.—*Mark Twain*

1545   The scenery in the play was beautiful, but the actors got in front of it. —*Alexander Woollcott*

1546   Whenever one has anything unpleasant to say, one should always be quite candid.—*Oscar Wilde*

1547   It is a pity that Chawcer, who had geneyus, was so unedicated; he's the wuss speller I know of.—*Artemus Ward*

1548   Miss Stein was a past master in making nothing happen very slowly. —*Clifton Fadiman*

1549   We hope that, when the insects take over the world, they will remember with gratitude how we took them along on all our picnics.—*Bill Vaughan*

1550   All the really good ideas I ever had came to me while I was milking a cow.—*Grant Wood*

1551   Don't jump on a man unless he's down.—*Finley Peter Dunne*

1552   *Sartor Resartus* is simply unreadable, and for me that always sort of spoils a book.—*Will Cuppy*

1553   Somebody's boring me . . . I think it's me.—*Dylan Thomas*

1554   The nearest thing to immortality in this world is a government bureau. —*General Hugh S. Johnson*

1555   I do not rule Russia; ten thousand clerks do.—*Nicholas I*

1556   Statistics indicate that, as a result of overwork, modern executives are dropping like flies on the nation's golf courses.—*Ira Wallach*

1557   Business will be better or worse.—*Calvin Coolidge*

1558   Underneath this flabby exterior is an enormous lack of character.—*Oscar Levant*

1559   The best way to keep children home is to make the home atmosphere pleasant—and let the air out of the tires.—*Dorothy Parker*

1560   By the time the youngest children have learned to keep the house tidy, the oldest grandchildren are on hand to tear it to pieces.—*Christopher Morley*

1561   The thing that impresses me most about America is the way parents obey their children.—*Duke of Windsor*

1562   Children are a great comfort in your old age—and they help you reach it faster, too.—*Lionel Kauffman*

1563   In a real-estate man's eye, the most exclusive part of the city is wherever he has a house to sell.—*Will Rogers*

1564   Our educational system disqualifies people for honest work.—*Peter Drucker*

1565   The Mets has come along slow, but fast!—*Casey Stengel*

1566   The older I grow, the more I listen to people who don't say much.—*Germain G. Glidden*

1567   Any pitcher who throws at a batter and deliberately tries to hit him is a Communist.—*Alvin Dark*

1568   It is not necessary to understand things in order to argue about them. —*Beaumarchais*

1569   Next to ingratitude, the most painful thing to bear is gratitude.—*Henry Ward Beecher*

1570   Drawing on my fine command of language, I said nothing.—*Robert Benchley*

1571   Journalists say a thing that they know isn't true, in the hope that if they keep on saying it long enough it will be true.—*Arnold Bennett*

1572   "Whom are you?" said he, for he had been to night school.—*George Ade*

1573   Money brings everything to you, even your daughters.—*Honoré de Balzac*

1574   A man likes his wife to be just clever enough to comprehend his cleverness, and just stupid enough to admire it.—*Israel Zangwill*

1575   It is the proud perpetual boast of the Englishman that he never brags. —*D. B. Wyndham Lewis*

1576   The audience strummed their catarrhs.—*Alexander Woollcott*

1577   If it isn't the sheriff, it's the finance company; I've got more attachments on me than a vacuum cleaner.—*John Barrymore*

1578   You never know what you can do without until you try.—*Franklin P. Adams*

1579   Hello! We heard you at the door, but just thought you were part of the bad weather.—*Arthur "Bugs" Baer*

1580   Lawyers are the only persons in whom ignorance of the law is not punished.—*Jeremy Bentham*

1581   I have made mistakes, but I have never made the mistake of claiming that I never made one.—*James Gordon Bennett*

1582   It is well, when one is judging a friend, to remember that he is judging you with the same godlike and superior impartiality.—*Arnold Bennett*

1583   I was a modest, good-humored boy. It is Oxford that has made me insufferable.—*Max Beerbohm*

1584   A clever, ugly man every now and then is successful with the ladies, but a handsome fool is irresistible.—*William Makepeace Thackeray*

1585   I've given up reading books; I find it takes my mind off myself.—*Oscar Levant*

1586   He can compress the most words into the smallest ideas of any man I ever met.—*Abraham Lincoln*

1587   The man who has become a thinking being feels a compulsion to give to every will-to-live the same reverence for life that he gives to his own.—*Albert Schweitzer*

1588   To profit from good advice requires more wisdom than to give it.—
John Churton Collins

1589   There he comes, in a snail's trot.—*George Colman*

1590   A "new thinker," when studied closely, is merely a man who does not
know that other people have thought.—*Frank Moore Colby*

1591   Middle age occurs when you are too young to take up golf and too old
to rush up to the net.—*Franklin P. Adams*

1592   What's on your mind—if you'll forgive the overstatement?—*Fred Allen*

1593   The God to whom little boys say their prayers has a face very like their
mother's.—*J. M. Barrie*

1594   I thought he was a young man of promise, but it appears he is a young
man of promises.—*Arthur Balfour*

1595   Friendships last when each friend thinks he has a slight superiority over
the other.—*Honoré de Balzac*

1596   All press agents belong to a club of which Ananias is the honorary
president.—*John Kendrick Bangs*

1597   In everything that relates to science, I am a whole encyclopedia behind
the rest of the world.—*Charles Lamb*

1598   Alteration is not always improvement, as the pigeon said when it got
out of the net and into the pie.—*Charles Haddon Spurgeon*

1599   Jazz will endure just as long as people hear it through their feet instead
of their brains.—*John Philip Sousa*

1600   When I take a gun in hand, the safest place for a pheasant is just
opposite the muzzle.—*Sydney Smith*

1601   Some folks are wise and some are otherwise.—*Tobias George Smollett*

1602   As to marriage or celibacy, let a man take which course he will, he will
be sure to repent.—*Socrates*

1603   Never speak ill of yourself; your friends will always say enough on that
subject.—*Charles Maurice de Talleyrand*

1604   Public office is the last refuge of the incompetent.—*Boies Penrose*

1605   So much of what we call management consists in making it difficult for
people to work.—*Peter Drucker*

1606   In a hierarchy every employee tends to rise to his level of incompetence.
—*Laurence J. Peter*

1607   Work is achieved by those employees who have not yet reached their level of incompetence.—*Laurence J. Peter*

1608   Walking isn't a lost art—one must, by some means, get to the garage. —*Evan Esar*

1609   When people are serving, life is no longer meaningless.—*John Gardner*

1610   Compared to Velázquez I am nothing, but compared to contemporary painters I am the most big genius of modern times . . . but modesty is not my specialty.—*Salvador Dali*

1611   One of my chief regrets during my years in the theater is that I couldn't sit in the audience and watch me.—*John Barrymore*

1612   Conscience is the inner voice that warns us that someone may be looking.—*H. L. Mencken*

1613   Consistency is the last refuge of the unimaginative.—*Oscar Wilde*

1614   Pop used to say about the Presbyterians, it don't prevent them committing all the sins there are; but it keeps them from getting any fun out of it.— *Christopher Morley*

1615   The trouble with her is that she lacks the power of conversation but not the power of speech.—*George Bernard Shaw*

1616   To speak ill of others is a dishonest way of praising ourselves.—*Will and Ariel Durant*

1617   I was so long writing my review that I never got around to reading the book.—*Groucho Marx*

1618   A critic is a man created to praise greater men than himself, but he is never able to find them.—*Richard Le Gallienne*

1619   In his private heart no man much respects himself.—*Mark Twain*

1620   Diplomacy is the art of saying "Nice doggie!" till you can find a rock. —*Wynn Catlin*

1621   An appeaser is one who feeds a crocodile—hoping it will eat him last. —*Winston Churchill*

1622   Appeasers believe that if you keep on throwing steaks to a tiger, the tiger will become a vegetarian.—*Heywood Broun*

1623   A real diplomat is one who can cut his neighbor's throat without having his neighbor notice it.—*Trygve Lie*

1624   A woman drove me to drink and I never even had the courtesy to thank her.—*W. C. Fields*

1625   An egotist is a man who thinks that if he hadn't been born, people would have wondered why.—*Dan Post*

1626   Egotism is nature's compensation for mediocrity.—*L. A. Safian*

1627   Contrary to popular belief, English women do not wear tweed nightgowns.—*Hermione Gingold*

1628   To err is human, but when the eraser wears out ahead of the pencil, you're overdoing it.—*J. Jenkins*

1629   We learn from experience. A man never wakes up his second baby just to see it smile.—*Grace Williams*

1630   The degree of one's emotion varies inversely with one's knowledge of the facts—the less you know, the hotter you get.—*Bertrand Russell*

1631   Get your facts first, and then you can distort them as much as you please.—*Mark Twain*

1632   If a man keep his trap shut, the world will beat a path to his door.—*Franklin P. Adams*

1633   Early to bed and early to rise, and you'll meet very few of our best people.—*George Ade*

1634   The men the American people admire most extravagantly are the most daring liars; the men they detest most violently are those who try to tell them the truth.—*H. L. Mencken*

1635   I like long walks, especially when they are taken by people who annoy me.—*Fred Allen*

1636   It is amazing how nice people are to you when they know you are going away.—*Michael Arlen*

1637   The playthings of our elders are called business.—*St. Augustine*

1638   Vice is a creature of such hideous mien that the more you see it, the better you like it.—*Finley Peter Dunne*

1639   You raise your voice when you should reinforce your argument.—*Samuel Johnson*

1640   The best way to convince a fool that he is wrong is to let him have his own way.—*Josh Billings*

1641   Why be disagreeable, when with a little effort you can be impossible?—*Douglas Woodruff*

1642   I could see that, if not actually disgruntled, he was far from being gruntled.—*P. G. Wodehouse*

1643   All the extraordinary men I have ever known were chiefly extraordinary in their own estimation.—*Woodrow Wilson*

1644   When I was young I used to think that money was the most important thing in life; now that I am old, I know it is.—*Oscar Wilde*

1645   He is every other inch a gentleman.—*Rebecca West*

1646   A reasonable amount of fleas is good for a dog; it keeps him from brooding over being a dog.—*Edward Noyes Westcott*

1647   Civilization is a race between education and catastrophe.—*H. G. Wells*

1648   There is but one pleasure in life equal to that of being called on to make an after-dinner speech, and that is not being called on to make one.—*Charles Dudley Warner*

1649   I am not a politician, and my other habits are good.—*Artemus Ward*

1650   Thieves respect property; they merely wish the property to become their property that they may more perfectly respect it.—*G. K. Chesterton*

1651   Why should a worm turn? It's probably just the same on the other side.—*Irvin S. Cobb*

1652   One of the difficult tasks in this world is to convince a woman that even a bargain costs money.—*E. W. Howe*

1653   Genius may have its limitations, but stupidity is not thus handicapped.—*Elbert Hubbard*

1654   It's pretty hard to tell what does bring happiness; poverty and wealth have both failed.—*Kin Hubbard*

1655   When the million applaud, you ask yourself what harm you have done; when they censure you, what good.—*Charles Caleb Colton*

1656   I sometimes wish that people would put a little more emphasis upon the observance of the law than they do upon its enforcement.—*Calvin Coolidge*

1657   He hasn't a single redeeming vice.—*Oscar Wilde*

1658   Hain't we got all the fools in town on our side, and ain't that a big enough majority in any town?—*Mark Twain*

1659   A piece of a churchyard fits everybody.—*George Herbert*

1660   There are two times in a man's life when he should not speculate: when he can't afford it, and when he can.—*Mark Twain*

1661   I fear explanations explanatory of things explained.—*Abraham Lincoln*

1662   There is a great deal of difference between the eager man who wants to read a book and the tired man who wants a book to read.—*G. K. Chesterton*

1663   When you have no basis for an argument, abuse the plaintiff.—*Cicero*

1664   I once knew a fellow who spoke a dialect with an accent.—*Irvin S. Cobb*

1665   Tact consists in knowing how far we may go too far.—*Jean Cocteau*

1666   Examinations are formidable even to the best prepared, for the greatest fool may ask more than the wisest man can answer.—*Charles Caleb Colton*

1667   He had the sort of face that, once seen, is never remembered.—*Oscar Wilde*

1668   He missed an invaluable opportunity to hold his tongue.—*Andrew Lang*

1669   George Moore wrote brilliant English until he discovered grammar.—*Oscar Wilde*

1670   All generalizations are dangerous, even this one.—*Alexandre Dumas*

1671   If a man is wise, he gets rich, and if he gets rich, he gets foolish, or his wife does.—*Finley Peter Dunne*

1672   All great ideas are controversial, or have been at one time.—*George Seldes*

1673   Apart from man, no being wonders at its own existence.—*Arthur Schopenhauer*

1674   It saves a lot of trouble if, instead of having to earn money and save it, you can just go and borrow it.—*Winston Churchill*

1675   The good end happily, the bad unhappily—that is what fiction means. —*Oscar Wilde*

1676   She is intolerable, but that is her only fault.—*Talleyrand*

1677   We have just enough religion to make us hate but not enough to make us love one another.—*Jonathan Swift.*

1678   He flung himself upon his horse and rode madly off in all directions. —*Stephen Leacock*

1679   The brain is a wonderful organ; it starts working the moment you get up in the morning, and does not stop until you get into the office.—*Robert Frost*

1680   A noisy man is always in the right.—*William Cowper*

1681   Depressions may bring people closer to the church, but so do funerals. —*Clarence Darrow*

1682   There are more fools than wise men, and even in the wise men himself there is more folly than wisdom.—*Nicolas Chamfort*

1683   Silence is the unbearable repartee.—*G. K. Chesterton*

1684   A lover of himself, without any rival.—*Cicero*

1685   In those days he was wiser than he is now; he used frequently to take my advice.—*Winston Churchill*

1686   I like criticism, but it must be my way.—*Mark Twain*

1687   The English country gentleman galloping after a fox—the unspeakable in full pursuit of the uneatable.—*Oscar Wilde*

1688   The emperor sent his troops to the field with immense enthusiasm; he will lead them in person—when they return.—*Mark Twain*

1689   The difference between literature and journalism is that journalism is unreadable and literature is unread.—*Oscar Wilde*

1690   An empty stomach is not a good political adviser.—*Albert Einstein*

1691   Animals are such agreeable friends; they ask no questions, they pass no criticisms.—*George Eliot*

1692   A lover is a man who tries to be more amiable than it is possible for him to be.—*Nicolas Chamfort*

1693   Young men think old men are fools; but old men know young men are fools.—*George Chapman*

1694   He's all buttoned up in an impenetrable little coat of complacency.—
Ilka Chase

1695   Most people enjoy the inferiority of their best friends.—*Lord Chester-field*

1696   He was dull in a new way, and that made many think him great.—
Samuel Johnson

1697   The first thing I do in the morning is brush my teeth and sharpen my
tongue.—*Oscar Levant*

1698   He is remarkably well, considering that he has been remarkably well
for so many years.—*Sydney Smith*

1699   When a man wants to murder a tiger, he calls it sport; when a tiger
wants to murder him, he calls it ferocity.—*George Bernard Shaw*

1700   I have no other but a woman's reason;
             I think him so because I think him so.
                        —*William Shakespeare*

1701   No man but a blockhead ever wrote except for money.—*Samuel John-son*

1702   You are never so easily fooled as when you are trying to fool someone
else.—*La Rochefoucauld*

1703   Many a man in love with a dimple makes the mistake of marrying the
whole girl.—*Stephen Leacock*

1704   I often quote myself; it adds spice to my conversation.—*George Ber-nard Shaw*

1705   The liar's punishment is not in the least that he is not believed, but that
he cannot believe anyone else.—*George Bernard Shaw*

1706   I have noticed my conscience for many years, and I know it is more
trouble and bother to me than anything else I started with.—*Mark Twain*

1707   Though I'm anything but clever,
             I could talk like that forever.—*W. S. Gilbert*

1708   The wonderful world of home appliances now makes it possible to cook
indoors with charcoal and outdoors with gas.—*Bill Vaughan*

1709   You can take a boy out of the country, but you can't take the country
out of a boy.—*Arthur "Bugs" Baer*

1710   I have never found in a long career of politics that criticism is ever inhibited by ignorance.—*Harold Macmillan*

1711   Young normal tigers do not eat people. If eaten by a tiger, you may rest assured that he was abnormal.—*Will Cuppy*

1712   The young may die, but the old must!—*Henry Wadsworth Longfellow*

1713   I owe much; I have nothing; the rest I leave to the poor.—*Francois Rabelais*

1714   He did nothing in particular,
                And did it very well.
                    —*W. S. Gilbert*

1715   Democracy means government by the uneducated, while aristocracy means government by the badly educated.—*G. K. Chesterton*

1716   The butler entered the room, a solemn procession of one.—*P. G. Wodehouse*

1717   Blessed is he who expects nothing, for he shall never be disappointed. —*Alexander Pope*

1718   I have been laid up with intentional flu.—*Samuel Goldwyn*

1719   We are so fond of each other because our ailments are the same.— *Jonathan Swift*

1720   There is no doubt that every healthy, normal boy (if there is such a thing in these days of Child Study) should own a dog at some time in his life, preferably between the ages of forty-five and fifty.—*Robert Benchley*

1721   Newfoundland dogs are good to save children from drowning, but you must have a pond of water handy and a child, or else there will be no profit in boarding a Newfoundland.—*Josh Billings*

1722   Dogs laugh, but they laugh with their tails.—*Max Eastman*

1723   The more a feller really amounts to, th' worse his clothes fit.—*Kin Hubbard*

1724   Madam, I have been looking for a person who disliked gravy all my life; let us swear eternal friendship.—*Sydney Smith*

1725   The fate of a nation has often depended upon the good or bad digestion of a prime minister.—*Voltaire*

1726   I learned more about economics from one South Dakota dust storm than I did in all my years in college.—*Hubert Humphrey*

1727   It's called political economy because it has nothing to do with either politics or economy.—*Stephen Leacock*

1728   A learned blockhead is a greater blockhead than an ignorant one.— *Benjamin Franklin*

1729   I understand that Harvard University is making its diplomas larger or smaller. I have forgotten which. This is a step in the right direction.—*Robert Maynard Hutchins*

1730   Talk to a man about himself and he will listen for hours.—*Benjamin Disraeli*

1731   To love oneself is the beginning of a lifelong romance.—*Oscar Wilde*

1732   I never hold a grudge, especially when I'm wrong.—*Oscar Levant*

1733   Experience is the name everyone gives to his mistakes.—*Oscar Wilde*

1734   Fame is delightful, but as collateral it does not rank high.—*Elbert Hubbard*

1735   I let my relatives support me. I never flinched. I knew they could do it.—*Robert Fontaine*

1736   Farming looks mighty easy when your plow is a pencil and you're a thousand miles from the cornfield.—*Dwight D. Eisenhower*

1737   At length the fox is brought to the furrier.—*George Herbert*

1738   Diogenes struck the father when the son swore.—*Robert Burton*

1739   When a 220-pound man laughs, there is twice as much of him having a good time as when a 110-pound man laughs. This is one of the advantages of being fat.—*Hal Boyle*

1740   A fellow who is always declaring he's no fool usually has his suspicions. —*Wilson Mizner*

1741   We have confused the free with the free and easy.—*Adlai E. Stevenson*

1742   Anyone can buy new things, but only a strong man can throw out old things.—*William Feather*

1743   I never think of the future. It comes soon enough.—*Albert Einstein*

1744   We should all be concerned about the future because we will have to spend the rest of our lives there.—*Charles F. Kettering*

1745   And remember, dearie, never give a sucker an even break.—*Attributed to W. C. Fields*

1746
>   Be generous, yet not too free;
>   Don't give the Fox the Henhouse Key.
>   *Arthur Guiterman*

1747   It's getting harder and harder to support the government in the style to which it has become accustomed.—*Farmer's Almanac*

1748   Nothing is so admirable in politics as a short memory.—*John Kenneth Galbraith*

1749   But no, that would be common sense—and out of place in a government.—*Mark Twain*

1750   He's simply got the instinct for being unhappy highly developed.—*Saki*

1751   What's the use of running when you are on the wrong road?—*W. G. Benham*

1752   You can't set a hen in one morning and have chicken salad for lunch. —*George Humphrey*

1753   Stay your haste: the Man who made time made plenty of it.—*Seumas MacManus*

1754   Life is futile and the man who wears a toupee should take his hat off to no one.—*Fred Allen*

1755   When I was six I made my mother a little hat—out of her new blouse. —*Lilly Daché*

1756   Hating people is like burning down your own house to get rid of a rat. —*Harry Emerson Fosdick*

1757   . . . The two women exchanged the kind of glance women use when there is no knife handy.—*Ellery Queen*

1758   I have gout, asthma, and seven other maladies, but am otherwise very well.—*Sydney Smith*

1759   The surest way to hit a woman's heart is to take aim kneeling.— *Douglas Jerrold*

1760   The art of being a good guest is to know when to leave.—*Duke of Edinburgh*

1761   The most popular laborsaving device today is still a husband with money.—*Joey Adams*

1762   A husband should tell his wife everything that he is sure she will find out, and before anyone else does.—*Lord Dewar*

1763   Weddings make a lot of people sad,
But if you're not the groom,
They're not so bad. . . .
                    —*Gus Kahn*

1764   If ignorance is bliss, why aren't there more happy people?—*Farmer's Almanac*

1765   For years I have been known for saying "Include me out."—*Samuel Goldwyn*

1766   George Washington set many precedents, which, as the first President, he was in a good position to do.—*Richard Armour*

1767   "Be yourself" is the worst advice you can give to some people.—*Tom Masson*

1768   The beaver is very industrious, but he is still a beaver.—*Will Cuppy*

1769   No one is so busy as the man who has nothing to do.—*Old French proverb*

1770   An "egghead" is a person who stands firmly on both feet in mid-air on both sides of an issue.—*Senator Homer Ferguson*

1771   A highbrow is the kind of person who looks at a sausage and thinks of Picasso.—*A. P. Herbert*

1772   The Irish are a fair people; they never speak well of one another.—*Samuel Johnson*

1773   People who throw kisses are mighty hopelessly lazy.—*Bob Hope*

1774   A man of vast and varied misinformation.—*William Gaynor*

1775   We're overpaying him, but he's worth it.—*Samuel Goldwyn*

1776   Anybody who has any doubts about the ingenuity or the resourcefulness of a plumber never got a bill from one.—*George Meany*

1777　He [P. G. Wodehouse] is, I believe, the only man living who speaks with equal fluency the American and English languages.—*Max Eastman*

1778　I never knew an auctioneer to lie, unless it was absolutely necessary.—*Josh Billings*

1779　Every man's life is a fairy tale written by God's fingers.—*Hans Christian Andersen*

1780
> Man always knows his life will shortly cease,
> Yet madly lives as if he knew it not.
>　　　　　　　　　—*Richard Baxter*

1781　We are but tenants, and . . . shortly the great Landlord will give us notice that our lease has expired.—*Joseph Jefferson*

1782　We break up life into little bits and fritter it away.—*Seneca*

1783　Literature was formerly an art and finance a trade: today it is the reverse.—*Joseph Roux*

1784　Literature is the orchestration of platitudes.—*Thornton Wilder*

1785　The last time I saw Fay he was walking down Lover's Lane, holding his own hand.—*Fred Allen*

1786　In love, one first deceives oneself and then others—and that is what is called romance.—*John L. Balderston*

1787　Nobody in love has a sense of humor.—*S. N. Behrman*

1788　Many a man has fallen in love with a girl in a light so dim he would not have chosen a suit by it.—*Maurice Chevalier*

1789　Love is like the measles; we all have to go through it.—*Jerome K. Jerome*

1790　We must believe in luck. For how else can we explain the success of those we don't like?—*Jean Cocteau*

1791　Secretary on telephone: "Our automatic answering device is away for repair. This is a person speaking."—*Eric Burgin*

1792　Eventually I have high hopes I'll be able to retire from the human race.—*Fred Allen*

1793　We are all alike—on the inside.—*Mark Twain*

1794   All I care to know is that a man is a human being—that is enough for me; he can't be any worse.—*Mark Twain*

1795   If a man has good manners and is not afraid of other people, he will get by even if he is stupid.—*Sir David Eccles*

1796   I don't recall your name, but your manners are familiar.—*Oliver Herford*

1797   If there is one beast in all the loathsome fauna of civilization I hate and despise, it is a man of the world.—*Henry Arthur Jones*

1798   Money talks, and it is the only conversation worth hearing when times are bad.—*Fred Allen*

1799
>   Money is honey, my little sonny,
>   And a rich man's joke is always funny.
>   —*T. E. Brown*

1800   There is no fortress so strong that money cannot take it.—*Cicero*

1801   When a man says money can do anything, that settles it: he hasn't any.
—*E. W. Howe*

1802   He was subject to a kind of disease which at that time they called lack of money.—*Francois Rabelais*

1803   The crab, more than any of God's creatures, has formulated the perfect philosophy of life. Whenever he is confronted by a great moral crisis in life, he first makes up his mind what is right, and then goes sideways as fast as he can.
—*Oliver Herford*

1804   Corruption and golf is two things we might just as well make up our minds to take up, for they are both going to be with us.—*Will Rogers*

1805   Behind every successful man stands a surprised mother-in-law.—*Hubert Humphrey*

1806   "The Ancient Mariner" would not have taken so well if it had been called "The Old Sailor."—*Samuel Butler*

1807   Sleep is an excellent way of listening to an opera.—*James Stephens*

1808   Unless they share our opinions, we seldom find people sensible.—*La Rochefoucauld*

1809
>   I hate the Pollyanna pest
>   Who says that All is for the Best.
>   —*Franklin P. Adams*

1810   I am an optimist. It does not seem too much use being anything else.
—*Winston Churchill*

1811   The best audience is one that is intelligent, well educated—and a little drunk.—*Alben W. Barkley*

1812   I guess a man never becomes an orator if he has anything to say.—*Finley Peter Dunne*

1813   Why don't the' feller who says, "I'm not a speechmaker," let it go at that instead o' givin' a demonstration?—*Kin Hubbard*

1814   The politicians were talking themselves red, white, and blue in the face.
—*Clare Boothe Luce*

1815   I seldom think of politics more than eighteen hours a day.—*Lyndon B. Johnson*

1816   It's a big job. It isn't going to be so bad. You've got time to think. You don't have all those people bothering you that you had in the Senate—besides, the pay is pretty good.—*John. F. Kennedy*

1817   A demagogue is a person with whom we disagree as to which gang should mismanage the country.—*Don Marquis*

1818   Once there were two brothers. One ran away to sea, the other was elected Vice President, and nothing was heard of either of them again.—*Thomas R. Marshall*

1819   Politics is the science of the second-best.—*John Morley*

1820   The statesman shears the sheep, the politician skins them.—*Austin O'Malley*

1821   You can always get the truth from an American statesman after he has turned seventy or given up all hopes of the Presidency.—*Wendell Phillips*

1822   That most delicious of all priviledges—spending other people's money.
—*John Randolph of Roanoke*

1823   The Senate is a nice, quiet sort of place where good Representatives go when they die.—*Thomas B. Reed*

1824   It could probably be shown by facts and figures that there is no distinctly native American criminal class except Congress.—*Mark Twain*

1825   Fastest way for a politician to become an elder statesman is to lose an election.—*Earl Wilson*

1826   I believe if we introduced the Lord's Prayer here, Senators would propose a large number of amendments to it.—*Senator Henry Wilson*

1827   After being turned down by numerous publishers, he decided to write for posterity.—*George Ade*

1828   One of the strangest things about life is that the poor, who need money the most, are the very ones that never have it.—*Finley Peter Dunne*

1829   Try praising your wife even if it does frighten her at first.—*Billy Sunday*

1830   I can live for two months on a good compliment.—*Mark Twain*

1831   God bless mother and daddy, my brother and sister, and save the King. And, oh God, do take care of yourself, because if anything happens to you we're all sunk.—*Adlai E. Stevenson*

1832   One of the best temporary cures for pride and affectation is seasickness: a man who wants to vomit never puts on airs.—*Josh Billings*

1833   And the Devil did grin, for his darling sin
Is pride that apes humility.
—*Samuel Taylor Coleridge*

1834   Never put off till tomorrow what you can do day after tomorrow just as well.—*Mark Twain*

1835   I don't think you can spend yourself rich.—*George Humphrey*

1836   When you have got an elephant by the hind leg, and he is trying to run away, it's best to let him run.—*Abraham Lincoln*

1837   I am a member of the rabble in good standing.—*Westbrook Pegler*

1838   I do not have a psychiatrist and I do not want one, for the simple reason that if he listened to me long enough, he might become disturbed.—*James Thurber*

1839   A chip on the shoulder is too heavy a piece of baggage to carry through life.—*B. C. Forbes*

1840   We prefer the old-fashioned alarm clock to the kind that awakens you with soft music or a gentle whisper. If there's one thing we can't stand early in the morning, it's hypocrisy.—*Bill Vaughan*

1841   Satire lies about literary men while they live, and eulogy lies about them when they die.—*Voltaire*

1842   Ten years ago the moon was an inspiration to poets and young sweethearts; ten years from now it will be just another airport.—*Rep. Carroll Kearns*

1843   I should not talk so much about myself if there were anybody else whom I knew as well.—*Henry David Thoreau*

1844   Silence is one of the hardest arguments to refute.—*Josh Billings*

1845   Better to remain silent and be thought a fool than to speak out and remove all doubt.—*Abraham Lincoln*

1846   I have offended God and mankind because my work didn't reach the quality it should have.—*Leonardo da Vinci*

1847   The only way to get rid of a temptation is to yield to it.—*Oscar Wilde*

1848   He's a good boy—everything he steals he brings right home to his mother.—*Fred Allen*

1849   Faint heart never won fair lady or sold any life insurance.—*Kin Hubbard*

1850   If we must disagree, let's disagree without being disagreeable.—*Lyndon B. Johnson*

1851   The penguin flies backwards because he doesn't care to see where he's going, but wants to see where he's been.—*Fred Allen*

1852   A hole is nothing at all, but you can break your neck in it.—*Austin O'Malley*

1853   It is hard to believe that a man is telling the truth when you know you would lie if you were in his place.—*H. L. Mencken*

1854   After a man gets rich his next ambition is to get richer.—*Reflections of a Bachelor*

1855   A man must have a certain amount of intelligent ignorance to get anywhere.—*Charles F. Kettering*

1856   I don't care what is written about me so long as it isn't true.—*Katharine Hepburn*

1857   Most people spend their lives going to bed when they're not sleepy and getting up when they are!—*Cindy Adams*

1858   No civilized person ever goes to bed the same day he gets up.—*Richard Harding Davis*

1859   Show me a smile that won't come off an' I'll show you a cheerful idiot. —*Kin Hubbard*

1860   There are only two kinds of coaches—those who have been fired and those who will be fired.—*Ken Loeffler*

1861   As a nation we are dedicated to keeping physically fit—and parking as close to the stadium as possible.—*Bill Vaughan*

1862   The toughest thing about success is that you've got to keep on being a success.—*Irving Berlin*

1863   Those who set out to serve both God and Mammon soon discover that there is no God.—*Logan Pearsall Smith*

1864   At any age the ladies are delightful, delectable and, most important, deductible.—*Goodman Ace*

1865   Women like silent men. They think they are listening.—*Marcel Achard*

1866   When I say "everybody says so," I mean I say so.—*Ed Howe*

1867   In two words: im-possible—*Samuel Goldwyn*

1868   I had always assumed that cliché was a suburb of Paris, until I discovered it to be a street in Oxford.—*Philip Guedalla*

1869   Never work before breakfast; if you have to work before breakfast, get your breakfast first.—*Josh Billings*

1870   There is nothing so irritating as somebody with less intelligence and more sense than we have.—*Don Herold*

1871   I like work; it fascinates me. I can sit and look at it for hours. I love to keep it by me: the idea of getting rid of it nearly breaks my heart.—*Jerome K. Jerome*

1872   And so we plough along, as the fly said to the ox.—*Henry Wadsworth Longfellow*

1873   Never buy anything with a handle on it. It means work.—*H. Allen Smith*

1874   Boy to girl as they are about to wash dishes: "You wash, I'll drop." —*George Wolf*

1875   Even the youngest of us may be wrong sometimes.—*George Bernard Shaw*

1876   If you steal from one author, it's plagiarism; if you steal from many, it's research.—*Wilson Mizner*

1877   Pleasure is frail like a dewdrop, while it laughs it dies.—*Rabindranath Tagore*

1878   I defined a bureaucrat as "a Democrat who holds some office that a Republican wants."—*Alben W. Barkley*

1879   Politics is the art of the next best.—*Prince Otto von Bismarck*

1880   Perhaps one of the most important accomplishments of my administration has been minding my own business.—*Calvin Coolidge*

1881   The middle of the road is where the white line is—and that's the worst place to drive.—*Robert Frost*

1882   There's some folks standing behind the President that ought to get around where he can watch 'em.—*Kin Hubbard*

1883   We'd all like t' vote fer th' best man, but he's never a candidate.—*Kin Hubbard*

1884   A good husband should be deaf and a good wife blind.—*French proverb*

1885   Marriage is a mistake every man should make.—*George Jessel*

1886   "Ma," I said, "I just got married." "That's nice," she said. "Did you practice the piano today?"—*Oscar Levant*

1887   I have now come to the conclusion never again to think of marrying, and for this reason: I can never be satisfied with anyone who would be blockhead enough to have me.—*Abraham Lincoln*

1888   She didn't think he was good enough for her, but she married him because she thought he was too good for any other woman.—*Douglas Yates*

1889   He gobbled pills like a famished chicken pecking up corn.—*Dale Kramer*

1890   I'm not smart, I try to observe. Millions saw the apple fall, but Newton was the one who asked why.—*Bernard M. Baruch*

1891   To be bored by essentials is characteristic of small minds.—*R. U. Johnson*

1892   A middle-of-the-roader is one who's apt to have trouble on the one hand and also on the other.—*Franklin P. Jones*

1893   Hail, the conquering hero comes,
                 Surrounded by a bunch of bums.
                         —*George E. Phair*

1894   History is simply a piece of paper covered with print; the main thing is still to make history, not to write it.—*Prince Otto von Bismarck*

1895   All the historical books which contain no lies are extremely tedious.—*Anatole France*

1896   He was honest except when he went out to rob (there was no paradox in that to him).—*Homer Croy, Jesse James Was My Neighbor*

1897   I find honorary degrees always tempting, and often bad for me: tempting because we all—even ex-politicians—hope to be mistaken for scholars, and bad because if you then make a speech the mistake is quickly exposed.—*Adlai E. Stevenson*

1898   Hope is merely disappointment deferred.—*W. Burton Baldry*

1899   Hope is the poor man's bread.—*George Herbert*

1900   The only time a horse gets scared on the road nowadays is when he meets another horse.—*Harry Oliver*

1901   Some fellers' idea o' being funny is breakin' a few bones when they shake your hand.—*Kin Hubbard*

1902   Courage is doing what you're afraid to do. There can be no courage unless you're scared.—*Eddie Rickenbacker*

1903   I think I can say, and say with pride, that we have some legislatures that bring higher prices than any in the world.—*Mark Twain*

1904   Don't forget until too late that the business of life is not business, but living.—*B. C. Forbes*

1905   A secretary came to Goldwyn saying, "Our files are so crowded that I suggest destroying all correspondence more than six years old." "By all means," said Goldwyn, "but be sure to make copies."—*Samuel Goldwyn*

1906   I realize that one man's cliché can be another man's conviction.—*Adlai E. Stevenson*

1907   With one hand he put a penny in the urn of poverty, and with the other took a shilling out.—*Robert Pollock*

1908   Do you know the difference between a beautiful woman and a charming one? A beauty is a woman you notice; a charmer is one who notices you.—*Adlai E. Stevenson*

1909   It is absurd to divide people into good and bad. People are either charming or tedious.—*Oscar Wilde*

1910   The hand that rocks the scales in the grocery store is the hand that rules the world.—*Finley Peter Dunne*

1911   Half the world does not know how the other half lives, but is trying to find out.—*E. W. Howe*

1912   It took me fifteen years to discover I had no talent for writing, but I couldn't give it up because by that time I was too famous.—*Robert Benchley*

1913   By trying we can easily learn to endure adversity—another man's, I mean.—*Mark Twain*

1914   Parents were invented to make children happy by giving them something to ignore.—*Ogden Nash*

1915   He writes his plays for the ages—the ages between five and twelve.—*George Jean Nathan*

1916   An Englishman thinks seated; a Frenchman, standing; and American, pacing; an Irishman, afterward.—*Austin O'Malley*

1917   The public is wonderfully tolerant—it forgives everything except genius.—*Oscar Wilde*

1918   There is only one thing in the world worse than being talked about, and that is not being talked about.—*Oscar Wilde*

1919   There may be some doubt as to who are the best people to have charge of children, but there can be no doubt that parents are the worst.—*George Bernard Shaw*

1920   Women now insist on having all the prerogatives of the oak and all the perquisites of the clinging vine.—*Irvin S. Cobb*

1921   If you don't say anything, you won't be called on to repeat it.—*Calvin Coolidge*

1922   Poor men want meat for their stomachs, rich men stomachs for their meat.—*Anthony Copley*

1923   Alfred Lunt has his head in the clouds and his feet in the box office.
—*Noel Coward*

1924   Our severest winter, commonly called the spring.—*William Cowper*

1925   The first half of our lives is ruined by our parents and the second half by our children.—*Clarence Darrow*

1926   I am an old man and have known a great many troubles, but most of them never happened.—*Mark Twain*

1927   My own business always bores me to death; I prefer other people's.—*Oscar Wilde*

1928   Be contented, when you have got all you want.—*Holbrook Jackson*

1929   Noble system, truly . . . where it is impossible to reward the most illustrious and fittest citizen with the Presidency.—*Mark Twain*

1930   Great Caesar's bust is on the shelf,
             And I don't feel so well myself.
                —*Arthur Guiterman*

1931 · It is indecent to suspect a man when you are sure of his guilt.—*Stanislaw J. Lec*

1932   You see what will happen to you if you keep on biting your nails.—*Noel Coward, written on a postcard containing a photograph of the Venus de Milo*

1933   Cultivate only the habits that you are willing should master you.—*Elbert Hubbard*

1934   Nothing so needs reforming as other people's habits.—*Mark Twain*

1935   Better a bald head than no head at all.—*Seumas MacManus*

1936   When red-haired people are above a certain social grade, their hair is auburn.—*Mark Twain*

1937   Why don't you get a haircut? You look like a chrysanthemum.—*P. G. Wodehouse*

1938   Our public men are speaking every day on something, but they ain't saying anything.—*Will Rogers*

1939   When I was a boy I never had much sympathy for a holiday speaker. He was just a kind of interruption between the hot dogs, and a fly in the lemonade.—*Adlai E. Stevenson*

1940   A product of the untalented, sold by the unprincipled to the utterly bewildered.—*Al Capp, comment on abstract art*

1941   Modern art is what happens when painters stop looking at girls and persuade themselves that they have a better idea.—*John Ciardi*

1942   There are two kinds of people in one's life—people whom one keeps waiting,—and the people for whom one waits . . .—*S. N. Behrman*

1943   No man can be a patriot on an empty stomach.—*William C. Brann*

1944   A conqueror is always a lover of peace.—*Karl von Clausewitz*

1945   Peace is better than war, because in peace the sons bury their fathers, but in war the fathers bury their sons.—*Croesus to Cambyses*

1946   A pessimist is one who has been intimately acquainted with an optimist.—*Elbert Hubbard*

1947   The man who is a pessimist before forty-eight knows too much; the man who is an optimist after forty-eight knows too little.—*Mark Twain*

Unusual Facts, Stories, and Quotations from Biography

1948 *The People*

Our Republic can be no better, no stronger than the states which comprise it; our states, no stronger than their local communities. The whole can be no stronger than the people it governs.—*Adlai E. Stevenson*

1949 *The Goal of Education*

We must make it clear that the goal of education is to teach Western man not just to survive, but to triumph; not just to defend himself, but to make man and the world what God intended them to be.—*Adlai E. Stevenson*

1950 *The Greatest Danger*

If I were asked what the greatest danger is today in the conduct of democracy's affairs, I suppose I would think first of war—but second, and immediately, of a very different kind of thing—of what seems to me the possibility that we in America are becoming so big, so organized, so institutionalized, so governmentalized—yes, and so standardized—that there is increasing danger that the individual and his precious diversity will be squeezed out completely.—*Adlai E. Stevenson*

1951 *Opposite of Truth*

Sir Winston Churchill once squashed Aneurin Bevan in the Commons by replying blandly to one of his questions: "I should think it hardly possible to state the opposite of the truth with more precision."

188

1952 *Even Bigger Crowd*

Sir Winston Churchill was stopped by a woman who said to him: "Doesn't it thrill you, Mr. Churchill, to know that every time you make a speech the hall is packed to overflowing?"

"It is quite flattering," Sir Winston replied. "But whenever I feel this way I always remember that if, instead of making a political speech, I was being hanged, the crowd would be twice as big."

1953 *A Winston Churchill Haircut*

To a barber who asked him how he would like his hair cut: "A man of my limited resources cannot presume to have a hair style. Get on and cut it."

1954 *To Reporters on His First Day as President*

Boys, if you ever pray, pray for me now. I don't know whether you fellows ever had a load of hay fall on you, but when they told me yesterday what had happened, I felt like the moon, the stars, and all the planets had fallen on me. —*Harry S. Truman*

1955 *Perfection*

No government is perfect. One of the chief virtues of a democracy, however, is that its defects are always visible and under democratic processes can be pointed out and corrected.—*Harry S. Truman*

1956 *Have a Program*

I don't believe in anti-anything. A man has to have a program; you have to be for something, otherwise you will never get anywhere.—*Harry S. Truman*

1957 *Depends on How Many You See*

I see in the papers that Barry Goldwater and Rockefeller have decided to cut down their appearances in California. This reminded me of the fellow in Texas who said to his friend, "Earl, I am thinking of running for sheriff against Uncle Jim Wilson. What do you think?"

"Well," said his friend, "it depends on which one of you sees the most people."

"That's what I figure."

"If you see the most, Uncle Jim will win. If he sees the most, you will win." —*Lyndon B. Johnson*

1958 *You May Crawl Back*

When you crawl out on a limb, you always have to find another one to crawl back on.—*Lyndon B. Johnson*

1959   *The Vice Presidency*

The Vice Presidency is a good place for a young man who needs experience. —*Lyndon B. Johnson*

1960   *Paul Revere*

You remember the very old story about a citizen of Boston who heard a Texan talking about the glories of Bowie, Davy Crockett, and all the rest, and finally said, "Haven't you heard of Paul Revere?" To which the Texan answered, "Well, he is the man who ran for help."—*John F. Kennedy*

1961   *History*

Some of us think it wise to associate as much as possible with historians and cultivate their good will, though we always have the remedy which Winston Churchill once suggested when he prophesied during World War II that history would deal gently with us. "Because," Mr. Churchill said, "I intend to write it!" —*John F. Kennedy*

1962   *Washington*

Washington is a city of Southern efficiency and Northern charm.—*John F. Kennedy*

1963   *Gathering of Talent*

I think this is the most extraordinary collection of talent, of human knowledge, that has ever been gathered together at the White House—with the possible exception of when Thomas Jefferson dined alone.—*John F. Kennedy, at a dinner honoring Nobel Prize winners*

1964   *So Costly a Sacrifice*

Dear Madam: I have been shown in the files of the War Department a statement of the Adjutant-General of Massachusetts that you are the mother of five sons who have died gloriously on the field of battle. I feel how weak and fruitless must be any words of mine which should attempt to beguile you from the grief of a loss so overwhelming. But I can not refrain from tendering to you the consolation that may be found in the thanks of the Republic they died to save. I pray that our heavenly Father may assuage the anguish of your bereavement, and leave you only the cherished memory of the loved and lost, and the solemn pride that must be yours to have laid so costly a sacrifice upon the altar of freedom.—*Abraham Lincoln, letter to Mrs. Bixby, Washington, November 21, 1864*

1965   *The Way It Works*

"If you get up earlier in the morning than your neighbor," said the town philosopher, "and work harder and scheme more and stick to your job more closely and stay up later planning how to make more money than your neighbor and burn the midnight oil planning how to get ahead of him while he is snoozing, not only will you leave more money when you die than he will, but you will leave it a lot sooner."

1966   *Wiser Still*

Some years ago, King Carol of Rumania told how he had selected fourteen of the brightest young men in Rumania for training in the government service. Seven he sent to England and seven to America, to study the economic and political systems of the two countries.

"The seven who went to England were very wise," said Carol, "and they all have important posts in Bucharest. But the seven we sent to America were wiser still—they stayed in America."

1967   *Read 'Em and Weep!*

Back in 1835, fabulous Delmonico's Restaurant in downtown New York served the following menu:

Cup tea or coffee	1 cent
Bowl tea or coffee	2 cents
Soup	2 cents
Fried or stewed liver	3 cents
Hash	3 cents
Pies	4 cents
Half pies	2 cents
Beef or mutton stew	4 cents
Beef steak	4 cents
Liver and bacon	5 cents
Veal cutlet	5 cents
Chicken stew	5 cents
Ham and eggs	10 cents
Hamburger steak	10 cents
Roast chicken	10 cents
Regular dinner	12 cents

1968   *Einstein*

Albert Einstein, dining on a train, found he had forgotten his glasses and couldn't read the menu. He turned to the waiter and said, "You read it for me, please."

The waiter shook his head sympathetically and replied: "I's ignorant, too, boss."

1969   *Friendly Encounter*

Years ago, before I entered the ministry, I worked with a man from Missouri by the name of H. C. Wantland. He was a personal acquaintance of Jesse James.

One day when Wantland was returning from a day of collecting for a concern for which he was employed, Jesse James came riding up alongside his buggy and the following conversation took place:

"Hello, Harry."

"Hello, Jesse."

"What you doing out here?"

"Been out collecting."

"Got any money on you?"

"Yes."

"How much?"

"About six hundred dollars."

"Don't you know better than that? Someone is liable to rob you."

And Jesse James accompanied Wantland into town for protection from any hold-up. —*Rev. George E. Blanchard, Sunshine Magazine*

1970   *Second Fiddle*

A friend once asked a famous conductor of a great symphony orchestra which instrument he considered the most difficult to play. The conductor thought a moment, and then said, "Second fiddle. I can get plenty of first violinists. But to find one who can play second fiddle with enthusiasm—that's the problem. And if we have no second fiddle, we have no harmony!"

1971   *How It Started*

It was at the St. Louis World's Fair, in 1904, that the ice-cream cone first entered the arena, to become the most popular individual serving of ice cream.

A Syrian gentleman named Hamwi had come from Damascus to sell zalabia at the fair. The concession next door to his on the Midway was an ice-cream booth. One day the ice-cream people ran out of clean dishes. Hamwi rolled one of his still soft zalabia into a cornucopia. The ice-cream vendor filled it with ice cream and handed it to a customer. Success was instantaneous.

1972   *Who Said It?*

Who first said: "Of the people, by the people, for the people"? The first ninety-nine persons out of a hundred will reply, "Lincoln." And the hundredth person will add, "in his Gettysburg Address."

The famous phrase, familiar to millions of schoolchildren and their elders, actually is 584 years old, and once appeared in the Bible!

In John Wycliffe's introduction to his translation of the Bible, published in England in 1382, these words occur: "The Bible is for the government of the people, by the people, for the people."—*Sunshine Magazine*

1973   *Power*

Property is a form of control, and in capitalist societies like ours, power is vastly more dispersed than in state-socialist societies. There is little equality in these other societies. There is enormous concentration of power at the top.—*Daniel Patrick Moynihan*

1974   *Skilled Yarn Spinner*

Perhaps the most skilled yarn-spinner in the Senate today is Dale Bumpers of Arkansas. He was debating Senator Russell Long, who had been citing a poll of businessmen in support of a Long tax proposal. "Sometimes," Mr. Bumpers suggested, "people misunderstand the question."

Then he told of the preacher who asked that everybody in the congregation who wanted to go to heaven should stand up. Everyone stood except for one man. "You, sir," the preacher demanded, "are you telling us that you don't want to go to heaven when you die?"

"Oh," said the man, "when I die, yes. I thought you were getting up a load for right now."—*Alan L. Otten, Wall Street Journal*

1975   *All Aboard!*

It was in 1826 near Quincy, Massachusetts, that the first American railroad was built over a distance of four miles to connect the quarries with tidewater. The first passenger-and-freight railroad in this country was built between 1828 and 1830. It was known as the Baltimore and Ohio, was sixty miles long, and the cars at first were drawn by horses. The steam engine *Tom Thumb* replaced the horses in August 1830. Later the *De Witt Clinton* sped from Albany to Schenectady at fifteen miles an hour.

1976   *A Wise Request*

The late Rev. Peter Marshall, chaplain of the U.S. Senate, left a rich heritage of sermons and prayers. From one of his Senate prayers comes this excerpt: "Give us clear vision, that we may know where to stand and what to stand for —because unless we stand for something, we shall fall for anything."

1977   *Short Speech*

Airplane pioneers Orville and Wilbur Wright were notoriously untalkative; they especially hated making speeches. Nonetheless, at one luncheon they attended, the toastmaster asked Wilbur to say a few words.

"There must be some mistake," the elder Wright stammered. "Orville is the one who does the talking."

Then, when the toastmaster turned to him, Orville rose and announced, "Wilbur just made the speech."

1978   God and Man

Julia Ward Howe one day was talking to Charles Sumner, the distinguished Senator from Massachusetts. She asked him to interest himself in the case of a person who needed some help. The Senator answered, "Julia, I've become so busy I can no longer concern myself with individuals." Julia replied, "Charles, that is quite remarkable. Even God hasn't reached that stage yet."—*Ralph W. Sockman*

1979   What to Remember

Twelve things to remember: 1. The value of time. 2. The success of perseverance. 3. The pleasure of working. 4. The dignity of simplicity. 5. The worth of character. 6. The power of kindness. 7. The influence of example. 8. The obligation of duty. 9. The wisdom of economy. 10. The virtue of patience. 11. The improvement of talent. 12. The joy of originating.—*Marshall Field*

1980   An Ideal

I should like to conclude with a quotation from that remarkable television series *Civilization* by Lord Kenneth Clark because it sums up so elegantly and concisely an ideal towards which one hopes all men of goodwill and good sense will continue to strive:

I hold a number of beliefs that have been repudiated by the liveliest intellects of our time. I believe that order is better than chaos, forgiveness to vendetta. On the whole I think that knowledge is better than ignorance, and I am sure that human sympathy is better than ideology. I believe that in spite of the recent triumphs of science, men haven't changed much in the last two thousand years; and in consequence we must still try to learn from history. Above all, I believe in the God-given genius of certain individuals and I value a society that makes their existence possible.

Such an ideal may not be easy to sustain in an age characterized by escalating violence and intemperance, but I believe it is the sole hope for our continuing existence on this planet—a fertile but delicate oasis and, as yet, our only individual and collective home.—*Duncan Williams*

1981   You Might Be Surprised

President William Henry Harrison, with a basket on his arm, did his own shopping for the White House.

Robinson Crusoe's real name was Alexander Selkirk.

The initial "S" in former President Harry S. Truman's name does not stand for a name. It is merely an alphabetical addition.

1982   *Michelangelo*

Michelangelo Buonarroti was an Italian boy who would stand for hours watching artists paint pictures, and then run home and draw and paint pictures of his own. Nobody in the world ever painted any finer pictures than Michelangelo when he grew older.

1983   *The Power of Gentleness*

Away back in the sixth century before Christ, the Chinese philosopher Lao-tze listed gentleness as the first quality required of a leader. "I have three precious things which I hold fast and prize," he said. "The first is gentleness; the second is frugality; the third is humility, which keeps me from putting myself before others.

"Be gentle and you can be bold; be frugal and you can be liberal; avoid putting yourself before others and you can become a leader among men."

More powerful than a push is the gentle magnetic pull of a big idea and a common purpose. First of all, the leader should be a gentleman.—*Wilferd A. Peterson, Sunshine Magazine*

1984   *Herbert Hoover on Fishing*

To go fishing is the chance to wash one's soul with pure air, with the rush of the brook or the serenity of a lake, and the shimmer of the sun on blue water. It brings meekness and inspiration from the decency of nature, charity toward tackle-makers, patience toward fish, a mockery of profits and egos, a quieting of hate, a rejoicing that you do not have to decide a darned thing until next week. And it is discipline in the equality of men—for all men are equal before fish.

1985   *Thomas Alva Edison*

There was "Tommie" Edison, who began as a newsboy, selling papers on a Grand Trunk railroad train. In order to do what he wanted to do, when he had finished his work, he fitted up a laboratory in a baggage car, where he tried all sorts of new things as the train sped along between stations. When "Tommie" grew up, he became the great Thomas Alva Edison, perhaps the greatest inventor in the world.

1986   *Henry Clay*

When Henry Clay was a boy, he was very poor, but he spent his spare time committing speeches to memory, and then recited them aloud in the woods, where only the birds could hear him. Henry Clay became one of the greatest orators of his time.

1987   *James Watt*

James Watt, when only six or seven years old, would lie for hours on the hearth in his home in Scotland, and draw all kinds of circles and angles and squares with chalk. When he became older, he invented the steam engine.

1988   *Abraham Lincoln*

When Abraham Lincoln was a boy, he walked miles to borrow books to read, and then, after his day's work was done and his folks had gone to bed, he would put a fresh log on the fire, and by its light would read until he fell asleep. Abraham Lincoln became a great President.

1989   *Curious Bible Versions*

Printers are always especially careful to safeguard against typographical errors in the Scriptures. Especially in earlier editions, however, some peculiar mistakes have occurred. For instance, have you heard of the "Vinegar Bible"? This was so named because the heading for Luke 20 appeared as "Parable of the Vinegar" instead of "Parable of the Vineyard." A Bible published in 1823 became known as the "Camel Bible" because it contains the statement, "Rebecca arose, and her camels," instead of "damsels."

An edition appearing in 1702 has been called the "Printers' Bible" because, instead of "Princes" in the Psalms, this version made David complain bitterly, "Printers have persecuted me without cause." In another edition, "Blessed are the peacemakers" became "Blessed are the placemakers."

Then there is the "Wife Hater Bible," which has Jesus saying, in Luke 14:26, that He must be first in our lives above all else, and that relatives, possessions, "yes, and his own wife also," must be held in secondary esteem. The correct word in this instance is "life." The so-called "Wicked Bible" was named because a printer's mistake omitted the word "not" from the commandment, "Thou shalt not commit adultery."—*Sunshine Magazine*

1990   *His Signature*

One Sunday morning, just before service, a note was handed to the Rev. Henry Ward Beecher. The famous clergyman discovered it contained a single word: "fool."

Mr. Beecher arose, described the communication to his congregation, and added, "I have known many an instance of a man writing a letter and forgetting to sign his name, but this is the first case I have ever known of a man signing his name and forgetting to write the letter."

1991   *The Time Will Come*

Hisses, groans and loud conversation went on throughout [the maiden speech of Benjamin Disraeli in the House of Commons]. . . . But it does not follow that the maiden speech of the member for Maidstone was a failure.

Mr. Disraeli wound up in these words: "Now, Mr. Speaker, we see the philosophical prejudices of Man. (Laughter and cheers) I respect cheers, even when they come from the mouth of a political opponent. (Renewed laughter) I think, sir, (Hear! Hear! and repeated cries of Question!) I am not at all surprised, sir, at the reception I have met with (continued laughter). I have begun several things many times (laughter), and I have always succeeded at last. (Question) Ay, sir, and though I sit down now, the time will come when you will hear me."

1992   *Galaxy*

Our Milky Way Galaxy is an enormous cartwheel of about 100 billion stars —one of which is our sun.

A galaxy of 100 to 200 billion widely separated stars is enormous, and you need something bigger than miles to measure it. You can use the light-year, which equals about six million-million earth miles! Astronomers estimate that the diameter, or the length of a line drawn straight through the middle, of the "Big Wheel" is about 100,000 light-years.

We cannot travel at the speed of light, which is 186,282 miles per second, but even if we could, it would take us "forever" to cross the Milky Way Galaxy from one side to the other!—*Sunshine Magazine*

1993   *Love Your Enemies*

Some months ago I was reading an interesting comic strip, which featured my favorite character, "Dennis the Menace." Dennis had been filled with the Bicentennial ingredients. His teachers had told him how George Washington had marched out on his great horse, and with a few ragged soldiers had wrested freedom from the hands of old King George, that scoundrel potentate of England who, in his way, tried to repress and oppress the colonists. So one evening, when Dennis knelt down to say his prayers, he started out with his routine; then toward the end he came in with his extemporaneous sayings. He said, "Lord, bless George Washington, and George Washington's horse, and bless all of George Washington's soldiers." He was about to get up and walk away when he remembered what his Sunday School teacher had said about loving his enemies. So Dennis got down on his knees again, and said, "Lord, and bless old King George, but not as much."—*Bishop Roy Calvin Nichols*

1994 *Incentive*

When Louis Pasteur, the French scientist, was stricken with a cerebral thrombosis, his condition seemed so hopeless that construction was stopped on a laboratory that the government was building for him. Pasteur noticed and declined rapidly. His friends appealed to Emperor Napoleon III, who ordered construction resumed. Pasteur then began to recover and in the new laboratory conquered rabies and half a dozen other diseases.—*Tom Mahoney, American Legion Magazine*

1995 *Fuller's Earth*

Do today's problems seem a bit on the tremendous side? Perhaps it will help you to see them in better perspective if you are reminded of some of the things R. Buckminster Fuller, the famous engineer and architect, has to say about size.

The earth, he tells us, is 8,000 miles in diameter, and it really is rather "small potatoes." The diameter of one star he knows about is greater than the diameter of the earth's orbit around the sun! This sun of "ours" which seems so important to us is only one of 100 billion other stars in our galaxy. And—hold on to your hats—our galaxy is just one of a billion other galaxies in the universe—each of which has 100 billion stars of its own.

All of these stars are hurtling through space at a speed we don't even have the mathematics to estimate. Yet, astonishingly, there is enough order in all these goings-on to permit scientists to predict where certain heavenly bodies will be a century from now.

Since—after the sun—our nearest star neighbor is trillions of miles away, we don't know much about the inhabitants, if any, in the great out there, but of one thing we can be certain: There is an Intelligence behind all this. And it is running our little speck of a world, too. God is as near as He is far!—*Sunshine Magazine*

1996 *Long-distance Flier*

The hummingbird, smallest of all birds, migrates all the way from Alaska to Brazil. It can fly in any direction, even backward, but it cannot walk. Crossing the Gulf of Mexico, it flies over five hundred miles in a night.

1997 *A Common Experience*

This year I borrowed the money to pay the government a tax of $100,000. They have a procedure where they pay it to the President with the left hand and take it out with the right.—*Lyndon B. Johnson*

1998 *Their Responsibilities*

The Secretary of Labor is in charge of finding you a job, the Secretary of the Treasury is in charge of taking half the money away from you, and the Attorney General is in charge of suing you for the other half.—*Lyndon B. Johnson*

1999   *Resolutions for All the Year*

Jonathan Edwards, who was a noted theologian and clergyman of the eighteenth century, made five resolutions for himself in his youth and lived by them faithfully:

1. Resolved: To live with all my might while I do live.
2. Resolved: Never to lose one moment of time, but to improve it in the most profitable way I possibly can.
3. Resolved: Never to do anything which I should despise or think meanly of in another.
4. Resolved: Never to do anything out of revenge.
5. Resolved: Never to do anything which I should be afraid to do if it were the last hour of my life.—*Sunshine Magazine*

2000   *Your New Year's Resolutions*

In case you forgot to make your New Year's resolutions on the first of the year, it's never too late. Start compiling them any time, and then do your resolving on any of the following New Year's days: Chinese—February 18; Persian—March 21; Siamese—April 1; Mohammedan—April 26; Alexandrine—August 29.

2001   *Franklin Roosevelt*

I am busy as a one-armed paperhanger with the itch!

2002   *William Allen White*

Bill supports me for three and a half years out of every four.—*Franklin D. Roosevelt*

2003   *Truman on the White House*

The finest prison in the world.

2004   *Invitation to the Ball*

Mrs. Eisenhower and I got a nice invitation to the Inaugural Ball saying "RSVP" and I told her to answer it and say we had another engagement.

2005   *Dwight D. Eisenhower on Golf*

You're going to hear a lot of laughing today. My doctor has given me orders that if I don't start laughing instead of cussing when I miss those shots, then he's going to stop me from playing golf. So every time I miss a shot today, I'm going to go ho-ho-ho.

2006   *Not Much Going On*

My experience in government is that when things are noncontroversial, beautifully coordinated, and all the rest, it must be that there is not much going on.
—*John F. Kennedy*

2007   *How We Spend Life*

An interesting analysis of the lifetime of an average person, which appeared in an issue of the *Ladies' Home Journal,* revealed the following: 6 years spent in eating; 11 years in working; 5½ years in washing and dressing; 3 years in education; 8 years in amusement; 6 years in walking; 3 years in reading; 3 years in conversation; 24 years in sleeping; and just six months in worshiping God.

2008   *He Didn't Make It*

When Charlie Chaplin was at the peak of his popularity, a theater had a Charlie Chaplin Contest. The person who made up to look most like Charlie was to receive a silver cup, and there were other awards for runners-up. The quixotic Charlie decided to enter the contest himself. He came in second.

2009   *Help Wanted*

One of the early want ads in a Philadelphia newspaper was this one, placed by George Washington: "Wanted: A steward for the household of the PRESIDENT of the UNITED STATES. Any person well qualified for and willing to act in this capacity, may learn particulars by inquiring at the President's house, Philad. Feb. 25."

2010   *The Grocery List*

Looking through a desk drawer in a house that once belonged to President James K. Polk, a researcher has turned up a grocery list for the White House dated January 7, 1847. Sample prices: rice, 6 cents a pound; shelled almonds, 25 cents a pound; ham, 12 cents a pound.

2011   *Are You in Love?*

To a young man learning to perform on the flying trapeze, a veteran of the circus said: "Throw your heart over the bars and your body will follow."

In every field of endeavor those who put their hearts in their work are the real leaders. Falling in love with one's job is one secret of success.

Luther Burbank fell in love with plants, Edison fell in love with invention, Ford fell in love with motor cars, Kettering fell in love with research, John

Patterson fell in love with salesmanship, the Wright brothers fell in love with airplanes. Someone has truly said, "Be careful what you set your heart on, for it will surely come true."

Work is not drudgery, toil, and labor to a man who loves his work. It is inspiration and joy. Life is worth living.—*Silver Lining*

2012   *Thrift*

Teach people that economy is the greatest revenue producer in the world. None of us has the moral right to spend all we make!—*Eddie Rickenbacker*

2013   *Dear Deer*

Rudolph the Red-nosed Reindeer was created in 1939 by Robert L. May, a Montgomery-Ward catalog copywriter, in a booklet for the store's Santas to give away to children. May says, "Rudolph's the first reindeer that ever kept the wolf from the door."

2014   *Golf*

If you've ever wondered, in a fit of disgust or discouragement, what you were doing out on a golf course anyway, you may find perverse satisfaction in this diatribe about the game:

Golf is the easiest game in the world before you take it up, and the toughest after you have been at it for ten or twelve years.

Golf is played with little white balls, and as many clubs as a player can afford. The course consists of eighteen holes, seventeen of them unnecessary but included simply to multiply frustration. A "hole" is a tin cup in the center of the green. A "green" is a small patch of grass costing $1.98 a blade, and usually located between a lake and a number of abandoned excavations called sand traps.

The idea is to hit the ball from a given point into each of the eighteen holes, using the fewest strokes and the most words. The ball must be propelled by any one of a number of ridiculous-looking implements, cleverly designed to provoke the owner.

After each hole, the golfer counts his strokes, subtracts six, and says, "Made that in five, just one over par." After the eighteenth hole, he shakes hands with those he played with, and thanks them for helping him enjoy a wonderful afternoon of sportsmanship, then goes home and takes it all out on his wife and children.—*Sunshine Magazine*

2015   *Traffic Problems*

Traffic problems are not new. This is from the Old Testament, Nahum 2:4: "The chariots shall rage in the streets, they shall jostle one against another in the broad ways; they shall seem like torches, they shall run like the lightnings."

2016 *Here Is Victor Borge*

I just noticed something unusual about my walking: I usually walk in single file.

My great-grandfather was a brilliant man. In fact, he invented the burglar alarm. Unfortunately, it was stolen from him.

In my youth I wanted to be a great pantomimist—but I found I had nothing to say.

When I came to the U.S. in 1941 I didn't know a word of English, but after three Berlitz lessons my teacher spoke perfect Danish.

I remember when people used to step outside a moment for a breath of fresh air. Now sometimes you have to step outside for days to get it.

I have a good way of keeping in shape. I sit down a lot.

Modern music hasn't been around too long—and hopefully won't be.—*From: My Favorite Impressions*

2017 *Beware*

An observation from former Representative Orin Harris: "Beware of the man who knows the answer before he understands the question!"

2018 *Winning*

Al McGuire, basketball coach: Winning is overemphasized. The only time it is really important is in surgery and war.

2019 *Progress*

In 1789 it took George Washington eight days to travel the 200-odd miles from his home, Mount Vernon, to the scene of his inauguration as President in New York City. The fact that it required eight days is not significant. The important fact is that the time was the same as it would have taken two thousand years before. No real progress had been made in transportation in twenty centuries. Moses or Nebuchadnezzar could have traveled just as rapidly. Julius Caesar could have stepped from the first century into the nineteenth more easily than Benjamin Franklin could have stepped into this century. Now, for the first time in history, no man dies in the historical epoch in which he was born.

2020 *Franklin's Self-written Epitaph*

The Body
of
Benjamin Franklin, Printer
(Like the cover of an old book

Its contents torn out,
And stripped of its lettering and gilding,)
Lies here food for worms.
Yet the work itself shall not be lost,
For it will (as he believes) appear once
more
In a new
And more beautiful Edition
Corrected and Amended
By
The Author

2021　*The Later Years*

History is replete with examples of people who continued to use and enhance their creative gifts into very old age. Verdi composed his "Ave Maria" at eighty-five. Pablo Casals played the cello, conducted orchestras, and taught up to the time of his death at ninety-six. Ralph Vaughan Williams composed his eighth and ninth symphonies in his eighties. Grandma Moses took up painting at the age of seventy-seven and continued to do her quaint and appealing work to the end of her life at ninety-nine. Michelangelo worked on his sculptures virtually until the day of his death at eighty-nine.

Arthur Fiedler vigorously conducted the Boston Pops orchestra in his eighties, and Arthur Rubinstein at eighty-eight received tremendous ovations for his piano concerts. Will Durant, with the collaboration of his wife, Ariel, wrote five volumes of the massive ten-volume *History of Civilization* between the ages of sixty-nine and eighty-nine.

You may say these are unusually gifted and exceptional people, and you would be right. But they give proof that creativity, freshness of ideas, and the power to enrich one's society and culture need not vanish with old age.

Professor [Archibald] MacLeish points out—and I agree—that creativity in one's later years does not fall like manna from heaven. It requires an abiding interest in life and a conviction that we can continue to grow, learn, and create to the very end of our days.—*Alice Van Landingham*

2022　*"I Am the Door"*

The four panels of a door in your home have in relief the sign of the Cross. This is no accident. The Woodcraftsmen's Guild in England in the Middle Ages took as their motto the words of Christ, "I am the Door." Then they wrought in each door the sign of the Cross. It is a beautiful pattern, suiting both the hand and the eye.

2023   *Courage*

On May 20, 1927, a tiny Ryan monoplane took off in the early morning hours from Roosevelt Field, Long Island, New York, carrying a young man whose interest in flying had led him to several years of "barnstorming" throughout Southern and Midwestern states. Competing for the prize of $25,000 offered for the first nonstop flight from New York to Paris, Charles Lindbergh had obtained financial backing from a group of St. Louis businessmen. During the next thirty-three hours and thirty-nine minutes, the lone pilot guided his fragile craft, *The Spirit of St. Louis,* eastward over the ocean and landed on the evening of May 21 at Le Bourget, Paris, where an anxious world waited to receive the unassuming young man with a tumultuous welcome.

2024   *More Books*

More books have been written about Abraham Lincoln than any other man in history. Napoleon held the record until Lincoln's world popularity began.

2025   *Education*

Andrew Johnson was the only President who had little, if any, formal schooling. It is said that his wife taught him to read and write. Two thirds of the Presidents have been college graduates.

2026   *Too Crowded*

Yogi Berra, asked if a certain restaurant in New York was as popular as ever, answered, "Naw, nobody goes there anymore. It's too crowded!"

2027   *His View*

When James K. Polk won the Presidential election, Fillmore said: "May God save the country; for it is evident that the people will not."

2028   *Same Thing Still Wrong*

When Lincoln was carrying two of his sons, Willie and Tad, and both were yelling, he was asked what was wrong.

"Just what's the matter with the whole world. I've got three walnuts and each wants two."

2029   *Forgave Quickly*

Commenting on his desire to forgive an old opponent, Lincoln remarked, "I choose always to make my statute of limitations a short one."

2030 *Exhibit A*

You don't live there [the White House]. You are only Exhibit A.—*Theodore Roosevelt*

2031 *Description*

President Wilson called a digestive disturbance a "turmoil in Central America."

2032 *Calvin Coolidge Writes*

To his stepmother: "I wish you were here to see the dresses my wife has. Folks who see them know why I cannot pay very high rent."

2033 *Hoover as President*

The things I enjoyed most were visits from children. They did not want public offices.

2034 *Seventeen Camels*

There once lived an old Arab who had three sons. On his deathbed, he called his three sons and said: "At my death, you are to divide my possessions." To his eldest son he promised half of his worldly goods; to his second son, a third; and to the youngest, a ninth. When he died, it was found that his entire estate consisted of seventeen camels, and each of the sons began clamoring for his share.

When they found a fair division impossible, they turned to an old friend of their father for counsel. He was poor, but he said to the sons: "I have only one camel, but I will add it to the herd so that you can settle your father's estate amicably." Whereupon the old man gave the eldest son his half-share of nine camels. To the second son, he gave six camels, representing his third, and to the youngest, he gave two camels, representing his ninth share. Then the old man looked about him and, lo, his own camel remained. So he turned his head to the east and bowed, saying, "The wisdom of Allah is beyond understanding."

2035 *Most Important*

On Arturo Toscanini's eightieth birthday, someone asked his son what his father ranked as his most important achievement. The son replied, "For him there can be no such thing. Whatever he happens to be doing at the moment is the biggest thing in his life, whether it is conducting a symphony or peeling an orange."

2036   *Novelty in 1828*

The Tremont Hotel in Boston, opened in 1828, introduced the novelty of having a lock on the door of every guest room, no two of which could be opened with the same key.

2037   *Thomas Jefferson's Inventions*

Thomas Jefferson was a man of many talents and accomplishments. He was the third President of the United States, author of the Declaration of Independence, and the founder and first president of the University of Virginia.

He was also an architect, builder, and carpenter. Into his stately Virginia home, Monticello, went gadgets that were designed to save time and energy for its occupants. He built a circular staircase to conserve space. He also installed a dumbwaiter to save the servants many needless trips up and down the stairs. There were folding tables, and chairs that folded back into the walls when not in use. Sliding panels were built into some of the walls so that dishes and other small objects could be passed from one room to another with ease.

Jefferson designed a trick bed. From one side he emerged to his study, from the other, to his breakfast. During the day the bed was raised overhead out of the way.

These are only a few of the clever gadgets which may be seen today when one visits beautiful Monticello.

2038   *Ideas*

A group can spark an idea, but only an individual can have one. As former President Griswold of Yale has so aptly asked: "Could Hamlet have been written by a committee? Or the Mona Lisa painted by a club?"—*W. John Upjohn*

2039   *Two Dates*

1976 was not only the Bicentennial year of the United States, it also marked the 1,500th anniversary of the fall of Rome in 476 A.D.

2040   *Concentrated Too Much*

I was being educated at Admiral Rickover's College of Nuclear Knowledge prior to being qualified to command a nuclear-powered ship. And I was a captain and things weren't going too well for me.

I'd been out of school for a good many years, and hadn't studied very hard in nuclear physics, and thermodynamics were not coming back to me very easily. After the first reporting period Admiral Rickover called me in and, as you know, he is a salty old gentleman.

And he said, "Holloway, this is the lousiest report I have ever had of any of my officers going through this course. Look at it, one D and four F's. What's the matter with you?"

I said, "Well, Admiral, I don't have much to say. I guess I concentrated too much on one subject."—*Admiral James L. Holloway III, Chief of Naval Operations*

2041   A Sad Ending

Last Christmas I bought a hobby horse for my granddaughter. It came in a large box which said it contained 189 parts and could be put together in one hour. Sure it could, if you've just graduated from MIT and have a machine shop in your basement. I decided I didn't have to accept that kind of indignity, so, when I went to pay for it, I tore my check in 189 pieces and wrote them a little note telling them if they like to put things together let them work on that. One sad ending to my story . . . they did!—*Bill Veeck*

2042   A Favorite Portrait

Gilbert Stuart, American painter born December 3, 1755, was the foremost portrayer of George Washington—and he had no qualms about copying his three Presidential portraits for any and all buyers. He sold at least ninety-four copies, over seventy of the "Athenaeum" portrait, called "the most famous picture in American history."

Ordered by Martha Washington, this original was kept by Stuart instead, who dashed off copies, sometimes in two hours, whenever he needed money. (An unwilling assistant, his daughter, once moaned, "That Washington! I don't see why I haven't stuck a palette knife through him!") Gazing at us from posters, primers, and postage stamps, this portrait has become America's traditional concept of the first President's appearance.

2043   One Billion Dollars

The word "billion" is being used more and more. Very few realize how much money one billion dollars really is. Suppose you stood at the Washington Monument for 12 hours a day, 365 days of the year, and gave out $1,000 an hour, how long would it take to get rid of one billion dollars, at $12,000 a day?

Figure it out: 365 times $12,000 comes to $4,380,000, the amount you could dispose of in one year; in 10 years you would be able to give away $43,800,000; in 100 years, $438,000,000. To get rid of a billion at this rate would take you between 228 and 229 years.

2044   Last Words of Socrates

The last words of Socrates to Crito and his disciples, before the Jailer entered with the hemlock: ". . . And though I have been talking at such length, comforting you and myself with the assurance that, when I have drunk the poison, I shall not remain here, but shall go to a better place, my words have had no effect upon Crito. Therefore what I have failed to do you must do for me, and convince Crito, when I am gone, that it is not me but only a body which remains. And do not let him cry out when he sees it being buried, or burned, as though it were hurting me. For it won't, Crito."

2045   Opinion

Winston Churchill, possibly the world's greatest talker, was unquestionably its worst listener. In the House of Commons, while listening to a member of the opposition, he began to shake his head, and got more attention than the speaker, who, finally, unable to control himself, aimed a forefinger at Churchill screaming, "I wish to remind the Right Honorable friend that I am only expressing my own opinion." Impishly looking up, Churchill replied, "And I wish to remind the speaker that I am only shaking my own head."—*David E. Green*

2046   Executive Dish

Calvin Coolidge, who invited members of Congress to breakfast meetings at the White House, startled his guests one morning by pouring coffee and cream into his saucer. In confusion, several others at the table did the same. Without a word, the President placed his saucer on the floor for his dog!

2047   The Language of the Bible

The Bible is a collection of various books and letters reflecting and illuminating the long life of a small, yet a great, people. If it were only that, its value would be imperishable.

But it is more. It has been termed "the noblest monument of English prose." Its words and phrases, images and similes have become part of our everyday speech.

In the course of a single day we clarify and illuminate our talk by the often unconscious use of Bible language. An unwelcome neighbor becomes "a thorn in the flesh"; a hated task, "a millstone about the neck"; we escape from one thing or another "by the skin of our teeth"; we earn our bread "by the sweat of our brow"; we "strain at gnats and swallow camels"; tired at night, we say that "our spirit is willing but our flesh is weak"; in moments of anger we remember that "a soft answer turneth away wrath"; we prophesy to our children that if they "sow the wind they shall reap the whirlwind"; the price of our generous friends is still "far above rubies"; we "heap coals of fire" upon the heads of others; we long for the time when men "shall beat their swords into ploughshares and their spears into pruning hooks."

The language of the Bible, now simple and direct in its homely vigor, now sonorous and stately in its richness, has placed its indelible stamp on our best writers from Bacon to Lincoln and even to the present day.

2048 *The Growth of TV*

The first TV sets offered for sale in the United States were introduced at the 1939 New York World's Fair. Six years later there were only nine commercial TV stations in existence. By 1976 there were 953 of them. In 1977 there were over 121 million sets in ninety-seven percent of the homes of this country.

2049 *No One Is Accountable*

What is happening in America is something that is foreign to the American way of life: a government presuming to know what is best for its people, at the expense of the people's freedom to make their own decisions.

Moreover, it is doubly wrong when appointed officials exercise life-or-death power over the sources of people's jobs and income, without being held accountable for what happens when that power is used indiscriminately or unwisely.

This has always been the nub of the problem with regulatory agencies.—*Edgar B. Speer*

2050 *The Third Kick*

When William Allen White, the man who made the *Emporia Gazette* a national newspaper, gave fifty acres of parkland to his home town, he explained his action this way: "This is the last kick in a fistful of dollars I am getting rid of. I have tried to teach people that there are three kicks in every dollar: one, when you make it—and how I love to make a dollar; two, when you have it—and I have the Yankee lust for saving. The third kick is when you give it away—and it is the biggest kick of all."

2051 *Johnny Appleseed*

Johnny Appleseed actually did exist. He planted orchards of apple trees across America in the early 1800's—sometimes arriving in wilderness areas before the pioneers. Johnny Appleseed became a folk hero, and eating apples became an American institution. We don't know who said, "An apple a day keeps the doctor away." But many of us follow the advice. A cynic has said, "A doctor a day keeps the apples away," because you can't afford them.

2052 *Word Power*

There's an old game which some of you may have played called conjugation of adjectives. It goes something like this: I am firm; you are obstinate; he's pigheaded. I'm neat; you, my friend, are fussy; he, my enemy, is compulsive about germs. I'm scholarly; you're pedantic, he's dry as dust. I'm flexible; you're flabby; he's wishy-washy. I'm bold; you're a bit pushy; he's got his nerve; and so on. I've noticed that it is a game frequently played in talk about power and politics on campus. My side shows shrewd tactics; your side sometimes cuts corners a bit; my enemies are unscrupulous. My side adapts its rhetoric to the needs of the audience; you cannot quite be relied on to tell the same story twice. —*Wayne C. Booth*

2053 *Rich*

Some years ago, right after Walt Disney had completed Disneyland in California, someone asked him if he were rich. He replied, "Of course I'm rich. No one could owe $7 million and not be rich."—*Sunshine Magazine*

2054 *Experience*

You can take all the experience and judgment of men over fifty out of the world and there wouldn't be enough left to run it.—*Henry Ford*

2055 *Couldn't Believe It*

President Andrew Jackson was never convinced that the earth was round and not flat.

2056 *Good Old Days*

In 1913 the tax on a $4,000 annual income was one penny.

2057 *As He Saw America*

On Carl Sandburg's seventy-fifth birthday, a group of friends gave a party for him. When the great literator, his hair snow white, arose to speak, he proved that he still had the heart of a boy, with faith and inspiration aglow. Among his words were these: "I see America, not in the setting sun of a black night of despair ahead of us. I see America in the crimson light of a rising sun fresh from the burning, creative hand of God. I see great days ahead, great days possible to men and women of vision."

2058 *To Win by Losing*

Probably no man had a longer or more distinguished career in sports than coach Amos Alonzo Stagg, who for forty-two years was the idol of students and graduates of the University of Chicago. He was especially admired for his uncompromising honesty.

On one occasion, it is said, Mr. Stagg's champion baseball team was defending its college title. The batter had singled, and one of Stagg's men was racing home with the winning run. Stagg shouted, "Get back to third base—you cut it by a yard!"

"But the umpire didn't see me!" the runner protested.

"That doesn't make any difference!" roared Stagg. "Get back!"

The game was lost, but a character battle was won.

2059   Emphasize Your Strength

Justice Harlan Fiske once gave this advice to a young lawyer: "If you're strong on the facts and weak on the law, discuss the facts. If you're strong on the law and weak on the facts, discuss the law. If you're weak on the law and weak on the facts—bang the table."

2060   Objective

Oscar Levant numbered among his friends a composer whose ego was so inflated that he referred to himself in the third person.

One night, when he did this in the presence of a stranger, the latter remarked: "What conceit!"

"It isn't conceit," explained Levant. "He just likes to be objective when he admires himself."

2061   Unbelievable

One night after a performance the manager of a New York theater told Ethel Barrymore that two ladies wanted to see her. "They say they went to school with you," he explained.

"They went to school with me?" said Miss Barrymore. "Well, wheel them in."

2062   Then He Could Work

When Leonardo da Vinci was working on his painting "The Last Supper," he became angry with a certain man. Losing his temper, he lashed the other fellow with bitter words and threats. Returning to his canvas, he attempted to work on the face of Jesus, but was unable to do so. He was so upset he could not compose himself for the painstaking work. Finally he put down his tools and sought out the man and asked his forgiveness. The man accepted his apology and Leonardo was able to return to his workshop and finish painting the face of Jesus.—*Bits and Pieces*

2063   Making Dreams Come True

Dreams can become realities through persistence.

Carrie Jacobs Bond, whose "The End of a Perfect Day" is a song that will last forever, was crippled with rheumatism, and left with a child to support. She began to sing away her misery.

George Gershwin was earning only $35 a week when he was catapulted into success by his song "Swanee." Louisa May Alcott, celebrated author of *Little Women*, led an early life of grinding poverty. Edward Berry quit school when he was fifteen. But he never quit learning. And he became a dean at Johns Hopkins.

No man knew the stars so well as Edwin B. Frost, onetime head of the famous Yerkes Observatory. He was blind! Freud, founder of psychoanalysis, afflicted with an incurable disease, worked between operations. Charles Darwin, John Burroughs, and Henrik Ibsen were "sick" men, yet became distinguished.

2064   *The Most Expressive Words*

Dr. Wilfred Funk, lexicographer and dictionary publisher, selected the ten most expressive words in the English language: The most bitter word is *alone;* the most reverent, *mother;* the most tragic, *death;* the most beautiful, *love;* the most cruel, *revenge;* the most peaceful, *tranquil;* the saddest, *forgotten;* the warmest, *friendship;* the coldest, *no;* the most comforting, *faith.*

2065   *America*

"Your Constitution," wrote Lord Macaulay to H. S. Randall, American historian and biographer, "is all sail and no anchor."

2066   *Failed in Chemistry*

American painter James A. McNeill Whistler flunked out of West Point. He would have graduated in the Class of 1855 had he not failed chemistry.

2067   *An Unsuccessful Dentist*

Zane Grey, one of the most prolific writers of modern times, had a hard time of it. He was an unsuccessful dentist; decided to take up writing and sent his hundredth attempt, a long thing called *Riders of the Purple Sage,* to a publishing house. He never heard from them.

One day he was in New York, and decided to see about his script.

"You've wasted enough of our time with your junk," the publisher shouted. "Why don't you go back to filling teeth? You can't write, you never could write, and you never will be able to write."

Grey sent the book on to another publisher—who bought it immediately. And it sold over a million copies.—*Sunshine Magazine*

2068   *It Never Looked Better*

When Grant Wood painted scenes of his native Iowa, he would usually take artistic license, painting the villages and fields the way he wished they looked, rather than as they were. Once, when he got through painting a neighbor's farm, having again improved something here and there, he showed the finished product to the farmer, who looked at it and remarked:

"Yep, looks just like it and thanks for cutting the weeds."

2069   Human Energy

Only as far back as 1850, ninety-four percent of our energy still came from one source: human or animal muscle power. Today, at less than one percent, we're hardly lifting a finger.—*Douglass C. Harvey*

2070   First Flight?

Charles A. Lindbergh was a passenger on one of the 747 jets to Europe out of New York. When the plane was airborne, the pilot introduced Lindbergh as a passenger without bothering to identify him further.

Lindbergh stood and nodded to his fellow passengers. As he sat down, he had a little trouble fastening his seat belt.

A flight hostess stepped up quickly, buckled the belt, and asked: "Is this your first crossing, Mr. Lindbergh?"

2071   The Labor of Others

A hundred times every day I remind myself that my inner and outer life depends on the labors of other men, living and dead, and that I must exert myself in order to give in the measure as I have received and am still receiving.—*Albert Einstein.*

2072   Something He Wrote?

A friend, who did not like the grimy horrors of William Faulkner's stories, met Faulkner one day and said: "Hello! How are you?" Faulkner said he wasn't feeling too well; he'd had some sort of stomach upset lately. "Ah," said his friend, "something you wrote, no doubt."

2073   He Would Finish

St. Francis of Assisi, hoeing his garden, was asked what he would do if he suddenly learned he was to die at sunset that day. He said, "I should finish hoeing my garden."

2074   He Agreed

During an election, Winston Churchill was interrupted by a man in the gallery shouting derisively: "I don't think!" Mr. Churchill immediately retorted: "I agree with the gentleman in the gallery entirely."

2075   *Not Soon Enough*

Sir Thomas Beecham was rehearsing Massenet's *Don Quichotte,* in which Chaliapin, the great Russian bass, was starring. In the last act, Dulcinea failed repeatedly to come in on the beat. "It's Mr. Chaliapin's fault," she protested, "he always dies too soon." "Fräulein," said Sir Thomas sadly, "you are in error: no opera singer has ever died half soon enough."

2076   *Another Story*

A friend of James Thurber told him that his firm had the idea of having him do new illustrations for *Alice in Wonderland.* Thurber said: "Let's keep the present illustrations and I'll rewrite the story."

2077   *Not New to Him*

On a hot day in Denver, Colorado, a friend entered the chambers of Judge Ben Lindsay to find him having a cup of hot coffee.

"Why don't you drink something cooling, Judge?" he asked. "Have you ever tried chilled gin and ginger ale?"

"No," said the Judge, "but I've often tried fellows who have."

2078   *Credit*

No man's credit is as good as his money.—*Henry van Dyke*

2079   *Two Great Men*

That nation has not lived in vain which has given the world Washington and Lincoln, the best great men and the greatest good men whom history can show. —*Henry Cabot Lodge*

2080   *Famous Inscriptions*

Over one of the doors of the Milan Cathedral is sculptured a cross beneath which are the words: "All that troubles is but for a moment." Under the great central entrance in the main aisle is the inscription: "That only is important which is eternal."

2081   *His Monument*

Sir Christopher Wren, architect of St. Paul's Cathedral, London, had the following inscription in Latin carved above one of the entrances: "If you seek my monument, look around you."

2082 *Revealing*

The biographer of the Duke of Wellington had little difficulty in gathering material for his book. He could find material on what the Duke had done, but not find much on what kind of man he was.

And then he found the Duke's old checkbook stubs. By examining these he gained more insight into the character of Wellington than he had found anywhere else.

The same would be true in our own lives. The places and things for which our money and time go reveal the kind of person we are and what our major interest is.—*William I. Boand, Sunshine Magazine*

2083 *What It Meant*

Orville and Wilbur Wright had tried repeatedly to fly a heavier-than-air craft. They had had one disappointment after another. Finally one December day, off the sand dunes of Kitty Hawk, they did it. They actually flew! They did what man had never done before. It was the greatest news scoop of the century. Elated, they wired their sister Katherine, "We have actually flown one hundred twenty feet. Will be home for Christmas." Hastily she ran down the street and shoved the telegram at the city editor of the local paper. "Well, well," he smiled, "isn't it nice that they will be home for Christmas."—*Sunshine Magazine*

2084 *He Will*

Oscar Wilde, on hearing a clever remark: "Oh, I wish I'd said that!"
James Whistler: "You will, Oscar, you will."

2085 *Determination*

Edison described his repeated efforts to make the phonograph reproduce an aspirated sound, and added: "From eighteen to twenty hours a day for the last seven months I have worked on this single word 'specia.' I said into the phonograph 'specia, specia, specia,' but the instrument responded 'pecia, pecia, pecia.' It was enough to drive one mad. But I held firm, and I have succeeded."

2086 *A Little Error*

When, on the death of President McKinley, Theodore Roosevelt succeeded to the high office, a New York editor desired to contrast the event with a recent event in Europe. But the compositor, coming to the word "oath" in the manuscript, struck a wrong key and the sentence appeared: "For sheer democratic dignity, nothing could exceed the moment when, surrounded by the Cabinet, Mr. Roosevelt took his simple bath as President of the United States."

2087   Be Careful

Duchess of Gordon, on her return to London: "Have you been talking as much nonsense as usual, Mr. Pitt?"

William Pitt: "I am not so sure about that, but I think that since I saw Your Grace I have not heard so much."

2088   Right Clever

Actor: "I'm a smash hit. Why, yesterday during the last act I had the audience glued in their seats!"

Oliver Herford: "Wonderful! Wonderful! Clever of you to think of it!"

2089   Correct

A British critic once reviewed a play called *Dreadful Night.* His review read: "Exactly."

2090   Glad

Shortly after President Coolidge had left the White House, he stayed at a hotel where he had to sign the register as usual. Under the head of "Occupation" he wrote: "Retired," and after "Remarks" he paused a moment and then wrote: "Glad of it."

2091   He Lost

In a music review, the critic wrote: "An amateur string quartet played Brahms here last evening. Brahms lost."

2092   His Calling Card

The American Ambassador in Warsaw, Hugh Gibson, was ill in the Embassy when he heard the piano being played in the living room. It was Beethoven's Moonlight Sonata, played as only Paderewski himself could play it. When the music stopped, Gibson told a servant to ask Paderewski, then Premier, to come in. "He has already left," the servant said. "He said he only wanted to let you know he had called."

2093   He Was Baggy

When a critic raved about Charles Laughton's acting, but criticized his "blue, baggy suit," Laughton replied indignantly: "The suit was brand new, it was me that was baggy."

2094 *No Statue Needed*

Rossini, the composer, discovered that some wealthy admirers in France proposed to erect a statue in his honor. "How much will it cost?" he asked. "About ten million francs," was the reply. "Ten million francs!" gasped the composer. "Why, for five million I'd stand on the pedestal myself."

2095 *Epitaph on Lord Peter Robertson:*

> Here lies the Christian, judge, and poet Peter,
> Who broke the laws of God, and man, and metre.
> —*John Gibson Lockhart*

2096 *Comprehensive*

The Abbé Maury had just preached a long sermon at the Tuileries in which he covered government, finance, politics, and the arts. Said the King of France, Louis XVI, "If he had just talked to us a little bit about religion, he would have talked about everything."

2097 *Hard to Believe*

College girl, on observing poet Louis Untermeyer at a New Year's Eve party, topped with paper hat and blowing a horn: "Huh! And you're Required Reading!"

2098 *Why Knowledge Increases*

Educator at a testimonial for Charles W. Eliot, president of Harvard: "Permit me to congratulate you on the miracles you have performed at the university. Since you became president, Harvard has become a storehouse of knowledge."

Eliot: "That's true, but I scarcely deserve the credit for that. It is simply that the freshmen bring so much knowledge in, and the seniors take so little out."

2099 *A Charity Ball*

George Bernard Shaw, at a benefit affair, asked a dowager to dance. She said, "Oh, Mr. Shaw, what made you ask poor little me to dance?" Replied Shaw, "This is a charity ball, isn't it?"

2100 *Self-Help*

Shakespeare learned little more than reading and writing at school, but by self-culture he made himself the great master among literary men.

2101 *Perfection*

Samuel Johnson said a man must turn over half a library to write one book. When an authoress told Wordsworth she had spent six hours on a poem, he replied that he would have spent six weeks.

2102   *High Opinion*

W. S. Gilbert once said of a certain man: "No man can have a higher opinion of him that I have—and I think he's a dirty little beast."

2103   *Persistence*

Beethoven probably surpassed all other musicians in his persistent application. There is scarcely a bar in his music that was not written and rewritten at least a dozen times. Gibbon wrote his autobiography nine times, and was in his study every morning, summer and winter, at six o'clock; and yet youth who waste their evenings wonder at the genius which can produce *The Decline and Fall of the Roman Empire,* upon which Gibbon worked twenty years. Even Plato, one of the greatest writers that ever lived, wrote the first sentence in his *Republic* nine different ways before he was satisfied with it. Burke wrote the conclusion of his speech at the trial of Hastings sixteen times, and Butler his famous "Analogy" twenty times. It took Vergil seven years to write his *Georgics,* and twelve years to write the *Aeneid.*

2104   *Couldn't Lose*

When Woodrow Wilson was president of Princeton University, an anxious mother was questioning him closely about what Princeton could do for her son. Wilson replied: "Madam, we guarantee satisfaction or you will get your son back."

2105   *A Paradox of Life*

One of the paradoxes of life is that the young are always wishing they were just a little older and the old are usually wishing they were a whole lot younger.

2106   *Question*

Former President Dwight D. Eisenhower at Mount Vernon inspecting a sword George Washington received as a gift: "Do you suppose they investigated him for getting a present?"

2107   *Times Have Changed*

In the old days folks boiled coffee and settled it with an egg; the only reds known were red flannels and a boy didn't think he had to have a vehicle in which to pursue happiness.

Ladies rode sidesaddle and when the preacher said a truth the people said "Amen."

A candidate had to be economy-minded to get elected to office; neighbors asked about your family and meant it; and when a man dressed for the evening he put on his nightshirt.

Parents were the only baby-sitters; and men worked for an honest living instead of wishing for one.

A man's word was his bond; Rip Van Winkle slept twenty years and no one asked him to endorse a mattress; and men made the same wife do a lifetime.—
Sunshine Magazine

2108   *Not the Same?*

Ambassador Henry Cabot Lodge, in some annoyance, inquired why "the gentleman" kept demanding the floor at the United Nations.

"I am not a gentleman, I am representative of the Soviet Union here," replied the Russian Ambassador.

Murmured Lodge, "The two are not necessarily mutually exclusive."

2109   *Even So, He Did Well!*

Shakespeare boasted that as a country schoolmaster he had never blotted out a line. Said Ben Johnson when he heard of this: "I wish he'd blotted out a thousand."

2110   *Right Now*

Abraham Lincoln, as a young lawyer, once had to plead two cases in the same day before the same judge. Both involved the same principle of law, but in one Lincoln appeared for the defendant, and in the other for the plaintiff. In the morning he made an eloquent plea and won his case. In the afternoon he took the opposite side and was arguing with the same earnestness. The judge, with a half-smile, asked him for the cause of his change of attitude. "Your Honor," said Lincoln, "I may have been wrong this morning, but I know I'm right this afternoon."

2111   *Wanted to Share*

Two Texas oilmen walked into a Cadillac showroom. One of them asked the salesman: "How much is this model?" "Ten thousand dollars," was the reply. "I'll take it," said the Texan, and began to count thousand-dollar notes from a fat roll. His friend, however, whipped out his wallet. "Oh, no you don't," he said. "After all, you paid for the lunch."

2112   *No Barriers*

The barriers are not yet erected which shall say to aspiring talent, "Thus far and no farther."—*Ludwig van Beethoven*

2113   *Happy to Be There*

Called upon to make a speech at a dinner in honor of W. C. Fields, Jack Benny said: "I'm happy to be at this dinner tonight to pay tribute to our guest of honor —and besides, it's my cook's night out."

2114   *At Home*

Bernard Shaw received an invitation from a celebrity stalker: "Lady —— will be at home Thursday between four and six." Shaw returned the card with this message underneath: "Mr. Bernard Shaw likewise."

2115   *Mellow*

On Christopher Morley: "He became mellow before he became ripe."—*Alexander Woollcott*

2116   *Different Viewpoints*

When Cornelia Otis Skinner opened in a revival of Shaw's *Candida,* there followed this exchange of cablegrams:
Shaw: "Excellent. Greatest."
Skinner, overwhelmed: "Undeserving such praise."
Shaw: "I meant the play."
Skinner: "So did I."

2117   *Trying to Do Right*

When we understand the other fellow's viewpoint—understand what he is trying to do—nine times out of ten he is trying to do right.—*Harry S. Truman*

2118   *Mozart*

The great Mozart, unable to afford heat in his room, wrapped his hands in woolen socks while writing some of his most immortal music. This great musical genius was first buried in a pauper's grave.

2119   *Hardship*

One of the leading magazines ridiculed Tennyson's first poems and consigned the young poet to temporary oblivion. Only one of Ralph Waldo Emerson's books had a remunerative sale. Washington Irving was nearly seventy years old before the income from his books paid the expenses of his household.

2120   *Only One Best Place*

One evening when Thomas Edison came home from work, his wife said to him, "You've worked long enough without a rest. You must go on a vacation."

"But where on earth would I go?" asked Mr. Edison.

"Just decide where you would rather be than anywhere else on earth," suggested the wife.

Mr. Edison hesitated. "Very well," he said finally, "I'll go tomorrow." The next morning he was back at work in his laboratory.

2121   *Cheaper Then*

A lady invited Fritz Kreisler, the great violinist, to a party she was giving. "Of course," she added, "you'll bring your violin." "In that case," said Kreisler, "my fee will be two thousand dollars." "In that case," snapped the lady, "I shall have to ask you not to mingle with my guests." "In that case," responded the famous violinist, "my fee will be only one thousand dollars."

2122   *Postmaster Lincoln*

When he was twenty-four, Abraham Lincoln served as the postmaster of New Salem, Illinois, for which he was paid an annual salary of $55.70.

The New Salem post office was closed in 1836, but it was several years before an agent arrived from Washington to settle accounts with ex-postmaster Lincoln, who was a struggling lawyer not doing too well.

The agent informed him that there was $17 due the government. Lincoln crossed the room, opened an old trunk and took out a yellowed cotton rag bound with string. Untying it, he spread out the cloth and there was the $17. He had been holding it untouched.

"I never use any man's money but my own," he said.—*Sunshine Magazine*

2123   *Nice Insult*

Josephine Baker, asked how she liked Frenchmen, said: "I like them very much because even when they insult you they do it so nicely."

2124   *Good Letters*

In reply to a letter from Professor Edward Sylvester Morse: "It was very pleasant to me to get a letter from you the other day. Perhaps I should have found it pleasanter if I had been able to decipher it. I don't think that I mastered anything beyond the date (which I knew) and the signature (which I guessed at). There's a singular and a perpetual charm in a letter of yours; it never grows old, it never loses its novelty. . . . Other letters are read and thrown away and forgotten, but yours are kept forever—unread. One of them will last a reasonable man a lifetime."—*Sunshine Magazine*

2125   *Full of Bash?*

The witty half of the Gilbert and Sullivan partnership was taken to task for using the word "coyful" in one of his librettos. "How can anyone be full of coy?" he was asked. "I don't know," he replied; "but, for that matter, how can anyone be full of bash?"

2126   *It Takes Time*

Gutzon Borglum was the sculptor who created the Mount Rushmore Memorial, a mammoth work carved into the native rock of a mountainside. Borglum was once asked if he thought his work perfect in every detail. "Not today," he replied. "The nose of George Washington is an inch too long. It's better that way, though. It will erode to be exactly right in ten thousand years."

2127   *French Monument*

Inscription on a monument in France marking the grave of a mule: "In memory of Maggie, who in her time kicked two colonels, four majors, ten captains, twenty-four lieutenants, forty-two sergeants, four hundred and thirty-nine other ranks, and one bomb."

2128   *A Little Thing*

It was a little thing for the janitor to leave a lamp swinging in the cathedral at Pisa, but in that steady swaying motion the boy Galileo saw the pendulum, and conceived the idea of thus measuring time.

2129   *A Great Hymn*

John Henry Newman wrote "Lead, Kindly Light" when he was thirty-two years old. He was to live to be almost ninety—to become a distinguished Cardinal of the Catholic Church and to write the brilliant *Apologia,* one of the world's immortal classics. But it is for the simple hymn he wrote one anguished afternoon, his humble prayer for guidance when he was lost in a torment of doubt and indecision, that he is today best remembered.

2130   *Undiscovered World*

I know not what the world will think of my labors, but to myself it seems that I have been but as a child playing on the seashore; now finding some prettier pebble or more beautiful shell than my companions, while the unbounded ocean of truth lay undiscovered before me.—*Sir Isaac Newton*

2131   *Our Standards*

To put the matter bluntly, two men were crucified because they were too bad, and one because he was too good. You see, as Henry Sloane Coffin says, "We level up with our standards of right, and we also level down. He who is above the conscience of the community is as likely to be slain as he who is below."— *Harold Cooke Phillips*

2132   *Victor Hugo in Les Misérables* about Waterloo

End of the dictatorship. A whole European system crumbled away. Was it possible that Napoleon should have won that battle? We answer no. Why? Because of Wellington? Because of Blucher? No. Because of God. . . . Napoleon had been denounced in the infinite and his fall had been decided on. He embarrassed God.

2133   *The Right Time*

Asked by a *Parade* reporter what primary lesson he had learned from life, comedian Red Skelton searched his memory for several minutes, finally declared: "I've learned that any kid will run any errand for you, if you ask at bedtime."

2134   *Great Was the Fall*

Once the great Roman Empire was more powerful than any nation of our own time. No nation could stand up against Roman legions. Yet that great empire sank down to failure. What were the causes?

Historian Edward Gibbon in his story of *The Decline and Fall of the Roman Empire* gives these five reasons for that failure:

1. The rapid increase of divorce; the undermining of the dignity and sanctity of the home, which is the basis of human society.

2. Higher and higher taxes and the spending of public monies for free bread and circuses.

3. The mad craze for pleasure; sports becoming every year more exciting and more brutal.

4. The building of gigantic armaments when the real enemy was within; the decadence of the people.

5. The decay of religion—fading into mere form, losing touch with life and becoming impotent to warn and guide the people.

Are we following in the footsteps of the Romans? Upon each of us rests the responsibility of making our nation stronger.—*Thomas Dreier, Sunshine Magazine*

2135   *Flock of Bluebirds*

The late William L. Stidger once called on William Allen White, of Emporia, Kansas, and gave this account of the meeting:

"Mr. White was showing me the manuscript of a half-completed life of Theodore Roosevelt. I read a few pages of it, deeply impressed, and said to him, 'You ought to finish it.'

"There was a wistful look in his eyes as he replied, 'Haven't the heart to go on with it. My daughter Mary was running in and out of this room while I was writing the first part of the book, asking me questions about it. Then, when she was killed in a horseback riding accident, her death took all the heart out of the enterprise for me.'

"Then we stood and talked for a few minutes about Mary White's death—and immortality. Our father hearts were drawn to each other. As the dim dusk of evening came on, Mr. White said quietly: 'Well, after all, we're just a flock of bluebirds gathering for their flight.' "—*Sunshine Magazine*

2136   *His Own Books*

His first book had been printed at his own risk in an edition of 1,000 copies and when, four years later, fewer than 300 had been sold, he had taken over the remainder with the wry comment: "I have now a library of nearly nine hundred volumes, over seven hundred of which I wrote myself."—*Joseph Wood Krutch speaking of Henry David Thoreau*

2137   *Immortality*

Sophie Tucker gave this tribute to Irving Berlin, America's great songwriter: "What a wonderful feeling it must be to know while you're still alive that you're immortal!"

2138   *Civilization*

You are dying. I see in you all the characteristic stigma of decay. I can prove to you that your great wealth and your great poverty, your capitalism and your socialism, your wars and your revolutions, your atheism and your pessimism and your cynicism, your immorality, your broken-down marriages, your birth control, that is bleeding you from the bottom and killing you off at the top in the brains—I can prove to you that those were the characteristic marks of the dying ages of ancient States—Alexandria and Greece and neurotic Rome.—*Oswald Spengler to Europe and America in Decline of the West*

2139   *Unusual Circumstances*

"Rock of Ages," one of the most popular Protestant hymns, was composed under unusual circumstances. In 1775, Augustus Toplady took shelter from a storm in a cleft of a large rock at Barrington Coombe in Somerset, England, and, while waiting for the rain to stop, wrote this famous song on the only piece of paper he could find—a playing card.

2140 *Founding Fathers*

The founding fathers who wrote the Declaration of Independence were not, as so many think, a bunch of graybeards. Three were in their twenties, and most of them were young.

2141 *Writing for Children*

The Russian writer Maxim Gorky, when asked how to write for children, answered: "Just as you would write for grown-ups, but better!"

2142 *Spirit*

When a man loses heart, he loses everything. The story of Nelson, Admiral of England, when he nailed six flags to his mast so that if even five were shot away no one would think that he had surrendered, is the spirit applicable to our every day.—*Harry Emerson Fosdick*

2143 *Release the Rascal*

Pope Leo XII, on a visit to the jail of the Papal States in 1825, insisted on questioning each of the prisoners as to how he had come to be there. Almost every man protested his innocence. Only one humbly admitted that he was a forger and a thief.

Turning to the prison superintendent, Pope Leo said sternly: "Release this rascal at once. I do not wish that his presence should corrupt all these noble gentlemen here!"—*Leaves from the Garden of St. Bernard*

2144 *Great Phrases*

Many of the world's speeches became classics because their creators were masters of the pat phrase. Roman Cato's "Carthage must be destroyed," Patrick Henry's "Give me liberty or give me death," Lincoln's "Government of the people, by the people and for the people," and Churchill's "blood, sweat and tears" not only pinpointed the theses of the speakers but also shaped the destiny of nations.—*Arthur Postle*

2145 *How We Justify It*

"Let but the cause seem beautiful, dear God, if we must die" is a prayer repeated down the centuries from the time of the siege of Troy.—*Edgar Ansel Mowrer*

2146 *Abraham Lincoln*

We have been the recipients of the choicest bounties of Heaven. We have been preserved these many years in peace and prosperity. We have grown in numbers, wealth, and power as no other nation has ever grown—but we have forgotten God!

We have forgotten the gracious hand that preserved us in peace, and multiplied and enriched, and strengthened us; and we have vainly imagined, in the deceitfulness of our hearts, that all these blessings were produced by some superior wisdom and virtue of our own.

Intoxicated with unbroken success, we have become too self-sufficient to feel the necessity of redeeming grace, too proud to pray to the God that made us.

It behooves us, then, to humble ourselves before the offended Power, to confess our national sins, and to pray for clemency and forgiveness.

I still have confidence that the Almighty, the Maker of the universe, will, through the instrumentality of this great and intelligent people, bring us through present difficulties as He has through all the other difficulties of our country.—*Clear Horizons*

2147   *Too Many Tastes*

William J. Hutchins, once president of Berea College and father of the well-known president of Chicago University, tells the story of a mountaineer who came to town and saw for the first time a stalk of bananas. "Want to try one, Jeff?" asked a friend. "No, I reckon not," Jeff answered. "I've got so many tastes now I kain't satisfy I ain't aimin' to take on any more."—*William P. King, Zions Herald*

2148   *Eternity*

I care more for that long age which I shall never see than for my own small share of time.—*Cicero*

2149   *Her Life*

Some years ago a mother was carrying her baby over the hills of South Wales. But she never reached her destination alive. A blizzard overtook her and a search party later found her frozen beneath the snow.

The searchers were surprised that she did not have outer garments on, but soon discovered why. She had wrapped them around her baby. When they unwrapped the child, they found baby David Lloyd George alive and well.

David Lloyd George grew up to become the prime minister of Great Britain during World War I and one of England's great statesmen. The vital contribution which he made to humanity was possible because his mother had given her life to save him.—*B. Charles Hostetter, Christian Life*

2150   *Put Down*

George Bernard Shaw once boasted that he knew how to make an excellent cup of coffee. A country parson wrote to him for the recipe. Shaw wrote it out, but, true to character, he ended his letter: "I hope that this is a genuine request, and not a surreptitious mode of securing my autograph."

The parson's reply: "Accept my thanks for the recipe for making coffee. I wrote in good faith and, in order to convince you of that fact, allow me to return what it is obvious you infinitely prize, but which is of no value to me—your autograph."

2151 *Silent Men*

Some men of history won fame because they didn't talk much. They said little and did much. They were not morose or unsocial. They were simply not loquacious.

George Washington was one of the silent men of our American scene. He talked when necessary, was not hesitant when directions were to be given or advice sought, but the famed Virginian was not given to small talk, nor noted as a conversationalist.

Lincoln had his silent hours when he appeared to be withdrawn from the social chatter about him, and was not of the mind to relate incidents of old Indiana and Illinois days. He had his brooding periods, which on occasion were shrouded in deep melancholy.

Inspirational Quotations and Illustrations

2152   *Sixty—the Happy Age*

A wise old gentleman of eighty tells his friends as they reach sixty: "You have spent sixty years in preparation for life; you will now begin to live. At sixty you have learned what is worthwhile. You have conquered the worst forms of foolishness. You have reached a 'balance' period of life, knowing good from evil, what is precious, what is worthless. Danger is past, the mind is peaceful, evil is forgiven, the affections are strong, envy is weak. It is the happy age."

2153   *A Baby*

A baby is God's opinion that life should go on.

Never will a time come when the most marvelous recent invention is as marvelous as a newborn baby.

The finest of our precision watches, the most super-colossal of our supercargo planes, don't compare with a newborn baby in the number and ingenuity of coils and springs, in the flow and change of chemical solutions, in timing devices and interrelated parts that are irreplaceable.—*Carl Sandburg*

2154   *That's All I Want*

One of the finest sermons ever preached was delivered by a little girl who was asked by her teacher to repeat the 23rd Psalm from memory. She didn't recite it as most of us know it, but what she said makes sense for our day and age. "The Lord is my shepherd," she began, "that's all I want."

2155 *The Foundation*

Without God there could be no American form of government, nor an American way of life. Recognition of the Supreme Being is the first—the most basic —expression of Americanism. Thus the founding fathers of America saw it, and thus, with God's help, it will continue to be.—*Dwight D. Eisenhower*

2156 *Give Thanks Every Day*

It is good that we should set aside a day in each year for Thanksgiving, but it would be better if we gave thanks every day. For the absence of thankfulness does not mean that we are merely ungrateful—it means that we are missing the thrill of appreciation and pleasure. There seems to me no greater misfortune than having so much that all of it becomes meaningless; than wanting what you haven't, rather than what you have. Seven of the wisest words I know are, "Only those are rich who desire little."—*Channing Pollock*

2157 *No Nobler Venture*

Here, under cover of darkness, the fast-dwindling company laid their dead, leveling the earth above them lest the Indians should know how many were the graves. Reader! History records no nobler venture for faith and freedom than of this Pilgrim band. In weariness and painfulness, in watching, often in hunger and cold, they laid the foundations of a state wherein every man, through countless ages, should have liberty to worship God in his own way. May their example inspire thee to do thy part in perpetuating and spreading the lofty ideals of our republic throughout the world!—*Inscription on Plymouth Rock Monument*

2158 *Memorial Day*

Memorial Day is a good time to remember our wonderful heritage and some of the blessings we so take for granted. We often treat with indifference the sound foundations of our nation's life that were laid by consecrated and industrious hands. We should be grateful for our Constitution which has safeguarded our liberty and not allowed it to be destroyed by malicious minds or by those blinded by prejudice.

We have come into the heritage of our nation and have with little effort or sacrifice become sharers of its wealth and partakers of its honor. Every day is not too often to remember the men of vision who bought our liberty, and particularly should they be remembered on Memorial Day.

2159 *The Cost*

We have enjoyed so much freedom for so long that we are perhaps in danger of forgetting how much blood it cost to establish the Bill of Rights.—*Felix Frankfurter*

2160   *Our Past*

If only we are faithful to our past, we shall not have to fear our future.—*John Foster Dulles*

2161   *Our Heritage*

Every man has leaned upon the past. Every liberty we enjoy has been bought at incredible cost. There is not a privilege nor an opportunity that is not the product of other men's labors. We drink every day from wells we have not dug; we live by liberties we have not won; we are protected by institutions we have not set up. No man lives by himself alone. All the past is invested in lives of others.—*Dr. Thomas Gibbs*

2162   *The American Idea*

As the world hums with the rising clamor of confusing opinion and propaganda, ever more positively, skillfully, dominantly presented, it is imperative that you and I understand clearly the significance of our citizenship and the American idea upon which it is firmly based.

For there *is* an American idea.

It came with the Pilgrim Fathers and the William Tells of many races, who found homes here.

It took as its emblem the freedom of the eagle and the independence of the pioneer.

It overleapt the hurdles that had blocked human progress in many other lands for centuries.

It blew through the sordid runways of outworn civilizations with the cleanness of mountain winds.

It amazed the world with the rich outpourings of its untrammeled spirit.

It made men cry: "Give me liberty or give me death."

It dedicated itself in strength, humility, and tolerance, to the care of the needy and sick in this land and in all others.

It brought forth a beneficent downpouring of free thought, free speech, a free press, and a free pulpit.

It proclaimed the dignity of labor and the right to the profits of personal effort.

It erected the little white church and synagogue in 250,000 communities.

It created a nation of men with free bodies, free minds, free opinions, and free souls.

It brought forth, in only 200 years, the greatest wealth and the highest standard of living any people in history have ever known.

That is the American idea.—*Herbert V. Prochnow*

2163   *A Wise Man's Prayer*

A wise man's prayer: "O God, give the world common sense, beginning with me."

2164   *The Joy of Giving*

Helen Hunt Jackson once wrote: "If you love me, tell me so. The realm of silence is large enough beyond the grave." Give "flowers" to the living. Praise the one who does something good and worthy—and do it today!

The one thing we know definitely is that love, only if it is expressed, grows and gives out fragrance all about it here in this life. One of the greatest joys of life is to give, and giving is in itself flavored with divinity.

2165   *Understanding*

A woman bought eggs and butter from a farmer who had a fine reputation not only for the quality of his products, but also for his promptness of delivery. Then one day, when she was expecting guests, he failed to come. On the next delivery she spoke harshly to him. At the end of her tirade he said quietly, "I'm sorry if I caused you any inconvenience, but I had the misfortune of burying my mother yesterday."

Ashamed, the woman determined never to speak harshly to anyone again until she fully understood the cause of the delay.—*Rev. A. Purnell Bailey*

2166   *Hard Work and Determination*

The pioneers cleared the forests from Jamestown to the Mississippi with less tools than are stored in the typical modern garage.—*Dwayne Laws*

2167   *Religion*

The problem of religion is to induce people to practice in their daily lives what they say in church they believe.

2168   *Faith*

Belief in God is acceptance of the basic principles that the universe makes sense, that there is behind it an ultimate purpose.—*Carl Wallace Miller: A Scientist's Approach to Religion*

2169   *One Vote*

Thomas Jefferson was elected President by just one vote in the Electoral College. So was John Quincy Adams. Rutherford B. Hayes was elected President by just one vote. His election was contested and referred to an electoral commission. Again he won by a single vote.

The man who cast that deciding vote for President Hayes was a lawyer from Indiana who was elected to Congress by the margin of just one vote. That one vote was cast by a client of his who, though desperately ill, insisted on being taken to the polls to cast that one vote.—*Americans Will Vote, Inc.*

2170 Kindness

The extraordinary thing about kindness is that the more you expend, the richer you become. Try it. Do a little quiet thinking about people around you. Make an effort to understand them better; then take the trouble to speak words that may lift their spirit, enhance their self-respect. You can never guess what a few kind words sincerely spoken may do for them—and for you.—*The Little Gazette*

2171 Thanksgiving

Tell us, Lord, what is it we should say
Of gratitude on this our thankful day?
Should prayers of thanks for food and health be said?
But DAILY prayers are for our daily bread.
No, this day calls for more than that—
A heart-deep, lasting, grateful thought
For inspiration, soaring, trouble-proof,
That You have given for a perplexed life.
This time of mem'ry of our origins,
Of folk whose faithful works outweigh their sins,
Who stood firm-rooted in their trust in You
Gives cause for deep rejoicing; it is true
Man can stand with fearless dignity
Amid his trials and turmoils sturdily
If, truly, reverence is his attitude.
For this sure knowledge, Lord, our gratitude.
                                        —*John A. Howard*

2172 Waiting

Too many are waiting for God to do something for them rather than with them.—*Ralph W. Sockman*

2173 Benefits from Adversity

It is not good for all your wishes to be filled; through sickness you recognize the value of health; through evil, the value of good; through hunger, satisfaction; through exertion, the value of rest.—*From an old Greek Book of Wisdom*

2174 *A Day for Thanksgiving and Praise*

His heart wrung with anguish over the suffering and death of so many Americans on the battlefields of the Blue and the Gray, President Abraham Lincoln still found much to thank Almighty God for in the grim October days of 1863, in a Thanksgiving Day Proclamation that has significance and meaning for all of us today.

Said the great Lincoln:

"The year that is drawing to its close has been filled with the blessings of fruitful fields and healthful skies. To these bounties, which are so constantly enjoyed that we are prone to forget the source from which they come, others have been added which are of so extraordinary a nature that they cannot fail to penetrate and soften the heart which is habitually insensible to the ever watchful providence of Almighty God. . . .

"Needful diversions of wealth and strength from the fields of peaceful industry to the national defense have not arrested the plow, the shuttle, or the ship. . . . Population has steadily increased. . . .

"No human counsel hath devised, nor hath any mortal hand worked out these great things. They are the gracious gifts of the Most High God, who, while dealing with us in anger for our sins, hath nevertheless remembered mercy.

"It has seemed to me fit and proper that they should be solemnly, reverently, and gratefully acknowledged as with one heart and one voice by the whole American people . . . by a day of Thanksgiving and praise to our beneficent Father who dwelleth in the Heavens. . . ."

2175 *Wealth*

The best definition of wealth is the possession of whatever gives us happiness, contentment, or a sense of one's significance in the scheme of things.—*Ernest Watson*

2176 *An Unexpected Answer*

Who owns American business? Many people have misconceptions about it.

Most people will answer, "the rich," "the elite," "two percent of the population," or something similar. But those people are wrong.

The correct answer is that a majority of Americans have a piece of the action —and many of them don't even know it. The fact is, private employee pension funds now own more than one third of business and industry, and it's predicted that in a few years will control fifty percent.

Every person who has a life-insurance policy also has a stake in business because of his insurance company's corporate holdings.

Then there are Employee Stock Ownership Plans which encourage employees to buy stock in the company where they work.

Ask yourself again: Who owns American business? If you fit into any of the categories above, the answer is: You do.—*Sunshine Magazine*

2177   *Long May It Wave*

The American flag which flies above public and private buildings all over the country is the twenty-seventh version of "The Stars and Stripes." A year following our national Bicentennial was the two-hundredth anniversary of the flag. It was on June 14, 1977, that Congress passed the "Flag Resolution," which consists of a single sentence: "Resolved that the flag of the United States be made of thirteen stripes, alternating red and white, that the union be thirteen stars, white in a blue field representing a new constellation."

Because there were no details, there were many variations of this country's first official flag, and it has changed numerous times until 1960, when the change was made following the admission of Hawaii, the fiftieth state.

2178   *The Amazing Patriot*

Who engraved the plates for the first paper money issued by the Continental Congress?

Who supervised the manufacture of gunpowder for the Continental army, and also cast cannon for it?

Who perfected the process of forging malleable copper and set up the first copper rolling mill in America?

Who produced the copper sheathing, bolts, spikes, and brass work for the frigate *Constitution* ("Old Ironsides")?

Who made the boilers for Robert Fulton's Hudson River steam ferryboats?

The answer to each is the night-riding hero of Longfellow's poem, Paul Revere.

It was written of Paul Revere: "He was a man of such numerous abilities and achievements that there will likely never be another like him." Such extravagant praise was not unmerited. To catalog all his astonishing accomplishments is difficult. To remember him only as a patriotic horseman riding down the centuries in a childish poem is indeed unworthy. Patriot, artist, technician, inventor, industrial pioneer—he combined them all into one useful American citizen with his ability always at the service of his country.

2179   *A Better Version*

At a family reunion the discussion turned to "Live each day as though it were your last."

"Well," said a grandmother, "that's a fine idea, but I have always lived by one that is slightly different. It's this: Treat all the people you meet each day as though it were their last day on earth."—*The Grain and Feed Merchant*

2180 Men Will Fly

In the year 1870 the Methodists in Indiana were having a Conference. (This is a true story.) At their annual conference, the Bishop was presiding and he was asking for some kind of interpretation of events, and the president of the college where they were meeting stood up and said, "I think we are in a very exciting age." (This is 1870, you must remember.)

The Bishop asked, "What do you see?"

The college president, who had a science background, said, "I believe we are coming into a time when we will see, for example, wonderful inventions. I believe men will fly through the air like birds." (1870, mind you.)

The Bishop said, "This is heresy, this is blasphemy; I read in my Bible that flight is reserved for the angels. We will have no such talk here in my area."

This Bishop, whose name was Wright, went home to his two small sons, Orville and Wilbur.—*Bruce Larson, clergyman*

2181 Every Person's Welfare

Morality requires that people we don't know should not be considered as strangers. That applies equally to those who are worse than strangers to us, because we feel an aversion toward them, or because they have shown hostility to us. Even such people we must treat as our friends. In the last analysis, the commandment of love means this: No one is a stranger to you; every man's welfare is your concern.—*Albert Schweitzer*

2182 Love

Albert Schweitzer was once asked which he considered the most important of the Ten Commandments. "Christ gave only one Commandment," he said, "and that was Love."

2183 It Is a Mistake

It is a mistake to believe that international friendship can be secured through gifts rather than through genuine common principles and purposes.

It is a mistake to believe that the moral character of a nation as a whole can be better than the moral character of its citizens as individuals.

It is a mistake to believe that if we keep experimenting long enough we will find a substitute for an honest day's work.

It is a mistake to believe that shorter hours and less work will produce a higher standard of living.

It is a mistake to believe that stealing is not stealing when the majority of voters vote in favor of it.

It is a mistake to believe that government can give things to the people without first taking it away from the people.—*Sunshine Magazine*

2184   *The True Christmas Spirit*

The annual Christmas playlet was the order of the day at a private school, and the coach chose an amiable, beautifully brought-up boy of seven to play the role of the innkeeper at Bethlehem.

The boy had trouble learning to turn away Mary and Joseph with a curt: "There is no room at the inn," but had his part down pat by the end of the rehearsal period.

Then came the big night, with his proud mother and father beaming at him from the first row. He boomed out his "There is no room at the inn" with great authority, but then he couldn't resist adding, "But come in, anyhow, and have some cookies and milk."—*Sunshine Magazine*

2185   *Wrong Emphasis*

Birds build their nests, rear their young, and make their annual flights to other climes. But so far as is known, no bird ever tried to build more nests than its neighbors; and no fox ever fretted because he had only one hole in the earth in which to hide; and no squirrel ever died in anxiety lest he should not lay up enough nuts for two winters instead of one; and no dog ever lost sleep over the fact that he did not have enough bones buried in the ground for his declining years. So we may put the emphasis upon the wrong things.—*Religious Telescope*

2186   *Be Thankful for Work*

Thank God every morning when you get up that you have something to do which must be done, whether you like it or not. Being forced to work, and forced to do your best, will breed in you temperance and self-control, diligence and strength of will, cheerfulness and content, and a hundred virtues which the idle never know.—*Charles Kingsley*

2187   *Try Praise*

In marriage, with children, at work, in any association—an ounce of praise, of sincere appreciation of some act or attribute, can very often do more than a ton of fault-finding. If we look for it we can usually find, in even the most unlikely, unlikable, and incapable person, something to commend and encourage. Doubtless it is a human frailty, but most of us, in the glow of feeling we have pleased, want to do more to please, and knowing we have done well, want to do better.—*Sunshine Magazine*

2188   *An Old-Fashioned American*

I believe in America. I believe it became great because of its faith in God, its hope for independence, and its love of freedom.

I am grateful for America's glorious past; I am awed by its unbelievable present; I am confident of its limitless future.

Like millions of Americans, I want a free choice, not a free handout. I prefer an opportunity to prove my abilities on the job rather than a license to demonstrate my frustrations in the street.

I am an old-fashioned American with a newfound determination to do my part to make democracy work.—*Sunshine Magazine*

2189   *Individual Responsibility*

Arthur B. Motley, publisher, once said: "All the freedom man has achieved to date has been achieved only because individuals accepted responsibility, assumed obligations, performed on promises, and delivered to the rest of mankind whatever gifts and talent with which they were endowed.

"For those in future generations who would be free and help others achieve freedom, there is no other course except to live our daily lives as individuals responsible for our own morals, our own character, our own family, our own industry, our own jobs."—*Sunshine Magazine*

2190   *For Their Souls*

We on this continent should never forget that men first crossed the Atlantic not to find soil for their plows but to secure liberty for their souls.—*Robert J. McCracken*

2191   *A Reason for Thanksgiving*

Throughout the history of our country, the reasons for celebrating days of Thanksgiving were varied, but each one was a good one and showed the relief of the colonists from anxieties. Early records show that most of the days were observed because of the bringing of food to settlements where the people were half starved. Other days were because of the coming of new colonists and much-needed craftsmen, and the arrival of ships with cattle and utensils badly needed. Whatever the reason, the colonists felt impelled to pause to give thanks for what they had received.—*Sunshine Magazine*

2192   *Our Flag*

This flag, which we honor and under which we serve, is the emblem of our unity, our power, our thought and purpose as a nation.

It has no other character than that which we give it from generation to generation.

The choices are ours.

It floats in majestic silence above the hosts that execute these choices, whether in peace or war.

And yet, though silent, it speaks to us—speaks to us of the past, of the men and women who went before us, and of the records they wrote upon it.— *Woodrow Wilson*

2193   *Her Finals*

Two little girls were discussing their families. "Why does your grandmother read the Bible so much?" asked one. Replied the other, "I think she's cramming for her finals."

2194   *A Prayer for Today*

This is the beginning of a new day. God has given me this day to use as I will. I can waste it—or use it for good, but what I do today is important, because I am exchanging a day of my life for it! When tomorrow comes, this day will be gone forever, leaving in its place something that I have traded for it. I want it to be gain, and not loss; good, and not evil; success, and not failure; in order that I shall not regret the price that I have paid for it.—*W. Heartsill Wilson, Young Employee News*

2195   *The Winter Is Past*

For, lo, the winter is past, the rain is over and gone; the flowers appear on the earth; the time of the singing of birds is come, and the voice of the turtle is heard in our land; the fig tree putteth forth her green figs, and the vines with the tender grape give a good smell. . . .

Awake, O north wind; and come, thou south; blow upon my garden, that the spices thereof may flow out.—*Song of Solomon 2:11–13, 4:16*

2196   *Understanding*

While on a walk one day, I was surprised to see a man hoeing his garden while sitting in a chair. "What laziness!" I thought. But suddenly I saw, leaning against his chair, a pair of crutches. The man was at work despite his handicap. The lesson I learned about snap judgments that day has stayed with me for years now: the crosses people bear are seldom in plain sight.—*Annette Ashe, Guideposts*

2197   *The Heaviest Burden*

Life's heaviest burden is to have nothing to carry.

2198   *The Family*

The traditional family—consisting of parents who consider themselves bonded for life and for whom children are a responsibility—is the best teacher of morality. The family is the building block of society, and even one family can make a difference.—*Ted Ward, Michigan State University*

2199   *Parents*

The greatest tragedy today is that parents themselves are so often without any convincing standards to offer for the guidance of their children. They have the sextant but no fixed star, the technique but no destiny, the material but no blueprints, the means but no ends.—*Bishop Fulton J. Sheen*

2200   *Not to Stay*

An old man surprised everyone with his continual cheerfulness since he seemed to have an unusual amount of trouble and relatively few pleasures. When asked the secret of his cheery disposition, he replied, "Well, you see, it's like this. The Bible says often 'And it came to pass,' but never says 'It came to stay.' "

2201   *A Peter Marshall Prayer*

The late Peter Marshall gave our country this prayer: "Lord, help me to admit when I am wrong, and make me easier to live with when I am right."

2202   *What It Takes*

It does not take great men to do great things; it only takes consecrated men.
—*Phillips Brooks*

2203   *A Great Professor*

A sociable professor with grown children, living near us, was raking his front yard, when a group of neighborhood children happened by and offered to help. From time to time the professor made interesting comments and sustained their interest to such an extent that when the job was done each child said, "Thank you for letting me help."

Next morning early, the professor's doorbell rang. His wife opened the door to a five-year-old girl, one of the helpers of the previous day. The little girl smiled and said shyly, "Can he come out to play?"

2204   *A New Year*

Chronology, the science of time, is something we all think about when one year rolls away and another begins. We are a year older in this arbitrary division we make of nights and days. Few people like it. Philip James Bailey, a nineteenth-century poet, tells us that years are no way of reckoning time:

We live in deeds, not years; in thoughts, not breaths;
In feelings, not in figures on a dial.
We should count time by heart-throbs. He most lives
Who thinks most—feels the noblest—acts the best.

2205   *Wisdom*

You can preach a better sermon with your life than you can with your lips.
The best way to ease your troubles is to ease the troubles of others.

2206   *The Fifth Verse of "America"*

The hymn we know as "America" or, as it sometimes appears, under the title
"My Country, 'Tis of Thee," was written by Samuel F. Smith (1808–1895). To
its four verses Henry Wadsworth Longfellow (1807–1882) added this fifth verse,
which is a most appropriate prayer for our time:

Lord, let war's tempest cease,
Fold the whole world in peace
Under Thy wings.
Make all the nations one,
All hearts beneath the sun,
Till Thou shall reign alone,
Great King of Kings.

2207   *Bible*

A young woman said to an elderly friend: "I like reading"—she mentioned
three or four best-selling novels—"but I find the Bible very dull." "My dear,"
the friend replied, "the other night I went to the movies. There was a glorious
racket. Trains whizzed past, people escaped from windows, there was no end of
hue and cry; and I was excited and thrilled. When I came out it was a lovely
night, with the moon and the stars shining bright above me; and I was not
interested a bit!"—*Robert J. McCracken*

2208   *Refusing Responsibility*

"If" is a negative word. We hear so many men and women lamenting their
lack of progress and happiness by its use: "If I had a new car; if I were twenty
years younger; if I had a better education; if I had a decent boss; if I had better
health." They hope to weather their sense of failure by refusing to acknowledge
that they have any responsibility for it.

2209   *Cosmetics*

A dear old Quaker lady was asked to explain her obviously youthful appearance, her appealing vivacity, and her winning charm. She replied sweetly, "I used
for the lips—truth; for the voice—prayer; for the eyes—pity; for the hands—

charity; for the figure—uprightness; for the heart—love." How's that for a makeup kit?—*Rabbi Abraham R. Besdin*

2210   *I Can*

All of the progress of civilization is due to the constructive thinking of people. The record of history is brilliant with the deeds of men and women who said "I can," while it is silent for the most part concerning those who said "I can't." Positive people believe that it is better to fail in carrying out a project than to not fail because they have not tried.—*The Royal Bank of Canada Monthly Letter*

2211   *Good Night*

List, good people all!
Past ten o'clock the hour I call.
Now say your prayers and take your rest,
With conscience clear and sins confessed.
I bid you all good night! Good night!
—*The Town Crier*

2212   *A Prayer*

I asked God for strength, that I might achieve,
I was made weak, that I might learn humbly to obey. . . .
I asked for health, that I might do greater things,
I was given infirmity, that I might do better things. . . .
I asked for riches, that I might be happy,
I was given poverty that I might be wise. . . .
I asked for power, that I might have the praise of men,
I was given weakness, that I might feel the need of God. . . .
I asked for all things, that I might enjoy life,
I was given life, that I might enjoy all things. . . .
I got nothing that I asked for—but everything I had hoped for,
Almost despite myself, my unspoken prayers were answered.
I am among all men, most richly blessed.
—*Prayer of an unknown Confederate soldier, reprinted on the*
greeting cards of Democratic Presidential candidate Adlai E.
Stevenson, Christmas 1955. Time, January 2, 1956

2213   *The Despair of Loneliness*

One evening in 1808 a gaunt, sad-faced man entered the offices of Dr. James Hamilton in Manchester, England. The doctor was struck by the melancholy appearance of his visitor. He inquired:
"Are you sick?"

"Yes, Doctor, sick of a mortal malady."

"What malady?"

"I am frightened of the terror of the world around me. I am depressed by life. I can find no happiness anywhere, nothing amuses me, and I have nothing to live for. If you can't help me, I shall kill myself."

"The malady is not mortal. You only need to get out of yourself. You need to laugh; to get some pleasure from life."

"What shall I do?"

"Go to the circus tonight to see Grimaldi, the clown. Grimaldi is the funniest man alive. He'll cure you."

A spasm of pain crossed the poor man's face as he said: "Doctor, don't jest with me: I am Grimaldi."—*John Summerfield Wimbish*

2214 No Duties

Phillips Brooks, returning from a trip to the Far East, was asked about what articles he had brought back with him and what customs duty he had to pay. The friend, facetiously, asked him too if he had tried to bring back a new religion. Brooks replied that he had not tried to do so; but if he had done so, there would have been no difficulty about customs duties, for America would be glad to import a religion "without any duties."—*Clarence Edward Macartney*

2215 How Is Mr. Adams?

A young woman once stopped John Quincy Adams on the street to ask, "And how is Mr. Adams today?" The elderly statesman was then ninety-one years of age. He replied somewhat like this: "Mr. Adams is very well, thank you. It is true that his house is falling apart. The foundations have settled, the rafters sag and the roof leaks a bit. He will be moving out almost any day now. But Mr. Adams is well, thank you, very well." Life had taught him, as it does all who grow up in faith, to believe in what lies beyond the rim of the visible.—*Kenneth Hildebrand*

2216 Faith

Whatever happens, abide steadfast in a determination to cling simply to God. —*Francis of Sales*

2217 Life

Life is a voyage that's homeward bound.—*Herman Melville*

2218 Our Minds

Our minds have unbelievable power over our bodies.—*André Maurois*

2219   *Courage*

Keep your fears to yourself, but share your courage with others.—*Robert Louis Stevenson*

2220   *Press Forward*

This one thing I do, forgetting those things which are behind. . . . I press toward the mark. . . .—*Philippians 3:13, 14*

2221   *Industry and Genius*

After a great deal of experience and observation, I have become convinced that industry is a better horse to ride than genius. It may never carry any man as far as genius has carried individuals, but industry—patient, steady, intelligent industry—will carry thousands into comfort, and even celebrity.—*Walter Lippmann*

2222   *A Weakness*

One of the weaknesses of our age is our apparent inability to distinguish our need from our greed.

2223   *No Substitute*

History teaches us that there is no substitute for the family if we are to have a society that stands for human beings at their best.—*Ray Lyman Wilbur*

2224   *Family*

To bring up a child in the way he should go, travel that way yourself once in a while.—*Josh Billings*

2225   *The Spirit*

If wrinkles must be written upon our brows, let them not be written upon the heart. The spirit should not grow old.—*James A. Garfield*

2226   *Liberty and the Rights of Man*

God grant that not only the love of liberty but a thorough knowledge of the rights of man may pervade all the nations of the earth, so that a philosopher may set his foot anywhere on its surface and say: "This is my country!"—*Benjamin Franklin*

2227   *One World*

I believe that our Great Maker is preparing the world, in His own good time, to become one nation, speaking one language, and then armies and navies will be no longer required.—*Ulysses S. Grant*

2228   *Today*

If we are ever to enjoy life, now is the time—not tomorrow, nor next year, nor in some future life after we have died. The best preparation for a better life next year is a full, complete, harmonious, joyous life this year. Today should always be our most wonderful day.—*Thomas Dreier*

2229   *Endure*

When the day returns, call us up with morning faces and with morning hearts, eager to labor, happy if happiness be our portion, and if the day be marked for sorrow, strong to endure.—*Robert Louis Stevenson*

2230   *Time*

There is nothing of which we are apt to be so lavish as of time, and about which we ought to be more solicitous; since without it we can do nothing in this world. —*William Penn*

2231   *Difficulties*

To strive with difficulties, and to conquer them, is the highest human felicity. —*Samuel Johnson*

2232   *Education*

Perhaps the most valuable result of all education is the ability to make yourself do the thing you have to do, when it ought to be done, whether you like it or not. It is the first lesson that ought to be learned.—*Thomas H. Huxley*

2233   *Confidence and Achievement*

So long as one does not despair, so long as one doesn't look upon life bitterly, things work out fairly well in the end.—*George Moore*

2234   *Unless*

No one is ever beaten unless he gives up the fight.—*W. Beran Wolfe*

2235   *Self-Discipline and the Development of Character*

I hope I shall always possess firmness and virtue enough to maintain what I consider the most enviable of all titles, the character of an "honest man."— *George Washington*

2236   *God's Work*

An honest man's the noblest work of God.—*Alexander Pope*

2237   *Honor*

To me the highest thing, after God, is my honor.—*Ludwig van Beethoven*

2238   *When You Give*

You give but little when you give of your possessions. It is when you give of yourself that you truly give.—*Kahlil Gibran*

2239   *The Family*

Families are enduring institutions. They have been the foundation for virtually every society known to history. They possess incredible strength and resiliency, especially when faced with adversity. The American people are a loving people. We cherish family life.—*Walter Mondale*

2240   *Brief Life*

Life is too short to be little.—*Benjamin Disraeli*

2241   *Peace*

Happy the man, of mortals happiest he,
Whose quiet mind from vain desires is free;
Whom neither hopes deceive, nor fears torment,
But lives at peace, within himself content.
                    —*George Granville*

2242   *In a Lifetime*

During one's lifetime a person may be rated by the number who serve him, but after his passing he is measured by the number he served.

Napoleon made himself master of France and most of Europe by the power of his marching legions, but Louis Pasteur made himself the servant of France and the world in fighting the germs of disease, and Pasteur outlives Napoleon.

Mussolini dominated Italy for a decade, and was dishonored. Signor Marconi put his electrical wizardry at the service of his nation and the world and is still honored.

Some nations go into Africa to divide and dominate, while Schweitzer devoted his life to healing the natives of Africa.

"Whosoever would be great among you, let him be your servant."

2243   *Not the Difficulties*

Meeting difficulties with courage and overcoming handicaps make character. It is not the difficulties, but the power gained by rising above them, that builds greatness and a place of leadership.

2244   *Materialism*

We are in the grip of a scientific materialism, caught in a vicious cycle where our security today seems to depend on regimentation and weapons which will ruin us tomorrow.—*Charles A. Lindbergh*

2245   *Politeness*

A polite man is one who listens with interest to things he knows all about, when they are told to him by a person who knows very little about them.

2246   *A Character Quiz—*
   1. If you found a pocketbook with $1,000, would you give it to the owner if no one would ever know you found it?
   2. If you could advance yourself by unfair methods, would you do it if no one would ever find out you were unfair?
   3. If the bus driver failed to collect your fare, would you voluntarily pay it?
   4. If there were no locks on any house, store, or bank, would you take anything if no one would ever find out?
   5. If your business partner died, would you pay his relatives their fair share, if you did not have to pay them?
   6. If you are an employer trying to hire an efficient, honest, and competent employee, would you hire yourself at your salary?
   7. If you are an employer, would you like to be working for yourself with the wages, hours, and working conditions you provide?
   8. If you are a parent, would you like to be the child of a parent just like you are?
   9. If you had your choice, would you like to live in a community with people working in church, civic, and community affairs just like you do?
   10. If you had to live with someone just like you are for the rest of your life, would you look forward to it as a wonderful opportunity and privilege?—*Herbert V. Prochnow*

2247   *The Tiredness Is Gone*

We are told that one of the Indian translations of the 23rd Psalm, instead of saying, "Thou anointest my head with oil," says, "He lays His hand upon my head and all the tiredness is gone."

2248   *The Pilgrims' Feast*

Those who may sometimes feel that all is lost, and civilization is doomed, should pull up their chairs to the first Christmas dinner on the *Mayflower.* It was December 25, and it had taken the Pilgrims sixty-three days to cross the Atlantic

—seventy-three men, twenty-nine women, and twenty children. They had landed only four days before. Not a chimney smoked, from their stern and rockbound coast clear through the wilderness to Puget Sound. But there was no wilderness in the hearts of those people. They celebrated Christmas as a day of hope and promise.

The frugal meal was eaten on the ship. What they ate we do not know. All they had was salt beef, ship biscuits, and dried peas. But they had something else —freedom!

2249   *A Bright Side*

There is a bright side to headaches. It has been estimated that the purveyors of various headache remedies are doing millions of dollars' worth of business every year. In other words, every headache contributes something to the prosperity of the country!

2250   *Character*

Someday, in years to come, you will be wrestling with the great temptation, or trembling under the great sorrow of your life. But the real struggle is here, now, in these quiet weeks. Now it is being decided whether, in the day of your supreme sorrow or temptation, you shall miserably fail or gloriously conquer. Character cannot be made except by a steady, long-continued process.—*Phillips Brooks*

2251   *The Right Estimate*

Humility is to make a right estimate of one's self.—*Charles Haddon Spurgeon*

2252   *The Best*

The fact that people do not understand and respect the very best things, such as Mozart's concertos, is what permits men like us to become famous.—*Johannes Brahms*

2253   *The Difference*

What makes the difference between a nation that is truly great and one that is merely rich and powerful? It is the simple things that make the difference. Honesty, knowing right from wrong, openness, self-respect, and the courage of conviction.—*Governor David L. Boren*

2254   *Misfortune*

If all our misfortunes were laid in one common heap whence everyone must take an equal portion, most people would be contented to take their own and depart.—*Socrates*

2255　　*Remembering*

To be wronged is nothing unless you continue to remember it.—*Confucius*

2256　　*Revenge*

Never does the human soul appear so strong as when it forgoes revenge, and dares forgive an injury.—*E. H. Chapin*

2257　　*Responsibility*

The reason parents no longer lead their children in the right direction is because the parents aren't going that way themselves.—*Kin Hubbard*

2258　　*Life Is Sacred*

A man is ethical only when life, as such, is sacred to him, that of plants and animals as well as that of his fellow man, and when he devotes himself helpfully to all life that is in need of help.—*Albert Schweitzer*

2259　　*The Aim*

The aim of education is the knowledge not of fact, but of values.—*W. R. Inge, Dean of St. Paul's*

2260　　*The Objectives*

Education today, more than ever before, must see clearly the dual objectives: education for living and educating for making a living.—*James Mason Wood*

2261　　*Be Careful*

Don't ever slam a door; you might want to go back.—*Don Herold*

2262　　*Honest Toil*

The truly American sentiment recognizes the dignity of labor and the fact that honor lies in honest toil.—*Grover Cleveland*

2263　　*Too Wonderful*

Goodbye . . . Goodbye to clocks ticking . . . and Mama's sunflowers. And food and coffee. And new-ironed dresses and hot baths . . . and sleeping and waking up. Oh, earth, you're too wonderful for anybody to realize you.—*Thornton Wilder*

2264　　*Essentials*

The grand essentials to happiness in this life are something to do, something to love, and something to hope for.—*Joseph Addison*

2265   *Pleasure*

The more a man finds his sources of pleasure in himself, the happier he will be. . . .—*Arthur Schopenhauer*

2266   *Prayer*

The sovereign cure for worry is prayer.—*William James*

2267   *It Will Pass*

As certain as stars at night, or dawn after darkness,
Inherent as the lift of the blowing grass,
Whatever your despair or your frustration—
This, too, will pass.
                                        —*Grace Noll Crowell*

2268   *In Your Power*

Make the best use of what is in your power, and take the rest as it happens.
—*Epictetus*

2269   *"Doin' Purty Good"*

I'm jes' a-keepin' even, which is doin' purty good.
Haven't made a fortune that I used to hope I would.
Haven't caused the trump of fame o'er distant hills to sound,
But kin allus face the music when the landlord comes around.

I've had my share of sunshine, an' I seen the flowers smile;
Have the rheumatiz, but only fer a while.
An' when I come to quit the scene of hope, an' likewise doubt,
I'll hardly leave enough for lawyer folks to fight about.

I've had my disappointments, an' I've had my silent fears.
But I reckon that the laughs will easy balance all the tears.
It ain't a brilliant record, but I want it understood
That I'm still a-keepin' humpin', which is doin' purty good!
                                        —*Sunshine Magazine*

2270   *A Drop of Water*

The power of ideals is incalculable. We see no power in a drop of water. But let it get into a crack in the rock and be turned into ice, and it splits the rock; turned into steam, it drives the pistons of the most powerful engines. Something has happened to it which makes active and effective the power that is latent in it.

So it is with ideals. Ideals are thoughts. So long as they exist merely as thoughts, the power latent in them remains ineffective, however great the enthusiasm and however strong the conviction with which the thought is held. Their power becomes effective only when they are taken up into some refined human personality.—*Albert Schweitzer*

2271   Education

The day after the circus came to town, a teacher received the following excuse for the absence of one of her pupils:

"Dear Teacher: Education, you know, is a lot of things. It is reading and writing and ciphering. It is 'yes, please' and 'yes, thanks,' and 'no, thank you.' It is the washing of our hands and the use of forks. It is pencils and scissors and paste and erasers and chalk dust. It is the excitement of vacations. It is autumn bonfires and sleds and puddle-wading.

"Education is a lot of things. It is a brass band blaring and a calliope tootling. Education is a woman shot from a cannon, a man on a tight rope, a seal playing a tune with his nose. It is sideshow barkers, clowns, lions, cotton candy, cowboys and spangles. Education is the wonderment of new things and new sensations. It is, in short, a circus!

"That's why Ginger wasn't in your classroom yesterday. Excuse it, please."
—*Sunshine Magazine*

2272   The Barefoot Boy

Blessings on thee, little man,
Barefoot boy with cheeks of tan!
Trudging down a dusty lane
With no thought of future pain;
You're our one and only bet
To absorb the national debt.
Little man, with cares so few,
We've a lot of faith in you;
Guard each merry whistled tune,
You are apt to need it soon. Have your fun now while you can;
You may be a barefoot man!

2273   Using Spare Time

Spare moments are the gold dust of time. Of all the portions of our life, the spare moments are the most fruitful in good or evil.

2274   Watch Your Words

A careless word may kindle strife;
A cruel word may wreck a life.
A bitter word may hate instill;
A brutal word may smite and kill.

A gracious word may smooth the way;
A joyous word may light the day.
A timely word may lessen stress;
A loving word may heal and bless.
                    —*Grenville Kleiser*

2275   *Savers*

There is a growing sentiment in America that regular saving should be ignored —that the government will take care of people when they get beyond a certain age. But it must be borne in mind that the people who earn and do save are the ones who take care of the government! Were it not for the thrifty and the willing worker, the government would be unable to take care of anybody.—*George Matthew Adams*

2276   *When God Measures*

When God measures a man, He puts the tape around the heart instead of the head.

2277   *Difficulties*

Many men owe the grandeur of their lives to their tremendous difficulties.—*Charles Haddon Spurgeon*

2278   *Great Deeds*

No great deed is done
By falterers who ask for certainty.
                    —*George Eliot*

2279   *One of the Best*

One of the best funeral orations of modern times was delivered by an American Indian standing by the grave of his chief. Here it is, beautiful, simple, true:

"You have merely lost the man. You still have the world in which he lived and which he so enjoyed. You still have its beauty and its loveliness, and you still have the blue skies to which he looked; you have the wind and the rain and the sun and the silvery moon. The stars still will glitter in the skies at night; the corn still will ripen; the deer will roam the forests of your fathers, and the fish will leap in the stream.

"The Great Spirit has only taken to Him the man. You lose only that. He will be happy there in the happy hunting grounds of our fathers. The great Spirit leaves all the other things and the memory of the son He has taken to His tepee."

2280   *In the Hearts of Children*

Great ideas and fine principles do not live from generation to generation just because they are good, nor because they have been carefully legislated. Ideals and principles continue from generation to generation only when they are built into the hearts of children as they grow up.—*Dr. George S. Benson*

2281   *Spring Once in a Century?*

I believe with Henry W. Longfellow that if Spring came but once in a century, instead of once a year, or burst forth with the sound of an earthquake, and not in silence, what wonder and expectation there would be in all hearts to behold the miraculous change! To most men only the cessation of the miracle would be miraculous, and the perpetual exercise of God's power seems less wonderful than its withdrawal would be.—*Sir Oracle*

2282   *Hope*

There is no medicine like hope, no incentive so great, and no tonic so powerful as expectation of something tomorrow.—*O. S. Marden*

2283   *Spring*

Spring—an experience in immortality.—*Henry David Thoreau*

2284   *Life Is*

Life just is. You have to flow with it. Give yourself to the moment. Let it happen.—*Governor Jerry Brown*

2285   *Live Life*

As I grow to understand life less and less, I learn to live it more and more. —*Jules Renard*

2286   *Beautiful*

The longer I live, the more beautiful life becomes.—*Frank Lloyd Wright*

2287   *Man*

Man—a being in search of meaning.—*Plato*

2288   *Marriage*

The great secret of successful marriage is to treat all disasters as incidents and none of the incidents as disasters.—*Harold Nicolson*

2289   *Our Young People*

Instead of casting a critical eye at our young people, it would be better for adults to stop and think what kind of a world we have built for our young people to live in. It is a world so full of tension and strife that it is difficult enough for grown-ups, much less youth, to feel secure.—*Billy Graham*

2290   *Inferior*

Remember, no one can make you feel inferior without your consent.—*Eleanor Roosevelt*

2291   *Thinking*

A great many people think they are thinking when they are merely rearranging their prejudices.—*William James*

2292   *Do What You Can*

Do what you can, with what you have, where you are.—*Theodore Roosevelt*

2293   *Last Judgment*

I shall tell you a great secret, my friend. Do not wait for the last judgment, it takes place every day.—*Albert Camus*

2294   *Know Your Bible*

A thorough knowledge of the Bible is worth more than a college education. —*Theodore Roosevelt*

2295   *The Bible*

When you have read the Bible, you will know it is the word of God, because you will have found it the key to your own heart, your own happiness, and your own duty.—*Woodrow Wilson*

2296   *Conscience*

In matters of conscience, the law of the majority has no place.—*Mohandas K. Gandhi*

2297   *Gratitude*

I remember those happy days and often wish I could speak into the ears of the dead the gratitude which was due to them in life and so ill-returned.—*Gwyn Thomas*

2298   *Equal*

Democracy means not "I'm as good as you are," but "You're as good as I am."
—*Theodore Parker*

2299   *Education*

The object of education is to prepare the young to educate themselves throughout their lives.—*Robert Maynard Hutchins*

2300   *You Can't Please Everybody*

I cannot give you the formula for success, but I can give you the formula for failure—which is: Try to please everybody.—*Herbert Bayard Swope*

2301   *Faith*

If the work of God could be comprehended by reason, it would be no longer wonderful, and faith would have no merit if reason provided proof.—*Pope Gregory I (St. Gregory the Great)*

2302   *To Pursue Fame*

Fame has also this great drawback, that if we pursue it we must direct our lives in such a way as to please the fancy of men, avoiding what they dislike and seeking what is pleasing to them.—*Baruch Spinoza*

2303   *Fame*

Passion for fame: a passion which is the instinct of all great souls.—*Edmund Burke*

2304   *Liberty*

The history of liberty is the history of resistance . . . [it is a] history of the limitation of governmental power.—*Woodrow Wilson*

2305   *To Be Useful*

When Henry Ford, on his seventy-fifth birthday, was asked when he planned to retire, he exclaimed: "I haven't given a bit of thought to it! I'm going to stay around as long as I can be of any use; and I want to be of use as long as I stay around!"

2306   *Greatness*

The price of greatness is responsibility.—*Winston Churchill*

2307   *Hard Work*

I studied the lives of great men and famous women, and I found that the men and women who got to the top were those who did the jobs they had in hand, with everything they had of energy and enthusiasm and hard work.—*Harry S Truman*

2308   *Happiness*

The greatest happiness you can have is knowing that you do not necessarily require happiness.—*William Saroyan*

2309   *Sin*

He that is without sin among you, let him first cast a stone.—*Jesus*

2310   *Useful*

No one is useless in this world who lightens the burdens of another.—*Charles Dickens*

2311   *Solitude*

One of the greatest necessities in America is to discover creative solitude.—*Carl Sandburg*

2312   *Suffering*

Out of suffering have emerged the strongest souls; the most massive characters are seared with scars.—*E. H. Chapin*

2313   *Wasted Hours*

I would I could stand on a busy corner, hat in hand, and beg people to throw me all their wasted hours.—*Bernard Berenson*

2314   *Old Values*

Today we are afraid of simple words like *goodness* and *mercy* and *kindness.* We don't believe in the good old words because we don't believe in the good old values anymore. And that's why the world is sick.—*Lin Yutang*

2315   *Aim High*

Make no little plans: they have no magic to stir men's blood. . . . Make big plans, aim high in hope and work.—*Daniel H. Burnham*

2316   *Loveliness*

What is lovely never dies,
But passes into other loveliness,
Star-dust or sea-foam, flower or winged air.
—*Thomas Bailey Aldrich*

2317   *Goodness*

Goodness is a special kind of truth and beauty. It is truth and beauty in human behavior.—*Harry Allen Overstreet*

2318   *Beauty*

Beauty is not immortal. In a day
Blossom and June and rapture pass away.
—*Arthur Stringer*

2319   *Aladdin's Lamp*

When I was a beggarly boy
And lived in a cellar damp,
I had not a friend nor a toy,
But I had Aladdin's lamp.
—*James Russell Lowell*

2320   *Natural Resource*

Children are our most valuable natural resource.—*Herbert Hoover*

2321   *A Child's Laugh*

One laugh of a child will make the holiest day more sacred still.—*Robert G. Ingersoll*

2322   *Dignity*

No race can prosper till it learns that there is as much dignity in tilling a field as in writing a poem.—*Booker T. Washington*

2323   *Virtue*

There was never yet a truly great man that was not at the same time truly virtuous.—*Benjamin Franklin*

2324   *Faith and Honor*

When faith is lost, when honor dies,
The man is dead!
—*John Greenleaf Whittier*

2325   *Humility*

Humility is the most difficult of all virtues to achieve; nothing dies harder than the desire to think well of oneself.—*T. S. Eliot*

2326   *Censure*

They have a right to censure, that have a heart to help.—*William Penn*

2327   *Help Us to Be Humble*

Why is there such a lack of grace today? There can only be one answer. The people have gotten away from humility. We must recognize it and face it. May God help us to be a humble people.—*Billy Graham*

2328   *Love's Cure*

There is no remedy for love but to love more.—*Henry David Thoreau*

2329   *Love Is Giving*

Love is not getting, but giving; not a wild dream of pleasure, and a madness of desire—oh, no, love is not that—it is goodness, and honor, and peace and pure living.—*Henry Van Dyke*

2330   *God Watches*

Behind the dim unknown,
Standeth God within the shadow, keeping watch above his own.
                                          —*James Russell Lowell*

2331   *Spring Showers*

And the glad earth, caressed by murmuring showers,
Wakes like a bride, to deck herself with flowers!
                                          —*Henry Sylvester Cornwell*

2332   *Understanding*

There is much satisfaction in work well done; praise is sweet; but there can be no happiness equal to the joy of finding a heart that understands.—*Victor Robinson*

2333   *America*

America means opportunity, freedom, power.—*Ralph Waldo Emerson*

2334   *A Tree*

> He that planteth a tree is the servant of God,
> He provideth a kindness for many generations,
> And faces that he hath not seen shall bless him.
> —*Henry Van Dyke*

2335   *Men with Purpose*

> Bring me men to match my mountains;
> Bring me men to match my plains,—
> Men with empires in their purpose,
> And new eras in their brains.
> —*Sam Walter Foss*

2336   *Blessings*

My God! how little do my countrymen know what precious blessings they are in possession of, and which no other people on earth enjoy!—*Thomas Jefferson*

2337   *A Choice*

America lives in the heart of every man everywhere who wishes to find a region where he will be free to work out his destiny as he chooses.—*Woodrow Wilson*

2338   *Destiny*

We recognize and accept our own deep involvement in the destiny of men everywhere.—*Dwight D. Eisenhower*

2339   *Greatest Test*

The greatest test of courage on earth is to bear defeat without losing heart.—*Robert G. Ingersoll*

2340   *Fear*

He has not learned the lesson of life who does not every day surmount a fear.—*Ralph Waldo Emerson*

2341   *Alone But for Faith*

Man is not born and does not die collectively. He enters this world and leaves it—alone. And through most of life's most meaningful experiences he is alone. Fortunate he is, in my judgment, whose aloneness is enveloped in a Faith that is abiding, satisfying, and inspiring.—*Milton S. Eisenhower*

2342   *Experience Fear*

You gain strength, courage, and confidence by every experience in which you really stop to look fear in the face.—*Eleanor Roosevelt*

2343   *We Give*

The only things we ever keep
Are what we give away.
                    —*Louis Ginsberg*

2344   *It's All Relative*

Give what you have. To someone, it may be better than you dare to think.—*Henry Wadsworth Longfellow*

2345   *In Kind*

One can never pay in gratitude; one can only pay "in kind" somewhere else in life.—*Anne Morrow Lindbergh*

2346   *Life*

Life is a mystery as deep as ever death can be;
Yet oh, how dear it is to us, this life we live and see!
                    —*Mary Mapes Dodge*

2347   *When a Father Prays*

This meaningful prayer eloquently expresses the heartfelt sentiments of a father for his son. It was reportedly written by General Douglas MacArthur and was often a part of his morning devotions:

"Build me a son, O Lord, who will be strong enough to know when he is weak, and brave enough to face himself when he is afraid; one who will be proud and unbending in honest defeat, but humble and gentle in victory.

"Build me a son whose wishes will not take the place of deeds, whose wishbone will not be where his backbone should be; a son who will know Thee—and that to know himself is the foundation stone of all true knowledge.

"Lead him, I pray, not in the paths of ease and comfort, but under the stress and spur of difficulties and challenge. Here let him learn to stand up in the storm; here let him learn compassion for those who fail.

"Build me a son whose heart will be clean, whose goal will be high; a son who will master himself before he seeks to master other men; one who will learn to laugh, yet never forget how to weep; one who will reach far into the future, yet never forget the past.

"And after all these things are his, add, I pray, enough of a sense of humor so that he may always be serious, yet never take himself too seriously. Give him a touch of humility, so that he may always remember the simplicity of true greatness, the open mind of true wisdom, and the meekness of true strength.

"Then, I, his father, will dare, in the sacred recesses of my own heart, to whisper, 'I have not lived in vain.' "—*Sunshine Magazine*

2348   *Five Magic Phrases*

1. Please.
2. Thank you.
3. I'm sorry.
4. Excuse me.
5. After you.

2349   *Life's Averages*

The best hitters in professional baseball have batting averages between .300 and .400. Out of every ten times they come up to the plate, they have to hit safely three or four times. And that's hitting!

But look at it another way. These great batters fail to hit more often than they hit. Time after time they step up to the plate and hit a grounder to an infielder, or fly out to an outfielder, or strike out.

All of which means one thing: success isn't figured by averages. Nobody will remember the times you struck out in the early innings—if you hit a home run with the bases full in the ninth.

2350   *Was This Your Boy?*

Lost! A boy! Not kidnaped by bandits and hidden in a cave to weep and starve and raise a nation to frenzied searching. No, his father lost him.

Too busy to sit with him at the fireside and answer his trivial questions during the years when Dad is the only great hero to a boy, he let go his hold.

His mother lost him, too. Engrossed in worthwhile programs, clubs with high aims, she let the baby-sitter hear his prayers and abdicated her place of influence.

2351   *Abuse of Power*

If nothing may be published but what civil authority shall have previously approved, power must always be the standard of truth; if every dreamer of innovations may propagate his projects, there can be no settlements; if every murmurer at government may diffuse discontent, there can be no peace; and if every skeptic in theology may teach his follies, there can be no religion.—*Samuel Johnson*

2352 *Contemplation*

It was the habit of Immanuel Kant, famous German philosopher, to rise in the morning at five o'clock and think for two hours. He had no apparatus; there was nothing in his hands. He sat and thought, he did not just sit.—*William Lyon Phelps*

2353 *Time*

A man who has taken your time recognizes no debt, yet it is the only debt he can never repay.—*Papyrus*

2354 *The Power of Thought*

Thoughts are the most powerful things. Buildings, cities, nations follow the thoughts of men. Men think—and out of the unknown come things. Every reformation is only a change of thinking.—*The Vagabond*

2355 *We Must Grow*

We must guard against being smugly satisfied with what we are and what we have done. We must grow. We are so small and life is so big.—*Circle C. Chats*

2356 *Be Christian*

The sermon will be better if you listen as a Christian rather than as a critic.
—*Construction Digest*

2357 *Overpaid*

In China an American woman journalist watched a frail Sister cleansing the gangrenous sores of wounded soldiers. "I wouldn't do that for a million dollars!" the visitor remarked. Without pause in her work, the Sister replied, "Neither would I."—*Catholic Digest*

2358 *Semantics*

The last public reference to sin we can recall offhand was President Coolidge's remark that his minister had preached on sin and was against it. In these new times sin is known by nicer names, such as delinquency, impropriety, indecorum, indiscretion, irregularity, laxity, and moral turpitude.—*The New York Times Magazine*

2359 *Links in a Chain*

The Chinese have a proverb: "If there is righteousness in the heart, there will be beauty in the character. If there be beauty in the character, there will be harmony in the home. If there is harmony in the home, there will be order in

the nation. When there is order in the nation, there will be peace in the world."
—*Daniel L. Mar, Cumberland Presbyterian*

2360   Pray and Work

Pray as though no work would help, and work as though no prayer would help.—*German proverb*

2361   Insecurity

The special insecurity in which we now live in an age in which one civilization is dying and another is powerless to be born is typical of the insecurity in which the children of man have always lived. Each New Year is an adventure into which we must, as did Abraham of old, go out, not knowing whither we go.—*Reinhold Niebuhr, Missions*

2362   Time Is Now

A child was overheard meditating aloud: "At Grandmamma's there isn't any We-don't-have-time-to-do-that. . . . Grandmamma doesn't have a watch on her arm. . . . At Grandmamma's I feel good."
In the child's world, time is not measured grudgingly. Time is now. Time is being.—*Lucy Nulton, Your Child's World*

2363   Five-minute Warning

If one were given five minutes' warning before sudden death, five minutes to say what it had all meant to us, every telephone booth would be occupied by people trying to call up other people to stammer that they loved them.—*Christopher Morley*

2364   Man Will Prevail

I decline to accept the end of man. . . . I believe that man will not merely endure; he will prevail. He is immortal, not because he alone among creatures has an inexhaustible voice, but because he has a soul, a spirit capable of compassion and sacrifice and endurance.—*William Faulkner*

2365   A Beautiful Obstacle

To some people a tree is something so incredibly beautiful that it brings tears to the eyes. To others it is just a green thing that stands in the way.—*William Blake*

2366   Research

Basic research is what I am doing when I don't know what I am doing.—*Wernher von Braun*

2367   *Go to Sleep*

It was a fine old bishop who, years ago, worrying his heart over what seemed to him the evils of a doomed world, tossing on his bed at midnight, thought he heard the Lord say, "Go to sleep, Bishop. I'll sit up the rest of the night."—*Arkansas Methodist*

2368   *Her Motto*

A young schoolgirl wrote an essay on Queen Victoria which ran in part: "When Queen Victoria was coronated, she took as her motto, 'I will be good.' She followed this motto passionately throughout a long and tedious life."—*Harry Emerson Fosdick*

2369   *Trust*

A lady passed three kids rollicking on the lawn. She found the oldest little girl taking care of her baby brother.

"Hello, Peggy," she said, "can't you go out and play?"

"No, ma'am," said Peggy wistfully. "You see, Mother trusts me so much that I never can have much fun."—*This Week*

2370   *Trustworthy*

A Louisville, Kentucky, woman, very active in church work, had walked over to the edge of the swimming pool to watch the youngsters at play. She was thoroughly enjoying their fun when a thirteen-year-old boy ran up to her and asked, "Say, lady, do you go to Sunday School?"

"Why, yes, I do," she replied, a bit surprised.

"Then," he said, "please hold this quarter for me while I go into the pool."
—*Christian Advocate*

2371   *She Helped*

When my mother suffered a stroke of paralysis, Anna Kerns, one of our neighbors, didn't say, "Now, if there's anything at all I can do . . ." She said, "Mary, I'll be there at seven thirty in the morning to do the washing for you." And she was, too.—*Ernie Pyle, The Woman*

Epigrams and Witticisms on Many Subjects

2372   When a subject becomes totally obsolete, we make it a required course.
—Peter Drucker

2373   The fellow who really has his ups and downs sits on the aisle seat in a movie theater.

2374   Intuition is that strange instinct a woman has that tells her she is right —whether she is or not.

2375   The main impact of the computer has been the provision of unlimited jobs for clerks.*—Peter Drucker*

2376   If a government commission had worked on the horse, you would have had the first horse who could operate his knee joint in both directions. The only trouble would have been that he couldn't stand up.*—Peter Drucker*

2377   Americans used to shout, "Give me liberty!" Now they just leave off the last word.

2378   A fool and his money are soon invited places.

2379   If you want to teach a child the value of a dollar, you'd better hurry up.

2380   Safety sign in front of school: "Watch out for schoolchildren, especially if they are driving cars."

2381 Few persons have more to talk about than the fellow who has just switched to bifocals.

2382 An optimistic gardener is a person who believes that what goes down must come up.

2383 Most of our time is taken up making good, making trouble, or making excuses.

2384 It's not too hard to live with your own faults, but it's hard to put up with the faults of others.

2385 The guy we don't like is the one who is always me-deep in conversation.

2386 A luxury is something you don't need but feel you can't do without.

2387 Tariffs between nations enable them to charge their people too much.

2388 If all men were equal, we wouldn't need laws to hold back the able.

2389 Nowadays no farmer counts his chickens till they cross the road.

2390 The fellow who embezzles the money always seems calm and collected.

2391 It's hard to realize that the whole American Revolution started over just one tax.

2392 One advantage in being stupid is that you don't get lonesome.

2393 No one worries now about the wolf at the door as long as you can feed him on the installment plan.

2394 If we could see ourselves as others see us, we would never want a second look.

2395 Some folks speak when they think and some oftener.

2396 Good manners consist in letting others tell you what you already know.

2397 There has been only one indispensable man, and that was Adam.

2398 The family that isn't in debt today is underprivileged.

2399 When you go on a vacation to forget everything, you generally find when you open your bag at the hotel that you have.

2400 The young man in love thinks nothing is good enough for the girl except himself.

2401 Early to bed and early to rise, and you'll miss hearing and seeing a great deal that would make you wise.

2402 "Hear no evil, see no evil, speak no evil," and you'll certainly be a dull companion.

2403   A sure way to keep crime from paying is to let the government run it.

2404   A great many people are already working a four-day week; it just takes them five days to do it.

2405   Things are pretty well evened up in this world. Other people's troubles are not as bad as yours, but their children are a lot worse.

2406   Too many people are ready to carry the stool when the piano needs moving.

2407   A chip on the shoulder is about the heaviest load a person ever carries. —*Roy L. Smith*

2408   In the old days every nation had rights except a small one. Now every nation has rights except a large one.

2409   If at first you don't succeed, so much for skydiving.

2410   George Washington was first in war, first in peace—and first to have his birthday juggled to make a long weekend.

2411   Travel flattens the purse, broadens the mind, and lengthens the conversation.

2412   To train children at home, it is necessary for both parents and children to spend some time there.

2413   Someone asks, "Why can't the nations of the world live as one big family?" The answer is they do.

2414   Most girls prefer the strong, solvent type.

2415   With a luncheon of hamburger, catsup, mustard, fries, coffee, and a fudge sundae, a stomach is an exciting workroom.

2416   The population of the United States is getting denser, but let's not get personal.

2417   Some persons are the kind of friends who stand by you—with their arms folded.

2418   If the universe is finite, as some scientists say, we should be able to find those golf balls we lose.

2419   A foreign official's visit to the U.S. Treasury is generally quite touching.

2420   The person who always finds something to harp on may not be so fortunate in the next world.

2421   The bridegroom fainted on the way to his wedding. Wait till he gets the first month's bills.

2422   A nation needs a foreign policy that isn't patterned after its weather policy.

2423   Plants grow better if you lengthen the day with electric light, and this is especially true of electric light plants.

2424   One thing you learn from experience is that you can't make money without working.

2425   Strangely, the less you see of some persons, the more you like them.

2426   An isolationist is a person who doesn't want to support the rest of the world in the style to which we have become accustomed.

2427   It may have been better in the old days when charity was a virtue and not an industry.

2428   A pessimist is an optimist who voted for a politician he thought would reduce government spending.

2429   A fashion note says that there will be little change in men's pockets during the next year.

2430   By the time you get enough experience to be able to watch your step, you may not be going anywhere.

2431   Most of us don't expect the Congress to do anything for us, but we hope they don't do anything to us.

2432   It's very doubtful whether even the meek would like to inherit the earth at present.

2433   George Washington never told a lie, but he never had Form 1040 to fill out either.

2434   We long for the good old days when we were young and knew everything.

2435   He wrote a very successful novel. He struck pay dirt.

2436   Sometimes we think the wicked fleece and no man pursueth.

2437   Nothing makes the President of the United States happier than to have some matter before him that requires a hands-off policy.

2438   When all is said and nothing done, a committee meeting is over.

2439   Leader of a flock of geese to the bird following: "Stop that infernal honking—if you want to pass, pass!"

2440   You can lose your shirt by putting too much on the cuff.

2441   Rice requires more moisture than most cereals except wild oats.

2442   With a satellite government, jitters can now be sent quickly from country to country.

2443   We understand several government departments have a large number of millions for emergencies which no doubt can be developed as needed.

2444   Baseball is better than football because you don't need a college education to get tickets.

2445   More people would try to do right if they thought it was wrong.

2446   A business recession is when you do without some necessities in order to keep on buying your usual luxuries.

2447   A brilliant conversationalist is a person who uses meaningless words to say a great deal about nothing.

2448   Someone who has apparently never read the *Congressional Record* has suggested that it carry advertising.

2449   The products are seldom as irritating as the commercials.

2450   The end of daylight-saving time means you have one less hour to put off until tomorrow things you should have done today.

2451   The dove of peace is out on the limb most of the time.

2452   If you don't know what to be thankful for, be thankful for all the trouble you haven't had.

2453   No one has inside information as good as the doctor's.

2454   In this country every husband is free to do just what his wife pleases.

2455   An old-timer is one who remembers when a kid who got a licking at school was in for another one when he got home.

2456   Thrift is a wonderful thing—and who hasn't wished his ancestors had practiced it more?

2457   Some persons think if they wear their best clothes on Sunday they're observing the Sabbath.

2458   When an apple a day costs more than keeping the doctor away, brother, that's inflation!

2459   The best thing parents can spend on children is time—not money.

2460   Where did you get the idea that swimming is good for the figure? Did you ever take a good look at a whale?

2461   The Treasury brought back the $2 bill. The $5 bill was still a little large for small change.

2462 A South American political leader said, "I can take it." Cash, we suppose.

2463 It is said the federal budget can be balanced. We prefer the word *is*.

2464 All of us work for the government. The trick is to get paid for it.

2465 Nothing is further than the distance between advice and help.

2466 Most ideas are not unusual, but the experience of having ideas is unusual.

2467 If you can't find it in the dictionary, the atlas, or the encyclopedia, ask for it at the drugstore.

2468 We have never heard anyone say he couldn't sleep last night because of his conscience.

2469 Some successful men who have air-conditioned offices were reared in homes where the snow blew in through chinks in the attic.

2470 If we didn't have confidence in each other, we couldn't live beyond our incomes.

2471 Success in life generally expands the waistband or the hatband.

2472 If the spring poets want to be realistic, they should find more words that rhyme with *slush*.

2473 Some housewives run charge accounts with four grocers because it makes the bills seem smaller.

2474 If every mischievous little boy got his reward in the end, we might do away with juvenile delinquency.

2475 Economics lesson: Increased earnings always bring increased yearnings.

2476 When someone says, "I do not wish to appear critical," it means he is going to let you have it.

2477 The summer tourist soon finds that the cheaper rooms in the beach hotel overlook the ocean—completely.

2478 Still, if there were no Communists, how could the Western nations scare themselves into being friends?

2479 Solomon said, "There is no new thing under the sun," but he didn't say it over color television.

2480 The world would be pretty bad if the teen-agers didn't have any more sense than we sometimes think they have.

2481   In many elections some good candidates get the solid support of all the good people who don't vote.

2482   Some families go right on putting money in a savings account or government bonds when they haven't got a mink coat in the house.

2483   The prices of evening dresses now are no more modest than the dresses.

2484   Some people not only believe everything they hear but repeat it.

2485   Nothing is more difficult than trying to find something wrong with yourself.

2486   Only the very rich can afford to be foolish, and not infrequently are.

2487   The reason the road to success is crowded is that it is filled with women pushing their husbands.

2488   When everyone approves of what you are doing, you ought to ask yourself what's wrong.

2489   You can measure the progress of civilization by who gets more applause—the clown or the thinker.

2490   Love makes the world go around, but so does a good swallow of hot mustard.

2491   If some people weren't stupid, how could we know who is intelligent?

2492   The course of true love isn't smooth, but the detours are worse.

2493   Time is what passes between paydays.

2494   If you bow at all, give it all you've got.

2495   On a bus there is no such thing as the rising generation.

2496   Everyone wants to divide the wealth if he will get more than he has now.

2497   It isn't easy to get an idea into a head filled with prejudices.

2498   The thing for a husband to do when he spills something on a rug at home is merely to listen.

2499   A cat doesn't have nine lives, but catty remarks do.

2500   Love your enemy and it will completely confuse him.

2501   Work is time you spend on jobs you get paid for, and leisure is time you spend on jobs you don't get paid for.

2502   It isn't easy for a husband to get back some of his take-home pay after he takes it home.

2503   The United States is the one country where it takes more brains to make out the income-tax return than it does to make the income.

2504   The fellow who watches the clock need not worry about his future because he probably hasn't any.

2505   We all want to live a long time, but no one wants to get old.

2506   The still, small voice used to be your conscience, but now it's your pocket radio.

2507   Destiny may shape our ends, but making ends meet is our responsibility.

2508   Remember the good old days when we had nothing to worry about but the number of dimes we would get back from our chain letters.

2509   He who laughs last must have time to waste.

2510   Years make all of us old and very few of us wise.

2511   Your best friends are generally those you don't meet very often.

2512   One thing comes to the man who waits, and that's whiskers.

2513   Most of us can stand adversity, but prosperity is another matter.

2514   There are so many ways of being a fool that it's hard to avoid them all.

2515   By the time you save enough so you can sleep late in the morning, you're so old you want to get up early.

2516   Life is pretty simple—you only need a comfortable bed and comfortable shoes, because you are in one or the other all your life.

2517   A reckless driver may get to places a little sooner—even the cemetery.

2518   You have to be nice until you earn your first million, and after that folks will be nice to you.

2519   If ignorance is bliss, we should have a great many more happy people.

2520   Women now get men's wages, but they always have.

2521   When a person starts bragging about what he has done, he is getting old.

2522   One of the things you can still get for a nickel is a penny's worth of time on a parking meter.

2523   Every nation smashes a counterfeit ring when it finds one, as no government wants competition with its own currency-inflation program.

2524   You can go crazy in the world today without anyone noticing it.

2525   Sometimes a man tries to make a name for himself by signing it to someone else's check.

2526   Many wise words are spoken in jest, but even more foolish words are spoken in earnest.

2527   No husband should be too sure that his wife can't take a joke.

2528   What this country doesn't need is a five-cent dollar.

2529   Don't complain if your hair falls out, because it would be worse if it ached and you had to have it pulled.

2530   Someday some smart government is going to get the idea of spending only what it can pay for.

2531   Misfortune is a point of view. Your headache feels good to an aspirin salesman.

2532   You can't believe everything you hear, but you can repeat it.

2533   It's strange that the fellow who always wants the most has the least with which to buy it.

2534   The Greeks had their idea of tragedy, but they never sat in the grandstand and watched an outfielder drop an easy one.

2535   Modern youngsters are precocious. They don't read, but name any record and they can tell you what's on the other side.

2536   Man has conquered the air, but so has our neighbor's radio.

2537   To a Communist, a wage slave is any American who earns $20,000 a year, drives a car, owns a television set, and has a bathroom.

2538   Adam was the first man to know the meaning of *rib roast*.

2539   We sympathize with the fellow who occupied two seats in the bus because half the time he didn't get any seat.

2540   The reason some children are on the streets at night is that they are afraid to stay home alone.

2541   All women's hats are different because a milliner doesn't make the same mistake twice.

2542   A man's hair is either parted or departed.

2543   The hardest dollar to earn is the one you have already spent.

2544   The person who leaves becomes the life of the party.

2545   You get along better if you bring home a little applesauce with the bacon.

2546   The great thing about your home is that you can say anything you wish and no one pays any attention to you.

2547   The good mother is one who gets through a rainy Saturday with the television set out of order.

2548   In the old days, dealing with juvenile delinquency in the woodshed with a strap may have been bad, but it was effective.

2549   There is no special relation between what you want and what you need, and this makes selling interesting.

2550   You can sleep on a matter before you decide, unless you have a competitor who doesn't need the sleep.

2551   An optimist is a person who thinks he will never be a sucker again.

2552   One of the strangest delusions in the mind of man is that the stock market has no top.

2553   If the nations agree not to use nuclear weapons, none will be used until the next war.

2554   What this country needs is a cheap substitute for money, and it may get it.

2555   We like the person who tells us all the nice things about ourselves that we always knew.

2556   A person who is articulate and ignorant is certain to go a long way.

2557   Women keep a secret well, but sometimes it takes quite a few of them to do it.

2558   Civilization is not only at the crossroads, but this is a cloverleaf job.

2559   Underprivileged: Not to have remote control for your color television set.

2560   Now that the elections are over, we won't find any perfect men until the next election campaign.

2561   It's always easier to have a courageous conviction after you know what the boss thinks.

2562   It only takes one to start a quarrel, but it takes two to keep it up.

2563   Nothing shocks most of us so much as finding that we may be wrong.

2564   Most of us are the kind of do-it-yourself persons who hit the nail right on the thumb.

2565   A gentleman is a person who offers his seat to a lady when he gets off the bus.

2566   What a woman needs is a purse with a zipper on the bottom so she can find things quickly.

2567   Many persons would like to do something for a living that doesn't involve work.

2568   Experience is what helps you recognize the same mistake as you keep on making it.

2569   No married man says an old dog can't be taught new tricks.

2570   After an election speech, the audience draws its own confusions.

2571   Distance lends enchantment to the view, but not when you have a flat tire.

2572   By piling on the dirt when you gossip, you can make a mountain out of a molehill.

2573   People who seldom speak aren't the only ones who don't say much.

2574   Your head is like your pocketbook because it's not how it looks but what's inside that counts.

2575   It's what the guests say after they say good night that counts.

2576   Just because you blow your top doesn't mean you have a dynamic personality.

2577   Regarding trade relations, some people would like to.

2578   Many city gardeners would like to know how big a garden has to be before the government will pay you for not planting it.

2579   Half the world doesn't know how many installments the other half is behind.

2580   Nothing is more trying than to have the neighbors buy things you can't afford.

2581   A man needs a good yarn to pull the wool over his wife's eyes.

2582   She is the kind of woman that makes men climb mountains and jump across the deepest rivers—a woman truck driver.

2583   It's easy to get lost in thought if it's not familiar territory to you.

2584   We often wonder why a man speaks of "my" car when he still has twenty-nine payments to go.

2585   There are two kinds of conceited persons: those who admit it and those who don't.

2586 The idea of the brotherhood of man surges within us whenever we need to borrow our neighbor's lawn mower or garden tools.

2587 There is always one person who will do the job if you make him chairman.

2588 Bumper sticker to end all bumper stickers: "DON'T YOU FEEL STUPID READING THIS BUMPER STICKER THAT HAS NO MESSAGE?"

2589 The only thing that gives you more for your money today than it did a year ago is a weighing machine.

2590 The world is composed of givers and takers. The takers may eat better, but the givers sleep better.

2591 There's no fool like an old fool. You just can't beat experience.

2592 Always borrow money from a pessimist—he never expects to be paid back.

2593 The bathtub was invented in 1850 and the phone in 1875. For twenty-five years you couldn've sat in the tub without having the phone ring.

2594 Last week I lost a fortune in the market. My shopping bag broke in the grocery store.

2595 Nothing stretches slacks like snacks.

2596 A lot of people have the reputation of being cheerful when they're really just proud of their teeth.

2597 Courage is what it takes to stand up and speak; courage is also what it takes to sit down and listen.

2598 The condition a man is in can best be judged from what he takes two at a time—stairs or pills.

2599 For losses on the stock market the bulls and bears are not so much to blame as the bum steers.

2600 The best substitute for experience is being seventeen years old.

2601 In the good old days policemen didn't hide at the side of a busy road, but took their chances in traffic like anyone else.

2602 About the time you catch up with the Joneses, they refinance.

2603 The older a man gets, the farther he had to walk to school as a boy.

2604 A reckless driver is one who passes you on the road, despite anything you can do.

2605   A good listener is one who can give you his full attention without hearing a word you say.

2606   The prices of wheat, wool, and corn go up and down, but the price of wild oats stays the same.

2607   A dog fills an empty place in a person's life. That is also true of hot dogs.

2608   The beginning of wisdom is silence. The second step is listening.

2609   One compensation for old age is that you don't have to go to picnics.

2610   Many American homes are on three shifts. Father is on the night shift, mother is on the day shift, and the children shift for themselves.

2611   We understand the three most prolific writers of our time are Anonymous, Old Subscriber, and Steady Reader.

2612   Variety may be the spice of life, but it's good old monotony that brings home the groceries.

2613   Those who say you can't take it with you never saw a car packed for a vacation trip.

2614   Early to bed and early to rise—till you make enough cash to do otherwise!

2615   Old gardeners never die; they just spade away.

2616   The trouble with having a doctor who doesn't make house calls is you have to be in pretty good health to find out how sick you are.

2617   Old termites never die. They just get board and lumber on.

2618   What on earth will today's younger generation be able to tell their children they had to do without?

2619   Why doesn't somebody cross electric blankets with toasters so that people would pop out of bed?

2620   Why can't life's problems hit us when we're eighteen, and we know it all?

2621   The trouble with people these days is that they want to reach the promised land without going through the wilderness.

2622   Old politicians never die—they just run once too often.

2623   Old mufflers never die, they just get exhausted.

2624   No matter what we have learned since 1492, we are inclined to feel today that the world is flat.

2625   When you begin to notice how much fun the young folks have, you are getting old.

2626   Those in favor of conserving gasoline, raise your right foot.

2627   Nowadays apples are so expensive, you might as well have the doctor.

2628   If you look like your passport photo, you aren't well enough to travel.

2629   If the knocking at the door is loud and long, it isn't opportunity, it's relatives.

2630   When life knocks you to your knees, you're in position to pray.

2631   A person never realizes how many friends he has until he rents a cottage at the beach.

2632   There's a book that tells you where to go on your vacation. It's called a checkbook.

2633   There's one advantage to the music the younger generation goes for today: nobody can whistle it.

2634   Train up a child in the way he should go, and when he gets older he will tell you how wrong you were.

2635   People are peculiar—they want the front of the bus, the back of the church, and the middle of the road.

2636   Don't be afraid of asking a dumb question! That's better than making a dumb mistake.

2637   A good wife laughs at her husband's jokes, not because they are clever, but because she is.

2638   One IBM card to another: "I'm fed up with your 'holier than thou' attitude."

2639   The nicest thing about being quiet and dumb is that you will seldom be picked to head a committee.

2640   THE MONTPELIER—Restaurant and Lounge
          LA PROVENCE—Coffee House
          THE RETREAT—Men's Grille

2641   A good test of your power of concentration is your ability to do your child's homework while he is watching television.

2642   Sign in a cafeteria: "Courteous efficient self-service."

2643   Silence is not always an indication of modesty. Sometimes a fellow can't think of anything else nice to say about himself.

2644   What is so simple even a small child can manipulate it? A grandparent.

2645   The wonderful thing about back-seat driving is that you never make a mistake.

2646   When you sing your own praises, it's generally a solo.

2647   You can say for the crossword puzzle that it has convinced some people that education really pays.

2648   If your conscience is your guide, you are living under a very flexible rule.

2649   It's surprising how long you remember a kind deed if you did it.

2650   The fellow who wants you to play ball with him generally wants you to do the catching.

2651   Most wallets wouldn't be so fat today if you took out the credit cards.

2652   If you want more leisure, get to your appointments on time.

2653   You can stand still and watch the world go by—and it certainly will.

2654   When we read some of the Soviet Union's propaganda we know that behind the Iron Curtain lies Russia.

2655   The fellow who is up to his ears in work may be lying down on the job.

2656   You get on best when you don't try to tell people where to get off at.

2657   It's not only the cost and the upkeep, but the turnover that makes a car expensive.

2658   No dream comes true until you wake up and go to work.

2659   By the time you get the installments paid, the luxury you bought is a necessity.

2660   We wonder what would happen if the Internal Revenue Service offered us our money back if we weren't satisfied.

2661   You may outbluff another driver, but the real question is whether you will outlive him.

2662   One thing you can say for illiteracy—it protects you from some literary trash.

2663   Nothing is so hard on a woman's clothes as another woman.

2664   Autumn is the most beautiful time of the year to the person who has no leaves to rake.

2665   You are young only once, and that excuse won't last forever.

2666   On any proposed Congressional tax reduction, never do so many wait so long for so little.

2667   I've never had any trouble deciding whether I would rather be miserably rich or happily poor.

2668   The world isn't getting smaller. The missiles just go farther.

2669   When business is slow, it's a good idea to give it a push.

2670   One thing about getting old is that you can sing in the bathroom while brushing your teeth.

2671   Occasionally you meet a person whose only job is spreading ignorance.

2672   If people said what they thought, our conversation would be very brief.

2673   A bachelor is a man with enough confidence in women to act on it.

2674   A person who lives within his income is sometimes crowded for space.

2675   All the Internal Revenue Service wants is what you have left.

2676   A pessimist's idea of a big party is to paint the town blue.

2677   In an argument a person is tactful when he says, "I couldn't fail to disagree with you less."

2678   No opportunity is lost; the other fellow takes it.

2679   When a woman says her ideal has been shattered, it probably means he is only broke.

2680   This is a free country and a good many people are getting it by agreeing to pay later.

2681   According to the latest magazine in my dentist's office, business is expected to reach new highs in 1969.

2682   It isn't as hard to get the things you want as it is to keep from getting the things you don't want.

2683   Maybe the Department of Agriculture could work out a plan for paying juvenile delinquents for not raising wild oats.

2684   Mind may have control over matter, but not in a golf ball.

2685   Some persons are dumb and others just look dumb so they can make a good trade.

2686   The first essential for leadership is a group of dumb guys to follow.

2687   You can't make trouble for others without a little of it rubbing off on you.

2688 Keeping everlastingly at it not only brings success but also a nervous breakdown.

2689 Sooner or later a person who carries tales makes a monkey of himself.

2690 The way to end an argument is to keep your mouth shut.

2691 An idle rumor is generally very busy.

2692 Three square meals every day and you will soon be round.

2693 Profits may be bad, but they meet the payroll better than losses.

2694 A man may be down but never out, unless he is a university football coach.

2695 There are still quite a few American families so poor they only have one car.

2696 Unfortunately, laziness is never fatal.

2697 With 110 million automobiles, there is no such thing anymore as the man-in-the-street.

2698 The Director of the Office of Management and Budget should be the kind of person who buys a two-pants suit.

2699 A swelled head always picks out an empty one to expand.

2700 Making money last is just as hard as making it first.

2701 A hammer may miss its mark, but a compliment never.

2702 Doing nothing gets pretty tiresome because you can't stop and rest.

2703 The more you know about people, the more you wonder why some feel superior to others.

2704 You may be a fine upstanding citizen, but it makes no difference on a slippery sidewalk.

2705 Some persons are poor listeners because it interferes with what they want to say.

2706 Getting rattled may be a sign that there is a screw loose somewhere.

2707 To get ahead you have to use a head.

2708 It's bad to be young and broke, but it isn't easy either to be old and bent.

2709 A girl loves a boy's voice when it has a ring in it.

2710 A loose nut can cause an auto accident, but so can a tight nut.

2711 You may be able to trace your family back a hundred years and not know where your children were last night.

2712 The fellow who keeps on sawing wood has the biggest woodpile.

2713 Today no one is so poor that he has to live within his income.

2714 Don't worry too much about what people think, because they seldom do.

2715 Americans generally have good manners, but there are still a few who discipline their children.

2716 The most effective way for abolishing war forever is to have World War III.

2717 There are 100,000 useless words in the English language, but they come in handy in college football yells.

2718 With a small boy, cleanliness is not next to godliness, but next to impossible.

2719 The brain seldom wears out, probably because it's seldom overworked.

2720 The fellow who says the church is losing ground is probably the same one who says the sun is losing heat.

2721 With television, radio, and phonographs, the American family is more sound than ever.

2722 We suppose the clinging-vine type of woman has disappeared because it has been harder and harder to find something to cling to.

2723 It's easier for a woman to get her face lifted than it is for her husband to lift his when the bill comes in.

2724 Some persons are born good and others have to make good.

2725 You can get along without education, as Henry Ford and Thomas Edison did, if you are a Ford or an Edison.

2726 The automobile may ruin some youngsters, but there are also some youngsters who ruin the automobile.

2727 Economists say two can live on $5,000 a year, but they don't say two what.

2728 With the checks and balances provided in the Constitution, the tax-payer provides the checks and the Treasury holds the balances.

2729 It's pretty hard to believe in improvement through evolution if you have been listening to television programs for two or three years.

2730   In the grammatically correct home the wife says, "You shall" and the husband says, "I will."

2731   The man who comes out on top may still be a loser if he is bald-headed.

2732   If you want to borrow trouble, you will find your credit is good.

2733   A successful businessman keeps his head up and his overhead down.

2734   We suggest that some new issue of postage stamps carry a picture of a weeping taxpayer.

2735   None but the brave can afford the fair.

2736   We should think they could balance the French budget with the mistakes in addition in Paris cafés in one tourist season.

2737   If you would like to be talked about, leave the party before the rest do.

2738   We like the fellow who says he is going to make a long story short, and does.

2739   We suppose a fat man dressed up is an illustration of spic and span.

2740   Someday we're going to give that Gideon Bible in our hotel room to the headwaiter in the dining room.

2741   We haven't heard of a movie director signing up the national spelling champion.

2742   We don't suppose competition in the automobile industry will end until they get to the last pedestrian.

2743   Every spring many Americans tell the Internal Revenue Service that their incomes are nothing to speak of.

2744   Most people can play at least one instrument—usually an automobile horn.

2745   What some persons seem to want is a five-day weekend.

2746   Where do bad boys and girls go? Just about everywhere.

2747   With lunch counters in every kind of store, you can eat almost anywhere except at home.

2748   When both a speaker and an audience are confused, the speech is profound.

2749   Why does a woman apologize when friends drop in unexpectedly and find the house looking like it usually does.

2750   The little savings banks that couldn't be opened until they were full are now antiques.

2751 Faint praise ne'er won fair lady, but it would certainly surprise many wives.

2752 A national conscience is a still small voice that tells one country when another country is stronger.

2753 Most women have a skin they love to retouch.

2754 June is the month when the bride who has never had a broom in her hand sweeps up the aisle.

2755 Nothing makes time pass more quickly than an income-tax installment every three months.

2756 Money has wings and most of us see only the tail feathers.

2757 Men are either born with consciences or marry them.

2758 A saver grows rich by seeming poor. A spender grows poor by seeming rich.

2759 The person who is ignorant can speak freely.

2760 As you grow older you find the after-dinner speeches worse or your back weaker.

2761 There must be something wrong in the world somewhere that doesn't need Uncle Sam's money.

2762 A civilized nation is one in which you decrease the death rate by disease and increase it by accident.

2763 Fortunately, there are always enough crises in the world to help us keep our minds off our personal problems.

2764 A free country is one in which no one in particular is to blame for the messes you get in.

2765 We'll never have a labor government in this country until Cabinet salaries are up to the union scale.

2766 We can't remember hearing of a man, when we were young, who hoed potatoes until he was a nervous wreck.

2767 Don't criticize the rooster. If you got up at four A.M., you'd crow too.

2768 A city farmer is a fellow who is willing to lose money farming if he can wear overalls.

2769 We have a peace-loving world with nations seldom paying pensions for more than three wars at a time.

2770   Nobody knows who invented the alarm clock, which is certainly a fortunate break for the guy.

2771   Many a husband goes to his church rummage sale to buy back his Sunday pants.

2772   One way to find out what a woman really thinks of you is to marry her.

2773   Indigestion happens when there has been too much of a good thing.

2774   He was the kind of thoughtful person who never forgot himself.

2775   The family Bible can be passed from generation to generation because it gets so little wear.

2776   The reason a man dies suddenly in harness is that he has been working like a horse.

2777   Freedom of speech is a great thing. It even permits some people to talk nonsense.

2778   The fellow who laughs at his troubles never runs out of things at which to laugh.

2779   Some persons think they aren't getting ahead unless they've cheated the other fellow.

2780   Conversation without a touch of scandal gets very dull for most people.

2781   Ignorance combined with silence is sometimes mistaken for wisdom.

2782   When the cat is in the birdcage, he isn't there to sing.

2783   When some persons abuse you, they can't understand why you resent "constructive criticism."

2784   The person who thinks before he speaks is silent most of the time.

2785   Honesty is the best policy, but difficult to follow in a letter of recommendation.

2786   When a man doesn't believe today what he believed yesterday, how can he be so confident today knowing that tomorrow is coming?

2787   It's difficult to understand how a person can be bored with life and yet hope for immortality.

2788   Why do we all want to talk about ourselves when that's the subject we know least about?

2789   A person who says, "I'm not dumb" is merely trying to quiet his own doubts.

2790   Man is peculiar. He will torture animals, but do nothing about a radio soprano or a singing commercial.

2791   No amount of misfortune will satisfy a man who reaches for a second hors d'oeuvre.

2792   A fisherman is the only person who tells a lie with his arms stretched out.

2793   Every young man knows when the right girl comes along because she tells him.

2794   Some movie stars diet to keep thin, but the movie plots stay that way.

2795   The most effective answer to an insult is silence.

2796   Some nations think they're showing their friendliness by offering to borrow money from us.

2797   A person may be as young as he feels, but he is not often as important.

2798   Remember the old days when the automobile windshield didn't have so many stickers you could look through it.

2799   One thing most nations have learned is that buying wars on the deferred-payment plan is expensive.

2800   You can't mind your own business if you haven't any mind and any business.

2801   There is no use in worrying about your old troubles when you know new ones will be coming along.

2802   We know about how many blondes and brunettes there are in the country, but we have no record of the number of blockheads.

2803   We sort of like the person who is dumb but keeps it to himself.

2804   A human being is the only animal that can be skinned more than once.

2805   It's surprising how soon a child learns how to train its parents.

2806   The one comforting thing about being an economist is that no one else can predict the future either.

2807   Why is it that what you hear is always less interesting than what you overhear?

2808   Perhaps the reason we have juvenile delinquency is that we don't have enough stern punishment.

2809   Unfortunately, all the dummies in the movies aren't thrown over the cliff.

2810   As Baron Rothschild is reported to have said, "To make a fortune you must buy low and sell too soon."

2811   A cow is the only animal with a built-in fly swatter.

2812   One comfort is that when you lose $5 now you don't lose as much as you used to.

2813   When some women promise to be on time, it carries a lot of wait.

2814   The person who frequently is tight as a drum is seldom fit as a fiddle.

2815   Some persons are so unlucky they don't recognize their duty in time to sidestep it.

2816   The way to get in *Who's Who* is to know what's what.

2817   If you try to get something for nothing, you must be certain you don't end up getting nothing for something.

2818   The way to kill time profitably is to work it to death.

2819   People who live in glass houses have to answer the doorbell.

2820   The longer you carry a grudge, the heavier it gets.

2821   Most women want a permanent wave. Most men would settle for permanent hair.

2822   The happiest moment in life is when the folks back of you in the movies finish their popcorn.

2823   Some persons don't know the difference between thinking for yourself and thinking of yourself.

2824   It's always easy to get up early in the morning the night before.

2825   By the time you learn to stand up for your rights you have flat feet.

2826   Some people are in debt because they spend what their friends think they make.

2827   Worry takes as much time as work and pays less.

2828   Some people believe anything you tell them if you whisper it.

2829   The boy who could never remember why his mother sent him to the grocery store grows up and is sent to Congress by the people.

2830   Fifty years ago a man who drove thirty-five miles an hour was a sensation and he still is, which shows that the more things change, the more they are the same.

2831   Keeping up with the Joneses isn't a good idea, but it's not as bad as trying to pass them on a hill.

2832   If compact cars get any smaller, they will have to hunt pedestrians in packs.

2833   As you grow older, you grow wiser, talk less, and say more.

2834   A fisherman has fun the whole year—ten days of fishing and 355 days playing with the tackle and equipment.

2835   The owner of a candid camera generally takes the worst view of everything.

2836   He bought her a big diamond—the five-year installment size.

2837   A penny isn't worth much unless it gets stuck in a parking meter where it's worth at least six hours.

2838   It's almost impossible to keep your mind and your mouth open at the same time.

2839   It's surprising how thoroughly you can be misinformed with a little reading.

2840   A wife expects a husband with rare gifts to bring them home to her.

2841   You are not really ignorant until somebody finds it out.

2842   We know a housewife who got enough premiums from trading stamps to furnish a bedroom but couldn't use the other seven rooms because they were full of groceries.

2843   When you see a man with a woman who looks young enough to be his daughter, it is probably his mother.

2844   A man is getting old when he starts letting his wife pick out his neckties.

2845   One advantage in being poor is that your closets aren't full of old clothes and junk.

2846   An honest fisherman is a pretty uninteresting person.

2847   It is getting harder and harder to find a courteous person who isn't trying to sell you something.

2848   By requiring licenses now for gambling, even the wages of sin are subject to tax.

2849   We have to admit the atom was all it was cracked up to be.

2850   When the newspapers speak of a Latin American political candidate running, you never know in which direction.

2851   The only nation that cuts government waste is indignation.

2852   The world may owe you a living, but you have to collect the hard way.

2853   As a rule, a quitter isn't a very good beginner either.

2854   Necessity may be the mother of invention, but so is an aversion to work.

2855   Flattery is falsehood to all but the flattered.

2856   The straight and narrow path never crosses Easy Street.

2857   We have never been in a position to know whether the guy who said money isn't everything was right.

2858   The way Congress spends money, we aren't sure whether it's Capitol Hill or Capital Hill.

2859   We have discovered that women used cosmetics in the middle ages. They still use them in the middle ages.

2860   We suppose the orchestral din in some restaurants is to drown out the complaints of the diners.

2861   We still think having money a little tight teaches sobriety to spenders.

2862   A person who talks out of both sides of his mouth says something on both sides of everything.

2863   Some back-seat drivers look on their husbands as automobile accessories.

2864   It's a pretty hard job to run the country as cheaply in peace as we do in war.

2865   The Christmas cooing is followed by the January billing.

2866   There are an increasing number of women preachers now, and they aren't all in pulpits.

2867   The family that isn't in debt today is underprivileged.

2868   Millions of people escaped being run over by an automobile last year, and we understand there are still a few who escaped the year before.

2869   In the old days most people tried to be out of debt before they died, which shows how backward they were.

2870   The Bible is such a great book that it survives all the translations made of it.

2871   Some students burn the midnight oil in the transmission instead of the lamp.

2872   Sometimes we like to go to an old-fashioned silent movie and see people open their mouths without saying anything.

2873   Sometimes we think an enterchurch movement is more important than an interchurch movement.

2874   The person who has too much money for his own good easily finds friends to share his misfortune.

2875   It's a delicate problem to cultivate your friends so you know them well enough to borrow from but not well enough to lend to.

2876   It's difficult to define the word *ignoramus* unless one has studied himself pretty carefully.

2877   It is not sillier for the rich to think the poor are happy than for the poor to think the rich are.

2878   The world's choice: Disarmament or Disbursement.

2879   To be unhappily married requires a good income, and to be incompatible a couple must be rich.

2880   Some persons never appeal to God unless they're getting licked.

2881   Without a single exception, we have always found that the narrow-minded bigots are the ones who disagree with us.

2882   A telephone isn't a vacuum cleaner, but some people can get a lot of dirt out of it.

2883   No horse goes as fast as the money you bet on him.

2884   All things come to him who crosses the street without looking.

2885   You may have a high opinion of yourself and still rate pretty low.

2886   No matter how much money talks, most people don't find it boring.

2887   A good idea can get very lonely in an empty head.

2888   If you say you are less wise than you are, people will think you are wiser than you are.

2889   The *Congressional Record* might reduce expenses by cutting out the advertising.

2890   If you know you don't know much, you know more than most people.

2891   Some persons who are too proud to beg and too honest to steal, borrow and forget to pay.

2892   The person who tells you his troubles keeps you from talking about yours.

2893   The knock on the front door may be opportunity, but it may also be another salesman.

2894   The one thing it's easy to do these days is to get confused.

2895   What this country needs is more persons who are willing to take a fifteen-minute break for work.

2896   No wonder food costs more when the farmer has to know the botanical name of his crops, the entomological name of the bugs, and the pharmaceutical name of the sprays.

2897   The grass on the other side of the fence may look greener, but it still has to be mowed once a week.

2898   Every time we get held up an hour in the five-o'clock traffic, we wonder why it's called the rush hour.

2899   Modern man looks ahead to going to the moon, but hesitates to move to the rear of the bus.

2900   No one reads fortunes like Dun and Bradstreet.

2901   One reason a child must not suck his thumb is that he may need it someday.

2902   One trouble in this country is that too many persons try to get something for nothing, and another trouble is that too many succeed.

2903   Sometime a soap will be discovered that doesn't do anything but get the dirt off.

2904   One good thing about some drip-and-dry suits is that they don't bag any worse at the knees than elsewhere.

2905   You have to go to church pretty early to get a good back seat.

2906   All men are born free and equal, and they stay that way up to the time they marry.

2907   Every once in a while you see one of nature's big mistakes—a small mind with a large mouth.

2908   The fellow who follows the horses generally finds the horses he follows follow the other horses.

2909   Most of us who brag about what we are going to do tomorrow did the same thing yesterday.

2910   Money can't buy happiness, but there are some mighty attractive substitutes.

2911   Fun is expensive, and the older you get, the more expensive it is.

2912   Things happen so fast now almost every day is the first or second anniversary of something awful.

2913   Nothing causes such interesting arguments as ignorance.

2914   Most of us can't stand prosperity, and the way we spend money we won't have to.

2915   Most of us make enough hay nowadays, but it's harder to stack it up.

2916   It's a smart child who can ask questions his parents can answer.

2917   There is nothing wrong with having nothing to say if you don't say it out loud.

2918   You can't take it with you, but you can't travel very far without it either.

2919   You can knock the chip off the other person's shoulder simply by patting him on the back.

2920   There is nothing wrong with the young folks that the old folks haven't outgrown.

2921   You can't take it with you, and you can't even keep it while you're here.

2922   Life is no joke and neither is the average joke.

2923   There are greater things in life than money, but the problem is convincing your wife.

2924   No one has more to learn than the person who knows everything.

2925   Nothing takes the starch out of you like a strict diet.

2926   Running into debt has its problems, but so does running into your creditors.

2927   If at first you don't succeed, you are like the rest of us.

2928   Keep smiling and it may look as if you are not smart enough to understand the world's problems.

2929   The fellow who is a good sport has to lose to prove it.

2930   When you blow your top, you will make the best speech you will ever regret.

2931   If you get into deep water, the only safe course is to keep your mouth closed.

2932   A person seldom loses anything by good manners, but some people don't even take a chance.

2933   Americans today seem to worry less about stable money than about filling-station money.

2934   We understand a burglar in a Washington, D.C., home was offered five percent by the owner if he found anything.

2935   The news from all over the world is sometimes bad and sometimes even worse.

2936   There are some Americans who are weary of well-doing, while others are weary of being well done.

2937   When you decide to know yourself, you may find the acquaintance isn't worth the effort.

2938   All of us are born in a state of ignorance and many of us never change residence.

2939   Money talks and in most families it's the mother tongue.

2940   A fish gains weight slowly, except the one that got away.

2941   We never get anything but sad news out of those envelopes with a window in front.

2942   We have more high-school and college graduates than ever before and fewer of them can read traffic signs.

2943   We never could understand how a moth lives eating nothing but holes.

2944   Only one American in two knows how to drive a car well, and she sits in the back seat.

2945   We live in a world of change, but it's hard to get your hands on any of it.

2946   The best speech you hear may be from the fellow who keeps his mouth shut.

2947   The average husband is worth about twice what his wife thinks of him and half what his mother thinks of him.

2948   There is something comforting about the other fellow's hard luck.

2949   Sometimes we think everybody sees television but the fellow who writes the commercials.

2950   If some people lived up to their ideals, they would be stooping.

2951   Honesty pays, but not enough to satisfy some people.

2952   Many a successful person has risen from obscurity to something worse.

2953   After-dinner coffee is never so pleasant as when it is mixed with a little gossip.

2954   No person has really seen life until he has talked with the ticket seller in a theater box office.

2955   Few persons are so economical that they won't give you a piece of their mind.

2956   Whatever else may ail the world, it isn't inexpensive government.

2957   If you have to go to the hospital, it may help you to remember there is no such thing as a dangerous operation for less than one thousand dollars.

2958   As a last resort we suppose the farmer can go to the city, where his sons and some of his profits have already gone.

2959   Occasionally one sees a sweet young girl, hurrying to the office in the morning, who is pink-cheeked on only one side.

2960   A scientist says everyone should live to be a hundred years old. If that includes everyone, science has gone a little too far.

2961   You can live a quiet life just by living inside your income.

2962   Our politicians have thought of about every way to help the farmer but to leave him alone.

2963   A dollar doesn't go so far as it used to because it meets so many installments due right at home.

2964   Many a poor relative has a rich skinflint he would love to touch.

2965   One of the chief causes of war is the conviction that you can lick the other guy.

2966   Impoliteness is never excusable, except when you try to get a seat in a crowded bus.

2967   Sometimes it seems the people want free speech, a free press, and a free Federal Treasury.

2968   With the income-tax blanks due on April 15, a good many Americans will have a blank look and a blank pocketbook.

2969   Uncle Sam not only comes across and sits in conferences, but he also just comes across.

2970   The smallest book in the world: *Who's Who in Russia.*

2971   With crime serials on television, every youngster in the United States is a private detective.

2972   Most of us dislike being reformed by someone who is no better than we are.

2973   As we understand it, foreign businessmen do not object so much to American manners as to American customs.

2974   What most Americans would like is a dollar that will go a long way but won't go very fast.

2975   A news headline says, "Graft is Charged." We suppose it is in the tax bills.

2976   If you are ready to give someone a piece of your mind, be sure you can get along on what you have left.

2977   It's very difficult to become famous by having common sense and good manners.

2978   We've seen our share of movies where they didn't throw the right dummies over the cliffs.

2979   In modern education, children learn how to spell a word at least two ways.

2980   A woman never makes a fool of a man, but she sometimes helps direct the performance.

2981   An honest wife is one who lies only about her age, her weight, and her husband's salary.

2982   When you ask whether something is worth what it costs, you're getting old.

2983   There are one or two countries so backward the people don't spend money until they have saved it.

2984   One of the great mysteries to a married man is what a bachelor does with his time and money.

2985   Some persons jump at conclusions while others dig for facts.

2986   Some people think life is dull if there isn't any place to go where they shouldn't be.

2987   Always put off until tomorrow the things you shouldn't do at all.

2988   Only a few people live on borrowed time compared to the number who live on borrowed money.

2989   A person who is alone isn't necessarily in good company.

2990   It makes a lot of difference in life whether you live and learn or just live.

2991   It's a man's world, but the property is in his wife's name.

2992   Few persons ever grow up. They merely change their playthings.

2993   Many persons who didn't save last month are certain they will next month.

2994   A fool and his money are welcome as long as it lasts.

2995   You are young only once, but you can be immature all your life.

2996   The modern girl's hair may look like a mop, but she doesn't know what a mop looks like.

2997   It is unfortunate that many citizens demand something for nothing and even more unfortunate that they get it.

2998   When a thought strikes a person, no one can tell what will happen.

2999   The person who hears on radio and TV all the things wrong with him is lucky he feels as well as he does.

3000   The main difference between death and taxes is that taxes get worse every time Congress meets.

3001   The person who is always harping on something isn't necessarily an angel.

3002   The person who has nothing to say often proves it.

3003   If absence makes the heart grow fonder, some persons are in love with the church.

3004   No two persons are alike, and this makes it possible for each of us to be conceited.

3005   Travel doesn't broaden you as much as all the food you eat traveling.

3006   A fool and his money can throw a lot of parties.

3007   "I think" is an overworked expression and almost always a gross exaggeration.

3008   It's not at his mother's knees but across them where a youngster learns his best lessons.

3009   The most difficult meal for a wife to get is breakfast in bed.

3010   If you want to get a job done, give it to a busy man and he will have his assistant do it.

3011   A person may know his own mind and still be ignorant.

3012   The man who has holes in his socks should either get married or divorced.

3013   It must be discouraging to be a garage mechanic with grease on your hands and no steering wheel to wipe it on.

3014   Nothing goes to a man's stomach like success.

3015   It has just dawned on us why they call some resort hotels "The Palms."

3016   He cut quite a figure among his friends, but his bank account looked like zero.

3017   Sweet are the uses of your neighbor's adversity.

3018   An Eskimo is the only person who sits on top of the world, and he lives in an igloo and eats blubber.

3019   If they ever do away with comic books, many American youngsters will quit reading.

3020   "Reading maketh a full man," but it depends on what he is full of.

3021   Everyone may love a fat man, but not when he has the other half of a seat on the bus.

3022   Before a person tries his hand at something, he ought to try his head at it.

3023   A pessimist is a person who says all nations will share the atomic bomb.

3024   Sin is an old-fashioned word used to describe what is now called sophistication.

3025   When a rock-and-roll record wears out, it's hard to tell the difference.

3026   To get ahead in life, remember you can't keep your foot on second base and steal third.

3027   You can say for some persons that they aren't always as disagreeable as they are sometimes.

3028   A person may not have many faults and still overwork those he has.

3029   The Communist nations have less than we have and they want to share it with us.

3030   You can fool all the people some of the time, but you can fool yourself all the time.

3031   In a modern city you pay fifty cents to park your car so you won't be fined two dollars while you make a thirty-cent telephone call.

3032   The person who picks a tough job won't have much competition.

3033   Every dog has his day, but the road hog takes Sunday afternoon.

3034   The fellow who lives in a house by the side of the road and watches the world go by now is in a trailer.

3035   Half the world is always ready to tell the other half how to live.

3036   The average family could spend more money than it earns and generally does.

3037   You seldom are so busy that you can't stop and tell others how busy you are.

3038   No one has as many relatives as the fellow who makes a million dollars.

3039   Any game in which you hold hands is generally expensive.

3040   Most of us believe we are as good as we never were.

3041   Nothing is better for youngsters than some loving discipline.

3042   How do you start a conversation in Hawaii, where the weather is the same all the year around?

3043   From the standpoint of education, you can get a lot of firsthand knowledge from a secondhand car.

3044   Did you ever notice how nice you can be to someone you think can do you a favor?

3045   Think twice before you speak and you may say something even more irritating.

3046   Hope springs eternal in the shopper who looks for a ripe canteloupe.

3047   Many persons expect to be buried from the church, but do nothing about keeping it open until the funeral gets there.

3048   It does your heart good to hear a small boy eat.

3049   There are few husbands who do not love their wives still.

3050   You have to be very pessimistic not to see some good in the other fellow's troubles.

3051   Money makes fools of famous people, but it also makes famous people of fools.

3052   If you test a man's friendship by asking him to sign your note and he refuses, he is your friend.

3053   One advantage about baldness is that it requires very little attention.

3054   People who offer good advice always offer it in the big economy size.

3055   It's only on matters of great principle that some people lie with a clear conscience.

3056   If ignorance is bliss, what's the sense of intelligence tests?

3057   Some persons think there is no difference between self-confidence and conceit.

3058   A Congressman says middlemen are a burden on farmers, but so are meddle men.

3059   If all the officers in a business agree, some of them aren't thinking.

3060   As you grow older, you stand for more and fall for less.

3061   A person has good manners if he is able to put up with bad ones in others.

3062   When a person is always right, there is something wrong.

3063   Progress continues. The other day a fourteen-year-old boy ate an entire apple pie in ninety-one seconds.

3064   No one is so inconsiderate as the person who wants you to listen when you want to talk.

3065   One wonders if the English are so fond of tea because they have tried their coffee.

3066   Everyone has fun at the fat man's expanse.

3067   You have to give the great Marconi credit. He not only invented the radio but also the little gadget for turning it off.

3068   We suppose every time a golf champion plays he finds it's another uneasy lie for a crowned head.

3069   Do you suppose that the reason so many people don't vote is that they vote the way they think?

3070   There is nothing wrong with teen-agers that trying to reason with them won't aggravate.

3071   We used to spare the rod, but now we spare the hot rod and give it to Junior to drive.

3072   In cases of juvenile delinquency you fail unless you get at the seat of the trouble.

3073   The fact that no one knows anything about the future makes an economic forecaster more confident.

3074   Summer is the period when the children slam the doors they left open all winter.

3075   The most courteous tax collector in the country is the filling-station man who also sells gas and oil as a sideline.

3076   We've never been sure whether Isaac Walton or Ananias was the patron saint of fishermen.

3077   What this country needs is a little less paternalism in government and a little more in homes.

3078   It's strange how an earthquake four thousand miles away seems less of a catastrophe than the first scratch on your new car.

3079   The standard of living you can afford is the one you were on before you got your last raise.

3080   A reasonable man is one who doesn't demand the benefit of the doubt when there isn't any.

3081   An itch for public office often settles in the palms.

3082   If the newspapers and magazines continue going more and more to pictures, we may be able to eliminate the reading courses in schools.

3083   If the federal budget is to be in balance in four years, some drastic changes will be necessary in the figures, even in the four-year figure.

3084   When you talk about what a fool you used to be, you probably haven't changed much.

3085   A well-trained husband is one who feels in his pocket every time he passes a mailbox.

3086   Your hometown is the place where they can't understand how you got as far as you did.

3087   Even when Congress adjourns, there are still a few things wrong with the country.

3088   A sense of humor helps some people get a laugh out of their friends' troubles.

3089   Only Americans have mastered the art of being prosperous though insolvent.

3090   When you consider the hundreds of thousands of marriages each year, life seems to be just a marry chase.

3091   Every husband knows how words can flail you.

3092   A scientist says that prehistoric man was neither stoop-shouldered nor bowlegged. Then came taxes.

3093   Some after-dinner speakers are not only loquacious, but they also talk too much.

3094   There is nothing wrong with our young people that becoming a parent and taxpayer won't cure.

3095   Money still talks as much as ever, but it makes less cents today.

3096   Famous last words: "If he doesn't dim his lights, I'll give him my brights."

3097   An economist is a person who explains later how the thing he didn't expect was inevitable.

3098   The reckless driver approached the coroner at ninety miles an hour.

3099   We've never had it so good nor had to spend it so fast.

3100   If the months were made shorter, we wouldn't have so much month left over at the end of the money.

3101   Late to bed and early to rise makes you stupid rather than wise.

3102   A man never becomes so confused in his thinking that he thinks the other person is smart.

3103   One way to reduce blood pressure is to live within your income.

3104   A neurotic builds castles in the air and a psychoanalyst collects the rent.

3105   Maybe we have juvenile delinquency because too few parents are on spanking terms with their children.

3106   A good many arguments about new cars start from scratch.

3107   A youngster who learns from his grandfather what a dollar used to buy must feel pretty discouraged.

3108   Nothing is a better tranquilizer than a clear conscience.

3109   The fellow who follows the advice "Know thyself" is pretty certain not to tell anyone about it.

3110   The person who counts his money after a vacation begins to realize how carefree he really was.

3111   Most of us enjoy defending a prejudice more than we do fighting for a principle.

3112   The way to a man's heart, and also his pocketbook, is through his hobby.

3113   All things come to him who goes down a one-way street in the wrong direction.

3114   Punctuality is disappointing if no one is there to appreciate it.

3115   Staying on the straight and narrow path doesn't necessarily help you move in the best circles.

3116   A safe and sane Fourth is a small objective compared to the safety of 115 million automobiles on three million miles of highway.

3117   The next great advance in society will come when people become as speechless as they are thoughtless.

3118   No person puts off until tomorrow what he can do at time-and-a-half today.

3119   A good scare is more effective than good advice.

3120   Only one safe-driving rule is needed—drive as if a police car were just behind you.

3121   The person who looks tired and worn out has probably just returned from a vacation.

3122   The only time the average family practices togetherness is when they can't start the car.

3123   One of the evils of air-conditioning is that it makes you comfortable listening to a boring speech.

3124   Nothing makes a modern girl blush like the corner drugstore.

3125   The ant may be industrious, but he doesn't get on the front page as often as the butterfly.

3126   Truth in advertising: "The latest in antiques."

3127   In the international money markets, every day is a long daze work.

3128   A good barber now earns as much per word as an author.

3129   Scientists say we may have to make war against insects, as appeasement through picnics hasn't worked.

3130   When you buy something for a song, the accompaniment is probably expensive.

3131   On the sea of matrimony you have to expect occasional squalls.

3132   The first lesson in golf: Never stand too close to the ball after you hit it.

3133   Man's inhumanity to man makes prizefights, wars, and buffet suppers.

3134   We suppose the committee in Congress that considers the deficit is the committee of the hole.

3135   Some people sit around all day wondering why they don't get their pay raised.

3136   The only benefit most of us get from algebra is that it helps us when our children need help with algebra.

3137   One wonders how many amendments the Ten Commandments would have had if Moses had been a Senator submitting his proposals.

3138   Indians in the past bartered away valuable land for glass beads. We are more civilized and pay $5,000 for a string of pearls.

3139   If we saved civilization in two world wars, we wonder where it is hiding!

3140   As Confucius say, "Salesman who cover chair instead of territory is on bottom all time."

3141   No young man ever expects to grow up and be as dumb as his father.

3142   If you have to keep reminding yourself of something, perhaps it isn't worth remembering.

3143   A bird in the hand is good, but remember it has wings.

3144   You can generally evade a difficult question with a long-winded answer.

3145   The best way to bluff is to keep your mouth shut.

3146   The leaders of some underdeveloped nations should remember that it's one thing to itch for something and another thing to scratch for it.

3147   "A penny saved is a penny earned" was true up to the invention of the sales tax.

3148   If you want to win friends and influence people, you have to lose arguments.

3149   Modern transportation may be bringing us closer together, but the population increase helps.

3150   The person who takes his time often takes yours too.

3151   If you are sure you are right, you can afford to keep quiet.

3152   A conceited person never gets anywhere because he thinks he is already there.

3153   A scientist says life is the metabolic activity of protoplasm, but it seems worse than that on Monday morning.

3154   No one can make a fool of himself all the time—he has to rest occasionally.

3155   Some persons won't suffer in silence because that would take the pleasure out of it.

3156   A lot of persons who say the boss is dumb would be out of a job if the boss were any smarter.

3157   It's a great thing for a man to be married because he never has to worry about making up his mind.

3158   Modern chemistry has done a lot, but its greatest contribution was giving the world blondes.

3159   One way to make others happy is to leave them alone.

3160   He who hesitates is last.

3161   A fool and his money get to go places.

3162   Sometimes you find a person who knows how to live everyone's life expertly but his own.

3163   It is always easy to see the silver lining in the other person's cloud.

3164   If you think you know it all, you haven't been listening.

3165   A man who is on a wild-goose chase all his life never feathers much of a nest.

3166   If you are too busy to feel miserable, you will be happy.

3167   Early to bed and late to rise and you won't see any soap operas or old movies on television.

3168   Remember way back when you wished you could earn as much as you do now so you could save.

3169   It's strange how conscience may hurt when everything else seems pretty good.

3170   We long for the good old days when we earned only $15 a day and spent $20.

3171   The trouble with the average man is just that.

3172   Nothing is as easy as it looks except spending money and getting into an argument.

3173   Experience is what helps you to recognize everyone's mistakes except your own.

3174   Schooldays are the happiest days parents have.

3175   Too many people determine what is right or wrong on the basis of which pays best.

3176   It's bad enough to make a fool of yourself, but it's worse if you don't know who did it.

3177   In the old days young people who wore blue jeans worked, but now they only work their parents.

3178   A penny won't buy much, but it's still enough to buy most people's thoughts.

3179   It's one thing to hold your head up, but it's another matter to have your nose at the same level.

3180   Early to bed and early to rise and it's certain you are tired of TV Westerns.

3181   The straight and narrow path would be wider if more people walked on it.

3182   A hobby is something you go nuts about to keep from going nuts about what you are doing.

3183   A husband may read his wife like a book, but he can't shut her up that easily.

3184   When you hear your best girl talk to her ten-year-old kid brother, you know how she will talk to you after marriage.

3185   A newspaper is what a man uses in a bus so he can't see the woman standing in front of him.

3186   Don't complain about getting old, because when you stop you are dead.

3187   You can pay as you go, but it's not smart to go too much.

3188   If you get along with some people and ahead of some others, you will be a success.

3189   It's difficult to be content if you don't have enough, and it's impossible if you have too much.

3190   The seven ages of woman—the right age and six guesses.

3191   It's hard for a youngster to learn good manners without seeing any.

3192   When the going seems easy, you may be going downhill.

3193 When a husband sees the kind of men most women marry, he is sure his wife did pretty well.

3194 Marriage is a mutual partnership if both parties know when to be mute.

3195 Too often television is merely an advertisement with knobs on it.

3196 When you look at Chaucer's spelling, you know he must have dictated what he wrote to his secretary.

3197 A generation ago most men who finished a hard day's work needed rest; now they need exercise.

3198 Tragedy at a rummage sale is for a woman to take off her $100 dress and have someone sell it for $4.

3199 There are five thousand languages and dialects in the world, and money speaks all of them.

3200 Doctors say you should lie on the right side. We agree. If you must lie, always lie on the right side.

3201 It's hard to get as excited over things as the radio and TV commentators expect you to be.

3202 Nothing is more useless than a life spent just making money unless it is a life spent just trying to make money.

3203 The Supreme Court's rule: Blessed are those who pray, but not on school time.

3204 Most of us say "no" to temptation once weakly.

3205 Rock music may not be dying, but it sounds as if it were suffering terribly.

3206 To become a great professional ice skater you have to practice for hours on end.

3207 One trouble with the world is that there are too many clowns who aren't in the circus.

3208 Nothing teaches you so much about your neighbor as when you rub fenders with him.

3209 Money doesn't make you happy, but it certainly quiets your nerves.

3210 Every day Gabriel toots the horn on a great many cars.

3211 A person who is overweight is living beyond his seams.

3212 I don't mind parking the car except for that crash you have at the end.

3213 If a buttercup is yellow, is a hiccup burple?

3214   He who hesitates misses the green light, gets bumped in the rear, and loses his parking place.

3215   When it's just a prank, it's only jubilant delinquency.

3216   A business boom is a period when a consumer borrows more than he can repay in a business recession.

3217   American tourists don't have much trouble with their French. But the French do.

3218   An expert says no new crime has been invented for years, but apparently he hasn't heard some of the new song hits.

3219   Just when you wonder whether you will ever be able to pay your income tax, some doctor announces we will all live five years longer.

3220   We're always a little suspicious of those restaurants where the menus are in French and the prices in dollars.

3221   It seems easier to get married on $10,000 a year than to stay married on $30,000 a year.

3222   When you drive seventy-five miles an hour, you ought to carry at least a first-aid kit in the glove compartment.

3223   An old master is an artist who could paint almost as well as those who have since copied his paintings.

3224   What the world needs is not people to rewrite the Bible, but people to reread it.

3225   Political axiom: No tax reduction ever offends a voter.

3226   The person who says nothing in the world is ever done as well as it might be never talked to a taxpayer.

3227   Too many people think work is a good thing if it doesn't take up too much of your spare time.

3228   Civilization is a slow and painful process by which we get rid of some of our prejudices and acquire others.

3229   The reason a girl can't catch a ball like a man is that a man is so much bigger and easier to catch.

3230   Sometimes we think the human race began with Cain.

3231   The Kremlin's strength lies in knowing exactly what it wants—everything.

3232   The average driver learns how to drive safely after about three cars.

3233   Knocking in an individual is an evidence of a lack of power, just as it is in an automobile.

3234   Just how do some of our large cities tell the difference when there is a crime wave?

3235   An advertisement says homes are cleaner than they were a generation ago. Well, for one thing, they're used less.

3236   Although some foreigners criticize us, our immigration quotas are always full.

3237   A politician who says he will stick to the facts has no respect for tradition.

3238   The person who always insists on speaking his mind doesn't necessarily have one.

3239   Friendship is what makes you think almost as much of someone else as you do of yourself.

3240   The children run about everything now but the lawn mower and the vacuum cleaner.

3241   In Barnum's day there was only one sucker born every minute, but we suppose time marches on.

3242   There are a great many books now on how to live longer, but none on why.

3243   This generation can drive automobiles, fly jet planes, and develop color television, but has trouble with juvenile delinquency.

3244   Public opinion is simply the private opinion of one person who made enough noise to attract some converts.

3245   With some married couples the big difference of opinion is whether he earns too little or she spends too much.

3246   You can't tell by the looks of a mink coat how many installments are past due.

3247   Obstacles are the terrible things you see when you take your eyes from the goal.

3248   Two can live as cheaply as one, and after marriage they do.

3249   Remember the old days when you didn't have to borrow money to pay your income tax?

3250   If you hold your head up and your chin in, and put your shoulder to the wheel and your nose to the grindstone, you may get there but you will look pretty stupid.

3251   As the repair shop said to the passing motorist, "May we have the next dents?"

3252   Anger gets us into trouble because it makes the mouth move faster than the brain.

3253   When day is done in some offices mighty little else is.

3254   Early to bed and early to rise, it takes lots of credit cards to be able to do otherwise.

3255   In these days when you see silver threads among the gold it's time for another color hair rinse.

3256   We can't understand why most people won't admit their faults, because we would—if we had any.

3257   A smart husband doesn't go home and complain about dinner, but takes his wife to a restaurant where they can both complain.

3258   Foresight is knowing when to close your mouth before someone suggests it.

3259   The hand that rocks the cradle today gets $2 an hour, use of the TV, supper, and a ride home.

3260   Nothing gets a college football player out of condition more than studying.

3261   Whatsoever a husband soweth, that also shall he rip.

3262   If at first you succeed, you probably haven't done very much.

3263   The only person more stupid than the person who thinks he knows it all is the person who argues with him.

3264   An agriculturist is a farmer with a station wagon.

3265   No man with money is short of cousins.

3266   Nothing relieves the monotony of a job like finding ways to improve it.

3267   A slip of the tongue will often cause greater damage than a slip of the foot.

3268   If you rest your chin on your hands when you think, it will help you to keep your mouth closed.

3269   Unless you can look interested when you are bored, you will never be a success socially.

3270   We never could understand why other people do not profit from their mistakes.

3271   Sometimes you find you are up against it because you backed up instead of going ahead.

3272   You can often judge a man's knowledge of human nature by his opinion of himself.

3273   A man who is always on the go often never gets there.

3274   Some people consider nothing is a luxury if they can afford it.

3275   A man should stand up for his rights, but not in the middle of a street intersection.

3276   When you criticize your child for not being smart, remember a wooden head is one thing that can be inherited.

3277   Some people are always taking the joy out of life, and a good many of them are in the Internal Revenue Department.

3278   Half a loafer is better than a whole loafer.

3279   Most of us spend a great deal of time just letting off esteem.

3280   When you buy on the installment plan, you don't need a calendar.

3281   It's good to have an open mind if you know what to let in.

3282   "Heaven is not reached on a single bound," says the poet, but it may be on a busy street corner.

3283   The faster a man runs into debt, the more he gets behind.

3284   We understand that the idea of refueling in mid-air started by eating at those high stools at lunch counters.

3285   It's impossible to push yourself ahead by patting yourself on the back.

3286   Whenever everything is said and done, more is generally said than done.

3287   Sometimes we miss happiness by looking too far for things nearby.

3288   To reach a great height a person needs to have depth.

3289   If you have trouble opening your pocketbook, there are always plenty of people to help you.

3290   The difference between an allergy and an itch is about $100.

3291 Most girls want a spendthrift before they're married and a man who has saved his money after they're married.

3292 To win an argument, you have to argue with someone who knows less than you do, and that isn't easy either.

3293 At about forty a woman is old enough to start looking younger.

3294 The fellow who slaps you on the back is probably trying to get you to cough up something.

3295 Just because your face is serious is no assurance that you are sensible.

3296 Many a business fails because of a swelled overhead.

3297 One thing wrong with the country is that we have so many Republican and Democratic statesmen and so few United States statesmen.

3298 When you see this civilization survive, you wonder what happened to the old ones.

3299 With seventy-five percent of the automobiles being bought on time, there should be a market for a long-lasting automobile paint.

3300 A nation's credit and currency can be inflated to a point where there is a blowout.

3301 The fellow who doesn't believe in hell has never had his back peel off from sunburn.

3302 The Library of Congress has almost every book available except one on how to balance the federal budget.

3303 No one is so disappointed as the person who gets what's coming to him.

3304 Conscience helps, but the fear of getting caught doesn't do any harm either.

3305 One way to reach old age is to quit feeling responsible for the entire world.

3306 Think—and you will be very lonely.

3307 Always put off until tomorrow what you are going to make a mess of today.

3308 When you get up tired without having been out the night before, you have reached middle age.

3309 A prosperous person has two cars in the garage, a boat in the driveway, and a note due at the bank.

3310 Most of us who are in debt could get along now if we could borrow from Peter to pay Paul without paying Paul.

3311   In bridge, what some of us call "a bonehead bid made on a fool hunch" is called a "psychic bid" by the experts.

3312   When the hatpin disappeared, it was the only case of successful disarmament in history.

3313   Another thing our space exploration has done is to encourage ambitious American architects to alter their plans upward.

3314   Some high prices have fallen in a few food-store chains, but so far we have heard of no fatal injuries.

3315   The emphasis placed on keeping your eye on the ball is the best proof that golf originated in Scotland.

3316   One advantage of a polka-dot tie is that one more spot doesn't matter.

3317   The world would be very dull if we didn't flatter ourselves occasionally.

3318   Be sure to insist on the right of way when you drive, as it may make you feel better in the hospital.

3319   The best business forecasting is done after the events occur.

3320   One of the things that keeps the world in turmoil is the unusual attraction of strong lungs for weak heads.

3321   Someday a new model automobile will be brought out with no improvements, and then we'll know national decay has set in.

3322   At international conferences we never seem to have any record of the still, small voice.

3323   It's one thing to guarantee free speech in a country, but it's another thing to guarantee its quality.

3324   If the desert areas of the world want a crop that will unquestionably grow, we recommend a mixture of dandelions and crabgrass.

3325   An explorer says a tiger will not hurt you if you carry a white walking cane—we suppose you must carry it real fast.

3326   A Congressman who deals in billions must find it hard to go back home and talk to people who speak respectfully of quarters, dimes, and nickels.

3327   It used to be that Father got those impossible neckties only at Christmas, and then some cynic thought up Father's Day.

3328   Lifting ourselves out of a budget deficit by taxing less and spending more is going to put a terrific strain on our bootstraps.

3329   Sometimes we wonder how many youngsters wrote thank-you letters to Santa Claus after Christmas.

3330   Thank heaven this is a free country and a man can do as his wife pleases.

3331   There is no unemployment among those who spend their time minding other people's business.

3332   A man who agrees with everything you say needs to be watched.

3333   About the time you are pretty well satisfied with your progress the Joneses buy a new car.

3334   It's pretty embarrassing to watch the boss do something you said couldn't be done.

3335   A good many young brides today can dish it out better than they can cook.

3336   We remember the good old days when nobody but the baseball umpire called strikes.

3337   The air-pollution people say there is always rubbish in the air. Yes, but you're not obliged to listen to it.

3338   The difference between psychoneurosis and nervousness is about $50.

3339   In a materialistic society your problem is to get your share of the material.

3340   Each Christmas season the economists say that the improvement in business is due to holiday buying. You can't beat these economic experts for sharp analysis.

3341   We have never been able to decide whether betting is a means of getting something for nothing or nothing for something.

3342   Americanism means finding fault with other countries for not solving their problems, while we wait without hope for the government to solve ours.

3343   It looks like we would have a substantial federal deficit this year. Congress will undoubtedly find ways to spend it.

3344   The real question is can we make automobiles fool-in-the-other-car-proof.

3345   As an educational institution, nothing beats the stock market.

3346   An optimist is a person who thinks he knows a friend from whom he can borrow, and a pessimist is one who has tried.

3347   Blooming idiots have no off season.

3348   Many persons do not leave their footprints on the sands of time, but they leave their skidmarks at the traffic intersections.

3349   Of course the country is prosperous. We have more money and it buys less.

3350   It's difficult to take advice from some people when you know how much they need it themselves.

3351   Have you ever thought what Swiss cheese might smell like if it were not ventilated?

3352   Nothing is as relaxing as getting back to the office after a relaxing vacation.

3353   How far a fisherman stretches the truth depends on the length of his arms.

3354   Posterity—what you write for after being turned down by publishers. —*George Ade*

3355   Man's inhumanity to man makes crossing the street a major hazard.

3356   Most laws seem reasonable until unreasonable cops try to enforce them against nice people like us.

3357   Good government pays, and so does bad government, but not the same people.

3358   Nothing comes nearer to perpetual motion than the protests of taxpayers.

3359   No matter how much war changes, the privates end up doing the fighting and the hard work.

3360   When opposing groups in a Latin American country bury the hatchet, they both know exactly where it is.

3361   Man is the only creature whose brains tell him he should save for the future, but the squirrels and bees do it a lot better naturally.

3362   If you think mankind can conceive nothing more horrible than nuclear war, you have lost faith in the progress of civilization.

3363   Vacation is the period when you spend two weeks in an old shack without conveniences so you can go back to your home with its comforts and complain.

3364   A library has a sign, "Only low talk permitted," and we understood it when we saw the covers on the paperback books.

3365   In some cities a thief who breaks into the city hall can steal the results of the next election.

3366   Why is it that the other fellow always thinks he is carrying the load when we know we are?

3367   Sympathizing with some persons is like patting a dog on the head—they both follow you around for more.

3368   The early worm gets the fishhook.

3369   No two women are alike and neither is any one woman.

3370   The way to be successful is to follow the advice you give others.

3371   Little things keep one awake at night, especially those from three to six months of age.

3372   The young man who drives with one arm will either walk down or be carried up a church aisle.

3373   In a Communist country a man can talk his head off very easily.

3374   As the attractive young lady said, "A man without a country is bad, but a country without a man is worse."

3375   One of the first things man learns is to talk, and later in life he learns to keep still.

3376   Short, fat people are said to be "easily adjustable"—except when you try to adjust three of them into the front seat of the car.

3377   Blessed are the peacemakers—they will never be unemployed.

3378   Sometimes we think the politicians ought to give one of those $100-a-plate dinners to cover the federal deficit.

3379   How can the people object to higher taxes? They saved the money for a rainy day and this is it.

3380   Believe only half you hear, but be sure it's the right half.

3381   With women now having equal rights, we wonder what the feminine is for *colonel* in Kentucky.

3382   A smart Secretary of Agriculture would draw the salary for his term in advance.

3383   Sometimes we wish the Gideons would leave a Bible at the hotel reservation desk.

3384   In public libraries, except in Boston, low conversation is permitted.

3385   A wise husband confides his business troubles to his wife—especially if she wants a mink coat.

3386 If you are right, what's the use of arguing, and if you are wrong, what's the use?

3387 Have you ever heard a radio announcer say he was going to make an important announcement and then follow it by an important announcement?

3388 If the government investigates the steel industry, we suppose they will make the startling discovery that it is a large industry.

3389 Some men would rather be right than be President, but others would rather be wrong than not be.

3390 You can cover three hundred miles in a half-hour in a jet plane, which is about the time it takes an employee to go next door for a coffee break.

3391 We sort of admire some leaders in the new nations who stage revolutions without borrowing any money from us.

3392 When a politican makes a pledge to spend more money, he always keeps it.

3393 A doctor says a man is sober if he can say, "Susie sat in the soup," but what about Susie?

3394 In the old days U.S. Grant meant a famous soldier and not foreign aid.

3395 We would almost like to hear that a train had been robbed, as it would indicate that some of them are still running.

3396 The American who has not seen an automobile is impossible to find, but not the person who has not seen one in time.

3397 The eternal struggle in popular government is to retain its popularity.

3398 Diplomats are unusual-looking persons, and you would be too if you went around with your tongue in your cheek all the time.

3399 When a dentist is down in the mouth, the other fellow feels even worse.

3400 Some idea of how much the country has deteriorated is evident when you realize that no present Presidential candidates were born in a log cabin.

3401 Sometime the Nobel Peace Prize should go to the fellow who finds a way to keep the diplomats from constantly upsetting the world.

3402 Business needs more orders from customers and fewer from the government.

3403 We've meant to inquire whether women who take a test for a driver's license do it from the back seat.

3404 With colleges increasingly critical, it is getting so an amateur can't make a living in any sport.

3405 Is anyone old enough to remember way back when women's hats looked like hats?

3406 No man is suspected of being dumb until he begins to talk, which makes you wonder why so many are willing to make speeches.

3407 The rulers of a great many countries come to the United States on a moneymoon trip.

3408 One day of good old-fashioned winter is generally enough to satisfy us.

3409 Many industries are closely related. Think of what the petroleum industry has done for accident insurance.

3410 Do the good really die young or is it the goodness of the good that dies young?

3411 A true idiot cannot read, and this makes you wonder who buys some of the paperback books.

3412 When a girl marries a hardworking young executive, the thing she misses most after marriage is her husband.

3413 We are warned paper money is covered with germs, but we continue to feel very well.

3414 It's a tragedy that all of the people who know how to run the country are newspaper columnists or TV commentators.

3415 Santa Claus's taste in neckties leaves something to be desired.

3416 One benefit of high prices is that you don't have enough money left now to buy the things you don't need.

3417 Red China apparently promotes an increase in population to be killed in wars of expansion to find room for the surplus population.

3418 The people who adopt "It can be done" as a motto never ask, "Does anyone want it done?" or "How much will it cost?"

3419 Capitalists and Communists are alike in that both want more than they have.

3420 Most of us find some of our ambitions nipped in the budget.

3421 We wonder whether women's feet are getting larger now that they fill men's shoes so often.

3422 A model wife will help her husband with housework.

3423 Nothing is a better example of faith than the colored pictures in a spring seed catalog.

3424   Flying to Europe in six hours is easy, but finding a good reason for the hurry is harder.

3425   When a woman is pensive she is probably just planning something very expensive.

3426   The recipe for success is almost the same as that for a nervous breakdown.

3427   With modern dish- and clothes-washers, the only thing in the home that isn't automatically washed is the family.

3428   Wealth may not bring happiness, but it's a pleasant way to be unhappy.

3429   "You are what you eat," says a doctor. In that case, we are a tough steak.

3430   "Easy payments" means "easy" except when you are making payments on everything in the house.

3431   Some people don't let their right hands know where their left hands got it.

3432   A woman's waistline moves up and down, but a man's merely expands.

3433   The voice of the people is the voice of God when it agrees with us, and the voice of the ignorant masses when it doesn't.

3434   Money doesn't go as far as it used to except the dime that rolls under the bed.

3435   We expect modern youth to be strong, courageous, and prepared to pay even more taxes than their fathers.

3436   It's a delicate art when you try to give people just enough social security to prevent a rude reaction to new taxes.

3437   We're expecting Alaska to petition the government for a central heating plant as a needed public-works project.

3438   The best flings in life are not free, and besides you have to report them now in detail on your expense account.

3439   In a committee one person does the work while the four other persons pat him on the back.

3440   Getting up and going to work every morning certainly breaks into your whole day.

3441   To do a superior job, a good man needs a plan and not quite enough time.

3442   Fishing is generally best before you get there or after you leave.

3443   One reason foreigners find English so difficult is that they try to speak it correctly.

3444   When you are warned to slow down by the doctor instead of the police, you have reached middle age.

3445   Just because the little woman is sad-eyed, it doesn't mean she has loved and lost. She may have got him.

3446   Every four years the farmers are assured of higher prices for all they sell and lower prices for everything they buy.

3447   A man may be in a class by himself, but it all depends on what class.

3448   The emptier the pot, the quicker it boils.

3449   The Russians are very considerate and only start trouble for us in other countries.

3450   The trouble with some persons having the last word is that they never get to it.

3451   We sometimes wonder why political parties feel they need big men to head their tickets when they so often win without them.

3452   We suggest a contest among the nations to see which one has run longest with an unbalanced budget.

3453   It takes something more than a two-by-four to be good Presidential timber.

3454   Washington was the wealthiest man of his time, but what would Washington do to Washington today?

3455   Any ideas an economist has about money are certain to be theoretical.

3456   Taxation without limitation is tyranny.

3457   The other fellow's pain is always more interesting if you have some of your own.

3458   An ounce of keeping one's mouth closed may be worth a pound of explanation.

3459   A wife may appreciate your giving her credit, but she appreciates your giving her cash even more.

3460   All of us are more or less foolish, but it's when we try to prove it that we get into real trouble.

3461   In the old days two could live as cheaply as one, but now one can live as expensively as two.

3462   A test pilot who can go twenty miles up in the air and come down again should make an excellent candidate for public office.

3463   Most political candidates are more candied than candid.

3464   The highway engineers apparently decided that it is easier to eliminate the grade crossings than to eliminate all the people who don't look and listen.

3465   Lincoln said, "You can fool some of the people all of the time," and the politician lavishes his attention on this group.

3466   It's easy to be beautiful and healthy, too, if you believe the TV commercials.

3467   There are repeated suggestions that English be made the world language, which means a good many Americans will have to learn it.

3468   The university professor who is running a course in "What Civilization Is" could be helpful if he could tell us where it is.

3469   Next to a baby there is nothing like a mortgage to cement a family.

3470   Youth should have its day, because it ages rapidly when taxpaying begins.

3471   When you get older, you can miss the picnics, but they still catch you on the buffet suppers.

3472   A Soviet scientist is trying to increase the life-span to 150 years, but more important is making it worthwhile to live that long in Russia.

3473   We understand that some nations looked on the arguments in Congress on foreign aid as "Mutiny Over the Bounty."

3474   The dollar is holding up well. A half-dime dated 1851 is now worth twenty cents.

3475   The doctors who are working to prolong human life have a lot of faith in the government's social-security resources.

3476   There's nothing more enjoyable then a good short visit with an old classmate.

3477   One way to solve the problem of leisure is to sit around and criticize those who are working.

3478   We have the fear that a tax-revision program which doesn't reduce taxes will be hit from both the Right and Left, which is the well-known one-two punch.

3479   With all the grades in which gasoline is now sold, we suppose the next step is to offer six or seven delicious flavors.

3480   No matter what kind of platform a politican runs on, he always loses the economy plank sooner or later.

3481   It's strange how the Department of Agriculture budget steadily rises over the years as we reduce the number of our farms and farmers.

3482   With all our troubles here and abroad, we've been fearful that next someone would debunk vitamin pills.

3483   A knot on the head may result from carrying a chip on the shoulder.

3484   A public official's success ought to depend on how much he can do, and not how many.

3485   We've never had it so good nor had it taken away from us so fast.

3486   Some foreign nations can't get along with American capital and can't get along without it.

3487   Perhaps the single greatest change in the world in our generation is that the Stars and Stripes has replaced the British Lion.

3488   Art is long, but artists are generally short.

3489   We have often wondered how a father with two knees gets along with quintuplets.

3490   More and more nations are arming to the teeth and they aren't wisdom teeth.

3491   Civilization has progressed so you not only drive a tin can now but live out of one also.

3492   The optimists see no chance of nuclear war, but those with more faith in mankind believe some kind of misunderstanding can be worked out.

3493   Some women have only three requirements for a husband—money, wealth, and property.

3494   What you don't know doesn't hurt you unless it's all those hidden taxes in the things you buy.

3495   Any person can criticize, complain, and find fault, and most of them do.

3496   Attending conventions is the big American pastime. The country is going to the pow-wows.

3497   To be great, the people of a nation need to have tender consciences and callused hands. The situation frequently is reversed.

3498   With present fast airline schedules, you can be robbed in the East in the morning and in the West in the evening.

3499 Every once in a while a Latin American ambassador has to go home to find out who he is working for.

3500 The number of Americans who can't speak English is over two million, and this includes announcers in airports.

3501 A woman loves bargains, but never tell her she is wearing one.

3502 A philanthropist recently said, "It is hard to give away a million." Brother, it's even harder to get it in the first place.

3503 With some people, "Get thee behind me, Satan" is an invitation for him to push.

3504 A safety foundation has announced that there are too many traffic deaths, but it didn't say what would be a good wholesome number.

3505 We suppose one of these days the government will investigate why the automobiles throw so much business to the doctors.

3506 A well-known movie actress was reported to have a severe cold in the head. Most of the time it is entirely unoccupied.

3507 Civilization today just doesn't make sense, which should make it a good subject for fiction writers.

3508 We have everything in the modern kitchen now except a cook.

3509 Sometimes a person can't tell whether he is thinking big or whether his conscience is stretching.

3510 You may not know when you are well off, but the Internal Revenue Service does.

3511 If you think you won't be missed, just leave town without paying some of your bills.

3512 Money may not bring happiness, but it is nice to find out for yourself.

3513 There is a rumor that Red China would like to change its name to Asia.

3514 "If it ain't broke—don't fix it." A basic philosophy of government as told to Bert Lance by Mister Ben, the old Georgia mountain man.

3515 Money talks, but it is certainly hard of hearing when you call it.

3516 Sometimes you don't know who is knocking—opportunity or temptation.

3517 In government the next step after planned economy is planned extravagance.

3518   Since the end of World War II, Western Europe recovered over 100 percent of her prosperity, including some of ours.

3519   Sometimes the United Nations has about as much influence as the average American husband.

3520   Sometimes a politician is popular because of his purseonality.

3521   Wages are what you get for doing what you are told, and salaries are what you get paid for doing things without being told.

3522   Everything comes to him who waits except the time he lost waiting.

3523   If we are here to help others, what are the others here for?

3524   Some persons have nothing to say, but you have to listen a long time to find out.

3525   With rising college tuition fees, education is getting almost as expensive as ignorance.

3526   The hardest thing for any young couple to learn is that other parents have perfect children also.

3527   It is about as hard for a rich man to enter heaven as it is for a poor man to pay all his installments.

3528   A small man behind a big title is sometimes as ferocious as a small dog behind a big fence.

3529   Most people today never stay long enough in one place to get homesick when they leave.

3530   When you get to the top of the long ladder of success, remember that it took a good many people to hold the ladder.

3531   No secret is harder to keep than your opinion of yourself.

3532   The earth revolves on its axis, but the nations revolve on their taxes.

3533   Wisdom on the part of a wife is to let her husband have her way.

3534   One way to get rid of weight is to leave it on the plate.

3535   The way to keep closets clean is to get a bigger garage.

3536   Some leading Presidential possibilities would make good professional football players. You can't tell whether they are going to run or pass.

3537   America averages over a million major crimes a year, not counting those of people who signal one way and turn the other.

3538   When we read about the number of traffic deaths, we think maybe the underdeveloped nations with no roads are not so bad.

3539   Thrift means to spend less than you earn, an obsolete word in government circles.

3540   In Latin American countries, finance ministers seldom succeed. They only succeed each other.

3541   An expensive winter resort recently established a bird sanctuary for guests, but what they need is a refuge for out-of-town fish.

3542   Some people say wild life is disappearing, but, from our observations, it is just moving to the cities.

3543   The part of a woman's work that is never done is what she asked her husband to do.

3544   Loneliness is the feeling you have when you are without money among relatives.

3545   The old-fashioned sermon on hell wasn't much different from the modern TV program on world events.

3546   Even the most conceited public speaker is a little surprised when the toastmaster tells the audience how great he is.

3547   With daylight saving, some of us get tired an hour earlier.

3548   "What will become of our young people?" wails a parent. Oh, they will grow old and worry about the young people.

3549   Civilization totters from time to time, but it totters forward.

3550   News headline: "Two Burglars Surprised by Policemen." They must have been.

3551   A Hollywood actor's life isn't so easy, because he has to sit through every picture he makes at least three times.

3552   Divorce should be harder to obtain. At least the departing person should be required to wave goodbye.

3553   At least an honest taxpayer knows that he will not have to hear Andrew Carnegie's reproach, that the man who dies rich dies disgraced.

3554   No smart girl visits no man's land on a vacation.

3555   No one can jump down your throat if you keep your mouth shut.

3556   An old philosopher says a man spends a large part of a short life doing work he doesn't like in order to buy things he doesn't need.

3557   Three burglars entered a night club and escaped without losing anything.

3558   We seem to be progressing. Modern youth would be bored by the dime novel that was considered a terrible menace to the youth of yesterday.

3559   Death and taxes are certain, but death isn't an annual event.

3560   Very few persons complain of the high cost of golf balls.

3561   It's difficult to make your friends believe you earn as much as you do and have the government believe you make as little as you do.

3562   We do not understand why a politician never seems as wise in Congress as he does in an election campaign.

3563   It's pretty hard sometimes to tell whether a politician is sound or is just making a lot of it.

3564   The way of the transgressor is hard—not only on him, but on everyone else.

3565   Only mosquitoes and nations receiving foreign aid bite the hand that feeds them.

3566   Noah was ready when the flood came, but he didn't have to get a tax-revision bill through Congress.

3567   If we ever have a politician who keeps his promises, there is some doubt whether the people will be ready for such a drastic change.

3568   A good name is rather to be chosen than great riches, and there is no tax on it either.

3569   When a person says he wants to give you constructive criticism, he is really constructing skids for you.

3570   Sometimes you begin to doubt whether the more the country owes, the more prosperous it will be.

3571   If you think you are well informed, name ten members of the House of Representatives.

3572   One trouble with modern civilization is that too many people stretch the cocktail hour into three or four.

3573   We like to dream about a million dollars, but we hate to think about all the work it takes to make it.

3574   An intellectual is a person who only knows how to spell a word one way.

3575   Some persons have read so much about the harmful effects of smoking that they have decided to give up reading.

3576   The superiority of men over animals is not so clear when you consider that a cow is now milked with a machine without a man, but never without a cow.

3577   With high sugar prices, we are reminded that three hundred tons of sugar are wasted every year in the bottom of cups. We hope this causes a stir.

3578   Civilization is a state of society in which it is possible for a book to be published on *Tap Dancing as a Career.*

3579   What the country needs is a chocolate bonbon with a lettuce center for women on a diet.

3580   If you give an automobile driver an inch, he will take half your lane.

3581   Someday a government is going to try something really new and cut taxes.

3582   Allies are nations that may or may not stand by you through troubles you wouldn't have if you didn't have allies.

3583   Nowadays they broadcast the details of hospital operations on TV and in magazine articles. In the old days the patient did it.

3584   Someday we may find that it hurts just as much to lose your money in the stock market under the SEC as it did in the old unethical days.

3585   A farmer always knows when it's dinnertime on Sunday, as the yard is full of cars of city relatives.

3586   Couldn't the refrigerator people develop something that would keep our international relationships permanently defrosted?

3587   We understand that thousands of Bibles are stolen from hotel rooms each year, and this leaves us confused.

3588   All men are born free and equal, but soon grow up into graduated income taxes.

3589   They say a tax cut will relieve taxpayers, and that's what we are afraid may happen.

3590   The question historians should study is not where civilization began, but when.

3591   It makes a lot of difference whether the scales are in the hands of Justice or in her eyes.

3592   A bride of eighteen faces the job of cooking fifty thousand meals unless she gets a can opener.

3593   California is much like Florida except that all of it isn't constantly for sale.

3594   A flu shot is something that makes you careful not to catch a cold again and have to take a flu shot.

3595   The best things in life are free or are available for a dollar down and a dollar a week.

3596   With present-day wigs, a woman's hair may be Titian or imi-Titian.

3597   Most authors use about the same number of words as Shakespeare, but they are arranged very differently.

3598   If the size of the dollar bill were reduced to keep it in proportion to its purchasing power, it would save a lot of paper.

3599   One great thing about winter is that you can reduce by filling a shovel with wet snow and throwing it over your shoulders 1,765 times each week.

3600   If Soviet Russia could thrive on five-year plans and promises, her people would be well fed and not buying wheat.

3601   A doctor says dentist's fingers may carry disease germs, which apparently means the dentist should be boiled.

3602   The successful businessman who enrolled recently in a graduate school of business probably wants to find out how he got that way.

3603   A State Department diplomat has to have a gambler's instinct to be sure he is putting the government's foreign-aid money on the right revolution.

3604   The only safe rule in buying an old painting is to let the other fellow buy it.

3605   There are two kinds of people who don't generally say much—quiet people and those who talk.

3606   They never locate the man higher up in the crime syndicates. It's almost impossible to find one lower down than most of those they occasionally arrest.

3607   In New York City they tear down thirty-five-story shanties to make way for sixty-story modern buildings.

3608   Sometimes you wonder whether we should try to manage Europe, Asia, Africa, and Latin America before we learn how to run one American city well.

3609   People who used to buy school shoes and bathrobes for gifts now buy cocktail shakers and sports cars, which shows that the children are growing up.

3610   Are we going to find someday that all is Confucian in Southeast Asia?

3611   Christmas used to come only once a year, but with installment payments it comes every week.

3612   We understand radio and TV add words to the listener's vocabulary. We imagine there are some that shouldn't be printed.

3613   When some people are asked to do civic or charity work, they will stop at nothing.

3614   There are two kinds of conceited people—those who admit it and the rest of us.

3615   The world is getting smaller, but it costs more to run it.

3616   A critic is a person who sees a finished job and knows he could have done it better.

3617   The trouble with the nations today is that they all want to play the big drum and no one wants to play second fiddle.

3618   Most people recognize their duty in time to avoid it.

3619   All play and no work makes it difficult to know what to do with your leisure.

3620   We are looking for a book on *How to Avoid Doing It Yourself.*

3621   The persons who live next door listen to both sides of a family argument.

3622   A scientist says the world will last a billion years longer, which doesn't help our present pessimism about world affairs.

3623   Sometimes a person may be quieter because he has more to be quiet about.

3624   You never need to do over a job you did well, unless it's weeding the garden.

3625   Poverty is not a disgrace, but that's its one advantage.

3626   A person with a million dollars may be a bad egg, but he generally gets by pretty well until he is broke.

3627   The person who shouts the loudest for justice generally means in his favor.

3628   If you sing when you are sad, others can be sad with you.

3629   A person who slaps you on the back probably does it to help you swallow what he is telling you.

3630   Time is a great healer, but it's not much of a beauty parlor.

3631   If the world was created out of chaos, we're now back about where we started.

3632   With so many compact cars on the streets, you have to look right, left, and down.

3633   It's surprising how many persons will agree with you if you keep your mouth shut.

3634   Some of the new nations are getting so efficient that a plotter against the government is polished off before you can say *habeas corpus.*

3635   Sometimes it seems Congress should be able to discuss a question of fact without lining all the Republicans up on one side and all the Democrats on the other.

3636   If economy is the way to balance a government budget, we're afraid this is a harder job than we thought.

3637   You have to be pretty well off not to be ashamed to ask the clerk for something cheaper.

3638   A hypocrite is a person who says he believes you when he knows you are not telling the truth.

3639   For each dollar the United States spends, it takes in about ninety cents. It is only the large number of dollars we spend which makes this work.

3640   The improvement in padlocks, burglar alarms, and nuclear bombs just about keeps up with the progress of civilization.

3641   When you visit a modern-art gallery, you realize that things are never as bad as they are painted.

3642   We suggest that some of the government's surplus food be used in hors d'oeuvres in place of the plastics now being served.

3643   Why do so many car drivers have dominating personalities?

3644   Everything comes to him who waits, but it usually isn't worth waiting for.

3645   We like to hear people laugh, but not when we're chasing our hat down the street.

3646   Some people may mean well, but their meanness is sometimes greater than their wellness.

3647   The person who is always happy may be too lazy to complain.

3648   If some of the rest of the people don't start worrying soon, we're going to quit, too.

3649   Too many persons want the kind of government that will give them more than they deserve.

3650   If those who have nothing to say would refrain from saying it, the world would be very quiet.

3651   The government does not expect to live within its income—only within yours.

3652   Some prayers are so long because a person prays for more than he works for.

3653   It always depresses us when we consider the kind of homes the home-made pies we buy must have come from.

3654   When the government looks into the causes of the high cost of living, it always fails to look in the obvious place.

3655   A dollar doesn't go as far as it did once, but it goes a lot faster.

3656   If you want to live on Easy Street, you have to save enough to buy a lot there.

3657   A duty is a job you look forward to with distaste, perform with reluctance, and brag about ever after.

3658   One advantage in being poor is that you use up the junk around the house instead of putting it in the attic or garage.

3659   The fellow who says he owes everything to his wife probably keeps her on a skimpy allowance.

3660   There may be some consolation in the fact that the dollar you haven't got isn't worth so much as it was.

3661   It's strange, but you may try to do something and fail and try to do nothing and succeed.

3662   Listening to advice may get you into trouble, but it makes the other person feel better.

3663   The persons who tells his dollars where to go saves money, and the person who wants to know where they went doesn't.

3664   One trouble with the country is that you can't pass enough laws to keep people from making fools of themselves.

3665   If you can't think of a smart, snappy retort, a slight yawn is just about as good.

3666   Occasionally all of us must wish others would tell a lie about us rather than the truth.

3667   Even a person who serves as a horrible example for others isn't entirely useless.

3668   An automobile is only as fast as the people in it.

3669   They were happily married, because she was his little treasure and he was her great big treasury.

3670   A man is endowed with certain inalienable rights, all of which he must fight for.

3671   A small town is a place where a person with a black eye can't say he ran into a door.

3672   A fool and his money get along now just about as well as the rest of us.

3673   The way of the transgressor may be hard, but it isn't lonely.

3674   An appendix is what the doctor takes out before he decides it's gallstones.

3675   A person who is heavily in debt on installments wants more out of life than there is in it.

3676   You can entertain most persons by sitting down and listening to them.

3677   A baby-sitter is a girl who plays the TV to keep your children awake.

3678   If you're going to make a pal of your boy, don't do it until after he has had quadratic algebraic equations.

3679   It is said we spend more on wild life than we do on child life in this country, but parents will find this a puzzling distinction.

3680   Matrimony is a process by which the grocer acquires an account the florist had.

3681   The best time to weed a garden is just after your wife tells you to.

3682   Worry is like a rocking chair: it gives you something to do, but it won't get you any place.

3683   You can make a fortune if you know the exact moment when a piece of junk becomes an antique.

3684   A secret is something that's not worth keeping or is too good to keep.

3685   One robin may not make a spring, but one lark may make a fall.

3686   You can always tell a person who can't save because he is full of ideas about how to spend other people's money.

3687   The person who says he trusts no one should include himself.

3688   Maybe the reason girls prefer beauty to brains is that young men can generally see better than they think.

3689   Most of us would like to have all the money we spent foolishly—so we could spend it foolishly again.

3690   If you punch a man in the nose when he calls you a fool, it may prove he was right.

3691   The cost of living is up because many of us put nothing down when we buy.

3692   No man is as unpopular in government as the fellow who has ideas for saving money.

3693   If everyone thought before he spoke, the world would be almost silent.

3694   As long as so many persons take themselves seriously, there will be a great deal of humor in the world.

3695   At a party the conversation never gets good until a few couples leave.

3696   Women frequently change fashions, but their designs are always the same.

3697   In winter we always think what Noah might have done for us if he had left that pair of flu germs out of the ark.

3698   A bagpipe is the only instrument that sounds as good when you are learning to play it as it does afterward.

3699   Radio and TV have added five hundred words to the language, not including the words that are mispronounced.

3700   Sometime someone will come right out and run for office on a program of planned extravagance.

3701   In rural areas now they don't lock the barn door after the horse is stolen. They open a summer theater.

3702   The danger in giving a politician a free hand is that he will put it in your pocket.

3703   The way governments in some nations clamp down on the news, they seem to think no news is good news.

3704   Our agricultural policy is simple: A high price is paid for products which are sold at a lower price as exports and the taxpayer foots the bill.

3705   This country has become so affluent that when a motorist has a flat tire, he changes cars instead of tires.

3706   It's surprising how well your own car runs after you ask the price of a new one.

3707   Any car will last a lifetime if you are not careful.

3708   Somehow we think that very few big jobs are held by men who like to honk a horn in a traffic jam.

3709   A doctor says hungry persons drive faster and more dangerously, and we suppose the same thing applies to those who are no longer thirsty.

3710   After five thousand years of civilization, the most famous persons today are those who can carry a football, tote a gun in a TV Western, or play the lead in *Cleopatra*.

3711   The National Park Service should warn tourists not to encourage bears to sit up and beg. They might go to Washington and demand relief on a more regular basis.

3712   An automobile is always as drunk as the driver.

3713   Every time someone makes his mark in the world, someone is waiting to use the eraser.

3714   Times change. In the old days it was prosperity that was always just around the corner. Now it's a balanced budget.

3715   Housework is said to be too great a strain for modern women, but how would they know?

3716   Regarding government deficits, we believe that you should repair a hole in the roof while the sun is shining, but what's the use as long as it's never going to rain again?

3717   Doctors who do not get paid at least know they have earned the ingratitude of the patients they made well.

3718   The best buy in real estate is always a corner lot, because sooner or later someone will want it for a filling station.

3719   What this country needs is more police-department heads who favor shake-ups instead of shake-downs.

3720   At Christmas half the people believe in Santa Claus and half in the government.

3721   A smart wife will back up her husband in an argument—up against the wall.

3722   The way to win friends is to lose arguments.

3723   The fellow who puts on the dog often puts off the creditors.

3724   If a man tries as hard to keep his wife after marriage as he tried to get her, they will get along well.

3725   No woman likes a perfect husband, because it doesn't give her anything to do.

3726   We have advanced so far that when we want to relax we have to work at it.

3727   It's bad manners to talk when your mouth is full or your head is empty.

3728   The person who can't find a parking place near the church on Sunday probably concludes virtue isn't its own reward.

3729   This country has some fine old ruins, but you have to go to a night club to see them.

Helpful Verses

Occasionally in a speech or introduction of another speaker it is possible to use a short verse effectively. This provides a change in the speaker's form of presentation and may also enable him to place particular emphasis upon some point.

Both humorous and serious verses are included in this chapter.

3730   *Artless Aerials*

Of TV programs some complain:
    "Too stupid," or "Too hectic";
But it's the TV aerials
    That make me apoplectic.
At least a million pleasant homes
    In countrysides Elysian
Have sacrificed artistic charm
    Installing television.
I think most modern gadgets great,
    But I'm for early burials,
Thru technological advance,
    Of television aerials!
                    —*Leverett Lyon*

3731   *Attention Parents*

>   Breathes there a parent with a soul so dead
>   Who never to himself has said,
>   "Get a load of that spoiled brat.
>   I'd spank my kid for a thing like that."

3732   *Right*

>   Roses are red,
>   Violets are blue,
>   But they don't spread
>   Like dandelions do.

3733   *Good Old Ham and Eggs*

>   She read the fancy recipes,
>   Each one a tempting winner;
>   Then dashing to her kitchen,
>   Fixed ham and eggs for dinner.

3734   *Social Climber*

>   Early to rise and ditto to bed
>   Makes a guy healthy but socially dead.

3735   *Too Late*

>   All things come to those who wait,
>   But when they come they're out of date.

3736   *April 15*

>   Three hundred sixty-five days in the year
>   You work like the dickens to make it.
>   And just when you're ready
>   To start eating steady,
>   The government's ready to take it.

3737   *It Certainly Does*

>   The honeybee is funny,
>   Its functions seeming double,
>   One end gives us honey,
>   The other gives us trouble.

3738   *No Prescience*

One thinks, schemes, plans, contrives, projects—
Aware that he is mental;
But still, a large part of one's life
Is just coincidental!
                                    —*Leverett Lyon*

3739   *Wake Me*

Now I set me down to sleep,
The speaker's dull, the subject deep.
If he should stop before I wake,
Give me a poke, for goodness sake.

3740   *Safety*

Stop and let the trains go by—
It hardly takes a minute.
Your car starts out again intact,
And better still—you're in it.

3741   *A Certainty*

One thing is certain,
And the rest is lies;
If you lose your credit card,
You're in for a surprise.
                                    —*Herbert V. Prochnow*

3742   *Fishing*

In northern lakes the fish are teeming,
Say ads that send us northward streaming.
But once you're up there, and afloat,
Just try to get one in a boat!
Disdaining worms, flies, plugs, and scheming,
The fish prefer to stay there—teeming!
                                    —*Leverett Lyon*

3743   *Music*

A squeak's heard in the orchestra
As the leader draws across
The intestines of the agile cat
The tail of the noble Hoss.
                                    —*George T. Lanigan*

3744 *Success*

> I sent my boy to college
> With a pat upon the back.
> I spent ten thousand dollars
> And got—a quarterback.

3745 *Malcontent*

> As a rule a man's a fool;
> When it's hot he wants it cool;
> When it's cool he wants it hot.
> Always wanting what is not.

3746 *Dedicated to the South*

> Flower in the crannied wall,
> I broke my leg to pick you-all.
> —*Herbert V. Prochnow*

3747 *Vicarious*

> I like to ride in Cadillacs;
> I'd like to own a few;
> But, having none, the next best thing,
> Is having friends who do!
> —*Leverett Lyon*

3748 *No Moaning*

> Sunset and evening star,
> And one clear call for me!
> And may there be no moaning at the bar
> When I order a pot of tea.
> —*Herbert V. Prochnow*

3749 *Frog*

> What a wonderful bird the frog are—
> When he stand he sit almost;
> When he hop, he fly almost.
> He ain't got no sense hardly;
> He ain't got no tail hardly either.
> When he sit, he sit on what he ain't got almost.
> —*Anonymous*

3750   *Correct*

> Most folks love to watch for mail,
> It brings them countless thrills;
> But all we ever seem to get
> Is loads of unpaid bills.

3751   *Golf*

> Though he majored in math while in college,
> Knows calculus, trig and much more,
> It all fails him, each hole, when he's golfing—
> He can't count as high as his score!
> *—Leverett Lyon*

3752   **Push and Pull**

> The halls of fame are very wide
>   And always very full.
> Some go in by the door called "Push,"
>   And some by the door called "Pull."

3753   **Old Rhyme, New Version**

> Hey, diddle, diddle,
> I'm watching my middle,
> I'm hoping to slim it quite soon;
> But eating's such fun
> It may not get done
> Till my dish runs away with my spoon!

3754   **The Dromedary**

> The Dromedary is a cheerful bird:
> I cannot say the same about the Kurd.
> *—Hilaire Belloc*

3755   **After Our Garden Party**

> There is no kind of folding chair
> For which I ever more will care,
> Except one speeding on its way
> Into the trash man's waiting dray.
> *—Leverett Lyon*

3756 *Infant*

> I recollect a nurse call'd Ann,
>   Who carried me about the grass,
> And one fine day a fine young man
>   Came up, and kiss'd the pretty lass.
> She did not make the least objection!
>   Thinks I, "Aha!
> When I can talk I'll tell Mamma"
>   —And that's my earliest recollection.
> > —*Frederick Locker-Lampson*

3757 *Modern Longfellow*

> Beneath the spreading chestnut tree
> The village smithy snoozes;
> No nag, since 1923,
> Has been to him for shoeses.

3758 *The Reckless Driver*

> Oh, why should the spirit of a driver be proud?
> Like a fast-flitting meteor, a fast-flying cloud,
> A flash of the lightning, a break of the wave,
> He goes through a stop sign on his way to the grave.
> > —*Herbert V. Prochnow*

3759 *A Is an Apple*

> A is an apple, sour and green,
> Working in Tommy but cannot be seen.
> > —*Anonymous*

3760 *Budget*

> Those who work out our federal budget
>   Have a policy—really a honey—
> We shall live on our national income,
>   Even if we must borrow the money!
> > —*Leverett Lyon*

3761 *The Speaker's Problem*

> The speaker's hair grows gray,
>   His voice is also sore,
> Yet some wise guy is bound to say,
>   "I've heard that joke before."

3762   *Better Not Tell Her*

> The fur on my wife looks good,
> But I think
> It was better
> On the mink.
> —*Herbert V. Prochnow*

3763   *On the Democracy of Yale*

> Here's to the town of New Haven,
> The Home of the Truth and the Light,
>   Where God talks to Jones
>   In the very same tones
> That he uses with Hadley and Dwight.
> —*Frederick Scheetz Jones*

3764   *Speeding*

> He did not hear the traffic cop,
> But raced ahead, pell-mell;
> So the doctor told the sexton
> And the sexton tolled the bell.

3765   *Nostalgia*

> I still love the nickel and dime store,
>   Remembering, far back, the time
> When one could actually buy there
>   Some things for a nickel or dime.
> —*Leverett Lyon*

3766   *Just One Slip-up*

> They have a colored TV set,
> Their station wagon's new;
> When they eat out, it's crepe suzette,
> They'd never order stew!
>
> They keep the Joneses on the string
> With fashion's latest raiments;
> They're up-to-date on everything except . . .
> The monthly payments.

3767   *Try Tomorrow*

> As I was going up the stair
> I met a man who wasn't there!
> He wasn't there again today!
> I wish, I wish he'd stay away!
> —*Hughes Mearns*

3768   **Resolutions**

> On New Year's Day, some years ago,
> I swore off alcohol;
> And, one year later, I eschewed
> Pipes, cigarettes, et al.
> The next, I quit profanity
> As something not too nice,
> And then abandoned slot machines,
> Card games, roulette and dice.
> Thus, curing faults each year, I reached
> A state of such perfection
> That I have not a single flaw
> Now calling for correction.
> But New Year's Day is now for me
> A ruined institution,
> For what is New Year's Day without
> A New Year's resolution?
> —*Leverett Lyon*

3769   **Engraved on the Collar of His Highness' Dog**

> I am His Highness' dog at Kew.
> Pray tell me, sir, whose dog are you?
> —*Alexander Pope*

3770   **Your Mistakes**

> To all my faults my eyes are blind;
> Mine are the sins I cannot find.
> But your mistakes I see aplenty;
> For them my eyes are twenty-twenty.

3771   **Coffee**

> The "coffee break," up in our tower,
> Were better called the "coffee hour"!
> —*Leverett Lyon*

3772   *Ancestors*

> From your blue heaven above us bent
> The gardener Adam and his wife
> Smile at the claims of long descent.
> —*Alfred Lord Tennyson*

3773   *Pedestrians*

> When I used to walk to get some place,
> Car drivers were a menace to the human race!
> But now that I, too, drive a car,
> I discover what fools pedestrians are.

3774   *Mandalay*

> By the old Moulmein Pagoda,
> Lookin' eastward to the sea,
> There's a Burma girl a-settin',
> An' she ain't a-drinkin' tea.
> —*Herbert V. Prochnow*

3775   *Slow Recovery*

> He proposed on his knees with a speech tender and sweet,
> And it took him ten years to get back on his feet.

3776   *Diplomats*

> I know just how to cure the world
>   And make it safe and stable;
> But I haven't time to do it,
>   And those that have, aren't able!
> —*Leverett Lyon*

3777   *A Certain Scholar*

> He never completed his History of Ephesus,
> But his name got mentioned in numerous prefaces.
> —*W. Craddle*

3778   *Inflation*

> Of all the words of tongue and pen,
> The saddest are, "It might have been."
> More sad are these we daily see:
> Prices rising for you and me.
> —*Herbert V. Prochnow*

3779　*So Easy to Do*

> If you want to keep from trouble,
> Here's a mighty easy way:
> Always put off till tomorrow
> What you shouldn't do today.

3780　*That Mary Again*

> Mary had a little lamb on a pizza with mushrooms,
> A burger topped with everything, and then some macaroons;
> She drank a giant milkshake, ordered ice cream to go—
> And when they carried Mary out, her face was white as snow.

3781　*Call the Ambulance*

> His fuel was rich,
> His speed was high.
> He parked in a ditch
> To let the curve go by.

3782　*Deep Stuff*

> Sampling the books the moderns bring,
> 　In honesty I must confess
> I liked the old Pierian spring
> 　More than the "stream of consciousness."
>
> 'Twas just a shallow, surface seep,
> 　That crystal, classic spring, I know,
> And yet, why should we bore so deep
> To get this muddy modern flow?
> 　　　　　*—Keith Preston*

3783　*Thanksgiving*

> We thank Thee, Lord, for giving us
> 　Thy gift of bread and meat.
> We thank Thee, too—a little more—
> 　That we are here to eat!
> 　　　　　*—Leverett Lyon*

3784　*Have Patience*

> To every person comes his day,
> So calmly wait your chance—
> Pedestrians have the right of way
> When in an ambulance.

3785   *The Little Tin Cup*

Drink to me only with thine eyes,
And I will pledge with mine;
Or leave some dimes but in the cup,
And I'll not buy on time.
                    —*Herbert V. Prochnow*

3786   *Books*

As I was laying on the green,
A small English book I seen.
Carlyle's Essay on Burns was the edition,
So I left it laying in the same position.
                    —*Anonymous*

3787   *No Old Ones*

Whatever trouble Adam had,
No man in days of yore
Could say, when Adam cracked a joke,
"I've heard that one before."

3788   *Money*

Workers earn it,
Spendthrifts burn it,
Bankers lend it,
Women spend it,
Forgers fake it,
Taxes take it;
I could use it.

3789   *A Young Gourmet*

A certain young gourmet of Crediton
Took some pâté de foie gras and spread it on
    A chocolate biscuit,
    Then murmured, "I'll risk it."
His tomb bears the date that he said it on.
                    —*Rev. Charles Inge*

3790   *They Flew*

A flea and a fly in a flue
Were imprisoned, so what could they do?

> Said the fly, "Let us flee,"
> Said the flea, "Let us fly,"
> So they flew through a flaw in the flue.
> —*Anonymous*

3791 *Progress*

> The smith, a mighty man is he,
> With large and sinewy hands,
> But now he makes a bundle
> With a chain of hamburger stands.
> —*Herbert V. Prochnow*

3792 *Not the Vacant Stare*

> She sat on the steps at eventide
> Enjoying the balmy air.
> He came and asked, "May I sit by your side?"
> And she gave him the vacant stair.

3793 *Pathetic Picture*

> A little boy at the end of his rope,
> Facing a towel, water, and soap.

3794 *Architect*

> Sir Christopher Wren
> Said, "I am going to dine with some men.
> If anybody calls
> Say I am designing St. Paul's."
> —*Edmund Clerihew Bentley*

3795 *Economist*

> John Stuart Mill,
> By a mighty effort of will,
> Overcame his natural bonhomie
> And wrote "Principles of Political Economy."
> —*Edmund Clerihew Bentley*

3796 *Nature*

> I'm glad the sky is painted blue;
>   And the earth is painted green;
> And such a lot of nice fresh air
>   All sandwiched in between.
> —*Anonymous*

3797   *The Little Crocodile*

> How doth the little crocodile
>   Improve his shining tail,
> And pour the waters of the Nile
>   On every golden scale!
>
> How cheerfully he seems to grin,
>   How neatly spreads his claws,
> And welcomes little fishes in
>   With gently smiling jaws!
> > —*Lewis Carroll*

3798   *Doctor Fell*

> I do not love thee, Doctor Fell,
> The reason why I cannot tell;
> But this alone I know full well,
> I do not love thee, Doctor Fell.
> > —*Thomas Brown*

3799   *Responsibility*

> I am the captain of my soul;
>   I rule it with stern joy;
> And yet I think I had more fun
>   When I was cabin boy.
> > —*Keith Preston*

3800   *Don't Make It Too Long*

> Most speeches to an hourglass
> Do some resemblance show;
> Because the longer time they run,
> The shallower they grow.

3801   *What the Old Dutchman Said*

> When Christmas comes already yet,
> Mit presents large and sweet,
> The tings I like in mein stockings best,
> By jiminy, are my feet!

3802   *Four O'Clock Slump*

> When the dry clack-clack of office noise
> Beats in my ears like pain,
> I close my eyes a minute
> And I think of summer rain.
> Summer rain a-falling

On meadows sweet with flowers,
I let it drench my spirit
With fresh and cooling showers.
I take deep breaths of rain-washed air
That purge and heal all pain,
Then open up my eyes—oh, well,
Back to work again!

3803 *Isn't It the Truth!*

I love the Christmastide, and yet,
I notice this each year I live:
I always like the gifts I get,
But how I love the gifts I give!

3804 *What He Thought*

"I saw you take his kiss!" " 'Tis true."
"Oh modesty!" " 'Twas strictly kept:
He thought me asleep—at least, I knew
He thought I thought he thought I slept!"
—*Coventry Patmore*

3805 *Life*

A man may drink and no be drunk;
A man may fight and no be slain;
A man may kiss a bonnie lass,
And aye be welcome back again.
—*Robert Burns*

3806 *Makes Them Stick*

I always eat peas with honey:
I've done it the whole of my life.
I know that it sounds kinda funny;
But it does make 'em stick to the knife.

3807 *King's English*

Lay still, his mother often said
When Washington had went to bed;
But little Georgie would reply:
I set up, but I cannot lie.
—*Father John Bannister Tabb*

3808   *How Beautiful*

> A little scrap of orange peel,
> A stump of a cigar,
> When trodden by a princely heel
> How beautiful they are!
> —*Allan M. Laing*

3809   *The Angler's Prayer*

> Give me, O Lord, to catch a fish
> So large that even I,
> In boasting of it afterwards,
> Shall have no need to lie.
> —*Allan M. Laing*

3810   *Poor Father*

> Mother makes her firm demand,
> Children add theirs, too,
> Dad uplifts assenting hand,
> He knows his day is through.

3811   *Every Person Has Worries*

> If every man's internal care
> Were written on his brow,
> How many would our pity share
> Who raise our envy now?
> —*Walter Savage Landor*

3812   *Protocol*

> When a diplomat's pinched
> For speeding at ninety,
> He doesn't start thinking of bail,
> For the judge only says:
> "We are sorry, your highness,
> It's the cop we are sending to jail!"
> —*Leverett Lyon*

3813   *Cease Repining*

> Be still, sad heart, and cease repining,
> Behind the clouds the sun is shining;

Thy fate is the common fate of all;
Into each life some rain must fall,—
Some days must be dark and dreary.
—*Henry Wadsworth Longfellow*

3814   *Ambition*

Ambition has but one reward for all:
A little power, a little transient fame,
A grave to rest in, and a fading name!
—*William Winter*

3815   *Appearance*

O wad some power the giftie gie us
To see oursel's as ithers see us!
—*Robert Burns*

3816   *Exclusive*

And this is good old Boston,
The home of the bean and the cod,
Where the Lowells talk to the Cabots,
And the Cabots talk only to God.
—*J. C. Bossidy*

3817   *Change*

All things must change
To something new, to something strange.
—*Henry Wadsworth Longfellow*

3818   *Triumph and Defeat*

Not in the clamor of the crowded street,
Not in the shouts and plaudits of the throng,
But in ourselves, are triumph and defeat.
—*Henry Wadsworth Longfellow*

3819   *The Place to Die*

But whether on the scaffold high,
Or in the battle's van,
The fittest place where man can die
Is where he dies for man.
—*Michael J. Barry*

3820   *Decision*

Once to every man and nation comes the moment to decide,
In the strife of Truth with Falsehood, for the good or evil side.
—James Russell Lowell

3821   *No Doubt*

Of that there is no manner of doubt—
No probable, possible shadow of doubt,
No possible doubt whatever.
—W. S. Gilbert

3822   *Prize Growl*

It's easy enough to be grouchy,
When things aren't coming your way,
   But the prize old growl
   Is the man who can howl
When everything's going O.K.

3823   *Time*

The Moving Finger writes; and having writ,
Moves on; nor all your Piety nor Wit
Shall lure it back to cancel half a Line,
Nor all your Tears wash out a Word of it.
—Omar Khayyam

3824   *Flea*

Great fleas have little fleas upon their backs to bite 'em,
And little fleas have lesser fleas, and so ad infinitum.
And the great fleas themselves, in turn, have greater fleas to go on;
While these again have greater still, and greater still, and so on.
—Augustus De Morgan

3825   *What I Live For*

For the cause that lacks assistance,
The wrong that needs resistance,
For the future in the distance,
And the good that I can do.
—George Linnaeus Banks

3826   *My Candle*

My candle burns at both ends;
   It will not last the night;

But, ah, my foes, and, oh, my friends—
It gives a lovely light.
—*Edna St. Vincent Millay*

2827   *Give Us Men*

God give us men. A time like this demands
Strong minds, great hearts, true faith and ready hands!
Men whom the lust of office does not kill,
Men whom the spoils of office cannot buy,
Men who possess opinions and a will,
Men who love honor, men who cannot lie.
—*J. G. Holland*

3828   *Fear*

But the beating of my own heart
Was all the sound I heard.
—*Richard Monckton Milnes*

3829   *This Was a Man*

His life was gentle, and the elements
So mix'd in him that Nature might stand up,
And say to all the world, This was a man!
—*William Shakespeare*

3830   *Nothingness*

Nothing to do but work,
    Nothing to eat but food,
Nothing to wear but clothes,
    To keep one from going nude.
—*Ben King*

3831   *The Affairs of Men*

There is a tide in the affairs of men,
Which, taken at the flood, leads on to fortune.
—*William Shakespeare*

3832   *Politics*

I always voted at my party's call
And I never thought of thinking for myself at all.
—*W. S. Gilbert*

3833   *Blow Your Trumpet*

If you wish in this world to advance,
Your merits you're bound to enhance;
You must stir it and stump it,
And blow your own trumpet,
Or, trust me, you haven't a chance.
                                        —*W. S. Gilbert*

3834   *Master of His Fate*

It matters not how strait the gate,
How charged with punishments the scroll,
I am the master of my fate:
I am the captain of my soul.
                                        —*W. E. Henley*

3835   *Thinks Too Much*

Yon Cassius has a lean and hungry look;
He thinks too much: such men are dangerous.
                                        —*William Shakespeare*

3836   *To Thine Own Self*

To thine own self be true,
And it must follow, as the night the day,
Thou canst not then be false to any man.
                                        —*William Shakespeare*

3837   *Ill Fares the Land*

Ill fares the land, to hastening ills a prey,
Where wealth accumulates, and men decay;
Princes and Lords may flourish, or may fade—
A breath can make them, as a breath has made—
But a bold peasantry, their country's pride,
When once destroy'd can never be supplied.
                                        —*Oliver Goldsmith*

3838   *Be Early*

Last night I found my sweetheart Flo
Posed 'neath a spray of mistletoe.

"How come," said I, "when Christmas Day
Is still a good long week away?"
"Ah, shucks!" she said. "Don't make me blush—
Shop early and avoid the rush!"

3839   *Yesterday*

But yesterday the word of Caesar might
Have stood against the world; now lies he there,
And none so poor to do him reverence.
                            —*William Shakespeare*

3840   **This World**

This world is all a fleeting show,
    For man's illusion given;
The smiles of joy, the tears of woe,
Deceitful shine, deceitful flow,—
    There's nothing true but Heaven.
                            —*Thomas Moore*

3841   *Folly*

All the world's a mass of folly,
Youth is gay, age melancholy:
Youth is spending, age is thrifty,
Mad at twenty, cold at fifty;
Man is nought but folly's slave,
From the cradle to the grave.
                            —*W. H. Ireland*

3842   *Art*

In art I pull no high-brow stuff,
I know what I like, and that's enough.
                            —*William W. Woollcott*

3843   **Childhood**

The childhood shows the man,
As morning shows the day.
                            —*John Milton*

3844   *Achievement*

He slept beneath the moon,
He basked beneath the sun;

He lived a life of going-to-do
And died with nothing done.
—*James Albery*

3845 *Modest*

Have more than thou showest,
Speak less than thou knowest.
—*William Shakespeare*

3846 *Fame*

Fame is a fickle food
Upon a shifting plate.
—*Emily Dickinson*

3847 *Shaping Our Lives*

There's a divinity that shapes our ends,
Rough-hew them how we will.
—*William Shakespeare*

3848 *Still Same Opinion*

He that complies against his will
Is of his own opinion still.
—*Samuel Butler*

3849 *Where You Are*

Seek not for fresher founts afar,
Just drop your bucket where you are.
—*Sam Walter Foss*

3850 *Vice*

Vice is a monster of so frightful mien.
As to be hated needs but to be seen;
Yet seen too oft, familiar with her face,
We first endure, then pity, then embrace.
—*Alexander Pope*

3851 *Hope*

Hope springs eternal in the human breast:
Man never is, but always to be, blest.
—*Alexander Pope*

3852   *Flattery*

> Tis an old maxim in the schools,
> That flattery's the food of fools;
> Yet now and then your men of wit
> Will condescend to take a bit.
> —*Jonathan Swift*

3853   *Vacation*

> Between the spring and the autumn,
> When the sun in its zenith doth climb,
> Comes a pause in the year's occupations
> That is known as vacation time.

3854   *Extremes of Fortune*

> Extremes of fortune are true wisdom's test;
> And he's of men most wise who bears them best.
> —*Richard Cumberland*

3855   *Genius*

> Genius, that power which dazzles mortal eyes,
> Is oft but perseverance in disguise.
> —*Henry W. Austin*

3856   *A Good Deed*

> How far that little candle throws his beams!
> So shines a good deed in a naughty world.
> —*William Shakespeare*

3857   *The Good and the Bad*

> There is so much good in the worst of us,
> And so much bad in the best of us,
> That it hardly behooves any of us
> To talk about the rest of us.
> —*Edward Hoch*

3858   *Power*

> How a minority,
> Reaching majority,
> Seizing authority,
> Hates a minority.
> —*L. H. Robbins*

3859   *Be Satisfied*

> No one bulldog yet could eat
> Any other bulldog's meat;
> If you have a good-sized bone,
> Let the other dog alone.

3860   *Masquerading*

> Things are seldom what they seem,
> Skim milk masquerades as cream.
> *—W. S. Gilbert*

3861   *Learning*

> A little learning is a dangerous thing :
> Drink deep or taste not the Pierian spring;
> There shallow draughts intoxicate the brain,
> And drinking largely sobers us again.
> *—Alexander Pope*

3862   *Gold*

> That for which all virtue now is sold,
> And almost every vice—almighty gold.
> *—Ben Jonson*

3863   *Biography*

> The art of biography
> Is different from geography.
> Geography is about maps,
> But biography is about chaps.
> *—G. K. Chesterton*

3864   *Hidden*

> O, what may man within him hide,
> Though angel on the outward side!
> *—William Shakespeare*

3865   *Ignorance*

> From ignorance our comfort flows,
> The only wretched are the wise.
> *—Matthew Prior*

3866   *Commencement*

> Each of June's new graduates
> Has left his college hall.
> The world is now his oyster,
> The future is his thrall.
>
> He thinks he knows a great, great deal
> More than his parents do—
> And, speaking of that state of mind,
> The chances are it's true!
>   *—Leverett Lyon*

3867   **Those Fool Drivers**

> I think that I shall never see
> Along the road, an unscraped tree,
> With bark intact and painted white,
> That no car ever hit at night.
> For every tree that's near the road
> Has caused some auto to be towed.
> Sideswiping trees is done a lot
> By drivers who are not so hot.
> God gave them eyes so they could see,
> Yet any fool can hit a tree.

3868   **Sunday Drive**

> Highway gleaming;
> Traffic teeming;
> Driver dreaming;
> Siren screaming;
> Bail, redeeming;
> Home, blaspheming!
>   *—Leverett Lyon*

3869   *Unselfish*

> He wrecked his car, he lost his job,
> And yet throughout his life,
> He took his troubles like a man—
> He blamed them on his wife.

3870 *Fleeced*

Mary had a little lamb,
Its fleece was white as snow,
But some of the places Mary went,
They fleeced her for her dough.
—*Herbert V. Prochnow*

3871 *Christmas Tree*

I think that I shall never be,
Sold on an artificial tree.
A Christmas tree with plastic limbs
Just doesn't stir me up to hymns;
A tree with needles made of foil,
That grew in factories, not soil;
And, though it will not burn nor shed,
Will neither be alive nor dead.
Perennial, yes, it may be,
And formed in perfect symmetry.
But only God can make a tree
To suit old-fashioned fools like me.

3872 *Nervous*

If I'm asked for impromptu remarks,
It gives my stomach impromptu upstarts.
If I'm asked for a prepared short talk,
It makes my stomach grumble and squawk.
If I'm asked for a serious address,
It makes my whole insides a first-class mess.

3873 *Romeo Owed*

'Twas in a restaurant they met—
Romeo and Juliet.
He had no cash to pay the debt;
So Romeo'd what Juliet.

3874 *Some Ogden Nash*

O money, money, money, I'm not necessarily one of those who
    think thee holy.
But I often stop to wonder how thou canst go out so fast when
    thou comest in so slowly.

3875   *More Ogden Nash*

So my advice to mothers is if you are the mother of a poet don't
    gamble on the chance that future generations will crown him.
Follow your original impulse and drown him.—*International Herald
Tribune, May 20, 1971, at time of his death*

3876   *All Together Now*

"Help one another," the snowflakes said,
As they nestled down in their fleecy bed;
"One of us here would not be felt,
One of us here would quickly melt;
But I'll help you, and you help me,
And then a big white drift we'll be!"

3877   *Please Be Mine*

Many are the words to rhyme
With the key word, Valentine:
Fine, and shine, and then entwine,
Thine, and sign, and then enshrine,
Wine and dine, and too, divine—
I might fill a mile-long line
If I only had the time;
But to three words I'll confine
My verse, dear—please be mine!

3878   *Not Always Wisdom*

Every speaker has a mouth,
An arrangement rather neat.
Sometimes it's filled with wisdom,
Sometimes it's filled with feet.

3879   *Modern Mother Goose*

There was an old woman who lived in a shoe,
With more children than she could handle.
When they'd grown up and all left home,
She moved into a sandal.
                    —*Uplifting Gems*

3880   *It's Christmas*

>Christmas comes with snow and ice,
>With mistletoe and all that's nice;
>But, brother, it almost gives me chills
>To think it also comes with bills.

3881   *First Class or Steerage?*

>Said Jonah one day to the whale,
>"My, my, you look hearty and hale.
>   When I go overseas,
>   Will you transport me please
>In a window seat near the tail?"

3882   *Expensive Tan*

>To Florida and elsewhere south
>Have scurried those who can—
>And soon they'll scurry home again
>To show their high-priced tan.
>   —*Leverett Lyon*

3883   *Visitors*

>That visitor can take a bow,
>Who, seeing me about to doze,
>Remarks, "I must be going now"—
>And goes.

3884   *She Didn't Stop*

>A quite sentimental young cop
>Saw a cute thing come out of a shop.
>   When he gave her the eye,
>   She went blushingly by.
>She'd just lifted twelve spoons and a mop!
>   —*Leverett Lyon*

3885   *Their Day*

>The turkeys seem restless,
>The geese acting queer—
>Can it be they are sensing
>That day is 'most here?
>   —*Leverett Lyon*

3886   *Boston*

Then here's to the City of Boston,
The town of the cries and the groans,
Where the Cabots can't see the Kabotschniks
And the Lowells won't speak to the Cohns.

3887   *Procrastination*

So many things I've left undone!
Like marching soldiers, one by one,
They pass before me in review,
The little things I meant to do!

3888   *Whole Duty of Children*

A child should always say what's true
And speak when he is spoken to
And behave mannerly at table;
At least as far as he is able.
— *Robert Louis Stevenson*

3889   *Critics*

Nature fits all her children with something to do,
He who would write and can't write, can surely review.
— *James Russell Lowell*

3890   *Diplomacy*

Diplomacy is to do and say
The nastiest thing in the nicest way.
— *Isaac Goldberg*

3891   *Greetings*

Don't tell your Friends about your Indigestion:
"How are you!" is a Greeting, not a Question.
— *Arthur Guiterman*

3892   *A La Carte*

It takes much art
To choose à la carte
For less than they quote
For the table d'hôte.
— *Justin Richardson*

3893   *Knowledge*

> I am the great Professor Jowett:
> What there is to know, I know it.
> I am the Master of Balliol College,
> And what I don't know isn't knowledge.
> *—Anonymous*

3894   *Point of Law*

> "In my youth," said his father, "I took to the law,
> And argued each case with my wife;
> And the muscular strength, which it gave to my jaw,
> Has lasted the rest of my life."
> *—Lewis Carroll*

3895   *Life's a Joke*

> Life is a jest, and all things show it:
> I thought so once, but now I know it.
> *—John Gay*

3896   *Courting*

> He that would the daughter win
> Must with the mother first begin.
> *—John Ray*

3897   *Accounting*

> Never ask of money spent
> Where the spender thinks it went.
> Nobody was ever meant
> To remember or invent
> What he did with every cent.
> *—Robert Frost*

3898   *Politics*

> There's not a particle of doubt
> We've turned a bunch of rascals out,
> And put a nice clean aggregation
> In very serious temptation.
> *—Keith Preston*

3899   *Smart*

And still they gaz'd,
And still the wonder grew,
That one small head
Could carry all he knew.
                    —*Oliver Goldsmith*

3900   **Thank God**

We ain't what we oughta be,
We ain't what we wanta be,
We ain't what we gonna be,
But thank God we ain't what we was.
—*Martin Luther King, Jr., quoted in*
        Yes I Can, *by Sammy Davis, Jr.*

3901   *Cabbages and Kings*

"The time has come," the Walrus said,
    "To talk of many things:
Of shoes—and ships—and sealing-wax—
    Of cabbages—and kings—
And why the sea is boiling hot—
    And whether pigs have wings."
                    —*Lewis Carroll*

3902   *From "Casey at the Bat"*

Oh, somewhere in this favored land the sun is shining bright;
The band is playing somewhere, and somewhere hearts are light,
And somewhere men are laughing, and little children shout;
But there is no joy in Mudville—mighty Casey has struck out.
                    —*Ernest Lawrence Thayer*

3903   *From "The Month of June"*

It is the month of June,
    The month of leaves and roses,
When pleasant sights salute the eyes,
    And pleasant scents the noses.
                    —*Nathaniel Parker Willis*

3904   *The Old Man of Nantucket*

There was an old man of Nantucket
Who kept all his cash in a bucket;

But his daughter named Nan
Ran away with a man—
And as for the bucket—Nantucket.
—*Dayton Voorhees*

3905   *Teeth*

The best of friends fall out, and so—
His teeth had done some years ago.
—*Thomas Hood*

3906   *'Tis Folly*

Where ignorance is bliss
'Tis folly to be wise.
—*Thomas Gray*

Great Thoughts of Distinguished Americans

3907   Labor is one of the great elements of society—the great substantial interest on which we all stand. Not feudal service or the irksome drudgery of one race subjected to another, but labor—intelligent, manly, independent, thinking and acting for itself, earning its own wages, educating childhood, maintaining worship, claiming the right to the elective franchise and helping to uphold the great fabric of the state. That is American labor, and all my sympathies are with it.—*Daniel Webster*

3908   If, over the long run, we all wish to be gainfully employed, to be at economic peace with one another, to provide opportunity for all to break out of the slough of poverty, to ensure real increases in our incomes, to make our savings a bulwark against the unknown instead of a gambling device, and to have the resources for just welfare programs, then we will have to make peace with the iron law that, over time, we cannot consume more than we produce, as a nation. This is to say that it is my view that reliable and lasting prosperity can rest only upon a real economy taking its gains out of its per capita increases in production.—*Philip C. Jackson, Jr., member of the Board of Governors of the Federal Reserve System*

3909   We know that there is no true and lasting cure for world tensions in guns and bombs. We know that only the spirit and mind of man, dedicated to justice and right, can, in the long term, enable us to live in the confident tranquility that should be every man's heritage.—*Dwight D. Eisenhower*

3910   Nobody can really guarantee the future. The best we can do is size up the chances, calculate the risks involved, estimate our ability to deal with them, and then make our plans with confidence.—*Henry Ford II*

3911   If you see in any given situation only what everybody else can see, you can be said to be so much a representative of your culture that you are a victim of it.—*S. I. Hayakawa*

3912   I place economy among the first and most important virtues, and public debt as the greatest danger to be feared. To preserve our independence, we must not let our leaders load us with perpetual debt. We must make our choice between economy and liberty, or profusion and servitude. If we can prevent the government from wasting the labors of the people under pretense of caring for them, we will be wise.—*Thomas Jefferson*

3913   Democracy is based on the conviction that man has the moral and intellectual capacity, as well as the inalienable right, to govern himself with reason and justice.—*Harry S. Truman*

3914   The riders in a race do not stop when they reach the goal. There is a little finishing canter before coming to a standstill. There is time to hear the kind voices of friends and say to oneself, "The work is done."—*Oliver Wendell Holmes*

3915   The university exists only to find and to communicate the truth.—*Robert Maynard Hutchins*

3916   Education does not mean a college education. The author of the Gettysburg Address and the Second Inaugural could hardly be called uneducated.—*Bergen Evans*

3917   Discussion is an exchange of knowledge; argument an exchange of ignorance.—*Robert Quillen*

3918   Always remember others may hate you, but those who hate you don't win unless you hate them. And then you destroy yourself.—*Richard M. Nixon*

3919   We Americans are the best informed people on earth as to the events of the last twenty-four hours; we are not the best informed as to the events of the last sixty centuries.—*Will and Ariel Durant*

3920   I hope I shall possess firmness and virtue enough to maintain what I consider the most enviable of all titles, the character of an honest man.—*George Washington*

3921   Our rise from nothing to unparalleled power and prosperity within two hundred years has been meteoric. But there is nothing to prevent our flashing out of the pages of history even faster than we came in, nothing except our own common sense and growing maturity.—*D. F. Fleming*

3922   It is curious and sad the way much of the intellectual climate of this country has changed. Once we roared like lions for liberty; now we bleat like sheep for security.—*Norman Vincent Peale*

3923   Tenacity is a pretty fair substitute for bravery, and the best form of tenacity I know is expressed in a Danish fur-trapper's principle: "The next mile is the only one a person really has to make."—*Eric Sevareid*

3924   After order and liberty, economy is one of the highest essentials of a free government.—*Calvin Coolidge.*

3925   Let it never be forgotten that glamour is not greatness; applause is not fame; prominence is not eminence. The man of the hour is not apt to be the man of the ages. A stone may sparkle, but that does not make it a diamond; a man may have money, but that does not make him a success. It is what the unimportant do that really counts and determines the course of history. The greatest forces in the universe are never spectacular. Summer showers are more effective than hurricanes, but they get no publicity. The world would soon die but for the fidelity, loyalty, and consecration of those whose names are unhonored and unsung.—*John R. Sizoo*

3926   If today's average American is confronted with an hour of leisure, he is likely to palpitate with panic. An hour with nothing to do? He jumps into a car and drives off fiercely in pursuit of diversion. We "catch" a train. We "grab" a bite of lunch. Everything has to be active and electric. We need less leg action and more acute observation as we go. Slow down the muscle and stir up the mind.—*Don Herold*

3927   I don't know what your destiny will be, but one thing I know: The only ones among you who will be really happy are those who will have sought and found how to serve.—*Albert Schweitzer*

3928   Life is work, and everything you do is so much more experience. Sometimes you work for wages, sometimes not, but what does anybody make but a living? And whatever you have, you must either use or lose.—*Henry Ford*

3929   There is no use whatever trying to help people who do not help themselves. You cannot push anyone up a ladder unless he be willing to climb himself.—*Andrew Carnegie*

3930
  I am only one,
  But still I am one.
  I cannot do everything,
  But still I can do something;
  And because I cannot do everything
  I will not refuse to do the something that I can do.
         —Edward Everett Hale

3931 The happiest men I know in all this unhappy life of ours are those leaders who, brave, loyal, and sometimes in tears, are serving their fellow men. *—Lincoln Steffens*

3932 We are participants, whether we would or not, in the life of the world. The interests of all nations are our own also. What affects mankind is inevitably our affair, as well as the affair of the nations of Europe and Asia.*—Woodrow Wilson*

3933 It is astonishing what an effort it seems to be for many people to put their brains definitely and systematically to work. They seem to insist on somebody else—often anybody else—doing their thinking for them.*—Thomas Alva Edison*

3934 We can no longer overwhelm our problems; we must master them with imagination, understanding, and patience.*—Henry Kissinger*

3935 When the One Great Scorer comes to write against your name—
  He marks—not that you won or lost—but how you played the game.
         —Grantland Rice

3936 If a man has a talent and cannot use it, he has failed. If he has a talent and uses only half of it, he has partly failed. If he has a talent and learns somehow to use the whole of it, he has gloriously succeeded, and won a satisfaction and a triumph few men ever know.*—Thomas Wolfe*

3937
  Books are not men and yet they are alive,
  They are man's memory and his aspiration,
  The link between his present and his past,
  The tools he builds with.
      —Stephen Vincent Benét

3938 The man who has done his level best, and who is conscious that he has done his best, is a success, even though the world may write him down as a failure.*—B. C. Forbes*

3939   These are the times that try men's souls. . . . What we obtain too cheap, we esteem too lightly; . . . and it would be strange indeed if so celestial an article as Freedom should not be highly rated.—*Thomas Paine*

3940   Yes, we did produce a near perfect Republic. But will they keep it? Or will they in the enjoyment of plenty lose the memory of Freedom? Material abundance without character is the surest way to destruction.—*Thomas Jefferson*

3941   No tax dollar, even though it is wisely spent by bureaucrats sitting down in Washington, can possibly bring with it that great, human, individual concern which means so much to all of us. Any private dollar is worth four government dollars.—*Dwight D. Eisenhower.*

3942   Bad will be the day for every man when he becomes absolutely contented with the life that he is living, with the thoughts that he is thinking, with the deeds that he is doing, when there is not forever beating at the doors of his soul some great desire to do something larger, which he knows that he was meant and made to do because he is still, in spite of all, the child of God.—*Phillips Brooks*

3943   Late one night in July 1776 a young man from the Massachusetts colony, exhausted from the day's labors but too emotion-charged to sleep, took quill pen in hand. Writing to his wife, Abigail, by candlelight from the stifling boardinghouse quarters, he described a momentous event which had just taken place in Philadelphia. In years to come, he predicted, that day would be remembered as "the great anniversary Festival."
The man? John Adams.
The event? Adoption of the Declaration of Independence, which he hoped would be commemorated as "the Day of Deliverance, by solemn acts of Devotion to God Almighty."
His vision was indeed prophetic.

3944   A society as affluent as ours can ill afford to neglect the poor, the elderly, the unemployed, or other disadvantaged persons, but neither can it afford to neglect the fundamental precept that there must be adequate rewards to stimulate individual efforts.—*Arthur F. Burns*

3945   Our nation was founded as an experiment in human liberty. Its institutions reflect the belief of our founders that men had their origin and destiny in God; that they were endowed by Him with inalienable rights and had duties prescribed by moral law, and that human institutions ought primarily to help men develop their God-given possibilities.—*John Foster Dulles*

3946   Our misconception of the capabilities of the elderly has often limited our vision and influenced our public policies. As a result, government often creates programs and policies which deter rather than encourage older people from living a full and productive life.—*Walter Mondale*

3947   When an American says he loves his country, he means not only that he loves the New England hills, the prairies glistening in the sun, or the wide rising plains, the mountains, and the seas. He means that he loves an inner air, an inner light in which freedom lives and in which a man can draw the breath of self-respect.—*Adlai E. Stevenson*

3948   The duty of America is to secure the culture and the happiness of the masses by their reliance on themselves.—*George Bancroft*

3949   I place Economy among the first and most important virtues, and public debt as the greatest of dangers to be feared.
    To preserve our Independence, we must not let our rulers load us with perpetual debt. If we run into such debts, we must be taxed in our meat and drink, in our necessities and our comforts, in our labor and our amusements.
    If we can prevent the government from wasting the labor of the people, under the pretense of caring for them, they will be happy.—*Thomas Jefferson*

3950   In my judgment, it is philosophy, not science, which should be uppermost in any culture or civilization, simply because the questions it can answer are more important for human life.—*Mortimer Adler*

3951   Short-term survival may depend on the knowledge of nuclear physicists and the performance of supersonic aircraft, but long-term survival depends alone on the character of man. We must remember that it was not the outer grandeur of the Roman but the inner simplicity of the Christian that lived on through the ages.—*Charles A. Lindbergh*

3952   You must give some time to your fellow men. Even if it's a little thing, do something for others—something for which you get no pay but the privilege of doing it.—*Albert Schweitzer*

3953   Each honest calling, each walk of life, has its own elite, its own aristocracy based on excellence of performance.—*James Bryant Conant*

3954   The greatest danger that faces this country is the danger of moral lassitude—liberty turned to license, rights demanded and duties shirked, the moral sense deteriorating, the traditions and standards of the nation weakened, the spiritual forces within it losing ground.—*Robert J. McCracken*

3955   Let us have done with the cult of the common man and begin to recognize and appreciate worth, talent, ability, and devotion wherever we find it. Gifted men have carried the world forward on their shoulders. Whatsoever progress we have made, we owe to them. Let us acknowledge it and be grateful for it, and not try to clip their wings and reduce them to the level of mediocrity. —*Howard E. Kershner*

3956   There are things that are worth dying for—the honor of one's country, the sanctity of the home, the virtue of women, and the safety of little children. But, if they are worth dying for, they are worth living for!—*George W. Truett*

3957   Throughout history, government has proved to be the chief instrument for thwarting man's liberty. Government represents power in the hands of some men to control the lives of other men.—*Barry M. Goldwater*

3958   All free governments, whatever their name, are in reality governments by public opinion, and it is on the quality of this public opinion that their prosperity depends.—*James Russell Lowell*

3959   Everybody likes and respects self-made men. It is a great deal better to be made in that way than not to be made at all.—*Oliver Wendell Holmes*

3960   If a man does not keep pace with his companion, perhaps it is because he hears a different drummer. Let him step to the music which he hears, however measured or far away.—*Henry David Thoreau*

3961   The security and elevation of the family and of family life are the prime objects of civilization, and the ultimate ends of all industry.—*Charles W. Eliot*

3962   There is the fear that we shan't prove worthy in the eyes of someone who knows us at least as well as we know ourselves. That is the fear of God. And there is the fear of Man—fear that men won't understand us and we shall be cut off from them.—*Robert Frost*

3963   Our present and future danger may lie in our failure to recognize that if we were to achieve freedom from responsibility, all our freedoms would be lost. All the freedom mankind has achieved to date has been achieved only because individuals accepted responsibility.—*Arthur H. Motley*

3964

Feast, and your halls are crowded;
Fast, and the world goes by.
—*Ella Wheeler Wilcox*

3965   Conspicuous consumption of valuable goods is a means of reputability to the gentleman of leisure.—*Thorstein Veblen*

3966   A government that is big enough to give you all you want is big enough to take it all away.—*Barry M. Goldwater*

3967   Were we directed from Washington when to sow and when to reap, we should soon want bread.—*Thomas Jefferson*

3968   The broad goal of our foreign policy is to enable the people of the United States to enjoy in peace the blessings of liberty.—*John Foster Dulles*

3969   The deadliest foe of democracy is not autocracy but liberty frenzied. Liberty is not foolproof. For its beneficent working it demands self-restraint.—*Otto Kahn*

3970   A liberty to do that only which is good, just, and honest.—*John Winthrop*

3971   Every step of progress the world has made has been from scaffold to scaffold, and from stake to stake.—*Wendell Phillips*

3972   Ships that pass in the night, and speak each other in passing,
Only a signal shown and a distant voice in the darkness;
So on the ocean of life, we pass and speak one another,
Only a look and a voice, then darkness again and a silence.
            —*Henry Wadsworth Longfellow*

3973   A retentive memory is a good thing, but the ability to forget is the true token of greatness.—*Elbert Hubbard*

3974   The true greatness of nations is in those qualities which constitute the greatness of the individual.—*Charles Sumner*

3975   No nation is fit to sit in judgment upon any other nation.—*Woodrow Wilson*

3976   The impersonal hand of government can never replace the helping hand of a neighbor.—*Hubert Humphrey*

3977   Peace is more than the absence of aggression. It is the creation of a world community in which every nation can follow its own course without fear of its neighbors.—*Lyndon B. Johnson*

3978   To pity distress is but human; to relieve it is Godlike.—*Horace Mann*

3979 To be President of the United States is to be lonely, very lonely at times of great decisions.—*Harry S. Truman*

3980 Make the most of yourself, for that is all there is of you.—*Ralph Waldo Emerson*

3981 We shall never solve the paradox of want in the midst of plenty by doing away with plenty.—*Ogden Mills*

3982 You pray in your distress and in your need: would that you might pray also in the fullness of your joy and in your days of abundance.—*Kahlil Gibran*

3983 It is never too late to give up our prejudices.—*Henry David Thoreau*

3984 Prosperity cannot be restored by raids upon the public treasury.—*Herbert Hoover*

3985 We must be willing, individually and as a nation, to accept whatever sacrifices may be required of us. A people that values its privileges above its principles soon loses both.—*Dwight D. Eisenhower*

3986 The personal right to acquire property, which is a natural right, gives to property, when acquired, a right to protection, as a social right.—*James Madison*

3987 The days of palmy prosperity are not those most favorable to the display of public virtue or the influence of wise and good men.—*Edward Everett*

3988 When we see a special reformer, we feel like asking him, What right have you, sir, to your one virtue?—*Ralph Waldo Emerson*

3989 There was worlds of reputation in it, but no money.—*Mark Twain*

3990 I have tried so hard to do right.—*Grover Cleveland, last words*

3991 If you don't want to work, you have to work to earn enough money so you won't have to work.—*Ogden Nash*

3992 And yet the same revolutionary beliefs for which our forebears fought are still at issue around the globe—the belief that the rights of man come not from the generosity of the state but from the hand of God.—*John F. Kennedy*

3993 It is my chore to ask you to consider the toughest proposition ever faced by believers in the free-enterprise system: the need for a frontal attack against Santa Claus—not the Santa Claus of the holiday season, of course, but the Santa Claus of the free lunch, the government handout, the Santa Claus of something-for-nothing and something-for-everyone.—*Barry M. Goldwater*

3994   My reading of history convinces me that most bad government has grown out of too much government.—*John Sharp Williams*

3995   History fades into fable; fact becomes clouded with doubt and controversy; the inscription moulders from the tablet: the statue falls from the pedestal. Columns, arches, pyramids, what are they but heaps of sand; and their epitaphs, but characters written in the dust?—*Washington Irving*

3996
      The course of life is like the sea;
      Men come and go; tides rise and fall;
      And that is all of history.
          —*Joaquin Miller*

3997   The universe is a stairway leading nowhere unless man is immortal.—*E. Y. Mullins*

3998   You and I know that there is a correlation between the creative and the screwball. So we must suffer the screwball gladly.—*Kingman Brewster, Jr.*

3999   The mind is no match with the heart in persuasion; constitutionality is no match with compassion.—*Everett M. Dirksen*

4000   The learned are seldom pretty fellows, and in many cases their appearance tends to discourage a love of study in the young.—*H. L. Mencken*

4001   Modern man worships at the temple of science, but science tells him only what is possible, not what is right.—*Milton S. Eisenhower*

4002   Common sense, in so far as it exists, is all for the bourgeoisie. Nonsense is the privilege of the aristocracy. The worries of the world are for the common people.—*George Jean Nathan*

4003   The stairway of time ever echoes with the wooden shoe going up and the polished boot coming down.—*Jack London*

4004
      The dark is at the end of every day,
      and silence is the end of every song.
          —*Edwin Arlington Robinson*

4005   I have Bloomington to thank for the most important lesson I have learned: that in quiet places reason abounds, that in quiet people there is vision and purpose, that many things are revealed to the humble that are hidden from the great.—*Adlai E. Stevenson*

4006   We sleep, but the loom of life never stops and the pattern which was weaving when the sun went down is weaving when it comes up tomorrow.—*Henry Ward Beecher*

4007   Perhaps the only true dignity of man is his capacity to despise himself. —*George Santayana*

4008   Society is frivolous, and shreds its day into scraps, its conversation into ceremonies and escapes.—*Ralph Waldo Emerson*

4009   I went to the woods because I wished to live deliberately, to front only the essential facts of life, and see if I could not learn what it had to teach, and not, when I came to die, discover that I had not lived.—*Henry David Thoreau*

4010   Let me give you some advice, Lieutenant. Don't become a general. Don't ever become a general. If you become a general you just plain have too much to worry about.—*Dwight D. Eisenhower*

4011   The soldier, above all other people, prays for peace, for he must suffer and bear the deepest wounds and scars of war.—*Douglas MacArthur*

4012   The human animal needs a freedom seldom mentioned, freedom from intrusion. He needs a little privacy quite as much as he wants understanding or vitamins or exercise or praise.—*Phyllis McGinley*

4013   Believe me, every man has his secret sorrows, which the world knows not; and oftentimes we call a man cold when he is only sad.—*Henry Wadsworth Longfellow*

4014   To me it seems as if when God conceived the world, that was Poetry; He formed it, and that was Sculpture; He colored it, and that was Painting; He peopled it with living beings, and that was the grand, divine, eternal Drama.—*Charlotte Cushman*

4015   We do not know, nor can we know, with absolute certainty that those who disagree with us are wrong. We are human and therefore fallible, and being fallible, we cannot escape the element of doubt as to our own opinions and convictions.—*J. William Fulbright*

4016   In time of war, truth is always replaced by propaganda.—*Charles A. Lindbergh*

4017   Logic is the art of going wrong with confidence.—*Joseph Wood Krutch*

4018   The highest form of vanity is love of fame.—*George Santayana*

4019 I'd rather see a sermon than hear one any day;
I'd rather one should walk with me than merely tell the way.
—*Edgar A. Guest*

4020

Before God we are all equally wise—equally foolish.—*Albert Einstein*

4021 In all ages the drama, through its portrayal of the acting and suffering spirit of man, has been more closely allied than any other art to his deeper thoughts concerning his nature and his destiny.—*Ludwig Lewisohn*

4022 Most modern plays are concerned with the relation between man and man, but that does not interest me at all. I am interested only in the relation between man and God.—*Eugene O'Neill*

4023 The highest of renown
Are the surest stricken down;
But the stupid and the clown,
They remain.
—*Eugene Fitch Ware*

4024 Personally, I do not feel that any amount can properly be called a surplus as long as the nation is in debt. I prefer to think of such an item as a reduction of our children's inherited mortgage.—*Dwight D. Eisenhower*

4025 The point to remember is that what the government gives it must first take away.—*John S. Coleman*

4026 Where is the politician who has not promised to fight to the death for lower taxes—and who has not proceeded to vote for the very spending projects that make tax cuts impossible?—*Barry M. Goldwater*

4027 Great men are they who see that spiritual is stronger than any material force, that thoughts rule the world.—*Ralph Waldo Emerson*

4028 Every man feels instinctively that all the beautiful sentiments in the world weigh less than a single lovely action.—*James Russell Lowell*

4029 A nation is molded by the tests that its peoples meet and master.—*Lyndon B. Johnson*

4030 The bravest sight in all this world is a man fighting against odds.—*Franklin K. Lane*

4031　　　　　Among the peaceful harvest days,
An Indian Summer comes at last!
—Adeline D. T. Whitney

4032　　I am long on ideas, but short on time. I expect to live to be only about a hundred.—*Thomas Alva Edison*

4033　　　　　Old loves, old aspirations, and old dreams,
More beautiful for being old and gone.
—James Russell Lowell

4034　　Here is our difference with the Communists—and our strength. They would use their skills to forge new chains of tyranny. We would use ours to free men from the bonds of the past.—*Lyndon B. Johnson*

4035　　To embody human liberty in workable government, America was born.
—Herbert Hoover

4036　　A conservative, briefly, has a philosophy based upon the proven values of the past. When we seek answers for the problems of today we look to the past to see if those problems existed. Generally, they have. So we ask: What was the answer? Did it work? If it did, let us try it again.—*Barry M. Goldwater*

4037　　My idea of a conservative is one who desires to retain the wisdom and the experience of the past and who is prepared to apply the best of that wisdom and experience to meet the changes which are inevitable in every new generation.
—Herbert Hoover

4038　　　　　The thing we long for, that we are
For one transcendent moment.
—James Russell Lowell

4039　　There will always be dissident voices heard in the land, expressing opposition without alternatives, finding fault but never favor, perceiving gloom on every side and seeking influence without responsibility. Those voices are inevitable.—*John F. Kennedy*

4040　　When death comes, he respects neither age nor merit. He sweeps from this earthly existence the sick and the strong, the rich and the poor, and should teach us to live to be prepared for death.—*Andrew Jackson*

4041　　The greatest part of the President's job is to make decisions. . . . He can't pass the buck to anybody.—*Harry S. Truman*

4042　　I strive for the best and I do the possible.—*Lyndon B. Johnson*

4043
>For the body at best
>Is a bundle of aches,
>Longing for rest;
>It cries when it wakes.
>—*Edna St. Vincent Millay*

4044　There are periods when the principles of experience need to be modified
. . . when in truth to dare is the highest wisdom.—*William Ellery Channing*

4045　Books are true levelers. They give to all, who will faithfully use them, the society, the spiritual presence, of the best and greatest of our race.—*William Ellery Channing*

4046　In the final analysis, our most basic common link is that we all inhabit this small planet. We all breathe the same air. We all cherish our children's future. And we are all mortal.—*John F. Kennedy*

4047　For, on this shrunken globe, men can no longer live as strangers. Men can war against each other as hostile neighbors, as we are determined not to do; or they can coexist in frigid isolation, as we are doing. But our prayer is that men everywhere will learn, finally, to live as brothers.—*Adlai E. Stevenson*

4048　The State cannot get a cent for any man without taking it from some other man, and this latter must be a man who has produced and saved it. The latter is the Forgotten Man.—*William Graham Sumner*

4049　The world is round. Only one third of the human beings are asleep at one time, and the other two thirds are awake and up to some mischief somewhere.—*Dean Rusk*

4050　The main point is getting some experience. The experienced people are better than the inexperienced. Think how it is in that tennis game or in that race or whatever it is. When the whistle blows you have only a limited amount of time to do what you have to do. You either do it then or you don't do it at all.—*Byron R. White*

4051　I would remind you that extremism in the defense of liberty is no vice. And let me remind you also that moderation in the pursuit of justice is no virtue! —*Barry M. Goldwater*

4052　If I were to paraphrase the two sentences in question in the context in which I uttered them, I would do it by saying that whole-hearted devotion is unassailable and that half-hearted devotion to justice is indefensible.—*Barry M. Goldwater*

4053   And if I should lose, let me stand by the road
And cheer as the winners go by!
—*Berton Braley*

4054   Death, the only immortal who treats us all alike, whose pity and whose peace and whose refuge are for all—the soiled and the pure, the rich and the poor, the loved and the unloved.—*Mark Twain, memorandum written on his deathbed.*

4055   In a democracy, the people have to want to do what must be done.—*Lyndon B. Johnson*

4056   The beauty of a Democracy is that you never can tell when a youngster is born what he is going to do with you, and that, no matter how humbly he is born . . . he has got a chance to master the minds and lead the imaginations of the whole country.—*Woodrow Wilson*

4057   Let us never negotiate out of fear. But let us never fear to negotiate.—*John F. Kennedy*

4058   If our history teaches us anything, it is this lesson: So far as the economic potential of our nation is concerned, the believers in the future of America have always been the realists. I count myself as one of this company.—*Dwight D. Eisenhower*

4059   The Forgotten Man works and votes—generally he prays—but his chief business in life is to pay.—*William Graham Sumner*

4060   Without ideals, without effort, without scholarship, without philosophical continuity, there is no such thing as education.—*Abraham Flexner*

4061   The recipe for perpetual ignorance is: Be satisfied with your opinions and content with your knowledge.—*Elbert Hubbard*

4062   When you reflect on it, the only thing that allowed the human race to stop living as animals and to start living as human beings was by adopting a set of rules—a system of justice. Maintaining a system of justice in an orderly society is essential to whatever else people accomplish.—*Frank W. Wilson, U.S. District Judge*

4063   There is no king who has not had a slave among his ancestors, and no slave who has not had a king among his.—*Helen Keller*

4064   Last, but by no means least, courage—moral courage, the courage of one's convictions, the courage to see things through. The world is in a constant conspiracy against the brave. It's the age-old struggle—the roar of the crowd on one side and the voice of your conscience on the other.—*Douglas MacArthur*

4065   Honor lies in honest toil.—*Grover Cleveland*

4066   No man needs sympathy because he has to work. . . . Far and away the best prize that life offers is the chance to work hard at work worth doing. —*Theodore Roosevelt*

4067   We prefer world law, in the age of self-determination, to world war in the age of mass extermination.—*John F. Kennedy*

4068   No man is above the law and no man is below it; nor do we ask any man's permission when we require him to obey it.—*Theodore Roosevelt*

4069   The interesting and inspiring thought about America is that she asks nothing for herself except what she has a right to ask for humanity itself.— *Woodrow Wilson*

4070
    The lyric sound of laughter
      Fills all the April hills,
    The joy-song of the crocus,
      The mirth of daffodils.
          —*Clinton Scollard*

4071   Every artist dips his brush in his own soul, and paints his own nature into his pictures.—*Henry Ward Beecher*

4072   Criticism is no doubt good for the soul, but we must beware that it does not upset our confidence in ourselves.—*Herbert Hoover*

4073   He is an incorrigible believer. He believes in everything that works.— *James Reston*

4074   When befriended, remember it; when you befriend, forget it.—*Benjamin Franklin*

4075
    Past my next milestone waits my seventieth year.
    I mount no longer when the trumpets call;
    My battle-harness idles on the wall,
    The spider's castle, camping-ground of dust,
    Not without dints, and all in front, I trust.
          —*James Russell Lowell*

4076   I feel about my work now as President Eliot felt about Harvard: "Things seem to be going fairly well, now that a spirit of pessimism prevails in all departments."—*Van Wyck Brooks*

4077   The tree is known by its fruits. If you want to understand the social and political history of modern nations, study hell.—*Thomas Merton, Seeds of Contemplation*

4078   Robert Frost said to a class of students, "I am not a teacher, but an awakener."

4079   The whole thing is gloriously unpredictable, occasionally tragic, often frustrating and sometimes uproariously funny. How democracy works nobody quite knows. It is the worst system of government in the world, says Winston Churchill, "except all those other systems."—*James Reston*

4080   Some of mankind's most terrible misdeeds have been committed under the spell of certain magic words or phrases.—*James Bryant Conant*

4081   In the long run all battles are lost, and so are all wars.—*H. L. Mencken*

4082   In our great pride at being the arsenal of democracy we must remember that we are also regarded as the arsenal of hope. Great leadership in such a righteous cause requires that a nation be humble—before its God and its fellow men.—*Omar N. Bradley*

4083   We think of tolerance as a virtue, but there are times when people speak of tolerance, and the word they ought to use is apathy.—*Robert J. McCracken*

4084   Politics is the only serious subject that men think themselves qualified to act upon without any previous education or instruction whatever.—*H. P. Hughes, American Mercury*

4085   If you get all the facts, your judgment can be right; if you don't get all the facts, it can't be right.—*Bernard M. Baruch*

4086   Too many of our prejudices are like pyramids upside down. They rest on tiny, trivial incidents, but they spread upward and outward until they fill our minds.—*William McC. Martin, Jr., American Magazine*

4087   What the church should be telling the workman is that the first demand religion makes on him is that he should be a good workman. If he is a carpenter, he should be a good carpenter. He should attend church by all means, but what use is church if, at the very center of life, a man defrauds his neighbor and insults God by poor craftsmanship?—*Dwight D. Eisenhower*

4088   Whenever anybody comes to me when we are starting a new thing, and says, "Don't you think you are going to have a lot of trouble?" I say, "Sure, any time you start to do something new we will guarantee the trouble." Success depends on whether you get through the trouble or not.—*Charles F. Kettering*

4089   Dr. Charles F. Kettering was once elaborately introduced as a great scientist. "Well," he responded, "after that introduction, I think I'd better give you my definition of science: Everything we do not understand is science."— *Thomas J. Watson, in Red Barrel*

4090   Wars to end wars are an illusion. Wars, more than any other form of human activity, create the conditions which breed more war.—*John Foster Dulles*

4091   One nation cannot defeat another today. That concept died with Hiroshima. War is like fire: You can prevent a fire, or you can try to put it out, but you can't "win" a fire.—*General H. H. Arnold*

4092   Give me the money that has been spent in war and I will clothe every man, woman, and child in an attire of which kings and queens will be proud. I will build a schoolhouse in every valley over the whole earth. I will crown every hillside with a place of worship consecrated to peace.—*Charles Sumner*

4093   There would never be another war if we fought it on a cash basis.— *Ray D. Everson*

4094   It would do the world good if every man in it would compel himself occasionally to be absolutely alone. Most of the world's progress has come out of such loneliness.—*Bruce Barton*

4095   If America is to be run by the people, it is the people who must think. And we do not need to put on sackcloth and ashes to think. Nor should our minds work like a sundial which records only sunshine. Our thinking must square against some lessons of history, some principles of government and morals, if we would preserve the rights and dignity of men to which this nation is dedicated.—*Herbert Hoover*

Humorous and Unusual Definitions

4096   *Ability:* The art of getting credit for all the home runs somebody else hits.

4097   *Absentminded:* When you forget in the winter to put Prestone in your water-filled mattress.

4098   *Action:* The last resource of those who know not how to dream.—*Oscar Wilde*

4099   *Adolescence:* The time when children answer the phone.

4100   *Adolescent:* One who is well informed about anything he doesn't have to study.

4101   *After-dinner Speaker:* The gust of honor.

4102   *Alarm clock:* A clock that scares the daylights into you.

4103   *Alarm clock:* A daylight-saving plan.

4104   *Ambidextrous:* Being clumsy with both hands.

4105   *Ambition:* The last refuge of the failure.—*Oscar Wilde*

4106   *American:* A person who believes in the absolute necessity of balancing the budget, but puts it off with the expectation that a miracle will come along and do the job.

4107 *American way:* Using instant coffee to dawdle away an hour.

4108 *Angling:* The name given to fishing by people who can't fish.—*Stephen Leacock*

4109 *Antique:* Something no one would want if there were two of them.

4110 *Applause:* The echo of a platitude.

4111 *Archeologist:* A person whose career lies in ruins.

4112 *Argument:* The worst sort of conversation.—*Jonathan Swift*

4113 *Army Draft Board:* The world's largest travel agency.

4114 *Atheist:* A person who prays when he can think of no other way out of his trouble.—*Prison Mirror*

4115 *Atheist:* A man who has no invisible means of support.—*Bishop Fulton J. Sheen*

4116 *Auction:* A place where, if you aren't careful, you'll get something for nodding.

4117 *Autobiography:* An unrivaled vehicle for telling the truth about other people.—*Philip Guedella*

4118 *Autumn:* The time of year when a man indulges in the vain fancy that next spring the grass will look greener on his side of the fence.—*Fletcher Knebel*

4119 *Baby-sitter:* A person who gets paid to watch television.

4120 *Baby-sitter:* Teen-ager who behaves like an adult while the adults are out behaving like teen-agers.

4121 *Bachelor:* A fellow who failed to embrace his opportunities.

4122 *Baloney:* The unvarnished lie laid on so thick you hate it.—*Bishop Fulton J. Sheen*

4123 *Bargain:* Anything that costs no more today than it did last week.

4124 *Bath Mat:* A little rug that children like to stand beside.

4125 *Big Head:* The sign of a small man.

4126 *Bigotry:* The anger of men who have no opinions.—*G. K. Chesterton*

4127 *Birth:* The beginning of death.—*Thomas Fuller*

4128   *Blarney:* Flattery laid on so thin you love it.—*Bishop Fulton J. Sheen*

4129   *Book:* What you look at when your TV goes dead.

4130   *Bookie:* A pickpocket who lets you use your own hands.—*Henry Morgan*

4131   *Broadmindedness:* Highmindedness that has been flattened by experience.

4132   *Bureaucrat:* A person who likes to experiment with a rugged individualist's money.

4133   *Calamities:* Misfortune to ourselves, and good fortune to others.—*Ambrose Bierce*

4134   *Camel:* A horse planned by a committee.

4135   *Canada:* A collection of ten provinces with strong governments loosely connected by fear.—*Dave Broadfoot*

4136   *Canadian:* Somebody who knows how to make love in a canoe.—*Pierre Berton*

4137   *Careful driver:* One who just saw the driver ahead of him get a traffic ticket.

4138   *Careless drivers:* Gamblers who play the hearses.

4139   *Caricature:* Rough truth.—*George Meredith*

4140   *Celebrity:* One who is known to many persons he is glad he doesn't know.—*H. L. Mencken*

4141   *Celebrity:* A person who is known for his well-knowness.—*Daniel Boorstin*

4142   *Chairman of the Meeting:* A person who introduces a speaker who doesn't need an introduction.

4143   *Character:* When you have the same ailments as the other person but refrain from mentioning it.

4144   *Charity:* A thing that begins at home and usually stays there.—*Elbert Hubbard*

4145   *Charm:* A glow within a woman that casts a becoming light on others.—*John Mason Brown*

4146   *Chatterbox:* A telephone booth.

4147   *Cheese:* Milk's leap toward immortality.—*Clifton Fadiman*

4148   *Childhood:* A series of happy delusions.—*Sydney Smith*

4149   *City life:* Millions of people being lonesome together.—*Henry David Thoreau*

4150   *Civilization:* A limitless multiplication of unnecessary necessaries.—*Mark Twain*

4151   *Clever men:* The tools with which bad men work.—*William Hazlitt*

4152   *College education:* A four-year plan for confusing a young mind methodically.

4153   *Communist:* A person who has given up all hope of becoming a capitalist.

4154   *Conceit:* Nature's compensation for inferiority.

4155   *Conceit:* A disease that makes everyone sick except the person who has it.

4156   *Conceit:* God's gift to little men.—*Bruce Barton*

4157   *Conclusion:* The place where you got tired of thinking.—*Martin H. Fischer*

4158   *Conference:* Where conversation is substituted for the dreariness of labor and the loneliness of thought.

4159   *Confidence:* The feeling you have when you are ignorant of the facts.

4160   *Confidence:* The feeling you have before you know better.

4161   *Conscience:* The thing that keeps you from doing the things you enjoy.

4162   *Conservative:* A man who does not think anything should be done for the first time.—*Frank Vanderlip*

4163   *Cookbook:* A volume that is full of stirring passages.

4164   *Cosmetics:* What women use to keep men from reading between the lines.

4165 *Courage:* Being brave when you know something isn't going to happen to you.

4166 *Coward:* A person who has a normal instinct to save his own hide.

4167 *Critic:* A person who can't write but knows what's wrong with another person's writing.

4168 *Cynic:* A man who is never happy unless he is unhappy.

4169 *Cynicism:* Disappointed idealism.—*Harry Kemelman*

4170 *Cynicism:* Intellectual dandyism.—*George Meredith*

4171 *Dancing:* Poetry of the foot.—*John Dryden*

4172 *Dawn:* A term for early morning used by people who don't have to get up.—*Oliver Herford*

4173 *Deficit:* What you have when you don't have as much as if you had nothing.

4174 *Dentist:* A person you see when your tooth aches so badly that it drives you to extraction.

4175 *Desk:* A wastebasket with drawers.

4176 *Diagnosis:* A physician's forecast of disease by the patient's pulse and purse.—*Ambrose Bierce*

4177 *Diet:* Something to take the starch out of you.

4178 *Diet:* What you keep putting off while you are putting on.

4179 *Digestion:* The great secret of life.—*Sydney Smith*

4180 *Diplomat:* A fellow that lets you do all the talking while he gets what he wants.—*Kin Hubbard*

4181 *Discretion for a married man:* When he is sure he is right, and then asks his wife.

4182 *Do-it-yourself person:* One who hits the nail right on the thumb.

4183 *Drama:* What literature does at night.—*George Jean Nathan*

4184 *Drama critic:* A man who leaves no turn unstoned.—*George Bernard Shaw*

4185   *Duty:* What one expects from other people.—*Oscar Wilde*

4186   *Earnest people:* People who habitually look on the serious side of things that have no serious side.—*Van Wyck Brooks*

4187   *Economist:* A person who knows tomorrow why the things he said yesterday didn't happen today.

4188   *Economy:* Spending money without getting any fun out of it.

4189   *Economy:* That mysterious something that impels us to pay too little for something we need and too much for something we want.

4190   *Editor:* A person who separates the wheat from the chaff and prints the chaff.—*Adlai E. Stevenson*

4191   *Education:* What you get from reading the fine print. Experience: What you get from not reading it.

4192   *Education:* What parents get when they talk to teen-agers.

4193   *Efficiency:* The ability to get someone to do your job.

4194   *Efficiency expert:* A person who can cope with your troubles but not with his own.

4195   *Egotism:* The anesthetic that dulls the pain of stupidity.

4196   *Egotist:* A person who thinks as much of himself as you think of yourself.

4197   *Egotist:* A person who never talks about other people.

4198   *Etiquette:* Knowing which finger to put in your mouth when you whistle for the waiter.

4199   *Evening:* The time when people do almost anything to keep from going to bed.

4200   *Executive:* A person who never puts off until tomorrow what he can get someone else to do today.

4201   *Executive:* A person who has trained others to discharge his responsibilities.

4202   *Exile:* One who serves his country by residing abroad, yet is not an ambassador.—*Ambrose Bierce*

4203   *Expert:* One who doesn't know more than you do but uses slides.

4204   *Fad:* Something that goes in one era and out the other.

4205   *Fair-weather Friend:* One who is always around when he needs you.

4206   *Fall Guy:* Any member of a Latin American cabinet.

4207   *Family Man:* The fellow who has replaced the currency in his wallet with snapshots.

4208   *Fanatic:* A person who redoubles his effort when he has forgotten his aim.—*George Santayana*

4209   *Fanatic:* One who can't change his mind and won't change the subject. —*Winston Churchill*

4210   *Farm:* Land which people leave to go to the city to make enough money so they can come back and live on it.

4211   *Fat chance:* Two words that mean the same as slim chance.

4212   *Fat man:* Only a little boy gone to waist.

4213   *Father:* A banker provided by nature.—*French proverb*

4214   *Father:* A person who wears last year's hat, drives this year's car, and lives on next year's income.

4215   *Feminine thrift:* Taking a bus to a mink-coat sale.

4216   *Financial success:* An accomplishment that helps you to see your relatives frequently.

4217   *Fishing:* A delusion entirely surrounded by liars in old clothes.—*Don Marquis*

4218   *Flattery:* The art of telling another person exactly what he thinks of himself.

4219   *Flattery:* A commodity that makes everybody sick except those who swallow it.

4220   *Flattery:* What makes husbands out of bachelors.

4221   *Football:* A sport that bears the same relationship to education that bullfighting does to agriculture.—*Elbert Hubbard*

4222   *Forgetfulness:* A form of freedom.—*Kahlil Gibran*

4223   *Friends:* People who dislike the same people we do.

4224   *Frustration:* When you have ulcers but still aren't a success.

4225   *Gambling:* The sure way of getting nothing for something.—*Wilson Mizner*

4226   *Garage sale:* A chance to purchase used articles from a neighbor's garage to store in your own garage.

4227   *Geneologist:* Clan digger.

4228   *Genius:* Elegant common sense.—*Josh Billings*

4229   *Genius:* Patience.—*Buffon*

4230   *Gentleman:* A person who "is at a big disadvantage these days."—*Kin Hubbard*

4231   *Gentleman:* One who never hurts anyone's feelings unintentionally.—*Oliver Herford*

4232   *Go-getter:* A person who gets his elbows on both arms of his theater seat.

4233   *Golf:* Another method of beating around the bush.

4234   *Golf:* Low-pasture pool.—*O. K. Bovard*

4235   *Golf:* A game in which you can't improve your lie. It differs from political oratory.

4236   *Golf:* A good walk spoiled.—*Mark Twain*

4237   *Good after-dinner speaker:* One who has a streamlined train of thought and a terminal.

4238   *Good executive:* A person who will share the credit with the one who did all the work.

4239   *Good manners:* Petty sacrifices.—*Ralph Waldo Emerson*

4240   *Good neighbor:* A person who could show you movies of his trip abroad but doesn't.

4241   *Gossip:* Mouth-to-mouth recitation.

4242   *Gossip:* Something that goes in one ear and over the back fence.

4243   *Gourmet:* A glutton with brains.—*Phillip W. Haberman, Jr.*

4244   *Government bureau:* Where the taxpayer's shirt is kept.

4245   *Grandmother:* A baby-sitter who doesn't hang around the refrigerator.

4246   *Great man:* The man who does a thing for the first time.—*Alexander Smith*

4247   *Grouch:* A person who has sized himself up and doesn't like what he saw.

4248   *Grudge:* The heaviest thing you can carry.

4249   *Hard work:* An accumulation of easy things that should have been done last week.

4250   *Helpless:* The feeling you have if you are "the owner of a sick goldfish." —*Kin Hubbard*

4251   *Highbrow:* A lowbrow who is smart enough to conceal it.

4252   *Historian:* An unsuccessful novelist.—*H. L. Mencken*

4253   *History:* A confused heap of facts.—*Lord Chesterfield*

4254   *History:* Romance that is believed.—*Horace Walpole*

4255   *History:* Mostly guessing; the rest is prejudice.—*Will and Ariel Durant*

4256   *History:* Something that never happened, written by someone who wasn't there.—*Unknown*

4257   *History:* The propaganda of the victorious.—*Ernst Toller*

4258   *Home:* The nursery of the infinite.—*William Ellery Channing*

4259   *Home:* Where the heart is.—*Elbert Hubbard*

4260   *Horn Blower:* A small boy left alone in the front seat of a car.

4261   *Horse sense:* The sense which keeps a horse from betting on the human race.

4262   *Hospital bed:* A parked taxi with the meter running.

4263   *Hush money:* Money that talks louder than any other kind.

4264   *Inflation:* Merely a drop in the buck.

4265   *Inflation:* Reducing a dollar bill without damaging the paper.

4266   *Inflation:* When everybody is so rich that no one can afford anything.

4267   *Inflation:* When the prices you get look good, and the prices you pay look awful.

4268   *Intellectual:* A person who cannot state a simple fact in simple terms.

4269   *Jelly:* A food usually found on bread, children, and piano keys.

4270   *Joint checking account:* One that lets a wife beat her husband to the draw.

4271   *Journalism:* History on the run.—*Thomas Griffith*

4272   *June:* When girls look at the bride side of life.

4273   *Junk:* Something you keep in the house ten years and then throw away just before you need it.

4274   *Laughter:* A tranquilizer with no side effects.—*Arnold Glasow*

4275   *Laughter:* The sensation of feeling good all over, and showing it principally in one spot.—*Josh Billings*

4276   *Lawyers:* Persons who write a 10,000-word document and call it a brief.

4277   *Laziness:* The love of physical calm.

4278   *Liberal:* A person whose own interests are not at stake in the position he takes on an issue.

4279   *Literary critic:* A person who interprets what the author didn't know he was writing.

4280   *Literature:* The orchestration of platitudes.—*Thornton Wilder*

4281   *Living wage:* Twice what you make.

4282   *Loafer:* A person who sees a completed job and is certain he could have done it better.

4283   *Logic:* The art of going wrong with confidence.—*Joseph Wood Krutch*

4284   *Man:* The only animal that contemplates death.—*William Ernest Hocking*

4285   *Man:* The only animal that does not know "that the principal business of life is to enjoy it."—*Samuel Butler*

4286   *Managed news:* When your wife waits until after you've eaten to tell you about the dented fender.

4287   *Management:* The art of getting three men to do three men's work.

4288   *Manners:* Noises you don't make eating soup.

4289   *Marriage:* A mistake every man should make.—*George Jessel*

4290   *Marriage:* A mutual partnership with the husband mute.

4291   *Martyrdom:* The only way in which a man can become famous without ability.—*George Bernard Shaw*

4292   *Mealtime:* That period when children sit down to continue their eating.

4293   *Medicine cabinet:* Nothing more than a home drugstore without sandwiches.

4294   *Melancholy:* The pleasure of being sad.—*Victor Hugo*

4295   *Memory:* The thing you have to forget with.

4296   *Middle age:* When a man has enough financial security to wear the flashy sports coats he didn't have the courage to wear when he was young.

4297   *Middle age:* When you are as young as ever, but it takes a lot more effort.

4298   *Middle age:* When you don't care where you go, just so you're home by nine P.M.

4299   *Middle age:* When your tripping becomes less light and more fantastic.

4300   *Miser:* A guy who lives within his income. He's also called a magician.
—*Alliston (Ontario) Herald*

4301   *Miser:* A home-loving body who seldom goes buy-buy.

4302   *Model wife:* One who spades the garden, picks up the fishworms, and saves them for her husband.

4303   *Modern man:* A person who drives a mortgaged car over a bond-financed highway on credit-card gas.

4304   *Modern parents:* Parents who can't or won't control their children at home, but expect others to control them in the schools and on the streets.

4305   *Modesty:* The gentle art of enhancing your charm by pretending not to be aware of it.—*Oliver Herford*

4306   *Money:* About the only thing that is handier then a credit card.

4307   *Moonlighter:* One who holds two jobs so he can drive from one to another in a better car.

4308   *Moral indignation:* Jealousy with a halo.—*H. G. Wells*

4309   *Morale:* When your hands and feet keep on working when your head says it can't be done.—*Admiral Ben Moreell*

4310   *Nerve specialist:* One thing Russia does not need.

4311   *News:* The first rough draft of history.—*Ben Bradlee*

4312   *Newspaper:* A circulating library with high blood pressure.—*Arthur "Bugs" Baer*

4313   *Night watchmen:* Yawn patrol.

4314   *Nonprofit agency:* The weather bureau.

4315   *Nostalgia:* Recalling the fun without remembering the pain.

4316   *Nostalgia:* The good old days multiplied by a bad memory.

4317   *Oboe:* A tramp to an Englishman.

4318   *Obstinacy:* The strength of the weak-minded.

4319   *Office:* A place where the man who arrives after nine A.M. is either an executive or will never be one.

4320   *Old age:* When your memory is short, your experience long, your breath short, your eyesight dim, and your safe-deposit box full.

4321   *Old-timer:* A person who can remember when people rested on Sunday instead of Monday.

4322   *Old-timer:* One who can remember when it cost more to run a car than to park it.

4323   *Old-timer:* One who remembers when you could promise a child the moon without having to buy a space suit.

4324   *Optimist:* A bridegroom who thinks he has no bad habits.

4325   *Optimist:* A cheerful guy who is blissfully unaware of what is going to happen to him.

4326   *Optimist:* A guy who has never had much experience.—*Don Marquis*

4327   *Optimist:* A man who gets treed by a lion but enjoys the scenery.

4328   *Originality:* Undetected plagiarism.—*W. R. Inge, Dean of St. Paul's*

4329   *Partisan:* A member of the other party.

4330   *Past:* Something to be forgotten.—*Oliver Herford*

4331   *Pawnbroker:* One who lives off the flat of the land.

4332   *Payroll:* The one role in which every politician is interested.

4333   *Perfect autumn day:* When the lawn no longer needs mowing and the leaves haven't started to fall.

4334   *Pessimist:* A person who is only happy when he is wrong.

4335   *Pessimist:* One who thinks all is lost because he is not running it.

4336   *Philosophy:* Common sense in a dress suit.

4337   *Platitude:* A truth we are tired of hearing.—*Sir Godfrey Nicholson*

4338   *Poetry:* A sort of dancing with the voice.—*Francis Searfe*

4339   *Poetry:* The impish attempt to paint the color of the wind.—*Maxwell Bodenheim*

4340   *Poise:* The ability to be at ease conspicuously.

4341   *Poise:* The art of raising the eyebrows instead of the roof.

4342   *Politics:* Getting votes from the poor and campaign funds from the rich by promising to protect each from the other.

4343   *Politics:* The diversion of trivial men who, when they succeed at it, become important in the eyes of more trivial men.—*George Jean Nathan*

4344   *Poverty:* A state of mind induced by the neighbor's new car.

4345   *Practical nurse:* One who falls in love with a rich patient.

4346   *Prejudice:* A timesaver that enables you to pass judgment without getting the facts.

4347   *Procrastination:* The art of keeping up with yesterday.—*Don Marquis*

4348   *Progress:* The exchange of one nuisance for another nuisance.—*Havelock Ellis*

4349   *Psychiatrist:* A person who owns a couch and charges you for lying on it.—*Edwin Brock*

4350   *Public servant:* Persons chosen by the people to distribute the graft.—*Mark Twain*

4351   *Publisher:* The one person to whom no author is a man of genius.—*Heinrich Heine*

4352   *Punctuality:* The art of guessing how late the other fellow is going to be.

4353   *Pure thought:* A glimpse of God.—*C. A. Bartol*

4354   *Puritan:* A person who pours righteous indignation into the wrong things.—*G. K. Chesterton*

4355   *Raving beauty:* The one who finishes last in a beauty contest.

4356   *Repartee:* What a person thinks of after he becomes a departee.—*Dan Bennett*

4357   *Republic:* A government in which those who don't vote criticize those who are elected.

4358   *Research:* Getting things out of many old books never read, and putting them into a new book which nobody is going to read.

4359   *Retirement security:* Making sure all the doors are locked before you go to bed.

4360   *Ringleader:* The first in a large family to take a bath on Saturday night.

4361   *Road map:* A map that tells you everything you need to know except how to fold it up again.

4362   *Romance:* History that is not believed.—*Horace Walpole*

4363   *Rummage sale:* Where you buy stuff from other people's attics to put in your own.

4364 *Salesmanship:* A puppy selling himself to a small boy.

4365 *Satellite:* An employee at a party the boss gives.

4366 *Second fiddle:* One of the most difficult instruments to play.

4367 *Second-story man:* One whose wife doesn't believe his first story.

4368 *Self-denial:* The effect of prudence on rascality.—*George Bernard Shaw*

4369 *Senior citizen:* A dropout from the school of hard knocks.

4370 *Shin:* A device for finding furniture in the dark.

4371 *Silence:* A conversation with an Englishman.—*Heinrich Heine*

4372 *Silence:* The unbearable repartee.—*G. K. Chesterton*

4373 *Silence:* The virtue of fools.—*Francis Bacon*

4374 *Skeptic:* Someone who won't take know for an answer.

4375 *Small boy's ambition:* To wash his mother's ears.

4376 *Sneer:* The weapon of the weak.—*James Russell Lowell*

4377 *Spring:* The time of year when big-league baseball players put on their contract lenses.

4378 *Squirrels:* Small animals who are like some people because they worry too much about nuttin'.

4379 *Statesman:* A successful politician who is dead.—*Thomas B. Reed*

4380 *Suburbanite:* A man who hires someone to mow his lawn so he can play golf for exercise.

4381 *Suburbanite:* One who thinks "dining out" means having charcoal-burned hot dogs in the backyard.

4382 *Success:* Doing what you want to do and making money at it.

4383 *Successful person:* One who has to borrow money to pay his income taxes.

4384 *Sucker:* A man who still has confidence in other persons.

4385 *Summer:* When the highway authorities close the regular roads and open up the detours.

4386   *Summer camps:* Places where little boys go for Mother's vacation.

4387   *Suspicion:* The feeling you have when an alderman moves from a $25,000 home into a $200,000 one.

4388   *Sweater:* A garment a child wears when his mother feels chilly.

4389   *Tact:* In the battle of existence, tact is the clever footwork.—*Wilson Mizner*

4390   *Tax collector:* The fellow who tells you what to do with the money you have already done something with.

4391   *Taxpayer:* A person who doesn't have to take a Civil Service examination to work for the government.

4392   *Taxpayer:* A person who has the government on his payroll.

4393   *Taxpayer:* A person who pays until it no longer hurts.

4394   *Tears:* The noble language of the eyes.

4395   *Television:* Burial place for old movies.

4396   *Television:* A device that permits people who haven't anything to do to watch people who can't do anything.—*Fred Allen*

4397   *Thoughtful wife:* One who has some steaks in the freezer when her husband returns from a fishing trip.

4398   *Tolerance:* The ability to keep your shirt on when you're hot under the collar.

4399   *Tomorrow:* The biggest laborsaving device ever invented.

4400   *Tongue twister:* A group of words that get your tang all tonguled up.

4401   *Tourist:* A person who travels thousands of miles to get a snapshot of himself standing beside his car.

4402   *Traffic light:* A device to get pedestrians halfway across the street safely.

4403   *Unhappiness:* Not knowing what we want and killing ourselves to get it.

4404   *Vacation:* The time when you spend all the money you have left after the installment payments to live higher than you can afford.

4405   *Vacation:* What we take when we can't take what we are taking any longer.

4406   *Vanity:* A parent trying to make his child just what he is.

4407   *Virtue:* The avoidence of the vices that do not attract us.—*Robert Lynd*

4408   *Waiter:* A person whose chief business is hiding out.

4409   *Walking:* The means by which you get to the bus or the garage.

4410   *War:* A series of catastrophes which result in victory.—*Georges Clemenceau*

4411   *Weather report:* Chili today and hot tamale.

4412   *Wig:* A new top on an old chassis.

4413   *Winter:* The time of the year when we try to keep the house as hot as it was in the summer, when we complained about it.

4414   *Wise child:* One "that owes his own father."—*Carolyn Wells*

4415   *Wise man:* A person who is certain of very few things, whereas a fool is certain of everything.

4416   *Wisecracking:* Calisthenics with words.—*Dorothy Parker*

4417   *Wit:* Cultured insolence.—*Aristotle*

4418   *Yawn:* A silent shout.—*G. K. Chesterton*

4419   *Yawn:* An honest opinion.—*Farmer's Almanac*

Toasts and Quotations for Special Occasions

April 19, 1775—Birthday of American Liberty

4420   On April 19 we mark the 200th anniversary of the opening of the American Revolution. On that day in 1775 colonists in Concord and Lexington fired upon British troops and forced them to retreat to Boston.

On the 100th anniversary of the event, Concord reconstructed its Old North Bridge and erected its Minute Man statue. It was for this monument to American freedom that Ralph Waldo Emerson wrote the immortal "Concord Hymn":

> By the rude bridge that arched the flood,
>   Their flag to April's breeze unfurled,
> Here once the embattled farmers stood,
>   And fired the shot heard round the world. . . .
> Spirit, that made those heroes dare
>   To die, and leave their children free,
> Bid Time and Nature gently spare
>   The shaft we raise to them and thee.

4421   Stand your ground. Don't fire unless fired upon, but if they mean to have a war let it begin here.—*Captain John Parker, addressing his men at Lexington Green at the outset of the Revolutionary War, April 19, 1775*

Arbor Day

4422   I like trees because they seem more resigned to the way they have to live than other things do.—*Willa Cather*

4423   I think that I shall never see
A poem lovely as a tree. . . .
Poems are made by fools like me,
But only God can make a tree.
            —*Joyce Kilmer*

4424   Woodman, spare that tree!
Touch not a single bough!
In youth it sheltered me,
And I'll protect it now.
        —*George Pope Morris*

4425   Arbor Day has brought about a revolution in American taste. From tree destroying we have come back to tree planting.—*John Wilson*

4426   A country, embracing within its borders the headwaters of all the streams and rivers that interlace it, when stripped of its forest covering becomes a barren waste, incapable of supporting man or beast.—*Warren Highley*

4427   He who plants a tree, he plants love.
Tents of coolness spreading out above
Wayfarers he may not live to see.
    Gifts that grow are best;
    Hands that bless are blest;
    Plant: Life does the rest!
Heaven and earth help him who plants a tree
And his work its own reward shall be.
                —*Lucy Larcom*

Autumn

4428   The melancholy days are come, the saddest of the year,
Of wailing winds, and naked woods, and meadows brown and sere.
Heaped in the hollows of the grove, the autumn leaves lie dead;
They rustle to the eddying gust, and to the rabbit's tread;
The robin and the wren are flown, and from the shrubs the jay,
And from the wood-top calls the crow through all the gloomy day.
                —*William Cullen Bryant*

4429   O, it sets my heart a-clickin' like the tickin' of a clock,
When the frost is on the punkin and the fodder's in the shock.
                    —James Whitcomb Riley

4430   My sorrow when she's here with me,
    Thinks these dark days of autumn rain
Are beautiful as days can be;
    She loves the bare, the withered tree;
    She walks the sodden pasture lane.
                    —Robert Frost

4431   Dread autumn, harvest season of the Goddess of Death.—*Horace*

4432   In autumn the tide ebbs; leaf and petal look down to the soil whence they came as if they heard a call and longed to go back and intermingle with their kin; softly the petal flings herself down, and the leaf is not long in following.—*Mary Webb*

4433   How bravely Autumn paints upon the sky
The gorgeous fame of Summer which is fled.
                    —Thomas Hood

Christmas

4434   Hark the herald angels sing,
"Glory to the new-born king."
Peace on earth, and mercy mild,
God and sinners reconciled!
                    —Charles Wesley

4435   Away in a manger, no crib for a bed,
The little Lord Jesus laid down His sweet head.
                    —Martin Luther

4436   Heap on more wood!—the wind is chill;
But let it whistle as it will,
We'll keep our Christmas merry still.
                    —Sir Walter Scott

4437   At Christmas play and make good cheer,
For Christmas comes but once a year.
                    —Thomas Tusser

4438
God rest you merry, gentlemen,
Let nothing you dismay,
For Jesus Christ, our Saviour,
Was born upon this day.

4439   Although the birthday of Christ was celebrated on various dates as early as the third century, its observance was not sanctioned officially until a century later. Until then, church fathers withheld their blessing because they feared the occasion would be tied in with pagan festivals. Finally, to satisfy growing Christian desire, Julius I, Bishop of Rome, authorized an investigation to determine Christ's probable birth date. This led to the selection of December 25. On that date in 354 A.D., the feast of the Nativity was first observed in Rome. —*Sunshine Magazine*

4440   Among the most popular Christmas decorations—along with holly and mistletoe—are the pine cones, which are used in their natural state, or are painted in bright colors, or in silver or gold. There is an interesting German legend which explains the origin of the pine cone, widely used at Christmastime. It tells of a poor woman climbing a mountain to pick up pine cones for fuel. She was approached by an elf who told her to "take only the cones under this tree." The good woman picked up the cones indicated and when she arrived home she found that they had all turned to pure silver. Thus, the silver pine cone which we know today.—*Sunshine Magazine*

4441   Christmas is a widely observed holiday on which neither the past nor the future is of so much interest as the present.—*F. G. Kernan*

4442   How seldom Christmas comes—only once a year; and how soon it is over—a night and a day! If that is the whole of it, it seems not much more durable than the little toys that one buys of a fakir on the street corner. They run for an hour, and then the spring breaks, and the legs come off, and nothing remains but a contribution to the dust heap.
    But surely that need not and ought not be the whole of Christmas—only a single day of generosity, ransomed from the dull servitude of a selfish year—only a single night of merry-making, celebrated in the slave quarters of a selfish race! If every gift is the token of a personal thought, a friendly feeling, an unselfish interest in the joys of others, then the thought, the feeling, the interest may remain long after the gift is forgotten.—*Henry Van Dyke*

4443   In many countries, the Christmas crèche resembles a rainbow in coloring. Portuguese representations of the Adoration in glazed ceramics are often exotically tinted in vivid blue, cerise, and bright green. Their artists also add such unexpected touches as a throne for the Christ Child's cradle and chickens as well as cattle around the crèche. In the wine countries of France, ground-up cork may be used instead of straw for the manger; the Mexican Christ Child is hailed by a gaudily painted Indian with wings and a feather headdress.—*Catholic Digest*

4444   Charles Dickens was inspired to write his masterpiece, *A Christmas Carol*, to arouse the people to the need of improving the conditions of the poor. The idea came to him after he had attended the ceremonies of the new Athenaeum at Manchester during the first week of October 1843. One week later he returned to London and started his composition. Unaware that he was writing a classic, he later admitted that as the story took form he fell under its spell, laughing and weeping in turn with his characters. For seven weeks he labored on the manuscript. On December 18, 1843, the first edition of six thousand copies appeared on the bookstalls of London, and within twenty-four hours was entirely sold out.—*Sunshine Magazine*

4445   Christmas is many things. It is a star shining brightly to guide Magi from the East to the baby Jesus. It is shepherds gazing with awe and wonder at the heavenly visitors who announced the birth of the King of Kings. It is peace in a world of war and unrest, joy in a time of bewilderment and sorrow, hope in a situation of anxiety and apprehension. But most of all Christmas is the Son of God cradled in the arms of Mary. God's great gift of salvation and reconciliation to all mankind.—*War Cry*

4446   I sometimes think we expect too much of Christmas Day. We try to crowd into it the long arrears of kindliness and humanity of the whole year.—*David Grayson*

4447   And it came to pass in those days, that there went out a decree from Caesar Augustus, that all the world should be taxed. . . .
    And all went to be taxed, every one into his own city.
    And Joseph also went up from Galilee, out of the city of Nazareth, into Judaea, unto the city of David, which is called Bethlehem, (because he was of the house and lineage of David,)
    To be taxed with Mary his espoused wife, being great with child.
    And so it was, that, while they were there, the days were accomplished that she should be delivered.
    And she brought forth her firstborn son, and wrapped him in swaddling clothes, and laid him in a manger; because there was no room for them in the inn.—*Luke 2:1–7*

4448   God rest ye, little children; let nothing you affright,
    For Jesus Christ, your Saviour, was born this happy night;
    Along the hills of Galilee the white flocks sleeping lay,
    When Christ, the Child of Nazareth, was born on Christmas Day.
                                        —*Dinah Maria Mulock Craik*

4449   For unto you is born this day in the city of David a Saviour, which is Christ the Lord.—*Luke 2:11*

4450

It came upon the midnight clear,
    That glorious song of old,
From angels bending near the earth
    To touch their harps of gold;
"Peace on the earth, good will to men
    From Heaven's all-gracious King"—
The world in solemn stillness lay
    To hear the angels sing.
                    —*E. H. Sears*

4451

O little town of Bethlehem,
How still we see thee lie!
Above thy deep and dreamless sleep
The silent stars go by.
Yet in thy dark street shineth
The everlasting Light;
The hopes and fears of all the years
Are met in thee tonight.
                    —*Phillips Brooks*

4452

Let's dance and sing and make good cheer,
For Christmas comes but once a year.
                    —*G. MacFarren*

4453   Last night John Elzy, watchman at the Grand Eagle Department Store, while making his rounds of the bargain basement, found the body of a man lying under a counter. He was thin to the point of emaciation, apparently in his middle thirties, and was shabbily dressed. His pockets were empty and there were no marks of identification upon his person. Store officials believe that he was trampled in the Christmas rush and crawled under the counter for shelter. But they are unable to account for what appear to be nail wounds in his hands. The police are investigating.—*The Saturday Review*

4454   A youngster walked into a bank the other day to open an account with $25. The bank's vice president gave him a benign smile and asked how he had accumulated so much money.

"Selling Christmas cards," said the lad.

"Well, you've done very well. Sold them to lots of people, obviously."

"Nope," said the little boy proudly. "I sold all of them to one family—their dog bit me."

4455   By the time a man has the shape for the job, his kids no longer believe in Santa Claus.

4456   In Scandinavian countries a little elf called Julenissen brings toys to good children on Christmas Eve. In England it is Father Christmas who brings the gifts. In France the gift-bearer is known as Bonhomme Noël and he is accompanied by Père Fouettard (Father Whipper), who leaves a birch rod for the unfortunate child who has been naughty during the year. In Spain and some other Spanish-speaking countries it is Balthazar, one of the Wise Men, who brings the gifts on the eve of Epiphany. In Syria the Good Camel brings the gifts. According to legend, he was the youngest of the camels that bore the Wise Men on their journey to the Christ Child. A little old woman called Befana brings the gifts in Italy. According to legend, the Wise Men were on their way to Bethlehem when they encountered the old lady cleaning her house. They asked her to join them on their journey, but she said she was too busy. And since that time she has been wandering around seeking the child Jesus.—*Survey Bulletin*

4457   "Father," asked Junior, "what is a financial genius?"
        "A financial genius, my son," replied his father thoughtfully, "is a man who can pay his family's Christmas bills in January."

4458   Blessed is the season that engages the whole world in a conspiracy of love.—*Hamilton Wright Mabie*

4459   The world is filled with the sounds of Christmas. If you listen with your outer ears, you will hear carols, bells, and laughter, and now and then a sob of loneliness. If you listen with the inner ear, you will hear the sound of angels' wings, the hush of inner expectation, and the sacred sound of the deepest silence, the vibrant whisper of the eternal Word.
    The world is filled with the sights of Christmas. If you look with your outer eyes, you will see gay trees, tinseled stars, flaming candles, and a crèche. If you look with the inner eye, you will see the Star of Bethlehem in your own heart.
—*Anna May Nielson, Sunshine Magazine*

4460   A group of youngsters in a California school were told to draw the pictures for Christmas cards they would give their parents, but to copy the verse from a card they found at home.
    That's why one mother and father received this greeting from their daughter: "It's been a pleasure to do business with you."

4461   It is good to be children sometimes, and never better than at Christmas when its mighty Founder was a child Himself.—*Charles Dickens*

4462   Christmas, of course, belongs largely to children. So it is fitting to note here a few touching passages from a little boy's diary:

> Dec. 25: Got an air gun for Christmas, but it's raining, can't go hunting.
> Dec. 26: Still raining, can't go hunting.
> Dec. 27: Still raining, can't go hunting.
> Dec. 28: Still raining. Shot Uncle Edgar.—*Hugh Scott, Today*

4463   A little girl was saying her prayers a few nights before Christmas when she stopped suddenly and asked her mother a question with a worried look: "What are we giving God for Christmas? What does God want for Christmas?"

We smile, but it is an important question. Is God on your Christmas list?—*Halford E. Luccock, Christian Herald*

4464   One of the first things a boy learns who gets a chemistry set for Christmas is that he isn't likely ever to get another one.

4465   Christmas is over. Uncork your ambition! Back to the battle. Come on, competition! Down with all sentiment, can scrupulosity! For the other 364 days. —*Franklin P. Adams*

4466   A five-year-old rehearsing at home for the school Christmas program sang:

> "Hark, the herald angels sing
> Glory to the new-born king!
> Peace on earth and mercy mild,
> God and sitters reconciled."
> —*Delta Kappa Gamma Bulletin*

4467   It was on Christmas Eve that one of the most beloved classics came into being. High in the Austrian Alps, in the little hamlet of Oberndorf, two men, Father Joseph Mohr and the village schoolmaster and organist, Franz Gruber, faced the alarming prospect of Christmas Eve services with no music. The church organ was broken! To provide a song that could be "sung without the organ accompaniment," the two men brought forth the beautiful carol "Silent Night, Holy Night." Since that night in 1818 this lovely favorite carol has been translated into sixty-eight languages.

4468

> We ring the bells and we raise the strain.
> We hang up garlands everywhere

And bid the tapers twinkle fair,
And feast and frolic—and then we go
Back to the same old lives again.
—*Susan Coolidge*

Easter

4469
Tomb, thou shalt not hold Him longer;
Death is strong, but Life is stronger;
Stronger than the dark, the light;
Stronger than the wrong, the right;
Faith and Hope triumphant say
Christ will rise on Easter Day.
—*Phillips Brooks*

4470
"Christ the Lord is risen today,"
Sons of men and angels say.
Raise your joys and triumphs high;
Sing, ye heavens, and earth reply.
—*Charles Wesley*

4471

The date upon which Easter Sunday falls was fixed in the year A.D. 325 by the Council of the Christian Churches which met in Nicea, Asia Minor, to draw up the Nicene Creed. It was decided that the commemoration of the Resurrection of Christ should be observed on the first Sunday following the first full moon on or after the vernal equinox, which is the twenty-first day of March. The reason for the timing was that the thousands of pilgrims who visited the Holy Land to celebrate the Resurrection needed a bright moon to travel by. Easter can occur as early as March 22 or as late as April 25. Between 1970 and the year 2000, unless the calendar system is changed, Easter will be in the month of March five more times.—*Sunshine Magazine*

4472   Our Saviour Jesus Christ . . . hath abolished death, and hath brought life and immortality to light through the gospel.—*II Timothy 1:10*

4473   An unknown soldier stood facing Jesus as He died. A warrior to whom no monument has been erected and whose forgotten grave remains undecorated —a Roman centurion in command of an execution squad. This is the language of an army officer who was in a position to see and hear everything during the Master's last hours, not because he wanted to, but because it was his duty. Had he had a choice he would have been elsewhere that Friday from nine in the morning to three in the afternoon. Yet, had he been elsewhere, he would have missed the most important turning point in his life, and we would have been the

poorer for not hearing his estimate of Jesus: "Truly this man was a son of God."
—*Paul L. Moore, Seven Words of Men Around the Cross*

Fourth of July—Independence Day

4474   When in the course of human events, it becomes necessary for one people to dissolve the political bonds which have connected them with another, and to assume among the powers of the earth the separate and equal station to which the laws of nature and of nature's God entitle them, a decent respect to the opinions of mankind requires that they should declare the causes which impel them to the separation.—*Thomas Jefferson*

4475   O beautiful for patriot dream
                             That sees beyond the years
                             Thine alabaster cities gleam
                             Undimmed by human tears!
                             America! America!
                             God shed His grace on thee,
                             And crown thy good with brotherhood
                             From sea to shining sea!
                                      —*Katharine Lee Bates*

4476   That which distinguishes this day from all others is that then both orators and artillerymen shoot blank cartridges.—*John Burroughs*

Friday the 13th

4477   Among the most common of superstitions is that Friday the 13th is a day on which hard luck is apt to befall. It is not certain just what started this idea, but a number of ancient beliefs have designated Friday as an unlucky day, and for centuries the number 13 has been considered an unfortunate number. It is no wonder that the combination of these two—Friday and the 13th—is thought to be an ominous day.

To substantiate this belief, these tragedies are cited as examples of Friday the 13th bad luck:

Friday the 13th, April 1906, a devastating earthquake struck Taiwan.

Friday the 13th, September 1907, the steamship *Lusitania* began its ill-fated voyage.

Friday the 13th, April 1923, a huge tidal wave hit the coast of Korea.

On the other hand, good things have also occurred on that fateful date:

The first telephone line for business purposes was opened on Friday the 13th, April 1877.

Electric lighting was first tried in London on Friday the 13th, October 1878.
—*Sunshine Magazine*

Lincoln's Birthday

4478   Next to Washington, Lincoln stands forth as the grandest patriot in our American life. Washington was the "Father of His Country"; Lincoln was her most loyal son; Washington brought the United States of America into being; Lincoln made that being immortal; Washington unfurled a new flag among the nations of the world; Lincoln made that flag a mighty power among those nations. Dead, they yet speak. The good they did will last through time and on through eternity. And so our Nation has most rightly and fittingly made the birthdays of these, her illustrious sons, legal holidays, to inspire us to a purer, nobler, holier manhood.—*George H. Smythe, Jr.*

Loyalty Day—May 1

4479   Loyalty Day has been celebrated each year since 1959 on May 1, by Presidential proclamation. It is the day on which all loyal American citizens, both youths and adults, individually and through their schools and churches— and many, many organizations—make public declarations and demonstrations of loyalty to our country and to its ideals. They do this with parades and with flag ceremonies and the Pledge of Allegiance, and with public meetings and stirring patriotic speeches. Seem a bit too ostentatious? Too much rah-rah-rah in the name of America? Maybe—but it is one small measure to counterbalance the bombastic howls of criticism by those who would destroy the America that still dares to be free. Freedom is not free. Those who have it and wish to keep it must continue to work for it.—*Sunshine Magazine*

Memorial Day—Decoration Day

4480

The little green tents where the soldiers sleep
And the sunbeams play and the women weep,
Are covered with flowers today.
—*Walt Mason*

4481

The muffled drum's sad roll has beat
The soldier's last tattoo;
No more on Life's parade shall meet
The brave and fallen few.
On Fame's eternal camping-ground
Their silent tents are spread,
And Glory guards, with solemn round,
The bivouac of the dead.
—*Theodore O'Hara*

Months

4482   Pale January lay
        In its cradle day by day,
        Dead or living, hard to say.
                    —*Alfred Austin*

4483   The blasts of January
        Would blow you through and through.
                    —*William Shakespeare*

4484   Come, ye cold winds, at January's call,
        On whistling wings, and with white flakes bestrew
        The earth.
                    —*John Ruskin*

4485   Late February days; and now, at last,
        Might you have thought that Winter's woe was past;
        So fair the sky was and so soft the air.
                    —*William Morris*

4486   If February give much snow,
        A fine summer it doth foreshow.
                    —*English rhyme*

4487   Good weather in February is regarded as an unfavorable symptom of
what is to come.—*Chambers*

4488   February's rain fills the barn.—*Torriano*

4489   All the months in the year curse a fair Februeer.—*John Ray*

4490   The bleak wind of March
        Made her tremble and shiver.—*Thomas Hood*

4491   The stormy March is come at last,
            With wind, and cloud, and changing skies;
        I hear the rushing of the blast,
            That through the snowy valley flies.
                    —*William Cullen Bryant*

4492   Ah, March! we know thou art
        Kind-hearted, spite of ugly looks and threats,
        And, out of sight, art nursing April's violets.
                    —*Helen Hunt Jackson*

4493   There's joy in the mountains;
There's life in the fountains;
Small clouds are sailing,
Blue sky prevailing;
The rain is over and gone.
    —William Wordsworth

4494   The sun was warm but the wind was chill.
You know how it is with an April day:
When the sun is out and the wind is still,
You're one month on in the middle of May.
    —Robert Frost

4495   The children with the streamlets sing,
When April stops at last her weeping;
And every happy growing thing
Laughs like a babe just roused from sleeping.
    —Lucy Larcom

4496   Oh, to be in England
Now that April's there.
    —Robert Browning

4497   Again the blackbirds sing; the streams
Wake, laughing, from their winter dreams,
And tremble in the April showers
The tassels of the maple flowers.
    —John Greenleaf Whittier

4498   Every tear is answered by a blossom,
Every sigh with songs and laughter blent,
Apple-blooms upon the breezes toss them,
April knows her own, and is content.
    —Susan Coolidge

4499   Oh, the lovely fickleness of an April day!
    —W. H. Gibson

4500   I have seen the lady April bringing the daffodils,
Bringing the springing grass and the soft warm April rain.
    —John Masefield

4501   Sweet April showers
Do bring May flowers.
    —Thomas Tusser

4502   April warms the world anew.
              —*William Shakespeare*

4503   April prepares her green traffic light and the world thinks go.—*Christopher Morley*

4504   It is not enough that yearly, down this hill, April comes like an idiot, babbling and strewing flowers.—*Edna St. Vincent Millay*

4505   'Tis a month before the month of May,
              And the spring comes slowly up this way.
                        —*Samuel Taylor Coleridge*

4506   When April steps aside for May,
              Like diamonds all the raindrops glisten;
              Fresh violets open every day:
              To some new bird each hour we listen.
                        —*Lucy Larcom*

4507   Sweet May hath come to love us,
              Flowers, trees, their blossoms don;
              And through the blue heavens above us
              The very clouds move on.
                        —*Heinrich Heine*

4508   As full of spirit as the month of May.
                        —*William Shakespeare*

4509   'Tis like the birthday of the world,
              When earth was born in bloom;
              The light is made of many dyes,
              The air is all perfume:
              There's crimson buds, and white and blue,
              The very rainbow showers
              Have turned to blossoms where they fell,
              And sown the earth with flowers.
                        —*Thomas Hood*

4510   By great good fortune May does follow April and redeems many promises that April has forfeited.—*Brooks Atkinson*

4511   In the wonderfully beautiful month of May.
                        —*Heinrich Heine*

4512   He has a hard heart who does not love in May.—*Guillaume de Lorris*

4513   Love, whose month is ever May.
        —*William Shakespeare*

4514   Among the changing months, May stands confessed
        The sweetest, and in fairest colors dressed.
        —*James Thomson*

4515   As it fell upon a day
        In the merry month of May,
        Sitting in a pleasant shade
        Which a grove of myrtles made.
        —*Richard Barnfield*

4516   He was as fresh as is the month of May.
        —*Geoffrey Chaucer*

4517   But winter lingering chills the lap of May.
        —*Oliver Goldsmith*

4518   For I'm to be Queen o' the May, mother,
        I'm to be Queen o' the May.
        —*Alfred Lord Tennyson*

4519   And what is so rare as a day in June?
        Then, if ever, come perfect days;
        Then Heaven tries the earth if it be in tune,
        And over it softly her warm ear lays.
        —*James Russell Lowell*

4520   It is the month of June,
        The month of leaves and roses,
        When pleasant sights salute the eyes
        And pleasant scents the noses.
        —*Nathaniel Parker Willis*

4521   Knee-deep in June.
        —*Alfred Austin*

4522   June is bustin' out all over.
        —*Oscar Hammerstein 2nd*

4523   Loud is the summer's busy song.
        The smallest breeze can find a tongue,
        While insects of each tiny size
        Grow teasing with their melodies,
        Till noon burns with its blistering breath
        Around, and day lies still as death.
        —*John Clare*

4524 The summer looks out from her brazen tower,
Through the flashing bars of July.
—Francis Thompson

4525 Hot July brings cooling showers,
Apricots and gillyflowers.
—Sara Coleridge

4526 Dead is the air, and still! the leaves of the locust and walnut
Lazily hang from the boughs, inlaying their intricate outlines
Rather on space than the sky—on a tideless expansion of slumber.
—Bayard Taylor

4527 In the parching August wind,
Cornfields bow the head,
Sheltered in round valley depths,
On low hills outspread.
—Christina Rossetti

4528 Before green apples blush,
Before green nuts embrown,
Why, one day in the country
Is worth a month in town.
—Christina Rossetti

4529 Thirty days hath September,
April, June and November.
All the rest have thirty-one,
Excepting February alone,
And that has twenty-eight days clear
And twenty-nine in each leap year.
—Richard Grafton

4530 Warm September brings the fruit,
Sportsmen then begin to shoot.
—Sara Coleridge

4531 I'm not a chicken; I have seen
Full many a chill September.
—Oliver Wendell Holmes

4532 And close at hand, the basket stood
With nuts from brown October's wood.
—John Greenleaf Whittier

4533   October is the month for painted leaves. . . . As fruits and leaves and the day itself acquire a bright tint just before they fall, so the year near its setting. October is its sunset sky; November the later twilight.—*Henry David Thoreau*

4534   October is the opal month of the year. It is the month of glory, of ripeness. It is the picture-month.—*Henry Ward Beecher*

4535   October's gold is dim—the forests rot,
The weary rain falls ceaseless, while the day
Is wrapped in damp.
                        —*David Gray*

4536   The brown leaves rustle down the forest glade,
Where naked branches make a fitful shade,
And the lost blooms of Autumn withered lie.
                        —*George Arnold*

4537   October turned my maple's leaves to gold;
The most are gone now; here and there one lingers;
Soon these will slip from out the twig's weak hold,
Like coins between a dying miser's fingers.
                        —*T. B. Aldrich*

4538   Samuel Taylor Coleridge, the English poet, once said: "Why is it that many of us persist in thinking that autumn is a sad season? Nature has merely fallen asleep, and her dreams must be beautiful, if we are to judge by her countenance." The lovely month of October is in no way a sad time, with the beautiful red and crimson of the leaves and the golden pumpkin in the fields. Someone has said that October is just the happy side of summer and the pleasant side of winter.

4539   The wild November comes at last
Beneath a veil of rain;
The night wind blows its folds aside,
Her face is full of pain.
The latest of her race, she takes
The Autumn's vacant throne;
She has but one short moon to live,
And she must live alone.
                        —*R. H. Stoddard*

4540   In rattling showers dark November's rain,
From every stormy cloud, descends amain.
                        —*John Ruskin*

4541   Dreary is the time when the flowers of earth are withered.
                              —*William Cullen Bryant*

4542   When chill November's surly blast
        Made fields and forests bare.
                      —*Robert Burns*

4543   And suns grow meek, and the meek suns grow brief,
        And the year smiles as it draws near its death.
                          —*William Cullen Bryant*

4544   Dull November brings the blast,
        Then the leaves are whirling fast.
                      —*Sara Coleridge*

4545   In cold December fragrant chaplets blow,
        And heavy harvests nod beneath the snow.
                          —*Alexander Pope*

4546   Ah, distinctly I remember it was in the bleak December.
                              —*Edgar Allan Poe*

4547   In December ring
        Every day the chimes;
        Loud the gleemen sing
        In the streets their merry rhymes.
        Let us by the fire
        Ever higher
        Sing them till the night expire.
            —*Henry Wadsworth Longfellow*

4548   The sun that brief December day
        Rose cheerless over hills of gray,
        And, darkly circled, gave at noon
        A sadder light than waning moon.
                —*John Greenleaf Whittier*

Mother's Day

4549   Most of all the other beautiful things in life come by twos and threes,
by dozens and hundreds. Plenty of roses, stars, sunsets, rainbows, brothers and
sisters, aunts and cousins, but only one mother in the whole world.—*Kate
Douglas Wiggin*

4550   You may have tangible wealth untold;
        Caskets of jewels and coffers of gold;

Richer than I you can never be—
I had a mother who read to me.
—*Strickland Gillian*

4551   A mother is the only person on earth who can divide her love among ten children and each child still have all her love.

4552   An old-timer is one who can remember when a baby-sitter was called mother.

4553   There was a place in childhood that I remember well,
And there a voice of sweetest tone bright fairy tales did tell.
—*Samuel Lover*

4554   Even He who died for us upon the cross, in the last hour, in the unutterable agony of death, was mindful of His mother, as if to teach us that this holy love should be our last worldly thought—the last point of earth from which the soul should take its flight for heaven.—*Henry Wadsworth Longfellow*

4555   Youth fades; love droops, the leaves of friendship fall;
A mother's secret hope outlives them all.
—*Oliver Wendell Holmes*

4556   The best academy, a mother's knee.
—*James Russell Lowell*

4557   In after-life you may have friends—fond, dear friends; but never will you have again the inexpressible love and gentleness lavished upon you which none but a mother bestows.—*Thomas Babington Macaulay*

New Year

4558   "Happy New Year," we say. But just when does the New Year begin? We reply, "That's easy, on January first." But does it? The early Christians appropriately observed March 25, the Resurrection season; and so England continued with the rest of Christendom until 1753 when she changed over to the Gregorian calendar on January first. The Hebrews have their ecclesiastical New Year at the spring equinox, and their civil New Year in October. The year is the measure of time that it takes the earth to revolve about the sun. So to be exact, we should start the New Year with the day it began to run its course. But who knows when that was?—*Sunshine Magazine*

4559   A little more happiness spread through the day,
A little more cheer to light up the way;

A little more thought for the chap at our side,
A little more credit for others who've tried.

A little more kindness in word and in deed,
A little more boosting that others may need;
A little more love for the folks that we know,
A little more effort so friendships may grow.

Just a little of these—as we plod along here—
Will make it a wonderful, wonderful year!
—*David William Moore*

4560   The Chinese New Year is a day of honor and celebration. On this day they have their feasts and festivities, but most significant of all is the fact that the Chinese undertake to pay off all indebtedness and obligations on that day. Friendships, which have been strained and broken, are restored so far as humanly possible. They then bow before Confucius or Buddha, stating their debts have been paid and friendships restored, and ask his New Year blessings.—*Personnel Consultant*

4561   A wonderfully appealing ideal of life is found in the words of G. B. Shaw in a letter to a friend: "This is the true job of life, the being used for a purpose recognized by yourself as a mighty one, the being thoroughly worn out before you are thrown on the scrapheap, the being a force of nature instead of a feverish little clod of ailments and grievances complaining that the world will not devote itself to making you happy." How about that for one of your aims for the New Year?—*Halford E. Luccock, Christian Herald*

4562   Usually nothing starts people off on the New Year with more good resolutions than a big New Year's Eve party.

4563   The New Year usually gives people a fresh start on their old habits.

4564   Alas! the fleeting years are passing away!—*Horace*

4565
          A little less impatient with those we deem too low;
          A little less of arrogance because of all we know;
          A little more humility, seeing our worth is slight;
          We are such trivial candles compared to stars at night!
          A little more forgiving and swifter to be kind;
          A little more desirous the word of praise to find;
          The word of praise to utter and make a heart rejoice;
          A little bit more careful to speak with gentle voice;

A little more true eagerness to understand each other;
A little more real striving to help a shipwrecked brother;
A little more high courage to each task that must be done;
These be our resolutions—and God help everyone!

—*Author unknown*

4566   A flower unblown; a book unread;
         A tree with fruit unharvested;
        This is the Year that for you waits
         Beyond tomorrow's mystic gates.
                —*Sunshine Magazine*

Spring

4567   Spring hangs her infant blossoms on the trees,
        Rock'd in the cradle of the western breeze.
                —*William Cowper*

4568   Came the Spring with all its splendor,
        All its birds and all its blossoms,
        All its flowers, and leaves, and grasses.
                —*Henry Wadsworth Longfellow*

4569   Spring in the world! And all things are made new!—*Richard Hovey*

4570   All the veneration of spring connects itself with love.—*Ralph Waldo
Emerson*

4571   And the glad earth, caressed by murmuring showers,
        Wakes like a bride, to deck herself with flowers.
                —*Henry Sylvester Cornwell*

4572   In springtime, the only pretty ring time,
        When birds do sing, hey ding a ding, ding;
        Sweet lovers love the spring.
                —*William Shakespeare*

4573   I wandered lonely as a cloud
         That floats on high o'er vales and hills,
        When all at once I saw a crowd,
         A host, of golden daffodils,
        Beside the lake, beneath the trees,
         Fluttering and dancing in the breeze.
                —*William Wordsworth*

4574   The discouraging thing about spring is that everything seems to come back but us.

Summer

4575   One swallow alone does not make the summer.—*Cervantes*

4576
>   Oh, the summer night
>   Has a smile of light
>   And she sits on a sapphire throne.
>   —*B. W. Procter*

4577
>   I question not if thrushes sing,
>   If roses load the air;
>   Beyond my heart I need not reach
>   When all is summer there.
>   —*John Vance Cheney*

4578   An English summer, two fine days and a thunderstorm.—*Michael Denham*

4579
>   Summer treads on heels of Spring.
>   —*Horace*

4580
>   The Indian Summer, the dead Summer's soul.
>   —*Mary Clemmer*

Sunday

4581   Sunday clears away the rust of the whole week.—*Joseph Addison*

4582   There are many people who think that Sunday is a sponge to wipe out all the sins of the week.—*Henry Ward Beecher*

4583
>   Of all the days that's in the week
>   I dearly love but one day,
>   And that's the day that comes betwixt
>   A Saturday and Monday.
>   —*Henry Carey*

4584   Remember the sabbath day, to keep it holy. Six days shalt thou labor and do all thy work: but the seventh day is the sabbath of the Lord thy God. —*Exodus 20:8–10*

4585 Day of the Lord, as all our days should be!
—*Henry Wadsworth Longfellow*

Thanksgiving

4586 Heap high the board with plenteous cheer, and gather to the feast,
And toast the sturdy Pilgrim band whose courage never ceased.
Give praise to that All-Gracious One by whom their steps were led,
And thanks unto the harvest's Lord who sends our "daily bread."
—*Alice Williams Brotherton*

4587 So once in every year we throng
Upon a day apart,
To praise the Lord with feast and song
In thankfulness of heart.
—*Arthur Guiterman*

4588   Thanksgiving is one of the great traditional American holidays, and yet it did not originate in America. About three thousand years before it was observed in this country, God spoke to Moses in the days when the great host of Israelite slaves had just escaped from Egypt. They were having their first experience in the wilderness of Sinai. The original proclamation from God is reported in the 23rd chapter of Exodus, 16th verse: "Thou shalt keep the feast of harvest, the first fruits of thy labors, which thou hast sown in the field: and the feast of in-gathering, which is in the end of the year, when thou hast gathered in thy labors out of the field."—*Sunshine Magazine*

4589   It is a good thing to give thanks unto the Lord.—*Psalms 92:1*

4590   O give thanks unto the Lord, for he is good: for his mercy endureth forever.—*Psalms 107:1*

4591 Let never day nor night unhallow'd pass,
But still remember what the Lord hath done.
—*William Shakespeare*

4592 Now thank we all our God,
With heart and hand and voices,
Who wondrous things hath done,
In whom His world rejoices.
—*Catherine Winkworth*

4593   Almighty God, Father of all mercies, we, thine unworthy servants, do give thee most humble and hearty thanks for all thy goodness and loving-kindness to us, and to all men.—*The Book of Common Prayer*

4594   Some people always sigh in thanking God.
                                        —*Elizabeth Barrett Browning*

4595   Let us then, as good citizens, as believers in God, gratefully keep
Thanksgiving Day. Let us crowd to his sanctuaries, and praise God, from whom
all blessings flow. Let households and friends gather about their firesides and
well-spread boards, and let charities to the poor brighten and commemorate the
day, that it may be to us all long a pleasant memory.—*J. B. Walker*

4596   Yet it is meet and proper that a nation should set apart an annual day
for national giving of thanks. It is a public recognition of God as the Author of
all prosperity. It is the erection of a memorial to the honor of him who has led
us through another year. The annual proclamations which call to the duty of
thanksgiving are calculated to remind the people of their indebtedness to God,
to stir in their minds and hearts emotions of gratitude and praise, and to call out
thanks and sincere worship which otherwise might not find expression. But if the
observance of the day be not marked by real remembering of mercies and by real
lifting of hearts to God in thanks, what blessing can possibly come with it?—
J. R. Miller

4597   "Lord God of Hosts, be with us yet,
                       Lest we forget—lest we forget!"
                                        —*Rudyard Kipling*

4598   Of the 102 pilgrims who had set sail on the *Mayflower* the previous
autumn, only 51 sat down at the festive board when the first Thanksgiving dinner
was held in the New World in 1621. The other 51—exactly half of the original
party—lay buried on a nearby hill in unmarked graves, smoothed over in order
that the Indians might not count the dreadful losses that had occurred because
of disease and privation. Yet those who remained recognized ample cause for
gratitude: harvest had been abundant, each family had its own cottage ready for
the oncoming winter, and the Indians, once hostile, were now friendly, and some
of them had even come to partake of the great feast with their white friends.
Although the Pilgrims thus originated the observance of Thanksgiving, this day
for the recognition of blessings did not attain the status of a national celebration
until 1863, when President Lincoln proclaimed, in the midst of the Civil War,
a day for expressing gratitude. Since then, it has been an annual observance.—
Sunshine Magazine

Washington's Birthday

4599   America has furnished to the world the character of Washington. And
if our American institutions have done nothing else, that alone would have
entitled them to the respect of mankind.—*Daniel Webster*

4600   Almighty God: We make our earnest prayer that Thou wilt keep the
United States in Thy holy protection; that Thou wilt incline the hearts of the

citizens to cultivate a spirit of subordination and obedience to government; and entertain a brotherly affection and love for one another and for their fellow citizens of the United States at large.

And, finally, that Thou wilt most graciously be pleased to dispose us all to do justice, to love mercy, and to demean ourselves with charity, humility, and pacific temper of mind which were the characteristics of the Divine Author of our blessed religion, and without an humble imitation of whose example in these things we can never hope to be a happy nation.

Grant our supplication, we beseech Thee, through Jesus Christ our Lord. Amen.—*George Washington's inaugural prayer*

4601   First in war, first in peace, and first in the hearts of his countrymen. —*Henry ("Light-Horse Harry") Lee*

4602   Labor to keep alive in your breast that little spark of celestial fire, conscience.—*George Washington*

4603   The propitious smiles of heaven can never be expected on a nation that disregards the eternal rules of order and right which heaven itself has ordained. —*George Washington*

4604   He errs as other men do, but errs with integrity.—*Thomas Jefferson*

4605   The father of his country.—*Francis Bailey*

Wedding Day

4606   If it were not for the Presents, an Elopement would be preferable.— *George Ade*

4607

> I saw the young bride in her beauty and pride,
> Bedecked in her snowy array.
> > —*Mary Stanley Bunce Dana*

4608

> Happiness untold awaits them
> When the parson consecrates them.
> > —*W. S. Gilbert*

4609

> Hail the Bridegroom—hail the Bride!
> When the nuptial knot is tied.
> > —*W. S. Gilbert*

4610   Nobody enjoys a wedding but the mother of the bride: she likes a good cry.—*Reginald Wright Kauffman*

4611   A happy bridesmaid makes a happy bride.—*Alfred Lord Tennyson*

4612   Whoso findeth a wife findeth a good thing.—*Proverbs 18:22*

4613   What is there in the vale of life
Half so delightful as a wife,
When friendship, love, and peace combine
To stamp the marriage-bond divine?
—*William Cowper*

4614   A woman must be a genius to create a good husband.—*Honoré de Balzac*

4615   Grow old along with me,
The best is yet to be,
I've got a credit card,
And you've got three.
—*Herbert V. Prochnow*

Winter

4616   But where are the snows of yesteryear?
—*François Villon*

4617   O the snow, the beautiful snow,
Filling the sky and earth below;
Over the house-tops, over the street,
Over the heads of the people you meet,
Dancing, flirting, skimming along.
—*James W. Watson*

4618   If Winter comes, can Spring be far behind?
—*Percy Bysshe Shelley*

4619   Oh the long and dreary Winter!
Oh the cold and cruel Winter!
—*Henry Wadsworth Longfellow*

4620   Winter comes but once a year,
And when it comes it brings the doctor good cheer.
—*Ogden Nash*

4621   Winter lingered so long in the lap of Spring, that it occasioned a great deal of talk.—*Bill Nye*

4622   Oh, every year hath its winter,
And every year hath its rain—
But a day is always coming
When the birds go north again.
—Ella Higginson

4623   Stern Winter loves a dirge-like sound.
—William Wordsworth

4624   On a lone winter evening, when the frost
Has wrought a silence.
—John Keats

4625   Beneath the winter's snow lie germs of summer flowers.
—John Greenleaf Whittier

Toasts

4626

There are no times like the old times—they shall never be forgot;
There is no place like the old place—keep green the dear old spot!
There are no friends like the old friends—may heaven prolong their lives!
There are no loves like the old loves,—God bless our loving wives!
Oliver Wendell Holmes

4627   A book of verses underneath the Bough,
A jug of Wine, a loaf of Bread—and Thou
Beside me singing in the Wilderness,
O Wilderness were Paradise enow!
—Omar Khayyam

4628   Here's to the hostess who has worried all day,
And trembled lest everything go the wrong way;
May the grace of contentment possess her at once,
May her guests—and her servants—all do the right stunts.
—Francis Wilson

4629   Age cannot wither nor custom stale
Her infinite variety.
—William Shakespeare

4630   A perfect woman, nobly planned,
To warm, to comfort and command.
—William Wordsworth

4631   Here's to our wives, who fill our lives
With little bees and honey!
They break life's shocks, they mend our socks—
But don't they spend the money!

Here's to the girl that's good and sweet,
Here's to the girl that's true;
Here's to the girl that rules my heart—
In other words, here's to you!

4632   Woman—the true source of all our joys! The mother, the sister, the
wife, the true sympathetic friend! Without her the first man found the Garden
of Eden but a desert; for her kings have given up their thrones, generals have
left their armies, and the course of empire has turned aside. When she ceases to
exist, the human race will no longer survive. She is to man "The rainbow in his
storms of life, the evening beam that smiles the clouds away, and tints the
morrow with prophetic ray!"—*James A. Cooper*

4633   Woman—she needs no eulogy, she speaks for herself.

4634   Here's to our wives and sweethearts! May our sweethearts become our
wives, and our wives ever remain our sweethearts!

4635   Here's to us all! God bless us every one!—*Charles Dickens*

4636   Grace was in all her steps, Heaven in her eye,
In every gesture dignity and love!
          —*John Milton*

4637   She is so free, so kind, so apt, so blessed a disposition.
          —*William Shakespeare*

4638   To earth's noblest thing,—a woman perfected!
          —*James Russell Lowell*

4639   I have known many, liked a few,
Loved but one—so here's to you!

4640   Here's to your good health, and your family's good health, and may
you all live long and prosper.—*Washington Irving*

4641   The greatest blessing heaven can send—a good wife.

4642   A good wife and health
Are a man's best wealth.

4643   The Ladies: We admire them for their beauty, respect them for their intelligence, adore them for their virtue, and love them because we can't help it.

4644   And in those eyes the love-light lies and lies—and lies—and lies.— *Anita Owen*

4645   But in spite of all temptations
               To belong to other nations
               He remains an Englishman!
                         —*W. S. Gilbert*

4646   I drink to the general joy 'o the whole table.
                         —*William Shakespeare*

4647   May all your troubles be little ones.—*Irish toast to a bridal couple.*

4648   He who thinks the most good and speaks the least ill of his neighbors —the man we love.

4649   Our President: May he always merit the esteem and affection of a people ever ready to bestow gratitude on those who deserve it.

4650   To the old, long life and treasure;
               To the young, all health and pleasure.
                         —*Ben Jonson*

4651   I wish you health,
               I wish you wealth,
               I wish you happiness galore,
               I wish you heaven when you die,
               What could I wish you more?
                         —*Irish toast*

4652   Some men are born lucky; others have luck thrust upon them. And then there's this fellow! A toast, gentlemen, to his extreme good fortune.

4653   Anniversaries may come and anniversaries may go—but your happiness will go on forever.

4654   Here's to you. No matter how old you are, you don't look it.

4655   A toast to Mother, who knows us so well, yet loves us.

4656   Long life and happiness—for your long life will be my happiness.

4657   To your health. You will find that two cannot live as cheaply as one. But then, it is well worth the difference!

4658   To Mother—may she live long enough to forget what little fiends we used to be.

4659   To Mother: May the love and appreciation of later days overshadow the worries we caused her in our childhood.

4660   Father. May the love and respect we express toward him make up, at least in part, for the worry and care we have visited upon him.

4661   I pay my most hearty respects to the man who has so singularly honored me—by being my Father.

4662   To Dad's continued health, Mother's continued happiness, and our continued fortune.

XI

The Proverbs of Many Nations

4663   How many things I can do without!—*Socrates*

4664   No one can boast of his modesty.

4665   A fool may make money, but it needs a wise man to spend it.

4666   There is no companion like money.

4667   When gold speaks, every tongue is silent.—*Italian*

4668   Give me money, not advice.—*Portuguese*

4669   It is easier to make money than to keep it.—*Yiddish*

4670   All men think all men mortal but themselves.

4671   Men are what their mothers make them.

4672   No mother has a homely child.—*Yiddish*

4673   One murder makes a villain, millions a hero.

4674   Necessity will teach a man, however stupid, to be wise.—*Greek*

4675   A picture is a poem without words.—*Latin*

4676   He laughs best that laughs last.

4677   The laughter of man is the contentment of God.

4678   No one is sadder than he who laughs too much.—*German*

4679   He who loves to laugh has teeth that are white.—*Russian*

4680   When you laugh, all see; when you weep, no one.—*Yiddish*

4681   There is no law without a loophole for him who can find it.—*German*

4682   A lean compromise is better than a fat lawsuit.—*Italian*

4683   Fear not the law, but the judge.—*Russian*

4684   As lazy as the dog that leaned against a wall to bark.

4685   A small leak will sink a ship.

4686   Leisure is the time for doing something useful.

4687   A liar needs a good memory.—*Latin*

4688   A lie grows in size as it is repeated.—*Latin*

4689   Live not for time, but eternity.

4690   If you would make a thief honest, trust him.—*Spanish*

4691   A thought may take a man prisoner.

4692   If men would think more, they would act less.

4693   Great thoughts come from the heart.—*French*

4694   To think is to converse with oneself.—*Spanish*

4695   Many a man threatens while he quakes with fear.

4696   If you put nothing into your purse, you can take nothing out.

4697   He who rides a tiger is afraid to dismount.—*Chinese*

4698   Time subdues all things.—*Arabian*

4699   Lost time is never found again.

4700   There is a time for all things.

4701   Time heals sorrow.

4702   Nothing is so dear and precious as time.—*French*

4703   A hundred years hence we shall all be bald.—*Spanish*

4704   One always has a good appetite at another's feast.—*Yiddish*

4705   A bad cause should be silent.—*Latin*

4706   To understand your parents' love you must raise children yourself.—*Chinese*

4707   The arguments of the strongest have always the most weight.—*French*

4708   Better ask ten times than go astray once.—*Yiddish*

4709   It is not the beard that makes the philosopher.—*Italian*

4710   A bargain is always dear.—*Yiddish*

4711   What a man desires he easily believes.

4712   They can conquer who believe they can.—*Vergil*

4713   While the great bells are ringing, no one hears the little ones.—*Danish*

4714   An inch of gold will not buy an inch of time.—*Chinese*

4715   When the messenger of death comes, all affairs cease.—*Chinese*

4716   When a child stumbles, a good angel puts his hands under.—*Yiddish*

4717   God made the country and man made the town.—*William Cowper*

4718   He that never climbed never fell.

4719   He that climbs high falls heavily.—*German*

4720   A cockroach is always wrong when arguing with the chicken.

4721   A candle lights others and consumes itself.

4722   Confidence is a plant of slow growth.

4723   We triumph without glory when we conquer without danger.—*French*

4724   I came, I saw, I conquered.—*Julius Caesar*

4725   A clear conscience can bear any trouble.

4726   If all your life you have had a clear conscience, you need not fear a knock at the door at midnight.—*Chinese*

4727   Conscience is the voice of God in the soul.

4728   Every cook commends his own sauce.

4729   Excessive politeness assuredly conceals conceit.—*Chinese*

4730   He that will not be counseled cannot be helped.

4731   Many would be cowards if they had courage enough.

4732   Better take eight hundred than sell for a thousand on credit.—*Chinese*

4733   Critics are like brushers of noblemen's clothes.

4734   It is rarely that an author is hurt by his critics.

4735   Everyone thinks his own cross is heaviest.—*Italian*

4736   He who does not mix with the crowd knows nothing.—*Spanish*

4737   A desperate disease must have a desperate cure.

4738   No day passeth without some grief.

4739   There are more foolish buyers than foolish sellers.

4740   From the day of your birth you begin to die as well as to live.—*French*

4741   The whole earth is a sepulcher for famous men.—*Greek*

4742   If you continually give, you will continually have.—*Chinese*

4743   Pale Death, with impartial step, knocks at the poor man's cottage and at the palaces of kings.—*Horace*

4744   He is rich enough who owes nothing.—*French*

4745   You can't pay your debts with tears.—*Yiddish*

4746   Poverty is the common fate of scholars.—*Chinese*

4747   One may outwit another, but not all the others.—*French*

4748   The surest way to be deceived is to think one's self more clever than others.—*French*

4749   Whatever is worth doing at all is worth doing well.

4750   A delay is better than a disaster.

4751   Delay is preferable to error.

4752   When a man's life is at stake, no delay is too long.—*Latin*

4753   Humble hearts have humble desires.

4754   The fewer desires, the more peace.

4755   It is wise to submit to destiny.—*Chinese*

4756   One meets his destiny often in the road he takes to avoid it.—*French*

4757   Diligence is the mother of good luck.—*French*

4758   Nothing is profitable which is dishonest.—*Latin*

4759   Hunger is cured by food, ignorance by study.—*Chinese*

4760   Dogs gnaw bones because they cannot swallow them.

4761   He that lieth down with dogs shall rise up with fleas.

4762   God never imposes a duty without giving the time to perform it.

4763   We have two ears and one mouth that we may listen the more and talk the less.—*Greek*

4764   It is good to be merry at meat.

4765   To lengthen thy life, lessen thy meals.

4766   It is only the ignorant who despise education.—*Latin*

4767   Love your enemies, for they tell you your faults.—*Benjamin Franklin*

4768   The mouse that has but one hole is quickly taken.—*Latin*

4769   Never do evil that good may come of it.—*Italian*

4770   We always weaken whatever we exaggerate.—*French*

4771   A face like a benediction.—*Spanish*

4772   Fame is but wind.

4773   Fame, like man, will grow white as it grows old.

4774   The father, in praising his son, extols himself.—*Chinese*

4775   The fault of another is a good teacher.—*German*

4776   We see only the faults of another.—*Yiddish*

4777   Fidelity gained by bribes is overcome by bribes.—*Latin*

4778   Since Adam's time, fools have been in the majority.—*French*

4779   Pitch him into the Nile, and he'll come up with a fish in his mouth.
—*Arabian*

4780   No one is satisfied with his fortune, nor dissatisfied with his intellect.
—*French*

4781   At length the fox is brought to the furrier.

4782   The fox may grow gray but never good.

4783   A fox sleeps but counts hens in his dreams.—*Russian*

4784   Though boys throw stones at frogs in sport, the frogs do not die in sport but in earnest.—*Greek*

4785   He that will have the fruit must climb the tree.

4786   Whatever I have given I still possess.—*Latin*

4787   One may go a long way after he is tired.—*French*

4788   What is good is never plentiful.—*Spanish*

4789   The goose hisses but does not bite.—*Dutch*

4790   Do not cut down the tree that gives you shade.—*Arabian*

4791   Gratitude is the music of the heart.

4792   Be not ungrateful to your old friend.—*Hebrew*

4793   The more thy years, the nearer thy grave.

4794   It is a rough road that leads to the heights of greatness.—*Latin*

4795   Good health and good sense are two great blessings.—*Latin*

4796   A happy heart is better than a full purse.—*Italian*

4797   The burnt child dreads the fire.—*Ben Jonson*

4798   No man is a hero to his valet.—*French*

4799   Home is where the heart is.—*Latin*

4800   In my own house I am king.—*Spanish*

4801   Too much humility is pride.—*German*

4802   Everything is funny as long as it happens to somebody else.

4803   A happy couple: the husband deaf, the wife blind.

4804   He that knows little often repeats it.

4805   Impulse manages all things badly.—*Latin*

4806   The sleeping fox catches no poultry.

4807   Earth produces nothing worse than an ungrateful man.—*Latin*

4808   The remedy for injuries is to forget them.—*Latin*

4809   Innocence is its own defense.

4810   A jest loses its point when the jester laughs himself.—*German*

4811   Jests that give pain are no jests.—*Spanish*

4812   He who is a judge between two friends loses one of them.—*French*

4813   The greatest king must at last go to bed with a shovel.

4814   A learned man has always riches in himself.—*Latin*

4815   All wish to know, but none to pay the fee.—*Latin*

4816   He who would eat the kernel must crack the shell.—*Latin*

4817   Why seekest thou rest, since thou art born to labor?—*Latin*

4818   Make yourself a lamb and the wolves will eat you.—*French*

4819   It is too late for the bird to scream when it is caught.—*French*

4820   He who comes late must eat what is left.—*Yiddish*

4821   Life is a perilous voyage.—*Greek*

4822   Live as if you were to die tomorrow.—*Latin*

4823   We break up life into little bits and fritter them away.—*Latin*

4824   It is easy to live—hard to die.—*Yiddish*

4825   Even a lion must defend himself against the flies.—*German*

4826   Who has no children does not know what love is.—*Petrarch*

4827   It is the superfluous things for which men sweat.—*Latin*

4828   Man is the only animal that blushes. Or needs to.—*Mark Twain*

4829   Nothing in life is certain for men, children of a day.—*Greek*

4830   It is not marriage that fails; it is people that fail.

4831   In the long run the sword is beaten by the mind.—*Napoleon*

4832   Misfortunes never come alone.

4833   Birds of prey do not sing.—*German*

4834   Only moderation gives charm to life.—*German*

4835   A world where nothing is had for nothing.

4836   Nothing is swifter than the years.—*Latin*

4837   Enjoy the season of thy prime.—*Greek*

4838   With all his genius, man has never learned how to restrain the flight of time.—*Herbert V. Prochnow*

4839   Zeal without knowledge is a runaway horse.

4840   Be quiet and people will think you are a philosopher.—*Latin*

4841   Everybody's business is nobody's business.—*Seventeenth-century proverb*

4842   No man's head aches while he is comforting another.—*Indian*

4843   Better do a kindness near home than go to a far temple to burn incense. —*Chinese*

4844   Even the hen lifteth her head toward heaven when swallowing her grain.—*African*

4845   You cannot prevent the birds of sorrow from flying over your head, but you can prevent them from building nests in your hair.—*Chinese*

4846   If you want a plan by which to stop drinking, look at a drunken man when you are sober.—*Chinese*

4847   If you cannot bite, never show your teeth.—*French*

4848   Patience opens all doors.

4849   A good citizen owes his life to his country.—*Russian*

4850   God is with those who persevere.—*Arabian*

4851 Everyone can navigate in fine weather.—*Italian*

4852 Wherever MacGregor sits is the head of the table.

4853 You must leave your possessions behind, when God summons.—*Yiddish*

4854 I praise loudly, I blame softly.—*Russian*

4855 While we are postponing, life speeds by.—*Latin*

4856 Prosperity destroys fools, and endangers the wise.

4857 We are corrupted by prosperity.—*Latin*

4858 A full purse never lacks friends.

4859 There's no repentance in the grave.

4860 The opposite of gossip is often the truth.—*French*

4861 Self-confidence is the first requisite to great undertakings.

4862 He that falls in love with himself will have no rivals.

4863 Common sense is not so common.—*French*

4864 Shrouds are made without pockets.—*Yiddish*

4865 Speak no ill of a friend, nor even of an enemy.—*Greek*

4866 Empty barrels make the most noise.

4867 If you have no honey in your pot, have some in your mouth.

4868 He who says what he likes hears what he does not like.—*Spanish*

4869 To spend much and gain little is the sure road to ruin.—*German*

4870 What you spoil in youth you can't correct in old age.—*Yiddish*

4871 The worth of a State is the worth of the individuals composing it.—*John Stuart Mill*

4872 The stone that lies in one place becomes covered with moss.—*Yiddish*

4873 Men strain at gnats and swallow camels.

4874 He who stumbles twice over one stone deserves to break his shins.

4875 Success is the child of audacity.

4876   Success in men's eyes is God, and more than God.—*Greek*

4877   Success has brought many to destruction.—*Latin*

4878   Many suffer for what they cannot help.—*French*

4879   He who suffers much will know much.—*Greek*

4880   The sun shines on rich and poor alike.—*Yiddish*

4881   If each one sweeps before his own door, the whole street is clean.—
Yiddish

4882   Cast not pearls before swine.—*Latin*

4883   Use not the sword against him who asks forgiveness.—*Turkish*

4884   When your own tooth aches, you know how to sympathize with one
who has a toothache.—*Chinese*

4885   No man limps because another is hurt.—*Danish*

4886   Our sympathy is cold to the relation of distant misery.

4887   People in distress never think that you feel enough.

4888   There are toys for all ages.—*French*

4889   In this world nothing is certain but death and taxes.—*French*

4890   He is either dead or teaching school.—*Greek*

4891   If you love instruction, you will be well educated.—*Greek*

4892   Who teaches, often learns himself.—*Italian*

4893   In youth, one has tears without grief; in age, grief without tears.—
French

4894   Tears are the silent language of grief.—*French*

4895   Nothing dries sooner than a tear.—*Latin*

4896   Don't tell everything you know.—*Yiddish*

4897   He who loses his temper is in the wrong.—*French*

4898   A thief passes for a gentleman when stealing has made him rich.

4899   When it thunders, the thief becomes honest.

4900   Every rascal is not a thief, but every thief is a rascal.—*Greek*

4901   The receiver is as bad as the thief.—*Greek*

4902   Empty heads love long titles.—*German*

4903   Rather an egg today than a hen tomorrow.

4904   Let not your tongue outrun your thought.—*Greek*

4905   The tongue is a sharper weapon than the sword.—*Greek*

4906   He travels best that knows when to return.

4907   He that travels much knows much.

4908   Travel teaches toleration.

4909   Only at trees bearing fruit do people throw stones.

4910   A twig in time becomes a tree.—*Latin*

4911   He has as many tricks as a dancing bear.

4912   Never trouble trouble till trouble troubles you.

4913   The truth is always the strongest argument.—*Greek*

4914   He threw my coat out the door, and I happened to be in it.—*Yiddish*

4915   An empty bag cannot stand upright.

4916   Vanity is the food of fools.

4917   "What a dust we kicked up," said the fly to the car wheels.

4918   The noblest vengeance is to forgive.

4919   Sell not virtue to purchase wealth.

4920   "Wait" is a hard word to the hungry.—*German*

4921   The more one has, the more one wants.

4922   Want is the mother of industry.

4923   War is the child of pride.

4924   War seldom enters but where wealth allures.

4925   War is sweet to those who have not experienced it.—*Latin*

4926   When war is raging, the laws are dumb.—*Latin*

4927   In a just cause the weak overcome the strong.—*Greek*

4928   Wealth conquered Rome after Rome had conquered the world. —*Italian*

4929   Better the cottage where one is merry than the palace where one weeps. —*Chinese*

4930   Weeping makes the heart grow lighter.—*Yiddish*

4931   A wicked man is afraid of his own memory.

4932   The wicked heart fears God only when it thunders.

4933   God bears with the wicked, but not forever.—*Spanish*

4934   Great boasters, little doers.—*French*

4935   Wisdom is a good purchase though we pay dear for it.

4936   Wisdom is to the soul what health is to the body.—*French*

4937   He that is wise by day is no fool by night.

4938   It is easy to be wise after the event.

4939   A wise man—a strong man.—*German*

4940   You can't get rich by wishing.—*Yiddish*

4941   It is bitter fare to eat one's own words.—*Danish*

4942   Soft words win hard hearts.

4943   Work is no disgrace; the disgrace is idleness.—*Greek*

4944   He who deals with a blockhead will have need of much brains.— *Spanish*

4945   A man without a smiling face should not open a shop.—*Chinese*

4946   A wicked book is the wickeder because it cannot repent.

4947   If the profits are great, the risks are great.

4948   In life, beware of the lawcourt; in death, beware of hell.—*Chinese*

4949   No one knows what he can do till he tries.—*Latin*

4950   Never was the absent in the right.—*Spanish*

4951   Advice is something the wise don't need and fools won't take.

4952   Nothing is given so freely as advice.—*French*

4953   Your old men shall dream dreams, your young men shall see visions.

4954   A wise man is never less alone than when alone.—*Latin*

4955   The fish that escaped is the big one.—*Chinese*

4956   As soon as Justice returns, the golden age returns.—*Vergil*

4957   He who spares the bad seeks to corrupt the good.—*Latin*

4958   Labor is the law of happiness.

4959   Learning without thought is labor lost; thought without learning is dangerous.—*Chinese*

4960   If you love learning, you shall be learned.—*Euclid*

4961   The God who gave us life gave us liberty at the same time.—*Thomas Jefferson*

4962   Look at the end of life.—*Greek*

4963   A little stone may upset a large cart.—*Italian*

4964   Praising what is lost makes the remembrance dear.—*William Shakespeare*

4965   Love me, and the world is mine.

4966   Love is stronger than death.—*French*

4967   There is no living in love without suffering.—*Latin*

4968   He loves thee well who makes thee weep.—*Spanish*

4969   The dainties of the great are the tears of the poor.

4970   The opinion of the majority is not the final proof of what is right.—*Johann Christoph Friedrich von Schiller*

4971   Men talk wisely but live foolishly.

4972   Man's inhumanity to man
                Makes countless thousands mourn.
                                        —*Robert Burns*

4973   As your wedding ring wears, you'll wear off your cares.

4974   Sorrow remembered sweetens present joy.

4975   How sweet to remember the trouble that is past!—*Greek*

4976   The mind is the man.—*Latin*

4977   The mirror shows everyone his best friend.—*Yiddish*

4978   Mention money, and the world is silent.—*German*

4979   Would you know what money is? Go borrow some.

4980   Necessity breaks iron.

4981   He made a virtue of necessity.—*French*

4982   He knocks boldly who brings good news.—*Italian*

4983   Coming events cast their shadows before.—*Thomas Campbell*

4984   A difference of opinion alienates only little minds.

4985   Pain is the price that God putteth upon all things.

4986   The Present is the living sum-total of the whole Past.—*Thomas Carlyle*

4987   Have patience, and endure.—*Latin*

4988   Never give the skin when you can pay with the wool.—*German*

4989   The tyranny of a multitude is a multiplied tyranny.—*Edmund Burke*

4990   He that pities another remembers himself.

4991   His bread is buttered on both sides.

4992   When one has a good table, he is always right.—*French*

4993   It is easier to praise poverty than to bear it.

4994   What can a poor man do but love and pray?

4995   Let thy speech be short, comprehending much in few words.
—*Apocrypha*

4996   Who knows most speaks quietly.—*Herbert V. Prochnow*

4997   A man shows his character by what he laughs at.—*German*

4998   Character is habit long continued.—*Greek*

4999   Do good and ask not for whom.—*Yiddish*

5000   Who cheateth in small things is a fool; in great ones, a rogue.

5001   Dogs show no aversion to poor families.—*Chinese*

5002   Give a child his will and he'll turn out ill.

5003   Anger manages everything badly.—*Statius*

5004   Seem not greater than thou art.—*Latin*

5005   Bread and circus games.—*Juvenal*

5006   Bribery and theft are first cousins.

5007   Children are the keys of Paradise.

5008   No road is long with good company.—*Turkish*

5009   Constant complaints never get pity.

5010   They conquer who believe they can.—*Latin*

5011   Who profits by a crime commits the crime.

5012   The longest day will have an end.

5013   Death makes equal the high and low.

5014   Those who expect to reap the blessings of freedom must undergo the fatigue of supporting it.—*Paine*

Index

All numbers in this index refer to numbers placed in numerical order at the left-hand margins of the pages. The 5,014 items of source material are completely indexed so that it is possible quickly to find all the items throughout the book which relate to a particular idea. To illustrate, under the classification, business, in the index, one can immediately locate the numbers of all quotations, epigrams, humorous stories, definitions and other items relating to this subject. In addition, almost every one of the 5,014 items has been classified in the index under several headings so the reader who is seeking a quotation, epigram, or humorous story to illustrate even a particular word or a relatively restricted idea may find it by using the index.